WORKBOOK

www.majortests.com

HW=20 new vocab words
& read = main idea
tone/mood

BELL CURVES SAT® WORKBOOK

The SAT® is a registered trademark of the College Board, which is not involved in the production of and does not endorse in this product.

ABOUT BELL CURVES

Bell Curves is an educational services company focused on helping individuals overcome barriers to educational success. Bell Curves partners with individuals and organizations to guide individuals toward the highest level of academic excellence. Combining customized materials with energetic and knowledgeable instruction, the Bell Curves team seeks to take education beyond mechanical memorization and routine methodology. Our professional staff and proven instructional philosophy will help students reach and exceed their academic goals. Bell Curves provides SAT, LSAT, GMAT and other test preparation products as well, such as those pertaining to the ACT and GRE exam.

ACKNOWLEDGEMENTS

Bell Curves would like to thank the following people for their contributions to this product:

Akil Bello, Ally Fields, Sarah Duncan, John Mahone, Meg Borree, Candace Hoefert, Clayton Harding, Dan O'Mahoney-Schwartz, Jasmynne Shaye, Aimee Slater, Roberto Colon, Glenn Ribotsky, Elizabeth Schmid, and the amazing, dedicated teaching staff at Bell Curves.

COPYRIGHT

© 2016 Bell Curves, LLC

All rights reserved. This workbook is exclusively for the use of students and staff of Bell Curves, LLC. No part of this book may be reproduced, stored in a retrieval system, distributed, or transmitted in any form, by any means– electronic, mechanical, photocopying, recording, or otherwise. Use is permitted under license; for personal use only.

For more information visit
www.bellcurves.com or contact us at:

Phone: 646.414.1586
Email: support@bellcurves.com

TABLE OF CONTENTS

INTRODUCTION	5
READING TEST	17
Action Plan	40
Practice	95
WRITING & LANGUAGE TEST	121
Grammar Action Plan	129
Arguments	174
Practice	191
MATH TEST	209
Basics	215
Problem Solving & Data Analysis	235
Heart of Algebra	270
Passport to Advanced Math	300
Geometry and Trigonometry	335
Practice	365
Practice Section (No Calculator)	415
Practice Section (Calculator)	422
THE ESSAY	435
Action Plan	450

© 2016 Bell Curves, LLC

CHAPTER 1
Introduction

College Knowledge
Terms and Acronyms

Before beginning to study for the SAT exam itself, let's pause for a moment to think about why we're here. We all have a similar goal: To get into college. While the SAT is an important piece of your application, it is equally important to increase your college knowledge so you can make well-informed decisions regarding your future. Therefore, throughout this book we will pause to increase your college knowledge.

Instructions: Select the choice that best completes each of the following sentences.

A trade school trains you to
❏ teach
❏ work in business
❏ work as a plumber, electrician, etc.

A college is the same as a university.
❏ false
❏ true
❏ mostly true

B.A. stands for
❏ Big Achievement
❏ Black Academy
❏ Bachelor of Arts

M.A. stands for
❏ Master of Academics
❏ Minority of Achievement
❏ Master of Arts

The single most important factor in college admissions is
❏ Family income
❏ HS transcript
❏ Essays

Bursar is a
❏ bar
❏ cashier
❏ dean of discipline

J.D. stands for
❏ Jury's Decision
❏ Law degree
❏ Jurist Doctorate

A community college is a
❏ school close to home
❏ bad college
❏ college that gives only 2-year degrees

A college is the same as a university in all ways that matter to me.
❏ I don't know
❏ false
❏ true

B.S. stands for
❏ Big School
❏ Bachelor of Sociology
❏ Bachelor of Science

A.P. stands for
❏ Academically Painful
❏ Advanced Placement
❏ Associated Press

Ph.D. stands for
❏ Medical Doctor
❏ Doctor of Philosophy (highest academic degree)
❏ Master of Arts

FAFSA stands for
❏ Free Application for Federal Student Aid
❏ Federal Association of Fair Student Admissions
❏ Federation of Awesome Fraternity and Sorority Activities

What are the 3 most important factors in college admissions?
❏ SAT, GPA, legacy
❏ SAT, essays, income
❏ SAT, GPA/transcript, extra-curriculars

The SAT | What's the Point?

So you plan to spend the next couple of months prepping for this exam. Since you plan to invest so much time in this, it's important to understand why.

It's Used to Compare Students for College Admissions

The SAT serves as a part of your application, which colleges use along with your grade point average, extra-curricular activities, recommendations, and any other unique qualifications, to determine whether to accept you into their school.

Remember, college admissions tests make up just one aspect of your application. For many students, and many schools, other factors are more significant. Circumstances that apply to your situation: athletic ability; a rare and valued field of study; a family with several generations of attendance at the school; a particularly high GPA in comparison with most students applying to the school, etc, may make your SAT score almost a formality. However, it never hurts to have a great SAT score. No one has ever gotten rejected because their score was too high.

So let's do our best to make this portion of your application work in your favor. If your score is significantly higher than the average incoming freshman class from last year at the school of your choice, that's one more thing that sets you apart as the admissions officers look at your application.

It's Used to Predict Your First Year Grades

According to the College Board, SAT scores, along with a student's GPA, can be used to predict first year college success. The SAT is not supposed to be, and certainly isn't, a college test or a predictor of career success. In fact there is evidence that it's not even a very good predictor of first year college grades.

Introduction

College Knowledge | College Ranges

SAT scores only matter in relation to the schools you want to attend. To fully understand your scores and where they are in relation to scores that will give you the best possibility of admission, you need to research the colleges and universities on your list. Below is a selection of schools and their corresponding middle 50% ranges of SAT scores that you can use for reference.

School	*SAT Range
Duke University	1380 – 1550
Columbia University	1330 – 1530
Emory University	1300 – 1470
Georgetown University	1290 – 1490
New York University	1240 – 1420
SUNY Binghamton	1160 – 1350
Florida State University	1070 – 1250
North Carolina A & T University	1000 – 1210
Baruch College (CUNY)	990 – 1200
Spelman College	980 – 1160
Arizona State University	970 – 1220
Hampton University	940 – 1160
Howard University	910 – 1370
University of Mississippi	940 – 1190
Florida A & M University	820 – 1070
North Carolina Central University	750 – 960
Virginia State University	750 – 920
Clark Atlanta University	690 – 1270

Based on the previous SAT

For homework, fill in the average SAT score ranges for your top 3 choice schools.

School	SAT Range

Online college search sites
www.collegeboard.com
nces.ed.gov/collegenavigator
www.collegeview.com

Test Knowledge | What's on the SAT?

Over the next "few" pages we're going to show you everything you need to succeed on the exam and get that score that will blow your admissions officers away. Though the SAT may seem like a daunting venture, but it can be manageable. That's why we're here!

Just by being here, you've taken the first step toward achieving the score you want. You've already increased your odds of improving your test score. However, this doesn't mean that you can daydream during class. To get everything out of your time here, actively participate by asking and answering questions during class. And your prep doesn't stop when you leave this room. Complete, to the best of your ability, any homework your teacher assigns, and come to class prepared to discuss anything you felt unsure about. We are here to help!

Get comfortable. The most important thing about succeeding on the SAT is being familiar with the SAT – ALL OF IT. That's right, the whole test, from front to back and back to front. You need to know about the structure and content, how your scores are generated, how you should approach the test, and how you can help yourself beat the system. We will take a look at all of these components to ensure that on test day you're comfortable with everything.

Now that that's out of the way, without further ado, here is the SAT.

FORMAT

Section	# of Questions	Time Allotted	Topics Tested		Scoring
Reading Test	52	65 minutes	Topic Literature Social Sciences Social Studies Natural Sciences	# of Questions 10-11 10-11 10-11 10-11	200 – 800
Writing and Language Test	44	35 minutes	Topic Expression of Ideas Standard English Conventions	# of Questions 24 20	
Math Test (No Calculator)	20 (5 Grid-Ins)	25 minutes	Topic Algebra Advanced Math Geometry	# of Questions 8 9 3	200 – 800
Math Test (Calculator)	38 (8 Grid-Ins)	55 minutes	Topic Algebra Problem Solving and Data Advanced Math Geometry	# of Questions 11 17 7 3	
Essay (Optional)	1	50 minutes	Essay Response		2 - 8 (3 Grades)

© 2016 Bell Curves, LLC

Introduction | Scoring

For each individual section of the SAT, you will receive a raw score and a scaled score. Let's take a look at each.

Raw Scores

Your raw score is the total number of actual points you have accumulated from answering questions correctly. A few things you should know about the raw score:
- Each right answer adds 1 point to your total raw score.
- Each wrong answer does not add or subtract points from your raw score.
- Unanswered questions do not add or subtract points from your raw score.

Scaled Scores

Scaled scores are generated by a complex and secret SAT formula from which a conversion chart (like the partial one shown below) is generated. You will receive a scaled score on both test sections. These scores are then added in order to generate your total score. College admissions officers will see both your scaled scores for each individual section, as well as your total score. However, they will not see your raw scores. Take a look at a sample piece of a conversion chart below. The Evidence-Based Reading and Writing score is an approximation, as that scaled score is calculated in a slightly different way that will be explained on the next page.

Scaled Score	Evidence-Based Reading and Writing Raw Score	Math Raw Score
800	96	58
790	95	57
780	94	56
770	93	55
760	92	54
750	91	53
740	90	52
730	88-89	51
720	87	50
710	85-86	49
700	84	48
690	83	46-47
680	81-82	45
670	80	44
660	78-79	43
650	76-77	41-42
640	74-75	40
630	72-73	39
620	70-71	38
610	68-69	37
600	67	36
590	66	35
580	63-65	34
570	60-62	33-32

Introduction | Scoring

The SAT includes several additional scores you can use to determine your strengths and areas of need. These scores are not quite as important as your section or total scores, but they can give you insights into your abilities.

Test Scores

You are given a score from 10–40 for each of the three tests on the SAT: the Reading Test, the Writing and Language Test, and the Math Test. Your Evidence-Based Reading and Writing section score is the sum of your Reading Test and Writing and Language Test scores multiplied by 10.

Cross-test Scores

Cross-test scores measure your ability to analyze texts and solve problems in two different subject areas: Analysis in History/Social Studies and Analysis in Science. These subject areas appear in questions in all three of the tests on the SAT and are also scored from 10–40.

Subscores

You are given seven subscores, from 1–15 each, which measure your abilities on several content areas throughout the tests. The Reading Test and the Writing and Language Test contribute to the Command of Evidence and Words in Context subscores. The Writing and Language Test also reports subscores for Standard English Conventions and Expression of Ideas. The Math Test provides three subscores for Heart of Algebra, Problem Solving and Data Analysis, and Passport to Advanced Math.

Chapter 1

Introduction | Pacing

So, we have discussed the test format and content, as well as how the test-makers generate your score. The key now is to know how you can start to improve that score. The most important step now is to determine a pacing plan and to stick with it. It's all about momentum – choosing the proper pace so you can maximize your score and last through the test.

To find an appropriate pace for you, follow the rules below:

1. **Take your foot off the gas pedal.**
   By rushing through a section with the objective of getting to each and every question, there is a higher possibility of making silly mistakes along the way and giving away points on questions you should be answering correctly.

2. **Know your goals.**
   Deciding on a target score and devising a pacing plan to achieve that target score is vital.

3. **Take points where you can get them.**
   Look for the questions YOU feel you can do the best on. As you work through this book you will discover that there are some question types you like and get right more often, and others that you dislike and get wrong more often. Use your time to get the points on the questions you are good at. However, NEVER leave a question completely blank. If you have no idea how to answer it, still bubble in a guess, as you never lose points for a wrong answer.

4. **Use the allotted time wisely.**
   The SAT is all about the efficient usage of your time. Spend the time for each section answering the number of questions that you need to achieve your target score. Almost no one should try to do every single question.

Remember, the people who write the SAT design it to put pressure on test-takers. This leads to stress and a tendency to rush – which leads to mistakes. Do yourself a favor: slow down, answer fewer questions, and stick to your pacing plan. If you do, you will see your score go up.

So, how do you know how many questions you should be answering in each section?

Introduction | Pacing

Determine Your Target Score and Improvement

In order to create your testing plan, you'll need to evaluate the scaled score you currently have and determine a reasonable target score.

Take a look at these two students and how they approached 20 SAT Math questions.

Joe Schmoe

Question	1	2	3	4	5	6	7	8	9	10	11	12	13	14	15	16	17	18	19	20
Correct	B	H	C	K	C	F	E	G	D	F	D	H	C	G	D	F	B	J	B	K
Student	✓	J	✓	F	✓	J	✓	✓	✓	G	A	-	B	✓	C	✓	D	✓	-	G

Total Correct Answers: 9 Total Wrong Answers: 9
Skipped Questions: 2 Guessed Correctly (of those skipped): 0 Raw Score: 9

Bell Curves Student:

Question	1	2	3	4	5	6	7	8	9	10	11	12	13	14	15	16	17	18	19	20
Correct	A	H	C	H	D	K	B	K	B	F	D	J	A	F	B	K	D	K	D	J
Student	✓	✓	✓	J	✓	✓	C	✓	C	✓	C	✓	✓	G	✓	✓	✓	✓	C	✓

Total Correct Answers: 14 Total Wrong Answers: 6
Skipped* Questions: 5 Guessed Correctly (of those "skipped"): 2 Raw Score: 14

* Note: Although we use the term skipped, we do not mean you should leave it blank. Instead, do not spend time on that question and just put in a guess without wasting time. (Notice that this score report has no blanks.) Always put in a guess, as you may get lucky.

To help you decide on a reasonable target final score, keep a couple of things in mind:

> 1. **Be Incremental.**
>   Have a target score in mind but work toward that target score in stages. Do not try to achieve all the score improvements on the first practice test.
>
> 2. **Be Realistic and Fair to Yourself.**
>   Huge score improvements are possible, but they take a lot of work. There is no one timetable that tells you how many hours per week you need to study to get a certain score. Just know that the bigger the score improvement, the more work you need to do – inside and outside the classroom.

How to Get Your Best Score

To get your best score you must get as many questions right as possible. This means you want to work slowly in order to avoid careless mistakes. However, you get no points off for a wrong answer, so you also want to answer **every** question. Here's what to do:
- Work slowly and carefully on your TARGET NUMBER of questions.
- Guess using a "letter of the day" for every question you skip or don't have time to get to.

Introduction | Pacing

To get your best score, you must maximize the number of points you get (right answers), reduce the number of questions you omit (blanks), and minimize the number of points you lose (wrong answers). To do this, you will follow your personal pacing plan.

Let's create one now, using the scores from your initial diagnostic exam. Everyone's pacing plan and target scores will be different, so don't just copy wyour neighbor's plan.

Fill in tables below with the results from your first diagnostic exam. Once you have this information, use it to see a realistic target for your next exam, and fill that information into the chart as well.

Once you have a target scaled scores in mind for your next test, figure out how many raw score points you would likely need to achieve that score. Remember to be realistic. While our goal is to have a perfect hit ratio, everyone makes some mistakes. (This means flipping back to the partial conversion chart on page 10. If you don't see your score on there, ask your teacher to help you estimate the number of raw points you would need to get in order to receive that score.) This should dictate how many questions you attempt on your next exam. (Remember that even those questions you choose not to "attempt" should be bubbled in in the hopes of stealing a point or two on questions you don't actually know.)

Reading Pacing Planner					
	Attempted	Right	Wrong	Raw Score	Scaled Score
Results from Last Test					
Targets for Next Test					

Writing & Language Pacing Planner					
	Attempted	Right	Wrong	Raw Score	Scaled Score
Results from Last Test					
Targets for Next Test					

Math Pacing Planner					
	Attempted	Right	Wrong	Raw Score	Scaled Score
Results from Last Test					
Targets for Next Test					

SAT-R Workbook v. 1.5

Chapter 1

Introduction | Informational Graphics

The SAT will include questions on informational graphics, or infographics, in each section. We have specific instructions for how to deal with these questions in their particular sections, but overall there are some important tips to remember when dealing with infographics.

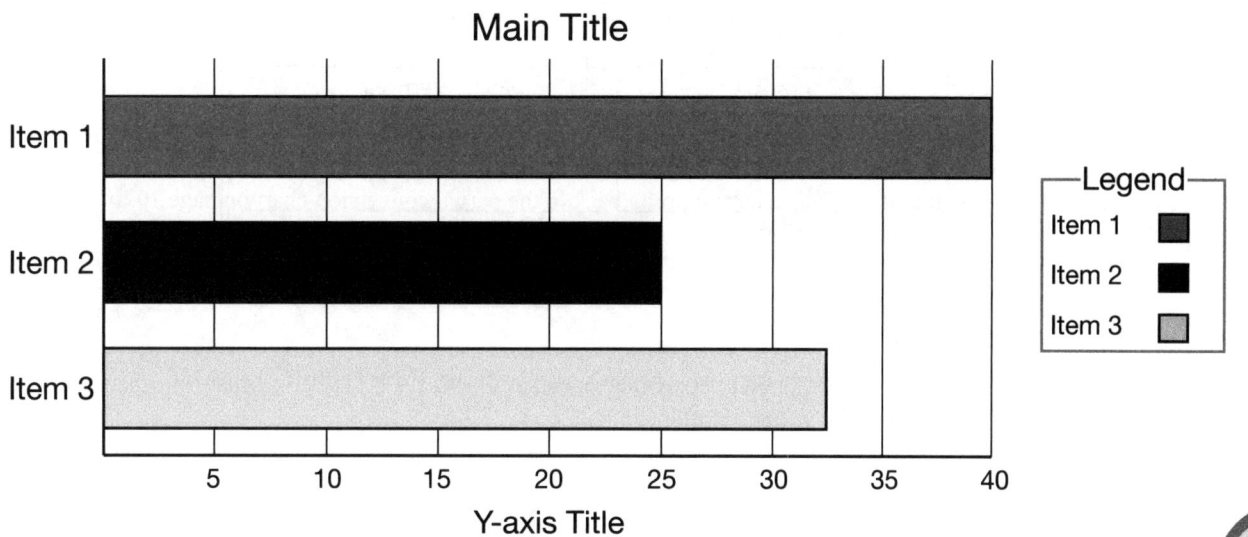

1. **Read All Labels.**
   Make sure you read and understand the main title, any axis titles, the axis markings, and/or the legend. Understanding these will allow you to correctly interpret the data in the graphic.

2. **Look for Trends and Extremes in the Data.**
   See if the data tend to follow any certain overall pattern. Also note the highest and lowest values and if there are any outliers.

3. **Connect the Data to the Question.**
   If the question asks you to refer to a piece of information on a chart or graph, read the relevant data carefully. If the question asks you to extend the graph or chart to include new data, follow the trends of the existing data.

© 2016 Bell Curves, LLC

Introduction | Exam Registration

When
The SAT is always offered on a Saturday morning (or Sunday morning for those with religious restrictions).

Test	Registration
October	September
November	October
December	November
January	December
March	February
May	April
June	May

*Please note that not every test is offered in every city and state. Check the SAT Web site sat.collegeboard.org for specific information about the testing locations in your area.

The Writing Sample
The SAT has an *optional* essay component. Students may choose to take the SAT with or without the essay. However, many universities require students to take the SAT with the writing sample. Please check the schools you are interested in applying to for their requirements.

How Often
The SAT can be taken as many times as a test-taker chooses, but should in most cases be taken only 2-3 times.

How Much
The cost is $43.00 for the SAT without the writing sample and $54.50 with the writing sample. Vouchers may be available from your guidance counselor for students who cannot afford the testing fee. If you qualify for a voucher, you are eligible to apply for free to up to four colleges from a list of over 2,000 participating schools. Additional fees may apply for situations such as standby testing, testing center location change or late registration.

QAS Service
If you choose to, you can order and pay for a Question and Answer Service (QAS) form and test. If you do so, you will receive a copy of the multiple-choice test questions, the answer key, scoring instructions, and a form for ordering your answer sheet. You can choose to order the QAS service when you register, or after you have taken the test. You are not given the option to request the QAS service during every administration of the exam.

The fee for the QAS service is $18.00.

Contact Info
Visit sat.collegeboard.org or call (866) 756-7346.

CHAPTER 2
The Reading Test

College Knowledge
Informed Decisions

Why Should I Go to College?

Here's some food for thought. Below is a chart that shows how much a person makes on average based on the highest degree that person has achieved. Though having a college degree does not guarantee you will make a lot of money, having it allows you many more opportunities to do so than just having a high school diploma. As we can see from the chart, on average a person with a bachelor's degree will make almost $20,000 more a year than someone with a high school diploma. Over a person's entire working life that will add up to almost a million dollars more.

Average Annual Earnings of Workers 25 to 64 Years Old by Level of Education

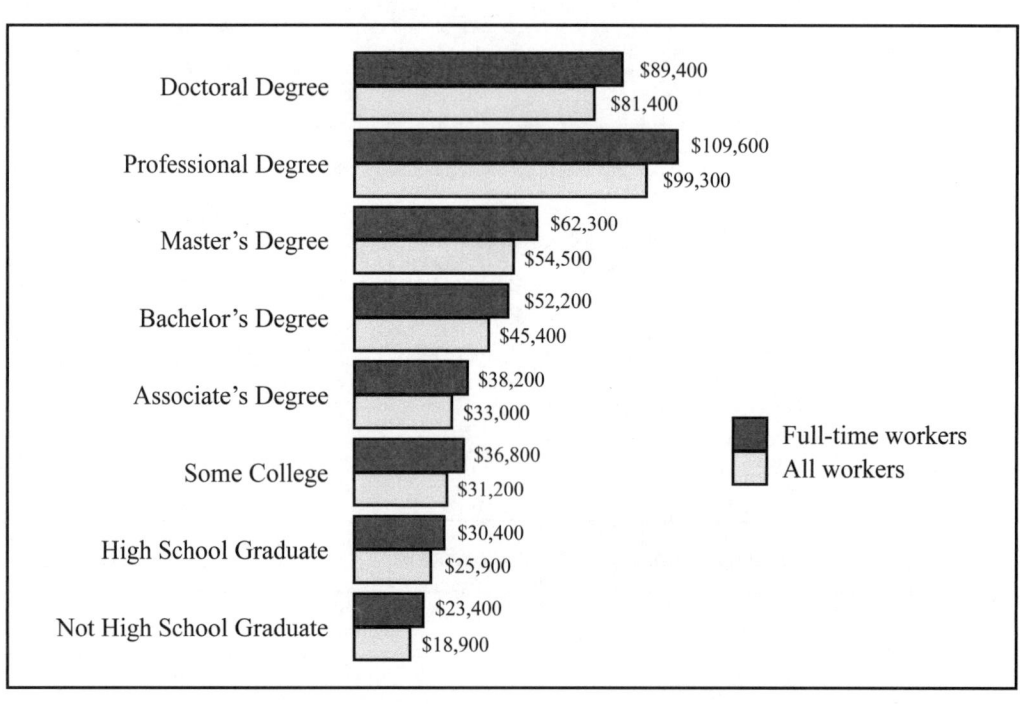

Chapter 2

Reading | Questionnaire

Instructions: *Answer the following questions about reading. There is no right or wrong answer. This survey is just to give you and your teacher a better understanding of how you view reading so we can best help you.*

	True	False
SAT passages are interesting.	☐	☐
SAT passages test topics I've never seen and that are difficult.	☐	☐
SAT passages use really difficult vocabulary.	☐	☐
SAT passages are way too long.	☐	☐
SAT passages are more difficult than other things I read.	☐	☐
SAT reading questions are tricky.	☐	☐
SAT reading questions are very easy to answer.	☐	☐

Reading | Format

The Reading Test composes 1/4 of your overall SAT total score, as it makes up half of the Evidence-Based Reading and Writing score.

The number of questions you get correct on this section will be converted into a test score, as is shown in the chart below. The conversion chart is slightly different for each administration, but these numbers give you a general idea of where you are scoring. The highest possible test score is a 40.

Raw Score	Test Score	Raw Score	Test Score	Raw Score	Test Score
0	10	18	21	36	30
1	10	19	22	37	31
2	10	20	22	38	31
3	11	21	23	39	32
4	12	22	23	40	32
5	13	23	24	41	33
6	14	24	24	42	33
7	15	25	24	43	34
8	15	26	25	44	34
9	16	27	25	45	35
10	17	28	26	46	35
11	18	29	27	47	36
12	18	30	27	48	37
13	19	31	28	49	37
14	19	32	28	50	38
15	20	33	29	51	39
16	20	34	29	52	40
17	21	35	30		

As mentioned earlier, this test score is then added to your Language and Writing Test score and the sum is multiplied by 10 to yield your scaled Evidence-Based Reading and Writing score, the highest score on which is an 800.

The SAT Reading Test will always consist of four single passages and one paired-passage. These five passages will always have 10 or 11 questions and be drawn from the following fields:

- One literature single passage drawn from American or world literature
- One social science single passage
- One social studies single or paired-passage drawn from American founding documents or global texts, and
- Two single passages, or one single and one paired-passage, drawn from the natural sciences.

Chapter 2

Test Knowledge | Reading Comprehension

The fundamental skills tested in the three types of Reading questions are the same: *the ability to read and extract information from what you've read.* To read and understand you must learn to read comprehensively and clearly *without adding, subtracting, or altering* what you read. This skill takes time to master, but it's very possible if you work at it!

How to Improve Your Comprehension:

- Read more challenging books, newspapers, magazines, blogs, etc.
- Constantly ask yourself why the author is saying something or why a certain character is doing something.
- Discuss your analyses with friends, family, teachers, etc.

Why You Should Improve Your Comprehension:

- Having good reading comprehension skills will help you correctly dissect and analyze any text. This is especially important in college as you will be reading a lot of material for every single class.
- Having good reading comprehension skills will help you communicate your ideas clearly.
- Most of the questions on the Reading sections of the SAT require good reading comprehension skills

Success in Critical Reading requires paying careful attention to the exact meaning of words.

www.bellcurves.com

Reading | Overview

The Keys to Success
Many people find the questions on the Reading Test of the SAT to be among the hardest to improve their score on. However this should not be the case! If you understand how the passages are structured and the keys for success you should be able to maximize your score and performance on these questions.

The keys to SAT Reading success are:

- Time Management
- Question Prioritization
- Translation

Time Management
Many people waste time reading passages multiple times when they take the SAT; once before looking at the questions, again to answer the questions, and finally to verify the answer selected. This is a huge waste of time and is an inefficient way to take a timed test. Instead of reading three times we're going to learn how to effectively attack and understand a question so we can spend our time thinking about the answers (since selecting the correct answer is what you get credit for). Learning what to read and when to read it are key to an effective plan for the Reading Test.

Question Prioritization
Questions for the Reading Test are *not* presented in order of difficulty (as they are in Math), so *you* have to decide which questions to answer, and which ones to skip. Typically, you will want to answer the detail questions with short line references (five lines or fewer) first, and save the longer line reference questions and the general questions for later (or, skip them altogether). General questions (main idea, tone, or overview questions) require much more reading and understanding of the passage than detail questions do, so saving or omitting them makes sense. *That* is efficient test-taking!

Translation
As you should remember from the previous chapter, the challenges in reading passages are that they are often difficult to translate into simple English from complex SAT-speak. We have to remember the keys to proper translation are:

• Read the passage literally.

• Read for what the author says, and why the author says it.

• Don't devour the passage– nibble at it!

Chapter 2

Understanding the SAT I Reading Passages

What's different about SAT reading?

SAT Reading is very different from most things you read in school. Understanding these differences will help you more effectively answer questions and address traps. One of the paragraphs is written in the style of the SAT, however, and the other is not.

Instructions: *Read the following passages and identify how the "SAT Passage" makes things more complex.*

Passage 1

The first detective fiction story was not E.T.A. Hoffmann's 1819 novel *Das Fräulein von Scuderi*, as some people believe. Instead, the detective fiction genre started in 1841 with Edgar Allen Poe's short story *The Murders in the Rue Morgue*. The central character of *The Murders in the Rue Morgue* is detective C. Auguste Dupin, who is described as "eccentric and brilliant." After *The Murders in the Rue Morgue*, Poe wrote more stories about C. Auguste Dupin. These stories further developed the detective fiction style, which continues to be used today. The plot in Poe's detective fiction focuses on determining truth primarily through careful gathering and analysis of evidence supported by logic, observation, and inference. This style of crime solving, with its emphasis on forensic detail, inspired the stories of Sherlock Holmes. In fact, Poe's story *The Murders in the Rue Morgue* is mentioned in the first Sherlock Holmes novel.

Passage 2

The 1819 novella *Das Fräulein von Scuderi*, by E.T.A. Hoffmann, is sometimes held up as the original detective story and a direct, influential antecedent to Edgar Allan Poe's *The Murders in the Rue Morgue*. However, detective fiction is more likely to have begun in 1841 with the publication of *The Murders in the Rue Morgue* itself, which featured "the first fictional detective: the eccentric C. Auguste Dupin." The formula for the detective story established by Poe in "Rue Morgue" and further developed in later C. Auguste Dupin tales continues to exist today with few alterations. In stories such as these, the primary concern of the plot is ascertaining truth, and the usual means of obtaining the truth is an abstruse and enigmatic marriage of intuitive logic, astute observation, and perspicacious inference. The key enabler of this style of analysis, with its attention to forensic detail, is the gathering of physical evidence. Poe's "Rue Morgue" set the tone for and perhaps acted as muse for the stories about the most famous of all fictional detectives: Arthur Conan Doyle's *Sherlock Holmes*. Indeed, Holmes mentions the Poe story in the first Conan Doyle

List 3 things that made the harder of the two passages harder to read?

1. _____

2. _____

3. _____

Which was more likely to appear on the SAT?

_____

New Vocabulary

www.bellcurves.com

The Scoop | SAT Reading Comprehension

Passage-based reading tests your reading and comprehension skills. In other words, it asks about the information in the passage, rather than your opinions. Passages will be drawn from a wide range of topics (from history to fiction) and be written in a variety of styles (some esoteric and dense, some cogent and simple), but the SAT cannot and will not test you on prior knowledge about a specific subject. SAT reading questions can only test you on the content of the passage or sentence in front of you. In short, this means that:

Reading passages give you all the information you need to answer the questions!

Reading comprehension questions are like questions on an open-book test. All of the support for the correct answers to questions about a passage must be in the passage. All you have to do is find them. Finding the information you need from the passage should be manageable as long as you remember:

SAT reading passages ...

- **are rarely black and white.**
- **often present complex and multi-faceted ideas.**
- **typically qualify most statements and arguments.**
- **require you to understand the reason for the information given.**

Drill | Understanding Meaning

Instructions: *For the questions below, determine the degree of truth of each statement based ONLY on the information provided in its accompanying passage/sentence.*

Most teenagers today believe that Lil Wayne is the best rapper ever.

1. Lil Wayne is not the best rapper ever.

[Must be true | Can't be true | (Could be true)]

2. Only one teenager thinks Lil Wayne is the best rapper ever.

[Must be true | (Can't be true) | Could be true]

3. At least one teenager does not think Lil Wayne is the best rapper ever.

[(Must be true) | Can't be true | Could be true]

4. Some people think that Lil Wayne stands among history's greatest rap artists.

[(Must be true) | Can't be true | Could be true]

5. Anyone who thinks that Lil Wayne is one of the best rappers in history is less than 20 years old but older than 12.

[Must be true | ~~Can't be true~~ | (Could be true)]

T.I. is not supposed to be here. He's not supposed to be on the cover of Vibe magazine. He's not supposed to be on MTV every Tuesday night subjecting at-risk teens to shock treatment on his new series, T.I.'s *Road to Redemption*. He's not supposed to be on the road doing shows to promote his blockbuster sixth album, *Paper Trail*. He's not supposed to be spearheading voting drives or voting for the first time in his life, as he did on October 28, 2008. To hear some tell it, Clifford "T.I." Harris, Jr., is not even supposed to be walking the Earth.

6. Some people believe that T.I. should be dead.

[Must be true | Can't be true | Could be true]

7. T.I.'s new album is not his first album.

[Must be true | Can't be true | Could be true]

8. T.I.'s show on cable is a hit.

[Must be true | Can't be true | Could be true]

9. T.I. is working with teens.

[Must be true | Can't be true | Could be true]

10. T.I. thinks Americans waste time voting.

[Must be true | Can't be true | Could be true]

Drill | Understanding Meaning

For many visitors to New York, the subway system is the most daunting part of travel around the city. Given New York City's 656 miles of track and many different alpha-numeric train lines, this fact is not surprising. What is surprising is how many of these tourists find it impossible to read the subway maps posted throughout the train system.

According to the above passage which statement in each of the following pairs is best supported by the passage?

11. [Most tourists have trouble navigating the subway | Some tourists have trouble navigating the subway]

12. [The author believes that people should be able to read a subway map | The greater portion of tourists cannot read subway maps]

13. [NYC's subway is the largest in the world | NYC's subway has more than 2 lines]

14. [All locals can read maps | Some locals may have skills tourists do not]

15. [A significant portion of visitors to New York City cannot use maps to navigate the subway system | All foreign tourists cannot understand what's written on the subway map]

16. [The author is surprised by the number of tourists who have trouble understanding the NYC subway map | The author is proud of the 656 miles of track that make up NYC's subway system.]

The consensus within the scientific community seems to be that if research continues as it has for the past decade, we will find intelligent and technologically advanced extraterrestrial life in distant parts of the galaxy. While the discovery of alien forms of life in other solar systems (if not in our own) seems likely, I find it most unlikely that myriad technologically advanced civilizations are out there, waiting to be discovered.

According to the above passage which statement in each of the following pairs is supported by the passage?

17. [There has been scientific research on the possibility of extraterrestrial life for at least a decade | There has been consensus on extraterrestrial life in the scientific community for at least a decade]

18. [The author agrees with the prevailing notion about aliens in certain regards | The author agrees with the scientific community]

19. [Scientists have found intelligent extraterrestrial life | Scientists continue to investigate the possibility of finding intelligent extraterrestrial life]

20. [The author has interest in certain scientific fields of study | The author is an expert in the study of astronomy]

21. [There is a scientific agreement about aliens | There appears to be a scientific agreement about types of extraterrestrial life to be discovered]

Chapter 2

Drill | Read Objectively

Remember the SAT cannot test you on your outside knowledge or personal associations with any topic. On the previous pages, you practiced how to read a text for literal meaning: read, digest, regurgitate. However, as SAT Reading Test gets harder, with more subtle, nuanced, and complicated phrases, you might find yourself tempted to make assumptions and leaps in logic about the meaning of a text. *Resist this temptation!* Never make assumptions or leaps in logic with Critical Reading! Instead, always ask yourself the same, basic questions: "What, literally, does the text say? What does it mean? Why?"

Let's look at some examples:

The sentence, "The woman's clothing was inappropriate," means:

Daniel's answer: The woman was scantily clad.

Patrice's answer: The woman was at a Fourth of July picnic in a wool business suit.

Angeline's answer: The woman was wearing red to a funeral.

Who, if anyone, is right? Why? _____

The sentence, "The woman's clothing was inappropriate, since her role in the company was that of a dish washer rather than an executive," means:

Daniel's answer: The woman should have had on a business suit.

Patrice's answer: The woman was wearing a suit.

Angeline's answer: The woman was dressed too formally given her position.

Who, if anyone, is right? Why? _____

> Question every choice and make the passage prove it to you.

www.bellcurves.com

Drill I Be Objective! B. E. Objective!

Instructions: *Read each of the following sentences and write down what they want you to assume and what they actually say.*

1. The question's difficulty needed to be adjusted.

    Assumption: _____

    Actual: _____

2. The cafeteria lunch made the students weep.

    Assumption: _____

    Actual: _____

3. Despite its obvious stylishness, many people questioned the value of the shirt.

    Assumption: _____

    Actual: _____

4. He arrived at work at a time other than his usual time.

    Assumption: _____

    Actual: _____

5. She cited irreconcilable differences as the reason for the divorce.

    Assumption: _____

    Actual: _____

6. The primary factor used to weigh the merits of an essay is its clarity.

    Assumption: _____

    Actual: _____

Remember to prove your answer in the passage. DON'T make assumptions.

Drill I Putting Answers in Your Own Words

Reading comprehension means understanding what you read. When you tackle SAT reading passages, your focus should be on what you were told, why you were told that thing, and how you were told that thing.

Instructions: *Read the following texts and answer the questions asked.*

1. I have little patience with shopping and little comprehension of those who enjoy doing it. For me, venturing into a store is an exercise in pragmatism; I venture into stores only when I have a particular need, be it for bread, toilet tissue, a new pair of pants, or a new mop.

   What are the author's feelings about shopping?

   _____

   How does he convey his feelings?

   _____

   _____

2. My addiction to the process and pleasure of shopping has often strained my budget. These days, venturing into a store is an exercise in self-control: I venture into stores only when I have a specific need, despite the lure of the "For Sale" and "50% Off" signs.

   What are the author's feelings about shopping?

   _____

   How does he convey his feelings?

   _____

   _____

3. Traditionally, having eyewitness testimony has been the ace in the hole in a prosecutor's case, in that having it usually results in a conviction. After all, seeing is believing, and the best testimony is one that is unwavering.

   What are the author's feelings about eyewitness testimony?

   _____

   How does she convey her feelings?

   _____

   _____

4. Traditionally, having eyewitness testimony has been the ace in the hole in a prosecutor's case, in that having it usually results in a conviction. After all, seeing is believing and the best testimony is one that is unwavering. But are witnesses reliable enough to merit their testimony having so much weight?

   What are the author's feelings about eyewitness testimony?

   _____

   How does she convey her feelings?

   _____

   _____

www.bellcurves.com

SAT Reading | What, Why, and How?

Discerning what a passage says will often require you to recognize and deal with subtle, convoluted, and often vague language. A significant aspect of understanding a passage is recognizing when something is said in an intentionally subtle or nuanced manner. Before you can answer questions accurately, you have to train yourself to efficiently and effectively identify *what* the author told you, as well as *why* and *how* he told it to you.

1. What?

After reading something, take the time to put *what* the author said into words that are clearer to you. Separate the main position from supporting ideas, details, and other information. In short, rephrase it in plain English so you understand what you've read.

2. Why?

Make sure you understand not only what the author is telling you but also *why* the author is telling it to you. The author always has a reason for providing you information: to support a position. You just need to understand the information and identify that position. Remember that supporting information does not contradict the main point.

3. How?

There is always more than one way to say something. Make sure you understand the *way* the author tells you the information. Think about what function the information you are reading serves in the passage as a whole. The *how* question-type is basically the opposite of the *why* question-type. Why does the author tell me this information? To back up his main point. How does he back up his main point? With the information he told me there.

Chapter 2

Drill I What, Why, and How?

Instructions: *Read the passage below, then answer the questions. Keep **what**, **why**, and **how** in mind.*

Familial dysfunction is not a new phenomenon. In fact, many seemingly innocuous fairy tales deal with this topic. In one of our most beloved stories, Cinderella was raised by her step-mother and two step-sisters after Cinderella's father remarries. Because Cinderella's father doted on her the few times when he was home, the envious women that married into the family mistreated Cinderella. In her father's absence, she was made to do all the household chores. According to the story, she worked so hard that her clothes were reduced to cinders and this is the source of her famous nickname.

1. What does the above paragraph imply about Cinderella's father?

    Daniel's answer:
    Her father was under a spell from her step-mother.

    Patrice's answer:
    Her father didn't have much say over Cinderella's raising.

    Angeline's answer:
    Her father was a wealthy and powerful man.

    Who's right? Why are they right?

    _____
    _____

2. How does the passage convey Cinderella's struggles?

    Daniel's answer:
    By explaining the difficulty of her daily life.

    Patrice's answer:
    By telling us how her Fairy Godmother's powers worked.

    Angelina's answer:
    By explaining how her mother passed away.

    Who's right? Why are they right?

    _____
    _____

3. Why does the passage mention that her clothes were "reduced to cinders"?

    Daniel's answer:
    It is an attempt to embarrass her father.

    Patrice's answer:
    To prove that hard work is rough on your wardrobe.

    Angeline's answer:
    To explain how she earned her nickname.

    Who's right? Why are they right?

    _____
    _____

Chapter 2

SAT Reading | Question Types

Reading for What, Why, and How

To do well on SAT reading questions, you simply have to find what they expect you to understand from each passage, question, and answer choice. Reading questions come in two basic types (*detail* and *general*), and ask three basic questions (*what*, *why*, and *how*).

What Questions

What questions ask *what* or *what else* the passage tells you. Typical types of *what* questions are:

> **Information Retrieval:** ask what the passage states
> **Inference:** ask what else must be true given what you were told
> **Vocabulary-in-Context:** ask what a word means as used in the passage
> **Main Point:** ask what the author's point is

Typical phrasing: Which statement about the Slater Paradox is supported by the passage?
In line 57, "claims" most nearly means
The comment about "the new artistic model" suggests that

Why Questions

Why questions ask you for the reason behind something the author does. Typical types of *why* questions are:

> **Purpose:** ask why the passage mentions the given reference
> **Primary Purpose:** ask for the reason that author writes the passage

Typical phrasing: The primary purpose of the statements in lines 4 - 6 ("One . . . of an age") is to
The author uses the phrase "rarified region" (line 23) to

How Questions

How questions ask the way in which the author does something. Typical types of *how* questions are:

> **Organization:** ask how the author structures the passage or a part of the passage
> **Tone:** ask how the author feels about a particular topic
> **Argument:** ask how the author supports his argument, or how you might weaken or strengthen it

Typical phrasing: The tone of the characterizations quoted in lines 11 - 12 is best described as
Which of the following would weaken the author's argument about the ape?

Chapter 2

Drill | Identifying Questions

Instructions: *In the exercise below, determine whether each question is a what, why, or how question. Then use the space below that question to translate it into a straightforward question beginning with one of our three question words!*

Question	Type		
The view of robotics held by the author can best be described as	❏ What	❏ Why	❏ How
The author uses the idea of the doors to	❏ What	❏ Why	❏ How
The author refers to the "cod fisherman" (line 53) primarily to illustrate	❏ What	❏ Why	❏ How
Lines 33-38 primarily serve to	❏ What	❏ Why	❏ How
The author of Passage 1 would most likely respond to the last statement in Passage 2 (lines 73-82) by asserting that	❏ What	❏ Why	❏ How
Which of the following rhetorical devices does the author use in the passage?	❏ What	❏ Why	❏ How
The African novelist's comment in lines 23-28 chiefly focuses on the	❏ What	❏ Why	❏ How
The statement in lines 56-64 ("But . . . fish") indicates that the author	❏ What	❏ Why	❏ How
The tone of the second passage is best described as	❏ What	❏ Why	❏ How
Which of the following best describes the relationship between the two passages?	❏ What	❏ Why	❏ How

www.bellcurves.com

Chapter 2

SAT Reading | Translation

Wicked Wording
Many questions, like the passages, use verbose, complicated language designed to hide what the questions are actually asking. The questions also often do not contain an actual question, but instead leave it to the answer choices to complete a thought started in the question. Furthermore, the questions often begin with a qualifier such as, "according to the passage," or, "according to the author," which is a pointless distraction since we should understand that everything used to answer the question will be based on the passage and author.

SAT-to-English Translation
To avoid the confusion caused by the questions, translate the questions from SAT-speak to a language you can understand. Pose the question with simpler language that still captures the real meaning of the question, but states it more simply. Be careful not to fall into the trap of regurgitating the question with synonyms or concepts that are as difficult as those in the original question. Consider the following example:

> The passage states that the primary reason traditional studies of financial markets and commercial structures in Latin American countries overlook imbalances in the allocation of financial resources is

Daniel thinks the question should be translated as:
What does the passage say is the principle reason that traditional studies of financial markets and commercial structures in Latin American countries don't consider imbalances in resource allocation?

Patrice thinks the question should be translated as:
Why are there imbalances in the allocation of financial resources in Latin American countries?

Angeline thinks the question should be translated as:
Why do studies of financial markets in Latin America ignore imbalances in the distribution of money?

Who's right? Why are they right?

_____

_____

_____

Reading | Question Types

Detail Questions

The vast majority of SAT Reading questions will be specific rather than general. Specific questions are questions that ask about the details in the passage and typically refer to a specific portion of the passage, either by directing you to highlighted text, a specific paragraph, or a specific topic.

General Questions

General questions are less common than their more specific kin. They will ask about the passage as a whole, or about large chunks of the passage at a time, often concerning themselves with the mood, tone, or intent of the passage.

Followup Questions

Followup questions will always ask for the "best evidence" to answer the previous question. The answer choices for these questions will always be line numbers. Use these questions as opportunities to get two points from a single piece of information.

Informational Graphics Questions

Informational Graphics questions will ask you to draw specific conclusions from tables, graphs, and charts. For these questions, use the strategy we discussed on the Informational Graphics skills page. You may be asked to analyze the graphic itself or connect the information to the text. They will only be in social science or natural science passages.

Reading | Question Types

Question Types

Let's further examine three specific question types we have already seen: Detail, Inference, and Main Idea. Detail questions ask you to recall information from the passage. Inference questions ask you to take what the author has said and extend it one step further. These questions ask what is implied by the author but not explicitly stated. Main Idea questions ask you to summarize either a paragraph or the entire passage. We've further categorized these types of questions below.

Detail Questions

- Identify and/or interpret details
    - ex: "According to the passage, other members of the genus *Laticauda* and the banded sea krait differ in which of the following ways?"
- Understand vocabulary in context
    - ex: "The author uses the word 'indifference' to indicate:"

Inference Questions

- Deduce the author's tone and point of view
    - ex: "Which of the following would the author most likely agree with?"
- Compare and contrast relationships
    - ex: "How does Martha's relationship with Linda differ from Martha's relationship with her own sister?"
- Understand cause and effect events and relationships
    - ex: "According to the author, what caused the dinosaurs to become extinct?"

Main Idea Questions

- Understand the main idea of a paragraph, multiple paragraphs, or the passage as a whole
    - ex: "The main point of the first paragraph is:"
- Make generalizations
    - ex: "Linda's mother is best described as:"
- Determine sequence of events
    - ex: "According to the passage, the experiments that led to the founding of the big bang theory began with:"

Chapter 2

Drill I SAT Reading Comprehension

Instructions: *Read the passage below, then decide who has the best answer to the question and explain why you chose that answer.*

Diana was becoming highly budget conscious and was consistently trying to reduce the needless expenses she had been prone to accumulate. So when she went to the supermarket, she bought a smaller pack of popsicles than usual.

1. Based on the passage, what is most likely true?

   Daniel's answer:
   Diana plans to go on a diet.

   Patrice's answer:
   Diana is willing to reduce her popsicle expenditures to save money.

   Angeline's answer:
   Diana plans to share at least some of her popsicles before they are no longer edible.

   Whose answer is best supported? Why?

   _____

   _____

High-speed space travel is so expensive and dangerous that intelligent alien civilizations, if they do exist, probably wouldn't even try it. After all, why should they try it, when radio communications are capable of providing all the information they might want?

2. In the above passage, "radio communications" are mentioned as an example of

   Daniel's answer:
   an outdated technology.

   Patrice's answer:
   a free way to listen to alien phone calls

   Angeline's answer:
   a more practical way to gather information

   Whose answer is best supported? Why?

   _____

   _____

> Be careful not to make assumptions based on outside information! The 'real world' is irrelevant when you take the SAT.

www.bellcurves.com

SAT Reading | Common Wrong Answers

Although the subject matter of SAT reading passages varies from section to section, and test to test, the basic types of wrong answer choices associated with those passages often remain the same. By familiarizing yourself with the patterns that wrong answers commonly follow, you will more readily be able to spot and eliminate likely wrong answer choices.

The most common wrong answers fall into one of the following categories:

Type	Explanation	Common Traits
Off-Topic	Off-topic answers bring up the wrong topic from the passage.	Mentions the topic, but an aspect of it which the author doesn't talk about or is not the answer to the question.
Extreme	Uses language stronger than that of the original passage.	Strengthens the emotions or tone of what the author says.
Vague	Requires you to guess what is meant by the wording.	Offers a general, and often true conclusion, but does not clearly connect to the question at hand.
Contradicts the Passage	Goes directly against the passage.	Comes from a dissenting opinion the author mentions.
Contradicts Reality	Ridiculous statements that contradict common sense.	Draws outlandish conclusions, or makes unsound assumptions.
Half-Right	Part of the answer is deceptively correct, but the other half is untrue.	Cites key phrases from the passages, but is ultimately made incorrect by one or more words.

Being able to spot trap answers helps you eliminate choices and make better guesses.

Chapter 2

Drill I Common Wrong Answers

Instructions: Read the following questions and answer choices (we did not give you the passages). Based on the common wrong answer types, see how many answer choices you can eliminate and check off which wrong-answer categories the choice falls into.

1. According to the passage, the Fermi Paradox depends most directly upon which assumption?

   A) Aliens and humans are already in contact.
   B) Extraterrestrial technology would develop at roughly the same rate as human technology.
   C) Extraterrestrial civilizations would inevitably use technology to destroy Earth.
   D) Science is a more powerful form of human knowledge than are art and literature.

	Off-Topic	Extreme	Vague	Contradicts Passage	Contradicts Reality	Half-Right
(A)						
(B)						
(C)						
(D)						

2. Lines 3-7 ("On the ... themselves") primarily serve to

   A) show the strong regard that people have for history.
   B) point out that Americans always experience radically different degrees of patriotism.
   C) cite history as a favored subject among a wide range of people.
   D) indicate the reverence people feel for Jefferson's words.

	Off-Topic	Extreme	Vague	Contradicts Passage	Contradicts Reality	Half-Right
(A)						
(B)						
(C)						
(D)						

SAT Reading | Action Plan

For many, the most daunting part of Reading is the length of the passages: 60-110 lines! Fortunately, following the steps below will make them less overwhelming.

1. **Read and digest the blurb.**

2. **Approach the questions one at a time.**
   The questions are almost always phrased as unfinished statements. Go to the first question and translate it into a real question that you can work with. Label it as a *what, why,* or *how* question, then decide whether it's a detail question you can attack now, or a general question to save for later. Do this for each question individually. If you don't understand a question, bubble in your letter of the day.

3. **Go back to the passage.**
   Find the portion of the passage that the question references, and read the **entire paragraph** that it is within. Use chronology or key words to find which paragraph to read if you don't have a line reference.

4. **Jot down the answer to the question in your own words.**
   You must know what answer you are looking for before reading the answer choices.

5. **Eliminate answer choices.**
   Eliminate any answer choice that is not similar to yours. If you are not sure what a choice means then keep it and come back to it.

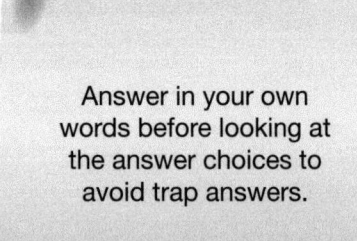

> Answer in your own words before looking at the answer choices to avoid trap answers.

Action Plan | Additional Strategies

For the Followup and Informational Graphic questions, while you still want to use your overall Action Plan, additional strategies are necessary. These question types are easy to identify and you can use the following methods for maximizing your efficiency on these question types.

Followup Questions:

1. Locate the Followup questions. You will actually answer these before answering the questions they follow (denoted here as "previous questions").
2. Read the previous question.
3. Using the answer choices in the Followup question, go back to the passage and read the cited lines.
4. Eliminate any answer choice that doesn't answer the previous question.
5. Using your answer to the Followup question, answer the previous question.

Informational Graphic Questions:

1. Locate the Informational Graphic questions. (These usually come at the end of a passage)
2. Read the question and determine the applicable information.
3. Break down the axes, legends, and/or any additional information that comes with the graphic.
4. Analyze the graphic and check the data against the relevant part of the passage.

Chapter 2

Additional Strategies | Drill

The ice cream industry did not begin to use the Dixie cup until approximately 1920, some 12 years after Hugh Moore had invented it. Initially the product was not the cups themselves, but rather water
5 from vending machines that used the disposable cups. Having been unsuccessful with the vending machines, Moore decided to sell the disposable paper cups in an attempt to replace the unsanitary tin cups that were commonly used for drinking water. Soon
10 after laws were passed in various states banning public sippers, demand for Moore's disposable cups skyrocketed. After years of success a new use for Moore's disposable cup emerged when he and the ice cream industry became acquainted.

Figure 1
Primary Uses for Moore's Disposable Cups in 1935

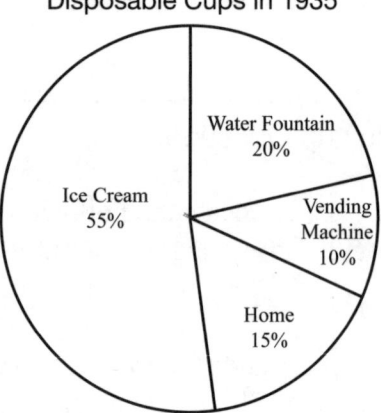

- Ice Cream 55%
- Water Fountain 20%
- Vending Machine 10%
- Home 15%

1. According to the passage, Moore's disposable cups became a success due to

   A) their durability.
   B) the ban on shared tin cups.
   C) the increasing popularity of vending machines.
   D) the rise of the ice cream industry.

   Which line reference in Question 2 best answers Question 1?

   _____

   _____

2. Which choice provides the best evidence for the answer to the previous question?

   A) Lines 1-3 ("The ice...invented it")
   B) Lines 3-6 ("Initially...cups")
   C) Lines 9-12 ("Soon...skyrocketed")
   D) Lines 12-14 ("a new...acquainted")

   Which answer choice in Question 1 matches the line reference you picked for Question 2?

   _____

   _____

3. The figure and the passage together show that the most popular use of the disposable cup

   A) changed between 1920 and 1935.
   B) was in home.
   C) declined after 1935.
   D) was no longer in vending machines.

   What information do we get from the labels on the infographic?

   _____

   _____

What information in the figure and the passage is relevant to the question?

_____

_____

How does the relevant information in the graphic connect with the relevant information in the passage?

_____

_____

SAT-R Workbook v. 1.5

Chapter 2

Reading | Drill

Read the passage below and answer the following questions using the Action Plan. Although passages on the SAT typically have 75 to 100 lines of text and 10-11 questions, for the purposes of this exercise, the passage below is shorter than what you'll typically see on the exam.

The following passage is an excerpt from an article on reptiles. The author discusses a particularly interesting species of snake.

While it is a zoologist's job to study animals (some of them rare), it is not every day that zoologists have the opportunity to study truly unique creatures. One such extraordinary creature is the banded sea krait, and those who are able to study it marvel at its distinctiveness. The banded sea krait (*Laticauda colubrina*) inhabits numerous warm water environments, though it is largely concentrated around the coastal coral reef regions of Australia and New Zealand. With the ability to live both on land and in water, the banded
10 sea krait is one of the few amphibious reptiles on the planet.

The sea krait is a type of sea snake that has undergone an evolution that is considered limited in comparison to other members of the genus *Laticauda*. A banded sea krait is easily identified by its small head and cylindrical-shaped
15 body that ends in a laterally compressed tail. As its name would indicate, the banded sea krait has bands running over the entire length of its 6 foot body. In addition to being able to survive extended periods of time on land or in water, *Laticauda colubrina* differs from other members of its
20 genus because it is ovoviviparous, meaning that it comes ashore to lay eggs. In exhibiting this behavior, sea kraits also distinguish themselves as one of the only reptiles to participate in group migrations. Similar to salmon, sea kraits usually return to the same area to lay their eggs. They do so
25 in migratory groups with numbers ranging from five to fifty participants.

Banded sea kraits also go ashore to engage in courtship, shed skin, and digest the food that they usually obtain by trapping small fish or eels in coral reef crevices and poisoning
30 their prey with an injection of venom via their small hollow fangs. While this venom is highly toxic (approximately ten times more toxic than cobra or rattlesnake venom), making *Laticauda colubrina* one of the most deadly animals on the planet, very few humans have been fatally wounded, owing
35 largely to the snakes' docile nature and small fangs.

1. The author's purpose in writing this passage is most likely to

   Your answer:_____

   _____

   _____

2. The author uses the verb "marvel" (line 5) to indicate that

   Your answer: they are amazed by it.

   _____

   _____

3. The main focus of the second paragraph (lines 11-26) in relation to the passage as a whole is

   Your answer:_____

   _____

   _____

4. Based on the passage, which of the following most likely contributes to the distinctive differences between banded sea kraits and other members of its genus?

   Your answer:_____

   _____

   _____

www.bellcurves.com

Reading | Drill

5. According to the passage, salmon and sea krait both

Your answer: _____

_____

_____

6. According to the passage, all of the following are reasons the banded sea krait comes ashore EXCEPT

Your answer: _____

_____

_____

7. According to the passage, which of the following pairs of reasons account for the lack of human fatalities from banded sea krait bites?

Your answer: _____

_____

_____

8. As it is used, the word "docile" in the line 35 most nearly means

Your answer: _____

_____

_____

Reading I Drill

1

The author's purpose in writing this passage is most likely to

A) define the characteristics that make animals extraordinary.
B) describe some of the distinguishing qualities of the banded sea krait.
C) argue for the protection of members of the genus *Laticauda*.
D) explain why the banded sea krait is more unique than other members of the genus *Laticauda*.

2

The author uses the verb "marvel" (line 5) to indicate that

A) many zoologists have never heard of the banded sea krait.
B) the banded sea krait is the most unusual sea snake in existence.
C) the banded sea krait inspires amazement and admiration in those who study it.
D) members of the genus *Laticauda* are extremely rare.

3

The main focus of the second paragraph (lines 11-26) in relation to the passage as a whole is

A) an analysis of the evolutionary forces that led to the unique adaptations of the banded sea krait.
B) a description of some of the unique characteristics of the banded sea krait compared to other animals.
C) a comparison of the banded sea krait's habitat to those of other members of the genus *Laticauda*.
D) support for the theory that the banded sea krait and the salmon share a common ancestor.

4

Based on the passage, which of the following most likely contributes to the distinctive differences between banded sea kraits and other members of its genus?

A) Evolutionary forces
B) Climate
C) Habitat
D) Food resources

5

According to the passage, salmon and sea krait both

A) lay their eggs on land.
B) return to the same area to lay their eggs.
C) migrate in groups of 5 to 50.
D) live in the waters of Australia and New Zealand.

6

According to the passage, all of the following are reasons the banded sea krait comes ashore EXCEPT

A) to shed its skin.
B) to find a mate.
C) to complete the digestive process.
D) to regulate its body temperature.

7

According to the passage, which of the following pairs of reasons account for the lack of human fatalities from banded sea krait bites?

A) The sea krait's passive nature and its hollow fangs
B) The sea krait's aggressive nature and its small fangs
C) The seak krait's unthreatening nature and its small fangs
D) The sea krait's cruel nature and its venomous fangs

8

As it is used, the word "docile" in the line 35 most nearly means

A) weak.
B) confused.
C) unassertive.
D) lethal.

Chapter 2

Reading | Literature

To answer Reading questions effectively, it is important to know what to look for and what to underline while reading. Below you will find a breakdown of the type of information included in each passage, as well as a guide to what will be important therein.

Literature

This is the only kind of fictional passage on the test. It is usually an intact short story or an excerpt from a short story or novel. For this type of passage, you should do the following:

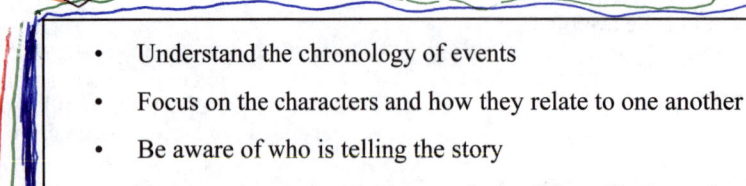

- Understand the chronology of events
- Focus on the characters and how they relate to one another
- Be aware of who is telling the story
- Pay attention to the dialogue and what it reveals about the characters
- Keep track of the tone/mood of the passage

Let's look at the following Literature passages and accompanying questions. Remember to look for the key points in the box above and apply our Action Plan as you answer the questions.

This passage is adapted from the short story "Gregorio" by Percy Addleshaw.

Gregorio found himself in Madam Marx's cafe, idly watching the passers-by. He was feeling happier, for he was amassing that which alone could insure his happiness. Each day some golden pieces were added to
5 the amount saved, and the cafe at Benhur seemed within his grasp. Security from want was his narcotic and soothed him, so that which should have troubled him scarcely interested him at all. Upon first seeing Xantippe and the Englishman together, his anger had
10 been violent; but when the futility of his rage became certain, his aggressive passion softened. He was contented now to sit all day with Madam Marx, and returned home in the evening when Xantippe was away. He had spoken to her only once since she had
15 told him she hated him. He had strolled out of the cafe about midday and entered his room. Xantippe was there, talking to her child, and quietly bade him go away.

"It's my room as well," Gregorio answered.
20 "It is my money that pays for it," she replied.
Xantippe told him that, if he stayed, she would grow to dislike her son since he was the father.

Gregorio was wise enough to stay calm. If she lost her love for the boy, his and the boy's chances
25 of prosperity would be destroyed. So he closed the door, ran downstairs, and never spoke to her again. He persuaded himself, sipping Madam Marx's coffee, that keeping in the background would cause Xantippe's hatred to dissipate. As for her feelings toward himself,
30 he ceased to care. The money was worth the cost of its attainment, and a woman's laugh was less sweet to him than the chink of gold and silver pieces.

Madam Marx brought her coffee and sat beside him. Her face betokened satisfaction, and she looked at
35 Gregorio with a possessive smile.

"Have you seen Xantippe since she turned you out? You are welcome here; it is foolish to go where one is not wanted."

"I've not seen her."
40 "If she had ever loved you, she would not have thrown you over. I should not have complained had I been in her place."

"It's that cursed Englishman who has spoiled her. I hate him."
45 "Why do you hate the Englishman? Because he has stolen your wife's love? It is lucky for both of you that this Englishman saw her. There are not men so rich as the English."

Madam Marx laid her fat hand upon Gregorio's
50 shoulder. It irritated him, but he didn't resist her.

"No. The money more than compensates me. But I hated the man when I first saw him at Paradise Cafe. There was a woman he talked to, and he could scarcely express himself. He had money, and he gave her
55 champagne and flowers. And I was starving, and the woman was beautiful."

"The woman can't interest you now. You have money—his money. Why worry about him? He won't follow you to Benhur, I fancy."
60 Darkness came, and Gregorio was impatient to see his son. He rose and left the cafe. He had promised the boy a boat, and blamed himself for having forgotten to buy it. Grumbling at his forgetfulness, he hurried along the street, determined to waste no time. He would hurry
65 always to obey the commands of the king, his son.

Soon he darted swiftly under the shadow of a wall, for he saw Amos. But the old man's sharp eyes detected the victim, and, following Gregorio into his hiding-place, Amos approached him.
70 "Why hide when we have so much to say to one another?"

Gregorio professed ignorance of the necessity for speech.

"My friend, the money you borrowed is still owing
75 in part."

"You will be paid. We are saving money; we cannot put by all we earn—we must live."

"I will be paid now; otherwise, you are to blame for the consequences."
80 And with a courtly salute Amos passed on. Gregorio realized he had been foolish not to pay something on account, but it hurt to part with gold. He determined, however, to send Amos something when he returned home. So good a watch had been kept, he
85 never doubted the child's safety. But what if Amos got him put in jail? So he reckoned up how much he could afford to pay, and, having bought the toy, returned eagerly home. He ran upstairs, singing loudly, and rushed into the room, waving the toy. "Here," he cried,
90 "is the ship! I have not forgotten it." But the room was empty.

With a heartbroken sob the man fell swooning on the floor.

Reading | Literature

1

According to the passage, Gregorio is saving money in order to

A) purchase a cafe.
B) move to another country with his family.
C) repay his debts.
D) buy an expensive gift for his son.

2

Which choice provides the best evidence for the answer to previous question?

A) Lines 4-6 ("Each . . . grasp")
B) Lines 51-52 ("'The money . . . cafe'")
C) Lines 64-65 ("'He would . . . son'")
D) Lines 81-84 ("Gregorio . . . home")

3

According to the passage, despite his current situation, Gregorio finds comfort in which of the following?

A) His conversations with Madame Marx
B) The prospect of financial security
C) The possibility of reuniting with Xantippe
D) Xantippe's relationship with the Englishman

4

According to the passage, how does Gregorio react to Xantippe's claim that his continued presence would cause her to dislike her son?

A) He decides to spend more time with her in an effort to save their relationship.
B) He becomes angry and storms out of the house.
C) He keeps his distance and spends his days at a local cafe.
D) He is saddened and consults Madame Marx for advice.

5

The author's use of the phrase on lines 31-32 ("a woman's . . . pieces") conveys the idea that Gregorio

A) finds material wealth to be meaningless without companionship.
B) values companionship less than he values material wealth.
C) believes that a romantic relationship would inhibit his ability to acquire wealth.
D) is afraid that a woman would attempt to take his money.

6

It can be inferred from the passage that Madame Marx

A) is romantically attracted to Gregorio.
B) has a motherly bond with Gregorio.
C) secretly wishes for Gregorio's demise.
D) wants to see Xantippe and Gregorio reconcile.

Reading | Literature

7

Which choice provides the best evidence for the answer to the previous question?

A) Lines 2-4 ("He . . . happiness")
B) Lines 14-15 ("He . . . hated him")
C) Lines 33-35 ("Madam Marx . . . smile")
D) Lines 64-65 ("He . . . son")

8

In line 59, the word "fancy" most nearly means

A) imagine.
B) hope.
C) know.
D) wish.

9

According to the passage, Gregorio's incentive for paying back Amos is

A) fear that Amos may have him arrested.
B) concern that Amos may harm his son.
C) the desire to maintain an upstanding reputation in his town.
D) worry that Xantippe will find out about his debts.

10

It can be inferred from the passage that Gregorio "fell swooning on the floor" (lines 92-93) because

A) he suspected that something terrible happened to his son.
B) he was disappointed that he would not be able to give his son the gift he had purchased.
C) he feared that Xantippe had left with the Englishman.
D) he was ashamed about owing money to Amos.

Reading | Literature

This passage is adapted from the novel *Sullen Soldier* by Russell Bell.

   Standing along the parapet of the rear porch, the Lieutenant had already begun to feel that he would not know what to do with himself from here on out. "It is like nothing I have ever seen. What more could a man ask?"
5 The words seemed like a very natural reaction given the splendor of his surroundings. Redwoods as fat around as a football huddle studded his son's land like birthday candles, sticking up at lower and lower heights as the property slung down into the arroyo of the adjoining
10 state preserve. On cool evenings, it seemed appropriate that only these old growth milemarkers of a bygone era, complete with their choirs of sparrows and buttertailed flycatchers, would be able to interrupt the setting sun, leaving behind a sky forgotten in tea browns and orange
15 blush. By the third sunset on that porch, itself overly-weatherized by hordes of workmen as if to sustain some yet to be seen California blizzard apocalypse, the Lieutenant had already unpacked his things twice. Nobody had known of his second unpacking; it had
20 been quickly reversed to avoid embarrassment. For an unexplainable reason, the first thing he found himself doing on his second morning in Tim's home was removing neatly folded shorts and pants from their day's rest in the dresser and replacing them in his travel trunk. If
25 it was a conscious action, it did not make any sense. The Lieutenant knew when he arrived, and first lightened that trunk of its denims and corduroys, that he would be here for good. And, as everyone had told him, it was for the best.
30   For the best or not, things were already moving in the direction he had imagined. They were going nowhere, and they were not doing it with much urgency. The thoughts that had cornered him against the passenger window on his civilian flight from Arlington seemed to have no
35 trouble fencing him in on a balcony expanse that would make most anyone else dizzy for all its endless sky and nameless vista. The Lieutenant quickly realized one thing: the empty house to "knock around in" was rarely empty for long. Blonde women with polish names and
40 inattentive looking men pulling boxes of tools on baggage carts would let themselves in to do housecleaning or scheduled work on the premises. They made the necessary apologies when they crossed paths in the cavernous home with this man of distinction, whom they presumed not to
45 disturb. But, for all their etiquette they were a disruption, he grumbled to himself. And as infrequent an overnight guest as his own diplomat son was in this, his very own dominion, it was clear that his son's hospitality would nevertheless be on display for his friends: their names
50 were blocked in as guests on the kitchen calendar for every foreseeable weekend. Most likely they too would be letting themselves in.
   Of course, these were not the things that had the Lieutenant absentmindedly gathering himself in
55 the morning to undo his arrival. For all his professed solemnity, worsened by the recent passing of his devoted wife, it was the absence of starting every day in the service of distinguished work that left him unsure of himself. Meeting the seasoned carpenters on his way for
60 a second or third cup of joe before noon, he would make inquiries into the nature of what they were doing, though he knew most everything had been carefully planned by his son. He could hardly decide on a tone with which to ask a simple question, usually with origins more in
65 mere curiosity than of any possessiveness of the house itself. It had long been the case that thirty years as an officer had left him unable to comfortably demonstrate an appreciation for a job well done without somehow sounding as if he was passing judgment, however
70 favorably. Where once he could feel that his daily responsibilities easily justified any lapses in his manner, he no longer felt as sure footed about casually needling people who were themselves merely doing their job. Having been cut loose for over a year, he could hardly say
75 the same for himself. The arrival of the workers every few days, whether craftsmen from a hiring hall or day laborers recruited to "winterize" the deck, could scarcely be said to interfere with the day of a pastured officer. They merely disrupted his ability to forget that for nearly a year he had
80 not done much of anything, by all accounts. And for all practical purposes, his closest family, with their hearty laughs, told him he better get used to it.
   Occasional visits to his last post in Arlington were no more uplifting. They were always cordial, but the
85 encounters reminded him that he was now misplaced on either side of the base's entry checkpoint. With Thea's passing, nothing else on the east coast held much sway over him; it had been as good a time as any to reevaluate his roles.
90   Returning to the vista one late afternoon from the kitchen, with the eastern windows already darkening, he nodded to a young man in a painter's hat holding the bottom of a ladder. The man above him was old enough to be graying, with one foot balanced on the top rung, and
95 one foot a rung below, as he taped over the mahogany trim within precious reach of those trembling fingers. The Lieutenant continued several paces more before thinking to himself that the ladder seemed to be at an awfully steep angle, its base only a shallow distance from

100 the wall. He shot another look at the workman stationed at eye level, careful not to seem as if he was getting ready to pry. The workman was already looking toward him. Again they nodded, but he did not say a thing.

1

The statement on lines 3-4 ("It is . . . ask?") relates to the passage as a whole by

A) demonstrating the Lieutenant's great fondness for nature.
B) showing how easily the Lieutenant is able to adapt to his current conditions.
C) testifying to the Lieutenant's enjoyment of a peaceful life.
D) illustrating the confusion the Lieutenant feels at not being satisfied with simple beauties.

2

The author's use of the sentence on lines 24-25 ("If it . . . sense") implies that the Lieutenant's mind

A) has been in decline for many years.
B) is persistently indecisive.
C) is preoccupied with thoughts unrelated to his actions.
D) is no more rational or troubled than that of his son.

3

According to the passage, the Lieutenant moved in with his son in order to

A) save money on living costs.
B) find a new direction in life.
C) put the memories of his past life behind him.
D) spend more time with his only living relatives.

4

Which choice provides the best evidence for the answer to the previous question?

A) Lines 25-28 ("The Lieutenant . . . for good")
B) Lines 37-39 ("The Lieutenant . . . for long")
C) Lines 57-59 ("it was . . . himself")
D) Lines 88-89 ("it had . . . his roles")

5

The tone of the passage could be best described as

A) melancholy.
B) upbeat.
C) combative.
D) unreasonable.

Reading | Literature

6

Based on the information in lines 63-70 ("He could . . . favorably") it can be inferred that the Lieutenant

A) was good humored but impatient.
B) was insincere but authoritarian.
C) was methodical but inconsiderate.
D) was demanding and not always polite.

7

As it is used in line 72, "needling" most nearly means

A) threading.
B) questioning.
C) twisting.
D) threatening.

8

As it is used in line 78, the word "pastured" conveys that the Lieutenant

A) has found an easy life in this new rural setting.
B) has grown tired of the meddling of his children.
C) is not especially busy in his retirement.
D) has been forgotten by those closest to him.

9

It can be inferred from the passage that the Lieutenant's wife, Thea, played what role in his moving in with his son?

A) She aggressively encouraged her husband to make the move.
B) She played no role in the decision of her husband to move in with his son.
C) She had been an influential factor in the Lieutenant's choice to be on the east coast.
D) She fretted about what the Lieutenant would do once he was on his own.

10

Which choice provides the best evidence for the answer to the previous question?

A) Lines 1-3 ("Standing . . .out")
B) Lines 55-59 ("For all . . .himself")
C) Lines 84-86 ("They were . . .checkpoint")
D) Lines 86-88 ("With Thea's . . .him")

Reading | Social Science

Social Science

Social Science passages present research on a particular issue from fields such as anthropology, archaeology, business, economics, sociology, psychology, education, or geography. With this type of passage, pay close attention to the following:

- Examples the author provides to illustrate his/her points
- The author's purpose
- Names associated with specific concepts
- Cause-effect relationships
- Comparisons/contrasts made by the author

Try the following Social Science passages and accompanying questions. Remember to look for the key points in the box above and apply our Action Plan as you answer the questions.

Reading I Social Science

This passage is adapted from the book *Free Culture* by Lawrence Lessig.

Since the inception of the law regulating creative property, there has been a war against "piracy." The precise contours of "piracy" are hard to sketch, but the animating injustice is easy to capture. As Lord Mansfield wrote in a case that extended the reach of English copyright law to include sheet music, "A person may use the copy by playing it, but he has no right to rob the author of the profit, by multiplying copies and dispersing of them for his own use."

Today the Internet has provoked a war against "piracy." Peer-to-peer (p2p) file sharing is among the most efficient of the technologies the Internet enables. Using distributed intelligence, p2p systems facilitate the easy spread of content in a way unimagined a generation ago.

This efficiency does not respect the traditional lines of copyright. The network doesn't discriminate between the sharing of copyrighted and uncopyrighted content. Thus there has been a vast amount of sharing of copyrighted content. That sharing in turn has excited the war, as copyright owners fear it will "rob the author of the profit."

The warriors have turned to the courts, legislatures, and technology to defend their "property" against this "piracy." A generation of Americans, the warriors warn, is being raised to believe that "property" should be "free." Forget tattoos, never mind body piercing—our kids are becoming thieves!

There's no doubt that "piracy" is wrong and that pirates should be punished. But before we summon the executioners, we should put this notion of "piracy" in some context. Though the term is increasingly used, at its core is an idea that is almost certainly wrong. The idea goes something like this: "Creative work has value; whenever I use or build upon the creative work of others, I am taking from them something of value. Whenever I take something of value from someone else, I should have his permission. Taking something of value from someone else without permission is wrong. It is a form of piracy."

This view runs deep within the current debates. It is what NYU law professor Rochelle Dreyfuss criticizes as the "if value, then right" theory of creative property—if there is value, then someone must have a right to that value.

This was the perspective that led a composers' rights organization, ASCAP, to sue the Girl Scouts for failing to pay for the songs their girls sang around campfires. There was "value" (the songs) so there must have been a "right"— even against the Girl Scouts.

This idea is certainly a possible understanding of how creative property should work. It might well be a possible design for a system of laws protecting creative property. But the "if value, then right" theory of creative property has never been America's theory of creative property. It has never taken hold within our law.

Instead, in our tradition, intellectual property is an instrument. It sets the groundwork for a richly creative society but remains subservient to the value of creativity. The current debate has this inverted. We have become so concerned with protecting the instrument that we are losing sight of the value.

The source of this confusion is a distinction that the law no longer takes care to draw—the distinction between republishing someone's work and building upon or transforming that work. Copyright law at its birth had only publishing as its concern; copyright law today regulates both.

Before the technologies of the Internet, this conflation didn't matter. The technologies of publishing were expensive; hence, the vast majority of publishing was commercial. Commercial entities could bear the burden of the law—even the burden of the Byzantine complexity that copyright law has become. It was just one more expense of doing business.

But with the birth of the Internet, this natural limit to the reach of the law has disappeared. The law controls not just the creativity of commercial creators but effectively that of anyone. Although that expansion would not matter much if copyright law regulated only "copying," when the law regulates as broadly and obscurely as it does, the extension matters greatly. The burden of this law now vastly outweighs any original benefit—certainly as it affects noncommercial creativity, and increasingly as it affects commercial creativity. Thus, the law's role is less to support creativity, and more to protect certain industries against competition. We may be seeing, as Richard Florida writes, the "Rise of the Creative Class." Unfortunately, we are also seeing an extraordinary rise of regulation of this creative class.

Reading | Social Science

1

The main purpose of the passage is to

A) explain why a recently common practice should not be illegal under any circumstance.
B) expose the consequences of the over-application of a law.
C) argue for a change to an established law.
D) question the appropriateness of applying a law in the age of the Internet.

2

The author's use of quotations around the word "piracy" serves to

A) demonstrate his doubt that piracy exists.
B) raise a question about the definition of the word.
C) minimize the severity that is often attached to the term.
D) mock those who use the term incorrectly.

3

What function do the first two paragraphs (lines 1-14) serve in the passage as a whole?

A) They explain the development of a recent phenomenon.
B) They summarize the findings of the author's research into a problem.
C) They introduce background to an argument the author later makes.
D) They give an overview of a problem that has not been sufficiently addressed by the experts mentioned in the passage.

4

According to the passage, America has traditionally viewed intellectual property as

A) a right.
B) a burden.
C) a commodity.
D) an instrument.

Peer to Peer File (Music) Sharing Versus Purchasing Music from 1995-2015

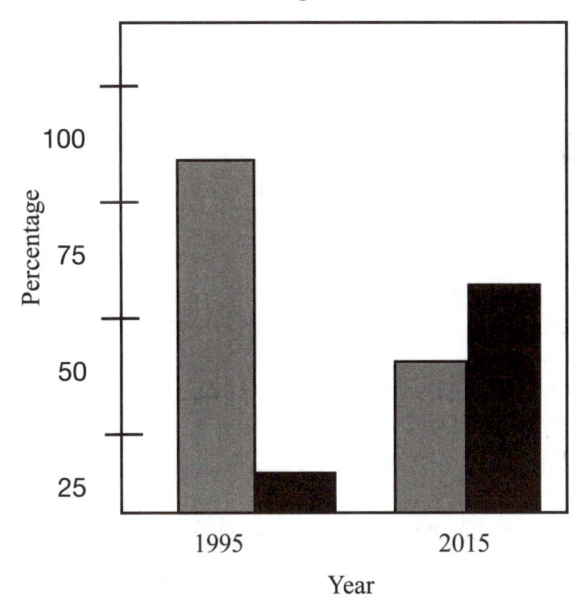

[Bar chart showing percentages for 1995 and 2015, with legend: p2p music file sharing (black) and acquiring content by purchase (gray)]

5

In line 57, "subservient" most nearly means

A) dominant.
B) beholden.
C) elusive.
D) helpful.

Reading | Social Science

6

The author believes that the current application of copyright law could result in

A) the mass arrest of American citizens.
B) the stifling of creativity.
C) the censorship of the Internet.
D) the breakdown of the justice system.

7

From the author's perspective, the main objective of current copyright law is to

A) protect certain industries against competition.
B) defend the creative freedom of artists.
C) assure that people will not use the Internet to commit crimes.
D) guarantee that creators will be adequately compensated for their work.

8

Which choice provides the best evidence for the answer to the previous question?

A) Lines 35-38 ("Whenever . . . piracy")
B) Lines 64-66 ("Copyright. . . both")
C) Lines 76-77 ("The law. . . anyone")
D) Lines 84-86 ("Thus. . . competition")

9

In line 68, "conflation" most nearly means

A) fusion.
B) tradition.
C) constraint.
D) belief.

10

The graph following the passage offers evidence that consumer preferences have

A) switched from file sharing to CD's.
B) made no significant change since 1995.
C) swung largely towards file sharing.
D) forsaken paying for music.

11

The graph following the passage adds supplemental evidence to the author's point that

A) the limits of the law has all but disappeared in the face of the internet and, subsequently, increased "piracy."
B) creative youth have less respect for art as property.
C) current copyright law regulates p2p file sharing only.
D) consumers of music are purchasing musical content far less in 2015 than in 1995.

Reading | Social Science

The following is excerpted from Mark Twain's "Purchasing Civic Virtue" essay.

The human race was always interesting and we know by its past that it will always continue to be so. It is monotonous; it is always the same; it never changes. Its circumstances change from time to time, for better or
5 worse, but the race's character is permanent and never changes. In the course of the ages it has built up several great and worshipful civilizations and has seen unlooked-for circumstances slyly emerge bearing deadly gifts which looked like benefits and were welcomed, whereupon the
10 decay and destruction of each of these stately civilizations has followed.

It is not worthwhile to try to keep history from repeating itself, for man's character will always make the preventing of the repetitions impossible. Whenever man
15 makes a large stride in material prosperity and progress he is sure to think that he has progressed, whereas he has not advanced an inch. Nothing has progressed but his circumstances. He stands where he stood before. He knows more than his forebears knew but his intellect is no
20 better than theirs and never will be. He is richer than his forebears but his character is no improvement upon theirs. Riches and education are not a permanent possession; they will pass away, as in the case of Rome and Greece and Egypt and Babylon, and a moral and mental midnight will
25 follow—with a dull, long sleep and a slow reawakening. From time to time he makes what looks like a change in his character but it is not a real change, and it is only transitory anyway. He cannot even invent laws and keep them intact; circumstances are stronger than he and all
30 his works. Circumstances and conditions are always changing, and they always compel him to modify his laws to harmonize with the new situation.

Republics have lived long but monarchs live forever. By our teaching we learn that vast material
35 prosperity always brings in its train conditions which debase the morals and enervate the nation—then the countries' liberties come into the market and are bought, sold, squandered, thrown away, and a popular idol is carried to the throne upon the shields or shoulders of the
40 worshipping people and planted there in permanency. We are always being taught—no, formerly we were always being taught—to look at Rome and beware. The teacher pointed to Rome's stern virtue, incorruptibility, love of liberty, and all-sacrificing patriotism—this when she
45 was young and poor; then he pointed to her later days when her sunbursts of material prosperity and spreading dominion came and were exultingly welcomed by the people.

The teacher reminded us that Rome's liberties
50 were not auctioned off in a day, but were bought slowly, gradually, furtively, little by little; first with a little corn and oil for voters who were not quite so poor, later still with corn and oil for pretty much every man that had a vote to sell—exactly our own history over again. At first
55 we granted deserved pensions, righteously and with a clean and honorable motive, to the disabled soldiers of the Civil War. The clean motive began and ended there. We have made many and amazing additions to the pension list but with a motive which dishonors the uniform and
60 the Congresses which have voted the additions, the sole purpose behind the additions being the purchase of votes. It is corn and oil over again, and promises to do its full share in the eventual subversion of the republic and the substitution of monarchy in its place. The monarchy
65 would come anyhow, without this, but this has a peculiar interest for us in that it prodigiously hastens the day. We have the two Roman conditions: stupendous wealth with its inevitable corruptions and moral blight, and the corn and oil pensions—that is to say, vote bribes, which have
70 taken away the pride of thousands of tempted men and turned them into willing, unashamed alms receivers.

1

On line 3, the author says that the human race is "monotonous" because

A) human nature itself is constant.
B) the appearance of change is temporary.
C) civilization has reached a point of equilibrium and there is no more room for advancement.
D) it only appears interesting in retrospect.

2

Which choice provides the best evidence for the answer to the previous question?

A) Lines 1-2 ("The human race. . . so")
B) Lines 3-6 ("Its circumstances. . . changes")
C) Lines 18-20 ("He knows. . . be")
D) Lines 40-42 ("We. . . beware")

Reading | Social Science

3

The statement on lines 9-11 ("whereupon . . . followed") is said to follow from

A) a failure to develop new technology to keep up with advancing civilizations.
B) an inability to plan ahead.
C) an acceptance of bribes from outsiders.
D) the unforeseen detriments of progress.

4

It can be inferred from lines 12-20 that intellectual progress itself is

A) ephemeral.
B) useless.
C) relative.
D) accumulated.

5

The phrase "moral and mental midnight" (line 24) most likely refers to

A) a time of public despair.
B) a period of intellectual inactivity.
C) the height of the empires mentioned previously in the passage.
D) the end of civilization.

6

The author's view of laws is best described as

A) critical.
B) old-fashioned.
C) inconsistent.
D) objective.

7

The statement on lines 33-34 ("Republics . . . forever) refers to the notion that

A) human nature tends to undermine democracy.
B) monarchies are better remembered in history.
C) monarchies are richer than republics.
D) democracy grants too much

8

Which choice provides the best evidence for the answer to the previous question?

A) Lines 12-14 ("It is . . . impossible")
B) Lines 28-29 ("He . . . intact")
C) Lines 30-32 ("Circumstances . . . situation")
D) Line 33-34 ("Republics . . . forever")

9

As it is used in line 35, "train" most nearly means

A) engine.
B) wake.
C) education.
D) practice.

10

The author implies that the politicians' primary motive for granting pensions after the Civil War was to

A) centralize political power.
B) increase their own wealth by controlling which soldiers received a pension.
C) eliminate poverty.
D) curry favor with the electorate.

11

The main function of the last paragraph (lines 49-71) is to

A) describe ancient Roman attitudes and explain how these attitudes led to the fall of the republic.
B) explain the drawbacks of the pension system established for Civil War soldiers.
C) relate an anecdote the author was told by his teacher.
D) provide a concrete illustration of a point previously made in the passage.

Reading | Social Science

The following is excerpted from Clarence Darrow's *Crime: Its Cause and Treatment*.

There can be no discussion of "crime" and "criminals" without an investigation of the meaning of the words. A large majority of people, even among the educated, speak of a "criminal" as if the word had a clearly defined
5 meaning and as if men were divided by a plain and distinct line into the criminal and the virtuous. As a matter of fact, there is no such division, and from the nature of things, there never can be such a line.

Strictly speaking, a crime is an act forbidden by the
10 law of the land, and one which is considered sufficiently serious to warrant providing penalties for its commission. It does not necessarily follow that this act is either good or bad; the punishment follows for the violation of the law and not necessarily for any moral transgression. No doubt most
15 of the things forbidden by the penal code are injurious to the organized society of the time and place. But even then it does not always follow that the violator of the law is not a person of higher type than the majority who are directly and indirectly responsible for the law.

20 It is apparent that a thing is not necessarily bad because it is forbidden by the law. Legislators are forever repealing and abolishing criminal statutes, and organized society is constantly ignoring laws, until they fall into disuse and die. Laws against witchcraft, and laws affecting religious beliefs
25 and many social customs, are well-known examples of legal and innocent acts which legislatures and courts have once made criminal. Every time a legislature meets, it changes penalties for existing crimes and makes criminal certain acts that were not forbidden before.

30 Judging from the kind of men sent to the State legislatures and to Congress, the fact that certain things are forbidden does not mean that these things are necessarily evil; but rather, that politicians believe there is a demand for such legislation from the class of society that is most
35 powerful in political action.

In this uncertainty as to the basis of good and bad conduct, many appeal to "conscience" as the infallible guide. What is conscience? It is not a distinct faculty of the mind, and if it were, would it be more reliable than the other
40 faculties? There is no doubt that all men of any mentality have what is called a conscience; that is, a feeling that certain things are right, and certain other things are wrong. This conscience does not affect all the actions of life, but probably the ones which to them are the most important. It
45 varies, however, with the individual. What reason has the world to believe that conscience is a correct guide to right and wrong?

The origin of conscience is easily understood. One's conscience is formed as his habits are formed—by the time
50 and place in which he lives; it grows with his teachings, his habits and beliefs. With some people the eating of pork would hurt their conscience; with others the eating of any meat; with some the eating of meat on Friday. Conscience is purely a matter of environment, education and temperament,
55 and is no more infallible than any habit or belief.

Some seek to avoid the difficulties of the problem by saying that a "criminal" is one who is "anti-social." But does this bring us nearer to the light? An anti-social person is one whose life is hostile to the organization or the society
60 in which he lives; one who injures the peace, contentment, prosperity or wellbeing of his neighbors, or the political or social organization in which his life is cast. In this sense many of the most venerated men of history have been criminals; their lives and teachings have been in greater or
65 lesser conflict with the doctrines, habits and beliefs of the communities where they lived.

No two men have the same power of adaptation to the group, and it is quite plain that the ones who are the most servile and obedient to the opinions and life of the crowd are
70 the greatest enemies to change and individuality. The fact is, none of the generally accepted theories of the basis of right and wrong has ever been the foundation of law or morals. The basis that the world has always followed, and perhaps always will accept, is not hard to find.

75 The criminal is the one who violates habits and customs of the community where he lives. These customs must be so important as to make their violation a serious affair. Such violations are considered evil regardless of whether the motives are selfish or unselfish, good or bad. Men
80 did not arrive at moral ideas by a scientific or a religious investigation of good and bad, of right and wrong, of social or anti-social life.

The author uses quotation marks around specific words throughout the passage in order to

A) question the sincerity with which the terms are used.
B) challenge the popular meanings of certain commonly used terms.
C) use irony to illustrate the absurdity of such terms.
D) provide explanations for unusual terms.

Reading | Social Science

2

According to the passage, which of the following is true about conscience?

A) It is useful for determining which actions are right and wrong.
B) It corresponds closely with laws.
C) It is relative and therefore not a universal tool for determining morality.
D) It is lacked by those who intentionally damage society.

3

The main function of the second paragraph (lines 9-19) in relation to the passage as a whole is to provide

A) a transition between a discussion of specific words to a discussion of specific events.
B) the prevalent definitions for terms examined throughout the passage.
C) a distinct example of the phenomenon mentioned in the first paragraph.
D) a counterpoint to the author's opinion.

4

The author mentions laws against witchcraft primarily to demonstrate

A) how what is deemed criminal by lawmakers may not actually be harmful.
B) that laws governing morality are necessary to stop such behavior.
C) the flawed ethics of legislators.
D) the effect that the politically powerful have on leglislation.

5

It can be inferred that the author considers politicians to be

A) morally inferior to many of the people they represent.
B) skilled at determining the validity of laws.
C) only worried about retaining their elected posts.
D) primarily concerned with appeasing certain constituents.

6

Which of the following provide the best evidence for the answer to previous question?

A) Lines 21-23 ("Legislators . . . laws")
B) Lines 27-29 ("Every . . . before")
C) Lines 30-31 ("Judging . . . Congress")
D) Lines 33-35 ("that politicians . . . action")

7

As it is used in line 37, "infallible" most nearly means

A) benevolent.
B) trustworthy.
C) maimed.
D) ludicrous.

8

According to the author, one who commits a crime

A) should face extreme punishment.
B) is likely to commit further crimes in the future.
C) lacks a conscience.
D) cannot be judged as either morally good or bad.

Reading | Social Science

9

With which of the following statements regarding the term "anti-social" would the author most likely agree?

A) It should be reserved only for the worst members of society.
B) It can be used to describe people who cause great social changes.
C) It is synonymous with the word "criminal."
D) It has more positive connotations than most people believe.

10

Which choice provides the best evidence for the answer to the previous question?

A) Lines 56-57 ("Some...'anti-social'")
B) Lines 58-60 ("An anti-social...lives")
C) Lines 62-64 ("In this...criminals")
D) Lines 70-72 ("The fact...morals")

11

The last paragraph (lines 75-82) differs from the rest of the passage in that it

A) cites an outside source.
B) states a conclusion against which the author argues.
C) uses real-world examples.
D) contains the author's thesis on the central issue of the passage.

Reading | Social Studies

Social Studies

This type of passage presents an essay or speech from U.S. founding documents or international texts influenced by them. These texts will be very similar to documents you analyze in history or social studies class. However, with these documents you do not need to have any outside knowledge. Everything needed to answer the questions is in the passage. With this type of passage, pay close attention to the following:

- Examples the author provides to illustrate his/her points
- The author's purpose
- Any specific stance the author takes
- How the author makes his/her case
- Comparisons/contrasts made by the author

Try the following Social Studies passages and accompanying questions. Remember to look for the key points in the box above and apply our Action Plan as you answer the questions.

Reading | Social Studies

This passage is adapted from Shirley Chisholm's address to Congress in 1970 about the proposed Equal Rights Amendment.

Resolution 264, before us today, which provides for equality under the law for both men and women, represents one of the most clear-cut opportunities we are likely to have to declare our faith in the principles
[5] that shaped our Constitution. It provides a legal basis for attack on the most subtle, most pervasive, and most institutionalized form of prejudice that exists. Discrimination against women, solely on the basis of their sex, is so widespread that is seems to many persons
[10] normal, natural, and right.

Legal expression of prejudice on the grounds of religious or political belief has become a minor problem in our society. Prejudice on the basis of race is, at least, under systematic attack. There is reason for optimism that
[15] it will start to die with the present, older generation. It is time we act to assure full equality of opportunity to those citizens who, although in a majority, suffer the restrictions that are commonly imposed on minorities, to women.

The argument that this amendment will not solve
[20] the problem of sex discrimination is not relevant. If the argument were used against a civil rights bill, as it has been used in the past, the prejudice that lies behind it would be embarrassing. Of course laws will not eliminate prejudice from the hearts of human beings. But that is no
[25] reason to allow prejudice to continue to be enshrined in our laws -- to perpetuate injustice through inaction.

What would be the economic effects of the equal rights amendment? Direct economic effects would be minor. If any labor laws applying only to women still
[30] remained, their amendment or repeal would provide opportunity for women in better-paying jobs in manufacturing. More opportunities in public vocational and graduate schools for women would also tend to open up opportunities in better jobs for women.

[35] Indirect effects could be much greater. The focusing of public attention on the gross legal, economic, and social discrimination against women by hearings and debates in the Federal and State legislatures would result in changes in attitude of parents, educators, and
[40] employers that would bring about substantial economic changes in the long run.

Sex prejudice cuts both ways. Men are oppressed by the requirements of the Selective Service Act, by enforced legal guardianship of minors, and by alimony
[45] laws. Each sex, I believe, should be liable when necessary to serve and defend this country. Each has a responsibility for the support of children.

This is what it comes down to: artificial distinctions between persons must be wiped out of the law. Legal
[50] discrimination between the sexes is, in almost every instance, founded on outmoded views of society and the pre-scientific beliefs about psychology and physiology. It is time to sweep away these relics of the past and set further generations free of them.

[55] Evidence of discrimination on the basis of sex should hardly have to be cited here. It is in the Labor Department's employment and salary figures for anyone who is still in doubt. Its elimination will involve so many changes in our State and Federal laws that, without the
[60] authority and impetus of this proposed amendment, it will perhaps take another 194 years. We cannot be parties to continuing a delay. The time is clearly now to put this House on record for the fullest expression of that equality of opportunity which our founding fathers professed.
[65] They professed it, but they did not assure it to their daughters, as they tried to do for their sons.

The Constitution they wrote was designed to protect the rights of white, male citizens. As there were no black Founding Fathers, there were no founding mothers -- a
[70] great pity, on both counts. It is not too late to complete the work they left undone. Today, here, we should start to do so.

1

The main issue that Chisholm describes in the passage is that women

A) do not hold positions of power to influence major decisions of government.
B) could be a major force of direct economic change if they were not burdened by current law.
C) face unequal treatment under the law to the detriment of society.
D) have a right to defend the country during times of war.

Chapter 2

Reading | Social Studies

2

As used in line 7, "institutionalized" most nearly means

A) relating to a school.
B) coming from an authority.
C) placed in an asylum.
D) culturally ingrained.

3

The second paragraph (lines 11-18) establishes a contrast between

A) the severity of different forms of discrimination.
B) the views of younger and older generations.
C) the majority and the minority of society.
D) optimism and pessimism.

4

Chisholm dismisses a line of criticism about the Equal Rights Amendment by

A) applying the same reasoning to civil rights legislation.
B) flatly rejecting the evidence for the argument.
C) challenging society to improve its moral character.
D) arguing that law can counter personal prejudices.

5

Chisholm contends that the economic impact of the Equal Rights Amendment will be

A) a drastic, positive shift in ecomonic production.
B) primarily felt in the future as the product of adjustments of perspective.
C) primarily felt in the present due to an increase of women in manufacturing.
D) minimal since women are already an integral part of the economy.

6

Which choice provides the best evidence for the answer to the previous question?

A) Lines 27-29 ("What would . . . minor")
B) Lines 29-32 ("If any . . . manufacturing")
C) Lines 35-41 ("The focusing . . . run")
D) Lines 55-56 ("Evidence . . . here")

7

It can reasonably be inferred that the Selective Service Act is

A) a major point of contention for advocates of the Equal Rights Amendment.
B) another example of legal injustice faced by women.
C) a bill that opposes the Equal Rights Amendment.
D) applicable only to men.

8

Chisholm uses the phrase "artificial distinctions" on line 48 to emphasize

A) the idea that society is the same as it was before is flawed.
B) the inaccuracy of the beliefs about differences in the genders.
C) how revolutionary recent scientific discoveries are.
D) the divisions between the current and subsequent generations.

9

Chisholm believes that ending discrimination based on gender will

A) force a major restructuring of governmental policies.
B) cause a largely negative backlash from men.
C) take over a century's worth of effort to achieve.
D) be a task for the children of the present generation.

10

Which choice provides the best evidence for the answer to the previous question?

A) Lines 49-54 ("Legal discrimination...them")
B) Lines 58-59 ("Its elimination...laws")
C) Lines 59-61 ("without...years")
D) Lines 65-66 ("They professed...sons")

Reading | Social Studies

This passage is adapted from a letter entitled To Every Englishman in India, written by Mahatma Gandhi.

    I wish that every Englishman will see this appeal and give thoughtful attention to it.

    In my humble opinion no Indian has co-operated with the British Government more than I have for an
[5] unbroken period of twenty-nine years of public life in the face of circumstances that might well have turned any other man into a rebel. I ask you to believe me when I tell you that my co-operation was not based on the fear of the punishments provided by your laws or any other selfish
[10] motives. It was free and voluntary co-operation based on the belief that the sum total of the activity of the British Government was for the benefit of India. I put my life in peril four times for the sake of the Empire. I did this in the full belief that acts such as mine must gain for my country
[15] an equal status in the Empire.

    So late as last December I pleaded hard for a trustful co-operation, I fully believed that Mr. Lloyd George* would redeem his promise to the Mussalmans and that the revelations of the official atrocities in the Punjab
[20] would secure full reparation for the Punjabis. But the treachery of Mr. Lloyd George and its appreciation by you, and the condonation of the Punjab atrocities have completely shattered my faith in the good intentions of the Government and the nation which is supporting it.

[25]   But though, my faith in your good intentions is gone, I recognise your bravery and I know that what you will not yield to justice and reason, you will gladly yield to bravery.

    See what this Empire means to India:

[30]   Exploitation of India's resources for the benefit of Great Britain. An ever-increasing military expenditure, and a civil service the most expensive in the world. Extravagant working of every department in utter disregard of India's poverty. Disarmament and consequent
[35] emasculation of a whole nation lest an armed nation might imperil the lives of a handful of you in our midst. Traffic in intoxicating liquors and drugs for the purposes of sustaining a top heavy administration. Progressively representative legislation in order to suppress an
[40] evergrowing agitation seeking to give expression to a nation's agony. Degrading treatment of Indians residing in your dominions.

    I know you would not mind if we could fight and wrest the sceptre from your hands. You know that we are
[45] powerless to do that, for you have ensured our incapacity to fight in open and honourable battle. Bravery on the battlefield is thus impossible for us. Bravery of the soul still remains open to us. I know you will respond to that also.

[50] I am engaged in evoking that bravery. Non-co-operation means nothing less than training in self-sacrifice. Why should we co-operate with you when we know that by your administration of this great country we are lifting daily enslaved in an increasing degree.
[55] This response of the people to my appeal is not due to my personality. People flock in their thousands to listen to us because we today represent the voice of a nation, a nation fighting for independence out from under iron heels.

[60]   My religion forbids me to bear any ill-will towards you. I would not raise my hand against you even if I had the power. I expect to conquer you only by my suffering.

    You are in search of a remedy to suppress this
[65] rising ebullition of national feeling. I venture to suggest to you that the only way to suppress it is to remove the causes. But this you cannot do unless you consider every Indian to be in reality your equal and brother.

    The other solution, namely repression, is open to
[70] you. I prophesy that it will fail. It has begun already. The Government has already imprisoned two brave men of Panipat for holding and expressing their opinions freely. Another is on his trial in Lahore for having expressed similar opinion. One in the Oudh District
[75] is already imprisoned. Another awaits judgment. You should know what is going on in your midst. Our propaganda is being carried on in anticipation of repression. I invite you respectfully to choose the better way and make common cause with the people of
[80] India whose salt you are eating. To seek to thwart their inspirations is disloyalty to the country.

*British Prime Minister from 1916-1922

1

Gandhi uses the words "wish" and appeal" in line 1 primarily to

A) demonstrate his genuine compassion for the many Englishmen in India.
B) highlight his own moral superiority.
C) use respect as a mediating tool in a difficult conversation.
D) stress the urgency of his address.

Reading | Social Studies

2

Gandhi indicates that the cooperation he describes in the passage

A) has turned him into a rebel.
B) was based primarily on his fear of punishment by the British Government.
C) has only now begun after 29 years of rebellion.
D) came from his initial belief that the British Government was beneficial to India.

3

According to the third paragraph (Lines 16-24), how have Gandhi's opinions of Mr. Lloyd George changed?

A) His affection and trust for Mr. Lloyd George have grown stronger.
B) His previous trust and respect in Mr. Lloyd George have been completely destroyed.
C) Although his faith in Mr. Lloyd George has been shattered, he now has hope this faith can be restored.
D) He believes there is slightly less of a chance Mr. Lloyd George will honor the requested reparations.

4

As it is used in line 27, "yield" most nearly means

A) grow.
B) holler.
C) stop.
D) surrender.

5

The long list of actions in lines 30-42 serves to demonstrate

A) the failings of India's economy.
B) the reach of Britain's ever-increasing military presence in India.
C) that poverty is pervasive in India.
D) that India has been subjected to copious amounts of British oppression.

6

The phrase on line 44 ("wrest . . . sceptre") most likelt means to

A) obtain weapons for the Indian army.
B) assasinate the King of England.
C) reclaim sovereign independence for India.
D) conquer England for India.

7

Which choice provides the best evidence for the answer to the previous question?

A) Lines 44-46 ("You . . . battle")
B) Lines 47-49 ("Bravery . . . also")
C) Lines 52-54 ("Why . . . degree")
D) Lines 56-59 ("People . . . heels")

8

The main purpose of the second to last paragraph (lines 64-68) is to

A) accuse the English of anti-Indian sentiment.
B) warn England that they will lose this battle.
C) insist that equality for Indians is the only answer to the current conflict.
D) mock the English Government's efforts to combat the uprising.

Reading | Social Studies

9

The central claim of the passage is that

A) the British Government will stop oppressing India either by choice or Indian bravery.
B) the British Government is using too much of India's salt.
C) the British Government must share their resources with India.
D) Gandhi will stop the British Government with his suffering.

10

As it is used in line 65, "ebullition" most nearly means

A) outpourings of emotion.
B) heat waves.
C) an overflow of opinions.
D) silence.

11

Which choice provides the best evidence for the answer to the previous questions?

A) Line 46-48 ("Bravery . . . us")
B) Lines 60-63 ("My . . . suffering")
C) Lines 77-78 ("Our . . . repression")
D) Lines 80-81 ("To . . . country")

Chapter 2

Reading | Natural Science

Natural Science

This type of passage presents a science topic and discusses its significance. One of the key differences between a Natural Science passage and a Social Science passage is that in a Natural Science passage, the author is concerned with relationships between natural phenomena, whereas in a Social Science passage, the author is interested in relationships between people. Do not be distracted by technical terminology with which you are unfamiliar. If knowing the definition of some term is important to answering a question, the passage will define the term, or you will be able to use context clues to ascertain its meaning. Take note of the following:

- Laws, rules, and theories presented, and to whom they are attributed
- How details and examples relate to larger ideas
- The author's perspective on the topic
- Cause-effect relationships
- Comparisons/contrasts between schools of thought

Look at the following Natural Science passages and accompanying questions. Remember to look for the key points in the box above and apply our Action Plan as you answer the questions.

Reading | Natural Science

This passage is adapted from the article "Diabetes Overview" published by the U.S. Department of Health.

An estimated 23.6 million people in the United States—7.8 percent of the population—have a condition known as diabetes. Of those, 17.9 million have been diagnosed, and roughly 5.7 million have not yet been.

Diabetes is a disorder of metabolism—the way the body uses digested food for growth and energy. Food is broken down into glucose, the main source of fuel for the body. After digestion, glucose passes into the bloodstream, where cells use it for growth and energy. For glucose to enter cells, insulin, a hormone produced by the pancreas, must be present.

When people eat, the pancreas automatically produces the right amount of insulin to transport glucose from the blood into cells. In diabetics, however, the pancreas produces little or no insulin. As a result, glucose builds up in the blood, overflows into the urine, and passes out of the body. Thus, the body loses its main source of fuel, even though the blood may actually contain an adequate amount of glucose.

There are three main types of diabetes: type 1, type 2, and gestational diabetes. Type 1 diabetes is an autoimmune disease, a disease that results when one's immune system turns against a part of the body. In diabetes, the immune system attacks and destroys insulin-producing beta cells in the pancreas. Scientists do not know what causes the body's immune system to attack the beta cells, but they believe that genetic and environmental factors, possibly viruses, are involved. Type 1 diabetes accounts for 5 to 10 percent of diagnosed cases in the United States. Although it develops most often in children and young adults, it can appear in people at any age. Symptoms of type 1 diabetes usually develop over a short period of time and may include increased thirst and urination, constant hunger, weight loss, blurred vision, and extreme fatigue. If not treated with insulin, a person with type 1 diabetes can lapse into a life-threatening coma known as diabetic ketoacidosis.

Roughly 90 to 95 percent of people with diabetes have type 2. This form is most often associated with old age, obesity, family history, previous history of gestational diabetes, physical inactivity, and certain ethnicities. About 80 percent of people with type 2 diabetes are overweight, so maintaining a reasonable body weight may help to prevent one from getting type 2 diabetes. Ethnicity also plays a role, as those of African American, Mexican American, or Pacific Islander descent show the highest rates of diagnosed diabete cases. When type 2 diabetes is diagnosed, the pancreas is usually producing enough insulin, but for unknown reasons the body cannot use it effectively. After several years of this, insulin production decreases and causes the same results as in type 1. Unlike in type 1 diabetes, however, the symptoms of type 2—fatuge, frequent urination, weight loss, blurred vision, and slow healing of woulds— develop gradually. Some people even exhibit no symptoms at all.

Some women develop the third type, gestational diabetes, late in pregnancy. It occurs more often in certain ethnic groups and among women with a family history of diabetes. It is caused by the hormones associated with pregnancy. Although this form of diabetes usually disappears after the birth of the baby, women who have had gestational diabetes have a 40 to 60 percent chance of developing type 2 diabetes within 10 years.

Diabetes is recognized as one of the leading causes of death and disability in the United States. It often leads to blindness, heart and blood vessel disease, stroke, kidney failure, amputations, and nerve damage. In 2006, it was the seventh leading cause of death. However, diabetes is likely to be underreported as the underlying cause of death on death certificates, as other things, such as heart disease, may be noted instead since diabetics often suffer from multiple health issues.

The prevalence of diabetes in the United States is likely to increase moving forward as there is a shift towards a more sedentary lifestyle. A large segment of the population is also aging, bringing a larger number of people into the age range most at risk. In addition, minority groups who genetically have an increased risk make up the fastest-growing segment of the U.S. population. Some doctors have claimed that the frequency of diagnosed diabetes cases will increase by 165% by the year 2050.

Despite this bleak outlook, in recent years, advances in diabetes research have led to better ways of managing and treating its complications. Major advances include the development of quick-acting and long-acting insulins, laser treatment for diabetic eye disease, and successful kidney and pancreatic transplantations. Researchers continue to look for ways to manage, prevent, or cure the disorder.

Chapter 2

Reading | Natural Science

Rates of Type 2 Diabetes Diagnosed Diabetes by Ethnicity

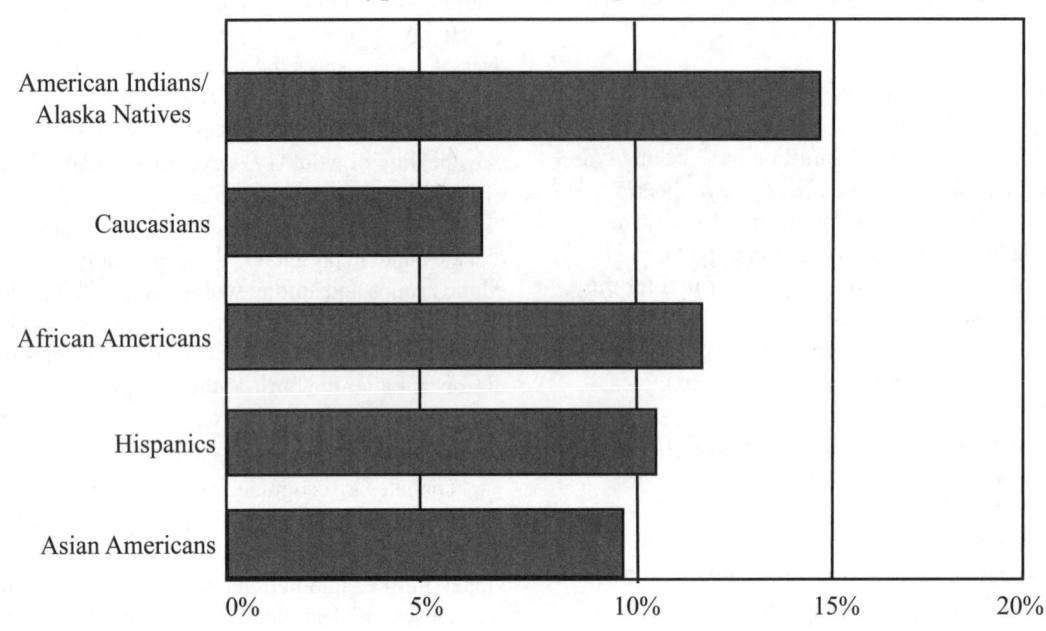

Ethnicity	Rate
American Indians/Alaska Natives	~14%
Caucasians	~6%
African Americans	~11%
Hispanics	~10%
Asian Americans	~9%

Adapted from the American Diabetes Association

1

As it is used in line 19, "adequate" most nearly means

A) scant.
B) boundless.
C) enough.
D) frequent.

2

According to the passage, type 1 diabetes occurs most often in

A) pregnant women.
B) children and young adults.
C) elderly men and women.
D) infants.

3

According to the passage, all of the following are symptoms of type 1 diabetes EXCEPT

A) decreased hunger.
B) extreme fatigue.
C) blurred vision.
D) increased thirst.

4

According to the passage, one difference between type 1 diabetes and type 2 diabetes is that

A) in type 1 diabetes the pancreas produces little to no insulin while in type 2 diabetes the pancreas usually produces enough insulin.
B) type 1 diabetes usually develops later in life while type 2 diabetes usually occurs in children.
C) type 1 diabetes occurs as a result of weight loss while type 2 diabetes occurs as a result of obesity.
D) in type 1 diabetes, glucose builds up in the pancreas while in type 2 diabetes glucose builds up in the blood.

Reading | Natural Science

5

Which choice best supports the article's implication that type 2 diabetes following gestational diabetes is not inevitable?

A) Lines 39-41 ("This form . . . ethnicities")
B) Lines 52-54 ("the symptoms . . . gradually")
C) Lines 60-63 ("Although . . . years")
D) Lines 73-74 ("The prevalence . . . forward")

6

Diabetes is likely to be underreported as the underlying cause of death in death certificates because

A) doctors often mistake diabetes for some other disease.
B) diabetes is not perceived as a potentially fatal illness.
C) many diabetics also suffer from another disease.
D) some diabetics are unaware that they have diabetes.

7

As it is used in line 75, "sedentary" most nearly means

A) solitary.
B) spry.
C) heavy.
D) inactive

8

According to the passage, all of the following are examples of major advancements in diabetes research EXCEPT

A) laser treatment for diabetic eye disease.
B) successful kidney transplantation.
C) development of quick-acting insulins.
D) development of early-detection tests.

9

Based on the graph, which choice gives the correct percentages of Asian Americans diagnosed with diabetes?

A) 14.8%
B) 9.7%
C) 8.5%
D) 12.2%

10

Does the information in the graph support the author's claim in lines 44-47 ("Ethnicity . . . cases")?

A) Yes, because African Americans have a rate of diagnosed diabetes cases of approximately 12%.
B) Yes, because American Indian/Alaska natives have the highest rate of diagnosed diabetes cases.
C) No, because Mexican Americans are not featured on the graph, so their rate of diagnosed cases must be minimal.
D) No, because because American Indian/Alaska natives have the highest rate of diagnosed diabetes cases.

Chapter 2

Reading | Natural Science

The following passage is adapted from a scientific journal published in 2005.

It would be too dramatic to suggest a conspiracy, but for nearly fifty years, physicists have actively ignored an ever-growing weed in a beautifully designed garden. The dilemma is as follows: There are two distinct pillars
5 supporting modern physics. At the smallest end of the scale there is quantum mechanics, a branch of physics that deals exclusively with the atomic world of molecules, including the subatomic particles that comprise it. At the other end is general relativity, which explains the
10 largest elements of the universe from stars and planets to solar systems and galaxies. Each concept has provided generations of physicists with powerful tools to accurately unlock the secrets of many worlds. Yet, when analyzed together, a shocking and ground-shattering conclusion
15 emerges: *the two theories are irreconcilable.*

It may seem incredible that you have never heard about this fundamental scientific contradiction. Seemingly, this disagreement would have created a grand debate between physicists. But because physicists usually
20 only work with either large, massive things (like stars and planets) or small, light things (like protons and electrons), a conflict between the two occurs infrequently, and only in the most extreme circumstances. Thus, physicists who use quantum mechanics and physicists who use
25 general relativity can, without consequence, disregard the equations that build the foundation of the opposing model. For this reason, quantum mechanics and general relativity have coexisted in near blissful ignorance for nearly half a century.

30 However, there *are* situations in which the universe is extreme. On the inside of a black hole, a gigantic mass can be effortlessly crushed to an atomic size. In addition, the big bang theory hypothesizes that the whole universe began as a miniscule, though massive, pebble that
35 violently erupted to form the immensity of the universe today.

Both of these examples require the concurrent use of both quantum mechanics and general relativity. But when brought together, the equations from the two models begin
40 to jerk and sputter like a broken-down garbage disposal.

Less figuratively, physicists who utilize an unpleasant amalgam of these two theories only find incongruous answers to their well-posed questions.

Even if you never desire to draw away the veil of
45 mystery surrounding the depths of a black hole or the origins of the universe, you can't help but feel that the animosity between quantum mechanics and general relativity poses a fundamentally destructive problem that requires resolution. Is it really possible that the
50 universe is ultimately divided into two levels, one that requires a set of laws for the unimaginably large and another contradicting set for things that are microscopically small?

Superstring theory, a modern structure compared
55 to the venerable pillars of quantum mechanics and general relativity, answers with a decisive no. Over the past decade, physicists and mathematicians around the world have meticulously researched this new approach to understanding matter at its foundational level. This
60 approach ultimately solves the conflict between quantum mechanics and general relativity. In reality, superstring theory does more than just resolve the tension between the two theories: within this framework, quantum mechanics and general relativity actually require each other
65 for the theory to be true. Because of superstring theory, the union between the two models is not just peaceful but necessary. Superstring theory has the potential to show that all the astounding events in the universe — from the vibrating dance of light's wave particles to the elegant
70 pirouette of a planetary orbit — are indications of one incredible physical principle, one inclusive equation.

1

As it is used in line 8, the word "comprise" most nearly means

A) amplify.
B) negotiate.
C) constitute.
D) encircle.

2

The primary purpose of the second paragraph (lines 16-29) is to

A) provide further evidence for a conflict introduced at the beginning of the passage.
B) summarize the ongoing conflict between two different sciences.
C) propose an alternative argument to the one that currently exists in the scientific community.
D) critique the separation of the two schools of thought, encouraging unity.

Reading | Natural Science

3

According to the passage, the two incompatible theories have peacefully coexisted to this point because

A) neither theory is still used by the scientific community.
B) physicists can effectively combine certain equations from both theories.
C) the theories only apply to a limited set of events.
D) physicists work in specific scales where these theories do not interact.

4

Which choice provides the best evidence for the answer to the previous question?

A) Lines 11-15 ("Each . . . irreconcilable")
B) Lines 19-23 ("But . . . circumstances")
C) Lines 23-26 ("Thus . . . model")
D) Lines 41-43 ("Less . . . questions")

5

The author's use of italics in line 30 serves primarily to

A) accentuate a well-known hypothesis.
B) substantiate a valid belief.
C) highlight an area of agreement.
D) underscore an important idea.

6

The author refers to black holes primarily to

A) represent the mysteries of the universe.
B) contrast them with the big bang theory.
C) provide an example of a situation in which the quantum scale intersects with general relativity.
D) raise a topic physicists know little about.

7

Which choice provides the best evidence for the answer to the previous question?

A) Lines 30-32 ("However. . . . size")
B) Lines 32-36 ("In . . . today")
C) Lines 37-38 ("Both . . . relativity")
D) Lines 38-40 ("But . . . disposal")

8

The author uses the phrase "garbage disposal" on line 40 most likely to suggest that the two theories

A) are inherently useless and should be thrown out.
B) can only be used by a professional.
C) do not work together effectively.
D) can be easily repaired when using superstring theory.

9

Which of the following, if true, would best refute the author's assertion about the "modern structure" in line 54?

A) Mathematical equations that reconcile the quantum mechanics with general relativity
B) Evidence that the laws governing the universe change according to the size of the object being studied
C) Speculation that the universe did not actually begin with the big bang
D) Confirmation the interior of a black hole is as dense as scientists have thought

10

The main idea of the final paragraph is to

A) clearly answer the question posited by the passage as a whole.
B) solve the aforementioned conflict by introducing, and expounding on a new theory and its benefits.
C) praise the scientific community for their grappling with an unprecedented change.
D) summarize recent physics experiments.

11

The author's main purpose in including the dance imagery in lines 68-70 is so as to

A) explain the way particles of light move.
B) stress the extremes found in the universe.
C) illustrate the complexity of a planetary orbit.
D) convey his regard for the laws governing the movement of objects in the universe.

Reading | Paired-Passages

One of the five passages you will deal with will be paired, meaning there will be two related passages with questions concerning each passage as well as questions concerning both passages together. If you see a dual passage, approach each passage and its respective set of questions as if it were separate from the other passage. This will make the method for dealing with dual passages similar to that of single passages, and we can use a similar Action Plan. See the approach for dual passages below:

Paired-Passages Action Plan

1. Focus on the questions that ask about only the first passage.
Dual passage questions will ask about Passage 1, Passage 2, or both passages. Isolate the ones that ask solely about Passage 1 and tackle those first.

2. Label line references in Passage 1.
Check to see if any of the questions you isolated have line references. Label these in the passage so you can answer them as you read through the first passage. Also, circle any important keywords to keep an eye out for as you read.

3. Read Passage 1.
Read Passage 1 starting at the beginning, making sure to stop and answer any questions as you come to any labeled lines or keywords.

4. Attack the remaining Passage 1 questions.
After you have finished reading Passage 1 and answering any questions with line references, answer the remaining questions pertaining to Passage 1. Remember, the SAT does not have a guessing penalty, so if you are struggling with a question, try to eliminate any answer choices you can, and then choose your best guess. Even if you can't eliminate any choices, always bubble in an answer.

5. Repeat steps 1-4 for Passage 2.
Isolate the questions that reference only Passage 2. Glance at these and label any line references. Read Passage 2, stopping at any labeled lines to answer the questions. After you have finished reading the passage, answer the remaining questions. Be sure to bubble in an answer for every question.

6. Answer any questions that reference both passages.
As you read through the second passage, try to understand how the two passages are similar and how they are different. Once you have finished all the questions for Passage 2, answer the questions that reference both passages.

Look at the following passages and accompanying questions. Apply our Action Plan as you answer the questions.

Passage 1 is from a 2001 book that examines Martin Luther King's historic "I Have a Dream" speech. Passage 2 is from an earlier biography of Martin Luther King, written by an African American historical scholar.

Passage 1

No matter how influential at the time, most speeches by America's great orators have failed to withstand the test of time. Perhaps the greatest exception to this rule is Martin Luther King's career-defining "I Have a Dream" speech, which simultaneously transformed race politics in America and stereotyped its author as a passive activist. Delivered in 1963, this speech is often held up as the quintessential King address. To many, this speech symbolizes King's nonviolent message of racial equality and justice. Yet the complex duality of his message of nonviolent rebellion and extreme militancy is often overlooked by casual readers and scholars alike. Some scholars suggest that this speech does not serve as a true rallying cry or revitalization of the Civil Rights Movement, as it lacks the power and call to action found in King's later orations. These same scholars would also note that the speech inaccurately solidified King as just a nonviolent dreamer rather than as a protester, a nonconformist, or an activist. To fully appreciate the power of King's message, one King scholar has recommended a moratorium on reading or listening to the "I Have a Dream" speech.

Any such ban on reading King's iconic address all but concedes that its narrow interpretation will continue to cloud the true intentions and sentiments of this speech. But King's inspirational speech could be immune to such pigeon-holing. The opening of this speech still stirs the emotions that people felt upon first encountering those words, and people still speak of these feelings with a reverence often reserved for a child or a venerated grandparent. Not least among the benefits of reading or hearing this speech is the opportunity to reminisce about a movement that, in ten short years, ended a system of civil injustice that had been untouched since the 1870s. While it is clear that the United States still has an arduous journey to achieve racial and social equality, this speech helps the United States make great strides on that journey. Segregation is no longer lawful or practiced in the United States; there are no longer German Shepherds attacking marchers in the streets of Southern cities; no black school children requiring police escorts. The recognition of King's ideas and dreams is invoked yearly during the celebration of Martin Luther King's birthday. This celebration observes King's influence on the racial progress that the United States has made with an emphasis on the progress that the country still has to make.

Passage 2

Martin Luther King's ideas, wisdom, and influence are largely based on those of past visionaries and philosophers from different, and often conflicting, backgrounds. King managed to amalgamate these various ideas and form the primary foundations for his beliefs concerning American equality. Although King is recognized for promoting nonviolence to achieve social equality, he also agreed with other visionaries who advocated that social equality could ultimately be achieved only by dismantling capitalism. Martin Luther King believed that capitalism had outlived its relevance as well as contributed to the persistence of social injustices around the world. Because of this economic structure, racially persecuted groups of people would never have the ability to change injustice embedded in the system unless they received or seized the power to reshape the system.

Most of King's admirers tend to neglect his complex ideas beyond those concerning nonviolent resistance. Indeed, these admirers are inclined to ignore or even disregard attacks contrary to classic "Kingisms" by transforming King into a nonviolent deity. Unfortunately, this transformation disintegrates the nature of his ideas into simple clichés, thus reducing the character of King himself. As a result, the world essentially experiences a watered-down version of King, rather than getting a complete picture of this complex Civil Rights leader. This simplistic version of King is further propagated by the constant and inappropriate use of his most popular phrases: "I have a dream," "At the center of nonviolence stands the principle of love," and "Darkness cannot drive out darkness." It is inevitable that upon hearing the first four lines of his famous "I Have a Dream" speech, we instantly board a time machine and travel back to the Smithsonian Mall on that summer's day in 1963. We can feel the heat of ire and optimism stemming not only from King's speech but also from the thousands of audience members seeking to change America's racial status-quo.

Reading | Paired-Passages

For many Americans, this image captures the core representation of King. "I have a dream" can be applied to anyone wanting change an unjust system – no matter that
95 person's background or beliefs, there will always have an instance in which she or he dreams for a better world.

1

It can be inferred that the scholars mentioned in line 13 would believe the complete image of King should

A) exaggerate the contradictions within King's beliefs.
B) compare King with other Civil Rights leaders.
C) observe King's powerful influence outside of the United States.
D) acknowledge King's multifaceted message.

2

The use of the words "some" and "suggest" in line 14 and the word "recommended" in line 22 contribute to the tone of the first paragraph by

A) creating an optimistic tone that makes it clear that the author does not think King's depiction is a serious discrepancy.
B) creating a diplomatic tone that makes it clear that the author believes this is one valid argument among many.
C) establishing a critical tone that makes it clear that the author believes those who find merit in the famous speech ought to change their beliefs in the face of better evidence.
D) establishing a casual tone that makes clear the authors are not invested in the way MLK is seen by the public.

3

In line 26, "cloud" most nearly means

A) obscure.
B) darken.
C) fabricate.
D) secure.

4

The author of Passage 1 mentions an "arduous journey" on line 37 primarily to

A) suggest King's acceptance by an international audience.
B) acknowledge King's influence on an enduring struggle.
C) demonstrate King's consistency as an eloquent public speaker.
D) validate King's use of imagery to express a point.

5

The statement on lines 39-43 ("Segregation . . . escorts") serves primarily to

A) dispute historical events.
B) express a strong desire for a better future.
C) contrast past events with future events.
D) underscore a point with concrete examples.

6

Lines 68-70 ("Most . . . resistance") are a transition within Passage 2 from

A) a discussion of King's influences to a dismissal of his legacy.
B) a recognition of King's views to an examination of people's interpretation of them.
C) an observation of King's significance to an examination of his lesser-known beliefs.
D) a defense of King's viewpoints to a disinterest in those who ignore them.

Reading | Paired-Passages

7

Which of the following statements best summarizes the second paragraph (lines 68-91) of Passage 2?

A) King is most famous for supporting nonviolence, but he was dually passionate about ending capitalism and its inevitable economic discrimination.
B) "I have a dream" and other noteworthy phrases are used inappropriately at great disservice to public perception of an intricate man.
C) Despite all criticism, the first four lines of the iconic speech are incomparably transporting.
D) A refusal to look at King's complexity has injured the legacy of a multifaceted Civil Rights leader.

8

In line 88, "ire" most nearly means

A) enthusiasm.
B) hope.
C) loathing.
D) anger.

9

The author of Passage 2 would most likely believe that the interpretation of King's principles mentioned in lines 44-46 of Passage 1 ("The recognition . . . birthday") is

A) foolish.
B) introspective.
C) inadequate.
D) unorthodox.

10

Which statement best characterizes the relationship between the two passages?

A) Passage 2 discusses a figure that is criticized in Passage 1.
B) Passage 2 overemphasizes a person who is neutrally characterized in Passage 1.
C) Passage 2 expounds on another facet of the problem presented in Passage 1.
D) Passage 2 negates the viewpoints promoted in Passage 1.

11

The authors of both passages would agree that King's "I Have a Dream" speech

A) has been influenced by many great thinkers.
B) was significant on the national and international level.
C) represented King's entire ideology.
D) had a lasting effect on many Americans.

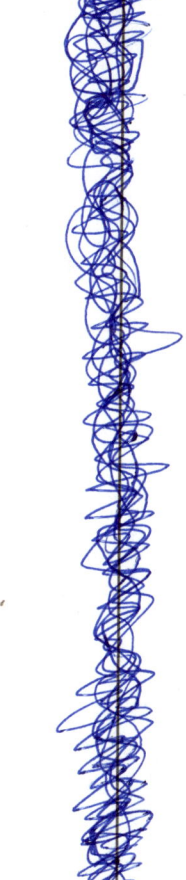

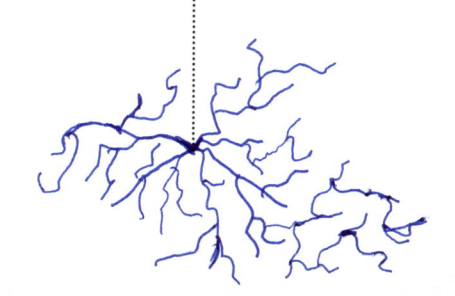

Reading | Paired-Passages

Passage 1 and Passage 2 are excerpts from 2009 articles on conservation.

Passage 1

    The public rise of conservationism has been startling both in its suddenness and in its breadth. People who only a decade or two ago were shopping for automobiles with a mind to bring their living
5 standard (and living room experience) to the road, are pressing automotive dealers for information on a vehicle's long term fuel efficiency and bio-diesel compatibility.
    More adventurous and proactive buyers are
10 flocking to waiting lists for vehicles with "hybrid" engines that run on both gasoline and rechargeable electric batteries. This has become especially apparent among younger and more educated drivers. There even seems to be an emerging trend among motorists to
15 petition their legislatures to set aside funding for the development of distribution stations for ethanol, an "earth friendly" bio-diesel.
    The 600 ethanol-blend pumps in the U.S. might be considered "odd ducks" indeed in a country
20 with tens of thousands of stations offering regular, super, and premium grades of gasoline. No less shocking is the persistence of such consumers to tolerate compromised performance and various refueling inconveniences while making the transition to more
25 conscientious fuel consumption. Nevertheless, all indicators seem to say it is a revolution in the making, with a front line of grass roots consumer advocates wearing their choices on their sleeves, and on their bumper stickers.

Passage 2

    There is a growing political trend to set mandatory
30 deadlines for fuel efficiency in automotive lines being proposed for future manufacture. While there are swaths of young, forward thinking constituencies petitioning their governments for fuel standards to be revised and energy conservation targets to be established, the real
35 benefits of such legislation will be limited to a few, opportunistic organizations. The major contributors to national productivity will be penalized for their energy saving innovations while disingenuous, predatory, or largely marginal businesses throw their weight behind
40 populist legislation written to serve a social good, but more likely to disinherit the electorate from the real time and energy saving gains that result from a re-investment of resources in traditional areas of technological advance.

45   For every conservation-minded piece of legislation to pass into law, there is an opportunistic multinational corporation that backs it to benefit its own bottom line to the detriment of industry-wide reinvestment of profit. Fuel economy laws are an excellent example. Seemingly a boon
50 for the environment, such legislation is often passed with the support of automotive manufacturers whose product lines are disproportionately concentrated into apparently "thrifty" sedans, while more diversified automotive manufacturers with investments in heavy trucks,
55 mechanical equipment, and diesel buses are unintentionally disadvantaged by an idealistic public.
    While such legislation is well-intentioned, it often creates harmful capital shortages for those businesses that are responsible for reinvesting in the most impactful
60 energy-saving research and developing things such as fuel-efficient diesel engines or mass transit designs. Such innovations save more fuel, per person, than even the most economical gas hybrid passenger sedans, and are spurred on by letting the companies that specialize in them raise
65 the capital to reinvest in the development cycle of these established technologies.

1

The main purpose of Passage 1 is to express

A) unease about unpredictable changes in public preferences.
B) disconcertion over the preoccupation of the public with untested energy alternatives.
C) disbelief that alternatives such as ethanol could ever rival proven energy sources of fuel such as petroleum.
D) astonishment at the emergence of a robust conservation movement.

Reading | Paired-Passages

2

The author of Passage 1 includes information about motorists "petitioning" their representatives for funding for ethanol distribution stations (lines 13-17) in order to

A) show that "proactive" buyers will have a very difficult time agreeing upon an alternative energy policy.
B) demonstrate how developed the conservation movement has become.
C) emphasize the difference between practical and frivolous approaches to political change.
D) hint at the inklings many in the conservation movement have towards political revolution.

3

The author uses the phrase "odd ducks" (line 19) most likely to

A) convey dissatisfaction with the limited distribution of alternative fuels.
B) disregard the efficacy of ethanol-based fuel alternatives.
C) insinuate that ethanol is still a long way from being a standard fuel source.
D) establish that ethanol refueling stations are an unlikely sight in most places.

4

In lines 45-48, the claim that there is always an opportunistic multinational corporation seeking to sponsor the legislation implies that

A) such legislation would not be able to pass without the support of multinationals.
B) such legislation is not as beneficial to conservation as it appears.
C) such legislation inevitably benefits some manufacturers while disadvantaging others.
D) such legislation is well thought out but poorly executed.

5

Passage 2's main objection regarding fuel efficiency mandates can be summed up as

A) fuel efficiency is not widely supported by the public.
B) focusing on fuel efficiency will always be an insufficient remedy to the nation's continuous thirst for new sources of energy.
C) mandating fuel efficiency will compel companies unequipped for fuel efficiency improvements to support sub-par innovations.
D) mandating fuel efficiency is a self-defeating approach to encouraging innovation in energy conservation.

6

It can be inferred from Passage 2 that one reason automotive manufacturers of heavy trucks and buses do not benefit from environmental legislation is that

A) heavy trucks and buses use more fuel per vehicle than do sedans.
B) manufacturers of sedans have a much better financed political lobby than do other manufacturers.
C) heavy trucks and buses may use less fuel than do sedans by some measurements, but the fuels on which they rely emit especially high levels of pollution into the environment.
D) heavy truck and bus manufacturers are innovators of technologies that are likely to have a significantly negative environmental impact.

Reading | Paired-Passages

7

As it is used in line 31, "swaths" most nearly means

A) cloths.
B) areas.
C) groups.
D) crowds.

8

In line 49, the word "boon" refers to

A) "thrifty" sedans which would appear to facilitate the conservation of energy.
B) the increased fuel economy of sedans.
C) legislation mandating new fuel economy provisions.
D) automotive manufacturers who are willing to research fuel economy improvements.

9

The primary difference between the purposes of Passage 1 and Passage 2 is that

A) Passage 1 clarifies the argument between advocates and detractors of alternative fuels while Passage 2 advances the agenda of those in favor of gradual change.
B) Passage 1 documents an unpredicted social movement while Passage 2 calls into question the sincerity of the advocates of that movement.
C) Passage 1 aims to raise awareness of the inadequacy of current sources of fuel, while Passage 2 debunks the myths put forth by Passage 1.
D) Passage 1 outlines the reasons for improving fuel efficiency while Passage 2 decries the inconsistency of consumer preferences.

10

The author of Passage 2 would most likely refer to the "motorists" discussed in line 14 of Passage 1 as

A) misguided.
B) deceived.
C) forward-thinking.
D) delusional.

11

The authors of both passages would most likely agree with which of the following statements?

A) Those advocating for revised fuel standards are unaware of whom this legislation will truly affect.
B) Conservationism has increased significantly within the past 15 years.
C) Although some of the advocates are young people, most of the motorists petitioning their government for fuel efficiency are over the age of 35.
D) Hybrid engines will radically change the automotive industry.

Reading | Practice

The following passage concerns an article written by an author who is nervously confronting its publication.

I unfolded the copy of *Le Figaro*. Why, here is an article on my subject! No! This is too bad, my very words, … I shall write to the editor, … but I said this, too, and here is my name at the bottom…. It is my
5 article! But for a moment, my thoughts, swept on by the impetus of this reaction, and perhaps already at this date grown rather the worse for wear, continue to believe it isn't, just as elderly people cannot arrest a movement once they have begun it. But quickly I return to the
10 thought: it is my article.

Then I pick up that sheet of paper which by a mysterious process of multiplication, preserving its singleness while withholding it from nobody, is both one and ten thousand, which is given to as many newsboys
15 who ask for it, and carried damp with morning fog and printer's ink, under the red span of sky over Paris to all those people who have just woken up and are about to drink their morning coffee. What I am holding in my hand is not only my own thought, it is thousands of
20 awakened attentions taking it in. And if I am to realize what is happening, I must abandon myself, I must be for a moment some one of the ten thousand readers whose curtains have just been drawn and on whose freshly awakened mind my thought is about to dawn in
25 a manifold surprise which fills me with more hope and faith than the sunrise overhead. So I pick up *Le Figaro* as if I did not know there was an article by me in it; I purposely avert my glance from the place where my words appear, trying to discover experimentally where it
30 would be likeliest to fall, and loading the dice by folding the page with that part hindermost, as someone who is waiting spaces out the minutes so that he may not be led away into counting them too fast.

I feel my lips purse up in the grimace of my reader
35 who expects to find nothing in particular, then my glance falls on my article, in the center of the page, and I begin to read. Every phrase conveys the image meant to call up. In every sentence the thought I wanted to express is made clear from the first words; but as it reaches
40 me in the sentence it is more abundant, more detailed, enriched—since I, the author, am for the time being the reader, and at the receiving end merely, and when I wrote I was at the producing end, and to the same thought which is now re-shaping itself in my mind I then
45 added harmonious amplifications which at the sentence's beginning had not entered my head, and whose ingenuity now amazes me.

I feel it is really impossible that the ten thousand who at this moment are engaged in reading my article
50 should not be feeling as much admiration for me as I feel for myself. And the thought of their admiration plugs the little gaps in my own. If I compared my article with the article I meant to write—as later on, alas! I shall do—instead of delightfully coherent passages I should probably find
55 palsied stammerings which even to the most well-wishing reader could barely hint at what, before I took pen in hand, I supposed myself able to express. That was how I felt when I wrote it, when I revised it; in an hour's time I shall feel so again; but at this moment each sentence that I extorted from
60 myself flows, not into my own mind, but into the minds of thousands on thousands of readers who have just woken up and opened *Le Figaro*.

1

The passage can best be described as

A) a discussion of how an article came into print.
B) a response to negative criticism.
C) a description of a thought experiment.
D) an analysis of the print process.

2

In line 8, "arrest" most nearly means

A) charge.
B) check.
C) retain.
D) seize.

3

The author repeatedly uses ellipses in the first paragraph most likely to convey the narrator's

A) displeasure at seeing his work in print.
B) thought process while reading the paper.
C) surprise at seeing his article in such a prestigious paper.
D) dismay at seeing how his words have been edited.

Reading | Practice

4

The authors use of the phrase on line 12 ("mysterious . . . multiplication") refers to

A) writing.
B) mathematics.
C) birth.
D) printing.

5

In lines 27-28, the narrator averts his glance in order to

A) lengthen the time he spends waiting before he begins to read.
B) show his disdain for his own words.
C) discover where an impartial reader's view would likely land on the page.
D) appreciate the imagery his words evoke.

6

An assumption made by the author is that the readers of his article

A) tend to be skeptical.
B) are inclined to peruse his article deeply.
C) are appreciative of his considerable writing skills.
D) are unlikely to fully grasp his technical abilities.

7

As used in line 50, "engaged" most nearly means

A) involved.
B) joined.
C) betrothed.
D) enlightened.

8

Which choice provides the best evidence for the answer to the previous question?

A) Lines 20-26 ("And . . . overhead")
B) Lines 34-37 ("I feel . . . read")
C) Lines 48-51 ("I feel . . . myself")
D) Lines 57-62 ("That. . . . Le Figaro")

9

It can be inferred from the passage that the narrator is usually very

A) wary of his audience.
B) solicitous of outside criticism.
C) confident in his ability.
D) critical of his own work.

10

Which choice provides thes best evidence for the answer to the previous question?

A) Lines 5-9 ("But . . . begun it")
B) Lines 18-20 ("What . . . in")
C) Lines 41-47 ("Since . . . me")
D) Lines 52-57 ("If . . . express")

The following passage is excerpted from a series of lectures on Shakespeare by A.C. Bradley.

What is the substance of a Shakespearean tragedy? What is the nature of the tragic aspect of life as represented by Shakespeare? What is Shakespeare's conception of tragedy? These expressions do not imply that Shakespeare himself ever asked or answered such questions. These imply only that Shakespeare, in writing tragedy, represented a certain part of life in a certain way. Therefore, through examination of his writings, we ought to be able to describe the tragic parts of life.

However, in doing so, we must remember two things, the first being that the tragic aspect of life is only one aspect. We cannot arrive at Shakespeare's whole dramatic way of looking at the world from studying his tragedies alone. Secondly, through studying his work, we can arrive at Shakespeare's dramatic view. We are not able to conclude whether this view corresponds directly with his opinions outside of his poetry - the opinions of the being whom we sometimes oddly call 'Shakespeare the man.'

In approaching this subject it will be best to start directly from the facts. Shakespeare's tragedies are preeminently the story of one person, the 'hero,' or at most of two, the 'hero' and 'heroine.' (It is only in the love-tragedies, Romeo and Juliet and Antony and Cleopatra, that the heroine is as much the center of the action as the hero. Therefore, for the sake of brevity, we will speak of the tragic story as being concerned primarily with one person.)

A tragedy depicts the troubled part of the hero's life, which precedes and leads up to his death. No play at the end of which the hero remains alive is, in the full Shakespearean sense, deemed a tragedy. An instantaneous death occurring by 'accident' in the midst of prosperity would not suffice. It is, rather, a tale of suffering, which, as a rule, is unexpected, and contrasted with previous happiness or glory. A tale, for example, of a man slowly worn to death by disease or poverty, however dreadful it might be, would not be tragic in the Shakespearean sense.

This exceptional suffering and calamity, which generally extends far and wide beyond the hero so as to create a whole scene of woe, are essential ingredients in a Shakespearean tragedy. They are chief sources of tragic emotions, especially that of pity. However, the proportions of pity in a tragedy naturally vary greatly. It plays, for example, a much larger part in King Lear than it does in Macbeth.

Shakespearean tragedy is concerned always with persons of 'high degree'; often with kings or princes; if not, with leaders in the state like Coriolanus, Brutus, Antony. And this characteristic of Shakespeare's tragedies, though not the most vital, is neither external nor unimportant. The pangs of unrequited love and the anguish of remorse are the same in a peasant and a prince. The story of the prince or the general, however, has a greatness and dignity of its own. His fate affects the welfare of a whole nation or empire; and when he falls suddenly from the height of earthly greatness to the dust, his fall produces a sense of contrast, of the powerlessness of man, and of the omnipotence of Fortune or Fate, which no tale of private life can possibly rival.

A Shakespearean tragedy, as so far considered, may be called a story of exceptional calamity leading to the death of a man in high estate. But it is clearly much more than this. No amount of calamity could alone provide the substance of its story. The calamities of tragedy do not simply happen; they proceed mainly from the actions of men.

We see human beings placed in certain circumstances; and we see, arising from the cooperation of characters in these circumstances, certain actions. This series of interconnected deeds leads, by an apparently inevitable sequence, to a catastrophe. The effect of such a series is to make us regard the sufferings which accompany it, and the catastrophe in which it ends, not only as something which happens to the persons concerned, but equally as something which is caused by them. This at least may be said of the hero, who always contributes in some measure to the disaster in which he perishes.

11

The 1st paragraph of the passage acts as

A) an introduction that introduces Shakespeare's emotional complexity.
B) an introduction that poses questions to be further answered in the passage.
C) an introduction that shows the reader the difference between tragedies and "love-tragedies."
D) an introduction that succintly explains Shakespeare's conception of tragedy.

Reading | Practice

12

According to the author, readers cannot capture the entirety of Shakespeare's worldview through studying his tragedies only because

A) tragedy is only one part of the human life experience, and also only one part of Shakespeare's work.
B) tragedy is overly dramatized in Shakespeare's work and as such is not a realistic portrayal of suffering.
C) Shakespearean tragedies only focus on the nobility.
D) Shakespeare purposefully obscured his own viewpoints from his tragedies.

13

Which of the following provides the best evidence for the answer to previous question?

A) Lines 4-6 ("These...questions")
B) Lines 10-14 ("However...alone")
C) Lines 25-27 ("Therefore...person")
D) Lines 31-33 ("An...suffice")

14

From the author's use of the phrase on line 18 ("Shakespeare . . . man"), the reader can infer that

A) Shakespeare intentionally separated his personal life from his work as an artist.
B) Shakespeare's poetry speaks often of his opinions of tragedy.
C) there is an important distinction to be made between Shakespeare as an individual and Shakespeare's writing itself.
D) there has been confusion previously regarding Shakespeare's gender.

15

In the love-tragedies such as Romeo and Juliet, the heroine

A) is the first to die in the story.
B) is an equally key part of the story as the hero.
C) is an important but secondary character.
D) evokes the most pity.

16

As it is used in line 25, "brevity" most nearly means

A) concision.
B) wit.
C) coherence.
D) education.

17

According to description in the fourth paragraph (lines 28-37), which of the following could NOT be the plot of a Shakesperean Tragedy?

A) An exiled King and his jester travel the world, and in the middle of the story the King dies.
B) A nobleman believes wrongly that his wife loves another man, and so he kills her and later, himself.
C) A prince seeks revenge for the death of his father, but eventually gives up and relocates to another country.
D) Two pairs of lovers find themselves in a bewitched woods overnight, and there experience a range of misfortunates and trickery.

18

The main purpose of the fifth paragraph (lines 38-45) is to

A) describe an entire scene of "woe."
B) explain that pity is a fixed component of great theatre.
C) prove that King Lear is more of a tragedy than Macbeth.
D) discuss and clarify the emotional components of a Shakespearen tragedy.

Reading | Practice

19

The author believes that "Shakesperean Tragedy" must not lack

A) the suffering and death of a hero or heroine.
B) an instantaneous, and often accidental, death of a leader.
C) a peasant character with integrity.
D) a great amount of pity.

20

Which of the following provides the best evidence for the answer to previous question?

A) Lines 51-53 ("The pangs . . . prince")
B) Lines 60-62 ("A Shakespearean . . . estate")
C) Lines 63-64 ("No . . . story")
D) Lines 64-66 ("The calamities . . . men")

21

The author of this passage would most likely agree that

A) tragedy is solely defined by an upsetting course of events.
B) tragedy is regularly brought on by those who suffer for it most.
C) all unfortunate events are equal in storytelling merit.
D) the goal of tragedy is to leave the reader or viewers with an understanding of their lack of control over their lives.

Reading | Practice

The following passage is an excerpt from the book *The Economic Aspects of Geology* by C.K. Leith.

　　Physiography is a phase of geology which investigates the surface features of the earth. It has to do not only with the description and classification of surface forms, present and past (physical geography or
5 geomorphology), but with the processes and history of their development. The subject is closely related to geography, climatology, sedimentation, and hydrology.
　　The central feature of physiography is the erosion cycle or topographic cycle. Erosion, acting
10 through the agencies of wind, water, and ice, is constantly at work on the earth's surface; the eroded materials are in large part carried off by streams, ultimately to be deposited in the ocean near the continental margins. The final result is the reduction of the land surface to an
15 approximate plain, called a peneplain, somewhere near sea level. Geological history shows that such peneplains are often elevated again with reference to sea level, by earth forces or by subsidence of the sea, when erosion again begins its work,—first cutting narrow, steep
20 gulches and valleys, and leaving broad intervening uplands, in which condition the erosion surface is described as that of topographic youth; then forming wider and more extensive valleys, leaving only points and ridges of the original peneplains, in which stage the
25 surface is said to represent topographic maturity; then rounding off and reducing the elevations, leaving few or none of the original points on the peneplain, widening the valleys still further and tending to reduce the whole country to a nearly flat surface, resulting in the condition
30 of topographic old age. The final stage is again the peneplain. This cycle of events is called the erosion cycle or topographic cycle. Uplift may begin again before the surface is reduced to base level; in fact, there is a constant oscillation and contest between erosion and
35 relative uplift of the land surface.
　　The action of the erosion cycle on rocks of differing resistance to erosion and of diverse structure gives rise to the great variety of surface forms. The physiographer sees these forms, not as heterogeneous
40 units, but as parts of a definite system and as stages in an orderly series of events. He is able to see into the topographic conditions beyond the range of immediate and direct observation. He is able to determine what these forms were in the past and to predict their condition in
45 the future. A given structure may, in different stages of topographic development, give quite diverse topographic forms. In such a case it is important to realize that the diversity is only superficial. On the other hand, a slight local divergence from the usual
50 topographic forms in a given region may reflect a similar local divergence in the underground structure. Thus it is that an appreciation of the physiographic details may suggest important variations in the underground structure which would otherwise pass undiscovered.
55 　　Many mineral deposits owe their origin or enrichment to weathering and other related processes which are preliminary to erosion. These processes vary in intensity, distribution, and depth, with the stage of erosion, or in relation to the phase of the erosion cycle.
60 They vary with the climatic conditions which obtain on the erosion surface. Mineral deposits are therefore often closely related to the topographic features, present and past, in kind, shape, and distribution.
　　For example, many of the great copper deposits of
65 the western United States owe their values to a secondary enrichment through the agency of waters working down from the surface. When this fact of secondary enrichment was discovered, it was naturally assumed that the process was related to the present erosion surface and to present
70 climatic and hydrologic conditions. Certain inferences were drawn, therefore, as to depth and distribution of the enriched ores. This conception, however, proved to be too narrow, as evidence was found to show that in many cases the copper deposits had been concentrated in
75 previous erosion cycles. The importance of this knowledge from an exploring and development standpoint is clear. It has made it possible to find and follow rich ores, far from the present erosion surface, which would otherwise have been disclosed solely by
80 chance. Studies of this kind in the copper camps are yet so recent that much remains to be learned. The economic geologist advising exploration and development in copper ores who does not in the future take physiographic factors into account is likely to go
85 wrong in essential ways, as he has done in some cases in the past.

22

The primary purpose of the first paragraph is to

A) persuade the reader to subscribe to a geological ideology.
B) explain the history of geomorphology.
C) identify and define an important term that is used through the passage.
D) discuss the five stages of the topographic cycle.

Reading | Practice

23

According to the second paragraph (lines 8-35), the central feature of physiography is
A) water.
B) wind.
C) the erosion cycle.
D) climatology.

24

A "peneplain" (line 15) can best be described as

A) land leveled by erosion over time.
B) an area of land significantly higher than sea level.
C) land in the first stage of the erosion cycle.
D) a featureless plain near the sea.

25

As it is used in line 34, "oscillation" most nearly means

A) argument.
B) stabilization.
C) fluctuation.
D) oxygenation.

26

According to the passage, the physiographer's role in studying the erosion cycle is to

A) carefully work to keep erosion from taking place.
B) ensure the cycle is perceived solely as heterogenous.
C) directly observe and record the erosion cycle.
D) holistically understand the process, causes, and consequences of erosion.

27

Which choice provides the best evidence for the answer to the previous question?

A) Lines 36-38 ("The action. . . . forms")
B) Lines 38-43 ("The physiographer. . . . observation")
C) Lines 47-48 ("In. . . . superficial")
D) Lines 51-54 ("Thus. . . . undiscovered")

28

The inferences referenced in the last paragraph were misguided because

A) evidence was found later on that challenged and expanded the initial theory.
B) these inferences did not take economic geology into account.
C) copper deposits were enriched through present erosion and climate conditions.
D) evidence was found that has called for an entirely new theory.

29

The author believes the science behind copper ores is important because

A) developing these ores is a dangerous task.
B) this knowledge has development and economic implications.
C) this knowledge is valuable to miners.
D) this knowledge ensures the preservation of copper ores in the future.

30

Which choice provides the best evidence for the answer to the previous question?

A) Lines 70-72 ("Certain . . . ores")
B) Lines 75-77 ("The importance . . . clear")
C) Lines 77-80 ("It . . . chance")
D) Lines 81-86 ("The economic . . . past")

Reading | Practice

31

Of the following choices, the best alternative title for this passage would be

A) The Cause and Effects of the Erosion Cycle.
B) The Economic Value of Copper.
C) How Peneplains Affect Topography.
D) Geological History.

32

The author would agree with which of the following statements?

A) Although much has been studied in the copper camps, there are many unanswered questions.
B) There is an erroneous perception that more research is needed on the erosion of copper ores.
C) A geologist does not need to concern herself with physiography, as geology and physiography are separate areas of study.
D) Because geologists in the past have made errors, all geologists should steer clear of the copper discussion.

Reading | Practice

The following passage is excerpted from the *Fireside Chats of Franklin D. Roosevelt.*

I want to talk for a few minutes with the people of the United States about banking—with the comparatively few who understand the mechanics of banking but more particularly with the overwhelming majority who use banks for the making of deposits and the drawing of checks. I want to tell you what has been done in the last few days, why it was done, and what the next steps are going to be. I recognize that the many proclamations from state capitols and from Washington, the legislation, the treasury regulations, etc., couched for the most part in banking and legal terms should be explained for the benefit of the average citizen. I know that when you understand what we in Washington have been about I shall continue to have your cooperation as fully as I have had your sympathy and help during the past week.

First of all let me state the simple fact that when you deposit money in a bank the bank does not put the money into a safe deposit vault. It invests your money in many different forms of credit— bonds, commercial paper, mortgages and many other kinds of loans. In other words, the bank puts your money to work to keep the wheels of industry and of agriculture turning around. A comparatively small part of the money you put into the bank is kept in currency— an amount which in normal times is wholly sufficient to cover the cash needs of the average citizen.

What, then, happened during the last few days of February and the first few days of March? Because of undermined confidence on the part of the public, there was a general rush by a large portion of our population to turn bank deposits into currency or gold—a rush so great that the soundest banks could not get enough currency to meet the demand. By the afternoon of March 3rd, scarcely a bank in the country was open to do business.

It was then that I issued the proclamation providing for the nation-wide bank holiday, and this was the first step in the government's reconstruction of our financial and economic fabric. The second step was the legislation promptly and patriotically passed by the Congress confirming my proclamation and broadening my powers so that it became possible in view of the requirement of time to extend the holiday and lift the ban of that holiday gradually. This law also gave authority to develop a program of rehabilitation of our banking facilities. Congress showed a devotion to public welfare and a realization of the emergency and the necessity for speed that is difficult to match in our history.

This bank holiday, while resulting in many cases in great inconvenience, is affording us the opportunity to supply the currency necessary to meet the situation. No sound bank is a dollar worse off than it was when it closed its doors last Monday. Neither is any bank which may turn out not to be in a position for immediate opening. The new law allows the twelve Federal Reserve Banks to issue additional currency on good assets and thus the banks which reopen will be able to meet every legitimate call. The new currency is being sent out by the Bureau of Engraving and Printing in large volume to every part of the country. It is sound currency because it is backed by actual, good assets.

As a result, we start tomorrow, Monday, with the opening of banks in the twelve Federal Reserve Bank cities—those banks which on first examination by the treasury have already been found to be all right. This will be followed on Tuesday by the resumption of all their functions by banks already found to be sound. On Wednesday and succeeding days banks in smaller places all through the country will resume business, subject, of course, to the government's physical ability to complete its survey.

It is possible that when the banks resume a very few people who have not recovered from their fear may again begin withdrawals. Let me make it clear that the banks will take care of all needs. It needs no prophet to tell you that when the people find that they can get their money—that they can get it when they want it for all legitimate purposes—the phantom of fear will soon be laid. People will again be glad to have their money where it will be safely taken care of and where they can use it conveniently at any time. I can assure you that it is safer to keep your money in a reopened bank than under the mattress.

The success of our whole great national program depends, of course, upon the cooperation of the public – on its intelligent support and use of a reliable system.

33

As it is used in line 10, "couched" most nearly means

A) articulated.
B) beset.
C) framed.
D) bedridden.

Reading | Practice

34

According to the passage, money deposited in a bank is

A) deposited securely in a safe.
B) given directly, as currency, to other citizens seeking loans.
C) invested, as credit, in mortgages and bonds.
D) used to pay taxes for social services.

35

The proclamation issued by Roosevelt was a step towards

A) establishing a nation-wide bank holiday in support of helping the banks restabilize.
B) giving the Bureau of Engraving and Printing extraneous time to print the needed funds.
C) encouraging citizens to only invest their money with the Federal Reserve Bank.
D) investigating widespread fraud and misuse of currency.

36

Which choice provides the best evidence for the answer to the previous question?

A) Lines 29-34 ("Because . . . demand")
B) Lines 36-39 ("It . . . fabric")
C) Lines 39-44 ("The second . . . gradually")
D) Lines 49-51 ("This . . . situation")

37

The primary purpose of the statement in lines 49-50 ("while . . . inconvenience") is to

A) criticize the banks for their inefficiency.
B) empathize with the frustrations of those individuals he is working to convince.
C) apologize to those his new proclamation will vex.
D) prepare the American people for a painful transition.

38

In the fifth paragraph (lines 49-61), Roosevelt's primarily argument is that the bank holiday will mostly benefit

A) America's foreign allies and affairs.
B) the smallest, rural banks, which gives aid to the poorest areas of the country.
C) every bank in the country, and consequently, American industry and agriculture.
D) the Federal Reserve.

39

Roosevelt believes individuals should stop withdrawing their money from the banks because

A) bank employees need time to rest.
B) it is their civic duty to share their money during wartime.
C) money loses value if it's kept under a mattress.
D) money is far safer in the banking system than anywhere else.

40

Which choice provides the best evidence for the answer to the previous question?

A) Lines 67-71 ("On . . . survey")
B) Lines 72-74 ("It . . . withdrawals")
C) Lines 81-83 ("I . . . mattress")
D) Lines 84-86 ("The . . . system")

41

The last sentence (lines 84-86) of the passage serves to

A) persuade the listeners of the importance of their actions during this crisis.
B) pressure the public into accepting the proclamation without question.
C) thank the public for their unending support and participation in democracy.
D) lambast the banks for taking advantage of the public's intelligence.

Reading | Practice

42

The overall tone of this passage could be described as

A) apologetic.
B) certain.
C) incensed.
D) pleading.

43

The reader can infer that Roosevelt would agree with the statement that

A) the banks are infallible.
B) the Federal Reserve can coexist healthily without public participation.
C) the American nation can only succeed if those goverened are willing to protect themselves first, the nation second.
D) the American nation can only succed with ordinary Americans trusting the establishment to do justly on their behalf.

44

According to the passage, Roosevelt's usage of the word "you" signifies that he is speaking to

A) congress.
B) wealthy Americans.
C) a small group of bankers.
D) the American population, regardless of income or occupation.

Reading | Practice

The following passage is excerpted from a scientific book about animals from the past.

   Fossils are the remains, or even the indications, of animals and plants that have, through natural agencies, been buried in the earth and preserved for long periods of time.
5   This may seem a rather meager definition, but it is a difficult matter to frame; fossils are not necessarily the remains of extinct animals or plants, neither are they, of necessity, objects that have become petrified or turned into stone. It is not essential for a specimen to have had
10 its animal matter replaced by some mineral in order that it may be classed as a fossil, for the Siberian Mammoths, found entombed in ice, are very properly spoken of as fossils, although the flesh of at least one of these animals was so fresh that it was eaten.
15   Many fossils, however, have been changed into stone by the slow removal of the animal or vegetable matter present and its replacement by some mineral, usually silica or some form of lime. Additionally, some of the best fossils may be merely impressions of plants or
20 animals and no portion of the objects themselves; some of our most important information has been gathered from these same imprints. Nearly all our knowledge of the plants that flourished in the past is based on the impressions of their leaves left on the soft mud or smooth
25 sand that later on hardened into enduring stone. Such, too, are the casts of the burrows of worms and the many footprints of the reptiles, great and small, that crept along the shore or stalked beside the waters of the ancient seas. The creatures themselves have passed away, their
30 massive bones even are lost, but the prints of their feet are as plain today as when they were first made.
   Impressions of vertebrates may be almost as good as actual skeletons, as in the case of some fish, where the fine mud in which they were buried has
35 become changed to a rock, similar to porcelain in texture; the bones have either dissolved away or shattered into dust at the splitting of the rock, but the imprint of each little fin-ray and every threadlike bone is as clearly defined as it would have been in a freshly prepared
40 skeleton.
   So why is it that fossils are not more abundant? Why, of the vast majority of animals that have dwelt upon the earth since it became fit for the habitation of living beings, does not a trace remain?
45   The answer to this query is that, unless the conditions were such as to preserve at least the hard parts of any creature from immediate decay, there was small probability of its becoming fossilized. The objects must be protected from the air, and, practically, the only way
50 that this happens in nature is by having them covered with water, or at least buried in wet ground. If an animal dies on dry land, where its bones lie exposed to sun and rain and frost and snow, it does not take these destructive agencies long to reduce the bones to powder; in the rare
55 event of a climate devoid of rain, mere changes of temperature, by producing expansion and contraction, will sooner or later cause a bone to crack and crumble.
   Usually, too, the work of the elements is aided by that of animals and plants. Everyone has seen a dog
60 make way with a pretty good-sized bone, and the Hyena has still greater capabilities in that line; and ever since vertebrate life began there have been carnivorous animals of some kind to play the role of bone-destroyers. Now and then we come upon a fossil bone, long since turned
65 into stone, on which are the marks of the little cutting teeth of field mice, put there long, long ago, and yet looking as fresh as if made only last week. These little beasts, however, are indirect rather than direct agents in the destruction of bones by gnawing off the outer layers,
70 and thus permitting the more ready entrance of air and water.
   Suppose, however, that some animal has sunk in the depths of a quiet lake, where the wash of the waves upon the shore wears the sand or rock into mud so fine that
75 it floats out into still water and settles there as gently as dew upon the grass. Little by little the bones are covered by a deposit that fills every groove and pore, preserving the mark of every ridge and furrow; and while this may take long, it is merely a matter of time and favorable
80 circumstance to bury the bones as deeply as one might wish. If, instead of a lake, our animal had gone to the bottom of some estuary into which poured a river turbid with mud, the process of entombment would have been still more rapid, while, had the creature been engulfed in
85 quicksand, it would have been the quickest method of all.
   At least two examples of the great dinosaur Thespesius have been found with the bones all in place, the thigh bones still in their sockets and the ossified tendons running along the backbone as they did in life.
90 This would hardly have happened had not the body been surrounded and supported so that every part was held in place and not crushed, and it is difficult to see any better agency for this than burial in quicksand.

Reading I Practice

45

The author views the definition of fossils as a "difficult matter to frame" because

A) contrary to what is popularly thought, the definition of what is considered a fossil does not include the remains of extinct animals and plants.
B) the criteria that must be met in order for an item to be classified as a fossil is so specific that it leaves out most items.
C) the definition of what is considered a fossil covers a few different categories of remains and indications, making a simple definition a challenge.
D) the impressions that vertebrates leave in mud are equally as good as any typical fossil.

46

The primary purpose of the statement in lines 30-31 "the prints . . . made" is to state that

A) the fossilized imprints look fairly ordinary.
B) despite many years having passed, the imprint does not look fossilized, but rather freshly created.
C) the feet of a certain animal long ago and the feet of the same animal in modern times look the same.
D) the footprints are barely visible on the fossils themselves.

47

The author's questions in lines 41-44 serve to

A) challenge a preceding point.
B) transition from an explanation of "what" to an explanation of "why."
C) transition from a discussion on imprint fossils to fossils that are created by entombment.
D) use rhetorical questions to keep the reader's interest.

48

As it is used in line 55, "devoid" most nearly means

A) at risk for.
B) full.
C) buoyant.
D) absent.

49

The main purpose of the sixth paragraph (lines 45-57) is to

A) link global water shortages with an upsurge in fossils.
B) factually answer the questions posed in the previous paragraph.
C) disprove a previously asserted claim.
D) describe a new theory of how fossilization takes place.

50

According to the passage, why are the field mice considered indirect agents of bone destruction?

A) The bones of the field mice don't decay fully upon burial.
B) The imprint of mice teeth mars the purity of the fossilized bone.
C) The mice gnaw much of the bone off, prompting it then to crack and crumble.
D) The mice gnaw off the outer layers of the bone, leaving the bone vulnerable to further damage.

Reading | Practice

51

Which choice provides the best evidence for the answer to the previous question?

A) Lines 51-54 ("If . . . powder")
B) Lines 58-59 ("Usually . . . plants")
C) Lines 63-67 ("Now . . . week")
D) Lines 67-71 ("These . . . water")

52

Which of the following examples would be most likely to successfully fossilize the fastest?

A) A dead rabbit strewn in the middle of a field
B) A dead rabbit at the bottom of a muddy river
C) A dead rabbit buried in quicksand
D) A dead rabbit buried in the snow

53

Which choice provides the best evidence for the answer to the previous question?

A) Lines 72-76 ("Suppose . . . grass")
B) Lines 76-81 ("Little. . . wish")
C) Lines 81-85 ("If . . . all")
D) Lines 86-89 ("At . . . life")

54

The author mentions the great Dinosaur Thespesius in order to

A) provide an example of the efficiency of bone fossilization through burial.
B) highlight the history of archeological research that focuses on dinosaurs.
C) remark on the rarity of the bones still being place upon discovery.
D) prove that quicksand, as opposed to mud, is better for the entombment process.

55

The main idea of the passage is that

A) fossilization by burial is most efficient.
B) the types and processes of fossilization vary.
C) there would be more traces of past life if natural elements did not impede fossilization.
D) there is some confusion over the definition of a fossil.

CHAPTER 2
PRACTICE

Reading | Practice

The following passage has been adapted from a 2002 novel about the lives of two brothers.

The two brothers had little in common but blood, and even that was shared begrudgingly. It was said that the newly-born Herman howled when Ishmael's flickering, candle-cast shadow fell upon the infant. It was the two brothers' first interaction, and it was to set the tone for all of those that followed.

Ishmael grew up tall and strong, a strapping lad with a well-defined chin whose only struggle was managing his various romantic conquests. Herman shared Ishmael's jawline, but was smaller and thinner, a pale boy who squinted in the sunlight. The two were known about town as the 'winsome chinsomes,' a moniker applied adoringly to Ishmael by pining lasses, and derisively to the morose Herman by nearly everyone. When Ishmael finally turned eighteen, he struck out on his own, eventually settling down in some metropolis which seemed barely to contain his oversized personality. Rumors and stories drifted back to his hometown in rural Arkansas. Ishmael was the CEO of a large corporation in New York. Ishmael had become Hollywood's newest star and was overseeing a project shrouded in secrecy. Ishmael was an artist in Paris, flitting enigmatically from studio to studio while the Louvre desperately sought his works. So said Marge at the pharmacy, in February, June, and December, respectively.

And what, then, of his brother? No rumors followed his life, for it was duly (and dully) documented. At seventeen, Herman got his first job as a car salesman at a small dealership in town. He did fairly well, and in a year or two, moved into his own apartment. After half a decade more of reliable sales, Herman met the lovely and charming Elizabeth, and in due time, asked her to marry him. Elizabeth encouraged Herman's career, but wished that he would further pursue his little-known but formidable skill with a paintbrush.

The exact events of the marriage's decline are somewhat hazy, but some facts are certain. It is certain that Ishmael exchanged silvery-tongued words with his sister-in-law which piqued her dissatisfaction. And it is known that Elizabeth walked out on Herman two months later. It is certain that Ishmael, resplendent in a white suit and shoes of shining leather, visited the happy couple during the fourth year of their marriage.

Herman wrote many letters to Elizabeth's father (for she had not left a forwarding address) asking after her, frantically seeking the reason for her disappearance. Her father, a local judge, eventually penned this short but imperious response: "Your brother told my Elizabeth that she was a saint for such charity, such an extraordinary girl living with a man of little repute. Elizabeth realized that pity is not love. I'll suffer no more letters, now that you've your answer." And so, Ishmael's campaign grew more apparent.

That was the beginning of Herman's decline. As his hours in bars grew longer and more regular, those at the dealership grew shorter and more irregular, and soon enough Herman held in his hands a paycheck with "Last one!" scrawled angrily upon the reverse side. When he tried to move back in with his parents, they told their lesser son that they had heard how Ishmael (who called frequently, they mentioned) had tried to save Herman's marriage. They told Herman that he needed to be more like his brother. Herman never even unpacked his bags. His brother, with his spite and charm, his cunning and cupidity, had won the day. Two days later, Herman was on a bus to Texas.

And now he flips burgers in a truck stop. Seven years over a grill have latticed his arms with burns, and most of his shirts have grease spots on them. His eyes are worse than ever, and the long hours of the dinner shift have taken their toll on his feet. Herman still paints - landscapes and portraits that are buried in a crowded closet upon completion, never to be seen again. And yet, despite his aching soles and scarred arms, he finds himself smiling. In Texas, at least, he is not the dour reflection of Ishmael. He is content at last; or at least as content as any younger brother could be.

Reading I Practice

1

The passage's characterization of Ishmael can best be described as

A) nondescript.
B) whimsical.
C) fabulous.
D) notorious.

2

As it is used in line 1, the word "blood" most nearly means

A) animating spirit.
B) familial ties.
C) common temperament.
D) long-standing animosity.

3

The author's intent in lines 2-4 ("It was . . . infant") is to

A) foreshadow the troubled nature of the brothers' relationship.
B) utilize personification to paint an image with words for the reader.
C) liken Ishmael to a candle to signify how he has always given light and goodness to others.
D) describe Herman's penchant for deep unhappiness.

4

What is the primary significance of the brothers' shared jawline?

A) It displays the hatred that existed between the two brothers.
B) It represented the only physical trait that the brothers shared.
C) It reflected the similar careers the brothers pursued.
D) It was an example of their attractive facial features.

5

Which of the following provides the best evidence for the answer to the previous question?

A) Lines 1-2 ("The two . . . begrudgingly")
B) Lines 7-9 ("Ishmael . . . conquests")
C) Lines 9-11 ("Herman . . . sunlight")
D) Lines 11-15 ("The two . . . everyone")

6

The statements in lines 27-32 ("And . . . apartment") provide examples of

A) Ishmael's early years in the workplace.
B) ambitious endeavors Herman undertook.
C) Herman's comparatively ordinary nature.
D) the aspects of Herman's life that impressed his neighbors.

7

As it is used in line 50, "imperious" most nearly means

A) apologetic.
B) curt.
C) domineering.
D) cruel.

8

The "campaign" mentioned in line 55 was "apparent" to

A) Herman.
B) Elizabeth's father.
C) Herman's parents.
D) Elizabeth.

Reading | Practice

9

The statement about younger brothers in lines 81-82 suggests that

A) they hardly reveal their true feelings.
B) their paintings express their true emotions.
C) they are often predisposed to be dissatisfied.
D) those that are most notable must outstrip their siblings.

10

Which of the following statements most accurately expresses Herman's feelings concerning his paintings in the final paragraph (lines 71-82)?

A) He is full of shame at the poor quality of his paintings.
B) His painting skill has diminshed as a result of his recently impaired eyesight.
C) He has improved his painting technique over seven years and has a sense of satisfaction in his work.
D) He paints for personal reasons, as he displays no desire to exhibit his works to anyone else.

This passage is excerpted from a 1992 article about the perception of philosophy and logic.

Mankind shows a remarkable propensity to accept conclusions without proof. This capability of our species, most typically called faith, exhibits itself in many aspects of our thought. We have faith in our family and friends
5 that they will not betray us or wrong us. Governments have faith in their people, and likewise, people trust in their government, in the hopes that it will act in the interest of its citizens. Believers of cultural norms are often dogmatically faithful, stalwartly trusting that the
10 attire, music, and food that they have grown accustomed to are "normal." However, perhaps the most ubiquitous form of faith is what we conceive of as its diametric opposite: logic.

We rely on logic to validate nearly every decision.
15 Even when we make emotional decisions, they may be traced back to logic based on flawed premises. When confronted with obstacles, we wield that uniquely human weapon, logic, with varying degrees of skill. Faith, we are told, is not kin but the direst opponent of logic;
20 logic demands proof to reach conclusions, and therefore cannot depend on faith. Doubting logic makes one seem foolish, and to do so is to disparage the only universal dogma humans share. However, logic relies on faith just as much as any intangible belief does since our beloved
25 logic depends wholly upon our nebulous senses. Take, for example, our everyday existence. Our memories tell us that we existed yesterday, as well as the day before that, up until the moment of our birth. Nonetheless, we do not remember every day we have lived through; if we
30 are lucky, one day in twenty stays stored in our fleshy, fallible memory banks. How, then, do we know that we have existed during the other nineteen days? We do this by simply making a jump of faith. Having no knowledge of experiencing gaps in our existence, we assume that it
35 hasn't happened.

And what of the days we do remember? Nobody can argue that his or her memory is infallible – every person has had proven wrong a vividly recalled memory. Our pasts must therefore be products of faith. What about
40 our presents (and presence)? Do we have any way of knowing that what our eyes show us is what is truly before us? We can never know if the "green" that you see and the "green" that I see are identical. We know that light takes time to travel, as does sound, and as do the
45 electrical impulses that convey sensory information to our brains. When we see a bird squawking, what we see and hear are not a bird and its noise, but their afterimages and echoes, lagging behind the bird itself. When we hold an apple, we feel old tactile information: not the apple,
50 but what the apple was at some point in the past.

Faith rules supreme not only over individual life, but also over the fates of civilizations. The only reason that each citizen of a nation continues his or her daily routine (be it work, school, or play) and adheres to his or her
55 duties and obligations is the faith-filled assumption that tomorrow will exist and will be much unchanged from today. Who would go to work on Tuesday if Wednesday might not exist? Indeed, for many people, Wednesday doesn't exist, but even against the inevitability of death,
60 we continue our life assuming that the reaper will not swing his mortal sickle at us on Thursday.

If we might generalize the character of human faith, it is that we believe that what happens in the present (or in the near past, given our senses' delayed intake of our
65 surroundings) will continue uninterrupted into the future. We do not tether ourselves to the ground, believing that gravity will fail; we do not worry that the sponge with which we wash dishes will suddenly become a piranha as it has never done so in the past. "Logic" involves
70 drawing conclusions from the past to predict the future. Ultimately, though, it is no more guaranteed than a soothsayer's crystal ball.

11

The passage as a whole suggests that the relationship between logic and faith is that of

A) two concepts linked through intrinsic similarities.
B) two distinct tools used to solve everyday problems.
C) similarly overvalued ways of reaching a conclusion.
D) ultimately incompatible systems of thought.

12

As it is used in line 1, "propensity" most nearly means

A) inability.
B) gift.
C) disposition.
D) enthusiasm.

Reading | Practice

13

The author suggests that to question logic is to risk being considered

A) insincere.
B) progressive.
C) emotional.
D) heretical.

14

The main purpose of the second paragraph (lines 14-35) is primarily to

A) emphasize the power of logic.
B) exhibit the infallibility of faith.
C) indicate the importance we imbue logic with and demonstrate its fundamental link to faith.
D) point out the flaws in faith.

15

The author views human memory as

A) a powerful tool for making logical decisions.
B) imperfect and lacking in detail.
C) a source of faith.
D) not subject to the rules of logic.

16

Which of the following provides the best evidence for the answer to the previous question?

A) Lines 4-5 ("We . . . us")
B) Lines 26-31 ("Our . . . banks")
C) Lines 40-43 ("Do we . . . identical")
D) Lines 62-65 ("If . . . future")

17

As it used in line 49, "tactile" most nearly means

A) fragile.
B) stirring.
C) cranial.
D) sensory.

18

The author would most likely describe the "daily routine" (line 53) as

A) ultimately based on an assumption.
B) unnecessary accoutrements of faith.
C) the unfortunate result of following logic.
D) evidence of the wholly positive power of faith-based thought.

19

The main function of the fourth paragraph (lines 51-61) in relation to the passage as a whole is most likely to

A) expand the scope of the point made in the previous paragraph.
B) transition between the two main points discussed in the passage.
C) provide an example to support the author's claim on memory.
D) conclude the author's discussion about logic.

20

The author uses the phrase "faith rules supreme" (line 51) to

A) hint that only the elite can truly control faith.
B) suggest that faith-based decisions are loftier than logical ones.
C) imply that leadership in particular relies upon faith.
D) emphasize the role faith plays on every scale.

21

The author mentions "a soothsayer's crystal ball" (lines 71-72) most likely in order to

A) exemplify how one can be guided by faith.
B) symbolize the limits of logic.
C) present an example of prophecy.
D) illustrate the speculative nature of logic.

Reading I Practice

The following passage is excerpted from a scientific journal concerning chimpanzees.

There is a tendency in popular consciousness to differentiate humans from other animals by regarding our social rules and hierarchies as uniquely human, but in fact, the pre-human species from which we descend
5 must also have been social. In other words, we were social before we were human. The chimpanzee, our 98.5% identical genetic relative, has a sophisticated set of social rules and habits, as do the more distantly related gorilla and orangutan, and the still more distant monkey.
10 As virtually all primates have complicated social rules, the common ancestor of humans and chimps, which lived more than five million years ago, must surely have had them, too. Human beings may be uniquely self-conscious, but they did not start with social blank slates.
15   One of the most conspicuous aspects of human society is power. Of the numerous ways to quantify power, one such measure is the capacity of one in power to reward oneself with privileges not afforded to those lacking power. Consider the following scenario: an older
20 sister petitions her parents for a raise in her allowance so that it is bigger than her younger brother's, on the grounds that she has more responsibility and greater expenses. The parents, persuaded, raise her allowance. In the simplest sense, the older sister is more powerful
25 than the younger brother because she is able to position herself to receive privileges that the younger brother, due to his age, is not. In this instance, the sister's age places her higher in the social order than her brother, and her resultant greater power is evidenced by her ability to gain
30 financial reward.
   Chimpanzee society has no concept of wealth, but it clearly has identifiable privileges, and power as access to such privileges is demonstrated with alarming consistency in the chimpanzee social order. Indeed,
35 chimpanzee society can often seem remarkably like human society. Males compete for dominance and dispense patronage; females build networks and smooth their sons' paths to power. Chimpanzee fights are not usually won, as are monkey fights, by brute force, but by
40 coalitions.
   So the alpha male may not be the strongest so much as the one who is best at making helpful friends. In the Mahale mountains of Tanzania, for example, there lives an alpha male chimp named Ntogi. He shares the
45 monkey meat he catches not only with his mother and his girlfriends, but also with older, middle-ranking males. He never gives meat to younger males or to his most senior rivals. Careful to maintain the relationships most advantageous to his status, he cultivates his most reliable
50 but least threatening constituents, who in turn help him to stay in power.
   Complicated human power schemes have been mirrored by the sophisticated tactics of a certain well-studied chimpanzee. The career of another chimpanzee
55 male, named Yeroen, in a colony at Arnhem zoo in the Netherlands, is reminiscent of the role Richard Neville played in the Wars of the Roses. Neville, aptly termed the "Kingmaker," attempted to wield power through the weaknesses of both Yorkist and Lancastrian competitors
60 vying for the throne of England: he first allied himself with the Yorkists, secured their victory, but then promptly joined the efforts of his one-time ally's rival to seize power. Just as Neville the Kingmaker shifted his support between the houses of York and Lancaster so as to keep
65 each one weak enough to be manipulated for his own purposes, so the alpha male's "right-hand man" Yeroen alternated between two contending alpha males to ensure that neither held the top job for long. As soon as one alpha felt secure enough to interfere with Yeroen's
70 privileges – principally his right to frequently mate with females in the troop – Yeroen would switch allegiance and begin building up the other. The resemblance between Yeroen's tactics and Neville's machinations to secure power is undeniable, and perhaps a tad
75 unsettling—are human lust for power and the lengths taken to secure it irrevocably woven into the fabric from which we are sewn?

22

"Social" as it is used in the first paragraph (lines 1-14) most nearly means

A) friendly and talkative.
B) popular with others.
C) organized in a cooperative group.
D) distinct from other animal species.

Reading | Practice

23

The mention of "our 98.5% identical genetic relative" (lines 6-7) emphasizes

A) how different humans are from chimpanzees.
B) impressive statistical accuracy.
C) genetic reasons for behavioral resemblance.
D) the belief that human behavior is inherently distinct from that of other animals.

24

According to the passage, which of the following would represent a shift in the balance of power between the older sister and the younger brother described in the second paragraph (lines 15-30)?

A) The younger brother is not allowed to watch T.V., while the older sister is allowed.
B) The older sister gets the largest piece of dessert.
C) The younger brother is permitted to play with his friends while the sister has to stay at home and clean her room.
D) The older sister gets a new CD player because of good grades on her report card.

25

Within the context of the passage as a whole, the third paragraph (lines 31-40) serves as

A) a counter example to the author's central thesis.
B) a continuation of the previous paragraph's consideration of human power structures.
C) a transition from a discussion focused on human social dynamics to chimpanzee social dynamics.
D) an introduction to the social hierarchies of a group of chimpanzees.

26

The statement on lines 38-40 ("Chimpanzee . . . coalitions") provides evidence to support that

A) like humans, chimps rise to power by developing social networks, rather than relying on sheer brawn.
B) monkeys use means other than physical force to establish dominance.
C) disputes should be settled calmly and rationally.
D) male chimps are instinctively more violent than females.

27

The "career" (line 54) of Yeroen and the "role" (line 56) of Richard Neville are analogous because of

A) their primitive, hostile environments.
B) their shared ancestry.
C) their sharing the spoils with those in power.
D) their capacity to shift allegiance for personal gain.

28

According to the passage, the author views society as

A) a constant struggle for power.
B) something that is particular to humanity.
C) easily manipulated by those in power.
D) derived from the social values of animals that lived over five million years ago.

29

Which choice provides the best evidence for the answer to the previous question?

A) Lines 15-19 ("One . . . power")
B) Lines 31-36 ("Chimpanzee . . . society")
C) Lines 52-54 ("Complicated . . . chimpanzee")
D) Lines 72-77 ("The resemblance . . . sewn")

Reading | Practice

30

The author's attitude towards the statement in lines 72-73 ("The resemblance . . . machinations") could be best characterized as

A) outraged.
B) uneasy.
C) euphoric.
D) secure.

31

As it is used in line 76, "irrevocably" most nearly means

A) dubiously.
B) irreversibly.
C) stagnant.
D) absently.

32

Which of the following best states what the passage is about?

A) How power dynamics within human society have changed over the course of history
B) How human tendencies to serve and prioritize power are reflected in other spaces
C) The alpha males of Tanzania
D) The difference in power relations among chimpanzess, monkeys, and apes

Reading | Practice

This passage is adapted from Thomas Paine, *Common Sense*. Originally published in 1776.

    Some writers have so confounded society with government, as to leave little or no distinction between them; whereas they are not only different, but have different origins. Society is produced by our wants, and
5 government by our wickedness; the former promotes our happiness positively by uniting our affections, the latter negatively by restraining our vices. The one encourages intercourse, the other creates distinctions. The first a patron, the last a punisher.
10   Society in every state is a blessing, but government even in its best state is but a necessary evil; in its worst state an intolerable one; for when we suffer, or are exposed to the same miseries by a government, which we might expect in a country without government, our
15 calamity is heightened by reflecting that we furnish the means by which we suffer. Government, like dress, is the badge of lost innocence; the palaces of kings are built on the ruins of the bowers of paradise. For were the impulses of conscience clear, uniform, and irresistibly obeyed, man
20 would need no other lawgiver; but that not being the case, he finds it necessary to surrender up a part of his property to furnish means for the protection of the rest; and this he is induced to do by the same prudence which in every other case advises him out of two evils to choose the
25 least. Wherefore, security being the true design and end of government, it unanswerably follows that whatever form thereof appears most likely to ensure it to us, with the least expence and greatest benefit, is preferable to all others.
30   In order to gain a clear and just idea of the design and end of government, let us suppose a small number of persons settled in some sequestered part of the earth, unconnected with the rest, they will then represent the first peopling of any country, or of the world. In this state
35 of natural liberty, society will be their first thought. A thousand motives will excite them thereto, the strength of one man is so unequal to his wants, and his mind so unfitted for perpetual solitude, that he is soon obliged to seek assistance and relief of another, who in his turn
40 requires the same. Four or five united would be able to raise a tolerable dwelling in the midst of a wilderness, but one man might labour out of the common period of life without accomplishing any thing; when he had felled his timber he could not remove it, nor erect it after it was
45 removed; hunger in the mean time would urge him from his work, and every different want call him a different way. Disease, nay even misfortune would be death, for though neither might be mortal, yet either would disable him from living, and reduce him to a state in which he
50 might rather be said to perish than to die.

    Thus necessity, like a gravitating power, would soon form our newly arrived emigrants into society, the reciprocal blessings of which, would supersede, and render the obligations of law and government
55 unnecessary while they remained perfectly just to each other; but as nothing but heaven is impregnable to vice, it will unavoidably happen, that in proportion as they surmount the first difficulties of emigration, which bound them together in a common cause, they will begin to
60 relax in their duty and attachment to each other; and this remissness, will point out the necessity, of establishing some form of government to supply the defect of moral virtue.
    I draw my idea of the form of government from a
65 principle in nature, which no art can overturn, viz. that the more simple any thing is, the less liable it is to be disordered; and the easier repaired when disordered; and with this maxim in view, I offer a few remarks on the so much boasted constitution of England. That it
70 was noble for the dark and slavish times in which it was erected, is granted. When the world was over run with tyranny the least remove therefrom was a glorious rescue. But that it is imperfect, subject to convulsions, and incapable of producing what it seems to promise, is easily
75 demonstrated.
    Absolute governments (to the disgrace of human nature) have this advantage with them, that they are simple; if the people suffer, they know the head from which their suffering springs, know likewise the remedy,
80 and are not bewildered by a variety of causes and cures. But the constitution of England is so exceedingly complex, that the nation may suffer for years together without being able to discover in which part the fault lies, some will say in one and some in another, and every
85 political physician will advise a different medicine.
    There is something exceedingly ridiculous in the composition of monarchy; it first excludes a man from the means of information, yet empowers him to act in cases where the highest judgment is required. The state
90 of a king shuts him from the world, yet the business of a king requires him to know it thoroughly; wherefore the different parts, by unnaturally opposing and destroying each other, prove the whole character to be absurd and useless.

Reading | Practice

33

The central purpose of the passage is to

A) argue against the establishment of democracies.
B) examine the effects of human behaviors.
C) discuss the function of a certain social institution.
D) call for the abolition of monarchies.

34

The main argument of the passage is that

A) humanity can achieve the most when working without the burden of others.
B) government is an imperfect, yet necessary condition.
C) society is the highest form of civilization.
D) constitutions are the best way to promote freedom in a country.

35

Paine states that the distinction between society and goverment is that

A) one seeks to harm humankind while the other tries to safeguard it.
B) one represents the good aspects of humankind while the other controls the evils.
C) one attempts to explain specific human conventions while the other defends their practice.
D) they both are separate parts that contribute to the formation of a civilization.

36

Paine contends that people join into social unions in order to

A) protect against the potentially negative motives of another or themself.
B) achieve wealth for themselves and their loved ones.
C) enjoy the personal status that one can only have in a group.
D) have a single source of authority ruling over them.

37

Which choice provides the best evidence for the answer to the previous question?

A) Lines 1-3 ("Some writers . . . them")
B) Lines 18-20 ("For were . . . lawgiver")
C) Lines 36-39 ("the strength . . . another")
D) Lines 51-60 ("Thus necessity . . . each other")

38

According to Paine, the essential duty of government is to

A) provide for the security of its citizens.
B) supply a source of aid when building shelter.
C) serve as a sign of advancement of a culture.
D) be as uncomplicated as possible.

39

The role of the third paragraph (lines 30-50) in the passage is a

A) warning of the dangers of a society without government.
B) a metaphor for tyrannical rule.
C) comparison between two systems of goverment.
D) real-world illustration of Paine's main point.

40

The phrase "defect of moral virtue" in lines 62-63 most likely refers to

A) the lack of integrity displayed by most people.
B) the act of demanding help from another without returning the favor.
C) the tendency of people to grow negligent over time.
D) the inability of humanity to form lasting bonds with each other.

Reading | Practice

41

Paine's feelings toward kings can best be described as

A) bafflement at their incompatible positions in society.
B) contempt for their puzzling decisions.
C) apprehension of the tremendous power they wield.
D) curiosity about how they attained their high rankings.

42

Which choice provides the best evidence for the answer to the previous question?

A) Lines 71-75 ("When the world . . . demonstrated")
B) Lines 76-78 ("Absolute governments . . . simple")
C) Lines 86-87 ("There is . . . monarchy")
D) Lines 89-94 ("The state . . . useless")

The following passage is adapted from an essay entitled "Labor's Martyrs" by Vito Marcantonio.

"These are my ideas. If you think that one can crush these ideas that are gaining ground more and more every day; if you think you can crush them by sending us to the gallows; if you would once more have people suffer the
5 *penalty of death because they have dared to tell the truth– and I defy you to show that we have told a lie–if death is the penalty for proclaiming the truth, then I will proudly and defiantly pay the costly price."* -August Spies, just before he was sentenced to death on October 9, 1886.

10   The man who spoke these words had no illusions. He knew the court he was facing was determined to stamp out all he stood for and believed in. He knew, also, that the movement he represented was bigger than the forces which were trying to crush it and that it would survive.

15   And survive it did. It became one of the most powerful factors on the American scene in the extension and preservation of democracy. Spies's fight laid the foundation for the American labor movement of the present day.

20   One of the main issues around which Spies, a metal worker by trade, and his fellow activists rallied was the fight for the eight-hour day. A contemporary of Spies, Albert Parsons, was only 36 when he was executed. He had spent more than ten years actively organizing
25 American workers. He was a printer, a member of the powerful International Typographical Union which had over 60,000 members. An able orator, he toured the United States, lecturing and recruiting supporters for the movement.

30   Spies carried the fight to the Central Trades Body of Chicago to which he was a delegate. His efforts bore fruit and the movement for the eight-hour day gained momentum. Union after union discussed the problem and went on record in favor of fighting for it, until finally the
35 slogan became: General Strike for the eight-hour day.

    The date set for the strike was May 1, 1886, a day that has now become the international fighting holiday of labor. In Chicago, the May Day strike was a great success. Thousands of workers filled the streets. Some paraded,
40 others gave out handbills, others went in committees from factory to factory calling the workers out on strike. Despite all the efforts of a hostile press to whip up hatred for the workers, to alienate the middle class, to spread the fear of disorder and raise the bogey of revolution, the day
45 passed in absolute peace.

    In many industries the workers decided to stay on strike after May 1. One of these was the McCormick Reaper Plant in Chicago. On May 3, August Spies was invited by the strike committee to address the pickets at
50 the factory gate. Just as he finished speaking, the police charged down upon the assembled workmen with clubs and guns. Chicago papers were quick to point out that only two had lost their lives, but this was untrue.

    That same evening a committee of trade unionists
55 decided to hold a protest meeting in Haymarket Square in Chicago. Several thousands of people attended. Spies opened the meeting and stated its purpose: to discuss the question of the eight-hour day and to protest the police shootings at the McCormick plant. Parsons, who had just
60 returned to the city from a speaking tour was hurriedly sent for and rushed over to lend a hand.

    The speakers addressed the crowd for about two hours. In the audience was the mayor of Chicago, Carter Harrison, who was quickly satisfied by its peaceful nature and went to
65 telephone Police Captain Bonfield with instructions to call off police reserves and send his men home as they would not be needed.

    Just as the last speaker, Samuel Fielden, was saying, "In conclusion...", a squad of armed police descended upon
70 Haymarket Square, despite having been instructed not to come, and yelled at protestors to disperse. The police then fell upon the assembled men and women with clubs and guns. At that moment, someone threw a bomb into the midst of the meeting, killing one policeman outright and
75 wounding scores of people.

43

The main purpose of the first paragraph (lines 1-9) is to

A) question an ideology.
B) analyze a reaction.
C) introduce a conflict.
D) describe a historic setting.

44

The phrase "the movement he represented" (line 13) most likely refers to

A) the labor rights movement.
B) the Haymarket Socialist movement.
C) the May Day strike.
D) the International Typographic Union.

45

Which choice provides the best evidence for the answer to the previous question?

A) Line 10 (The man . . . illusions)
B) Lines 17-19 (Spies's . . . day)
C) Lines 25-27 (He was . . . members)
D) Lines 47-48 (One . . . Chicago)

Reading | Practice

46

As it is used in line 27, "orator" most likely means

A) operator.
B) speaker.
C) writer.
D) organizer.

47

The author uses the phrase "bore fruit" in lines 31-32 to indicate that the protestor's tireless efforets

A) were beginning to produce tangible results.
B) led to working class people receiving more food to eat.
C) had very small positive effects preceding an onslaught of violence.
D) led to workers immediately earning the right to an eight hour work day.

48

According to the passage, the "press" in line 42

A) was somewhat unsupportive of the workers.
B) was openly antagonistic towards the workers, deliberately spreading misinformation and fear.
C) sided with the workers and helped spread pamphlets campaigning for the 8 hour workday.
D) hid the news of the strikes from the middle class.

49

Which choice provides the best evidence for the answer to the previous question?

A) Lines 33-35 ("Union . . . day")
B) Lines 39-41 ("Thousands . . . strike")
C) Lines 42-45 ("Despite . . . peace")
D) Lines 50-52 ("Just . . . guns")

50

The author includes the Mayor's opinions of the worker's speeches and actions in order to

A) analyze the communication between the Mayor, the protestors, and the police.
B) establish the context for the upcoming violence.
C) demonstrate the strong moral character of the Mayor of Chicago.
D) criticize the Mayor for not protecting his constituents.

51

As it is used in line 71 "disperse" most nearly means

A) dissuade.
B) leave.
C) quiet.
D) freeze.

52

The main purpose of the passage is

A) provide the historical background of an issue.
B) stress the current importance of an issue.
C) highlight the danger of free speech.
D) question the validity of journalism.

Questions 42 - 52 are based on the following passages

Passage 1 is adapted from *Curiosities of Civilizations* ©1860 by Andrew Wynter. Passage 2 is adapted from *The Complete Story of the San Francisco Horror* ©1908 by Hubert D. Russell.

Passage 1

Among the more salient features of the metropolis which instantly strike the attention of the stranger are the stations of the Fire Brigade. Whenever he happens to pass them, he finds the sentinel on duty, he sees the "red artillery" of the force; the polished axle, the gleaming branch, and the shining chain, testify to the beautiful condition of the instrument, ready for active service at a moment's notice.

No sooner comes the alarm, than one sees with a shudder the rush of one of these awe-inspiring engines through the crowded streets, the heavy vehicle swerving from side to side, and the black helmeted attendants swaying to and fro. The wonder is that horses or men ever get safely to their destination: the wonder is still greater that no one is ridden over in their furious drive as they race to save the day.

The scene which a London fire presents can never be forgotten: the shouts of the crowd as it opens to let the engines dart through it, the foaming head of water springing out of the ground, the black, snake-like coils of the leather hose rising and falling like things of life whilst a hundred arms work at the pump, the applause of the people watching that rings out clear above the roaring flame as the adventurous band throw the first hissing jet.

Suddenly there is a loud shrill cry, and the bank of human faces is upturned to where a shrieking person hangs frantically to an upper windowsill. A deafening shout goes forth, as the huge fire-escape comes full swing upon the scene: a moment's pause, and all is still, whilst every eye is strained towards the fluttering garments flapping against the wall. The blood in a thousand hearts runs cold, and then again break forth a thousand cheers to celebrate a daring rescue. Such scenes as this are of almost nightly occurrence in the great metropolis.

Passage 2

Only the outer fringe of the city was left, and the flames which swept unimpeded in a hundred directions were swiftly obliterating what remained. Nothing worthy of the name of building in the business district and not more than half of the residence district had escaped. Of its population of 400,000 nearly 300,000 were homeless.

Gutted throughout its entire magnificent financial quarters by the swift work of thirty hours and with a black ruin covering more than seven square miles out into her very heart, the city waited in a stupor. All the hospitals except the free city hospital had been destroyed, and the authorities were dragging the injured, sick and dying from place to place for safety.

All day the fire, sweeping in a dozen directions, irresistibly completed the desolation of the city. Nob Hill district, in which were situated the home of Mrs. Stanford, the priceless Hopkins Art Institute, the Fairmount hotel, a marble palace that cost millions of dollars and homes of a hundred millionaires, was destroyed. It was not without a struggle that Mayor Schmitz and his aides let this, the fairest section of the city, suffer obliteration. Before noon when the flames were marching swiftly on Nob Hill, but were still far off, dynamite was dragged up the steep debris laden streets. For a distance of a mile every residence on the east side of Van Ness Avenue was swept away in a vain hope to stay the progress of the fire.

The stricken people who wandered through the streets in pathetic helplessness and sat upon their scattered belongings in cooling ruins reached the stage of dumb, uncaring despair. The city dissolving before their eyes had significance no longer.

After sucking dry even the sewers the fire engines were either abandoned or moved to the outlying districts. They were of no help. Water was gone, powder was gone, hope even was a fiction. The fair city by the Golden Gate was doomed to be blotted from the sight of man.

Reading I Practice

53

The author of Passage 1 includes the information in lines 4-8 ("He finds . . . notice") primarily to

A) illustrate the importance of the Fire Brigade in London.
B) highlight the unique features of the Fire Brigade.
C) reverently describe the scene at a Fire Brigade station.
D) explain why the Fire Brigade strikes the attention of all strangers.

54

What function does the third paragraph (lines 17-25) serve in Passage 1?

A) It examines the reasons why fires are so prevalent in London.
B) It describes a memorable nightly scene in the metropolis.
C) It analyzes the causes and effects of fires.
D) It explains the importance of fighting fires effectively.

55

As used in line 15, the word "furious" most nearly means

A) belligerent.
B) boisterous.
C) angry.
D) hurried.

56

Which choice provides the best evidence for the answer to the previous question?

A) Lines 9-11 ("No sooner . . . streets")
B) Lines 17-18 ("The scene . . . forgotten")
C) Lines 32-34 ("The blood . . . rescue")
D) Lines 34-36 ("Such . . . metropolis")

57

The author of Passage 1 indicates that fires in London

A) happen infrequently.
B) are more dangerous because they are in a metropolis.
C) occur often.
D) are always safely extinguished by the Fire Brigade.

58

The tone of Passage 2 can best be described as

A) despondent.
B) sanguine.
C) nostalgic.
D) deafening.

59

As used in line 46, the phrase "black ruin" most nearly means

A) helplessness.
B) urban sprawl.
C) inferno.
D) ashes.

60

Which statement best describes the relationship between the passages?

A) Passage 2 illustrates the effects of an event described in Passage 1.
B) Passage 2 provides an example of why an event from Passage 1 occurs.
C) Passage 2 and Passage 1 describe a similar type of event with vastly different outcomes.
D) Passage 2 contradicts a central claim made in Passage 1.

Reading I Practice

61

The author of Passage 2 would most likely respond to the description of fire engines in Passage 1 in lines 9-16, by claiming that such a description

A) rightfully glorifies an integral piece of technology.
B) wrongfully diminishes the role of people on the engine itself.
C) correctly portrays the role of fire engines in a metropolis.
D) overstates the value of fire engines.

62

Which choice provides the best evidence for the answer to the previous question?

A) Lines 44-47 ("Gutted . . . stupor")
B) Lines 51-52 ("All day . . . city")
C) Lines 62-65 ("For a . . . fire")
D) Line 73 ("They . . . help")

63

How do the "people" in Passage 2 (Line 66) differ from the "people" in Passage 1 (Line 23)?

A) In Passage 1 they are expressing despair, while in Passage 2 they are celebrating.
B) In Passage 1 they are watching an event unfold and in Passage 2 they are reacting to the effects of an event.
C) In Passage 1 they are fire fighters and in Passage 2 they are residents of the city.
D) In Passage 1 they are excited by fire and in Passage 2 they are afraid of it.

Reading | Practice

The following passage is an excerpt from a book, published in 1997, about the preservation of the English language.

While the English language may have to its credit the elegance of Shakespearean drama and the noble verse of Tennyson, even the most well-turned phrase would not be able to halt the storm cloud which now overshadows
5 it. Once, English flourished in its most refined form; from simple letters to the eloquent exchanges of the gentry, English speakers paid dutiful heed to the conventions of the language. Now, however, ignorance of English's rules has relegated proper grammar to only the strictest
10 of academic and literary settings. The cause of this neglect seems obvious. English is the world's most ubiquitous language, but with this popularity comes the host of linguistic misunderstandings introduced by those to whom English is not a native language.
15 Furthermore, the increasing popularity of "quick and dirty" communication, whether through instant messages, text messages, or social networking websites, has made commonplace the brusque sacrifice of correct spelling and grammar on the bloody altar of efficiency. That the
20 younger generations, in whose hands the fate of our language rests, are the primary users of this abridged form of electronic shorthand, so-called "netspeak," seems to virtually guarantee the decay of our language.

Professors and editors are foremost among those
25 who complain about the abuse of English, blaming grammatical errors and stylistic blunders on poor education, as well as the aforementioned "netspeak." However, some linguists have commented on the lack of flexibility in formal, academic English, attributing its
30 decline to its unappealingly rigid and uncompromising nature. They claim that most people, not knowing the overly complex and seemingly arbitrary rules of the language, find it easier to simply write what seems natural. These linguists claim that the inevitable, and
35 indeed desirable, future for the language involves the organic incorporation of new conventions and idioms, although they may at present seem casual and slang-like. For example, when Latin was in its heyday, Roman noblemen often criticized the bastardization of their
40 native tongue. However, these barbaric-sounding dialects evolved into the Romance languages: French, Spanish, and Italian. While "proper" Latin stagnated and withered away, linguists claim that English is a particularly thriving language because of the constant flood of new
45 linguistic material.

The implications of this debate reach beyond the English language, as its outcome will likely be a decisive blow struck in an everlasting war between those who wish to preserve culture and those who see its evolution
50 as something to be encouraged. Entire communities and governments have taken stances on this issue by enforcing or disallowing signs which have their messages translated into multiple languages. Governments are infamous for having banned content they deemed
55 unsuitable for their people. While those who encourage preservation do so fearing the dilution and destruction of their native cultures, proponents of change are wary of preservationists who would freeze culture in time. Should this happen, the culture would gradually lose
60 relevance, like a language which refuses to admit a word for "email."

Linguists who oppose preservation point out that many users of social networking sites and instant messengers avoid in other settings the slang they use
65 so freely online. These linguists insist that "netspeak" is not an accurate measure of the health of English more generally. They cite other evidence such as the dramatically increasing levels of literacy worldwide, or that students today can still understand the English of
70 Chaucer and Shakespeare, writers whose English hails from centuries ago. Their argument disregards individual examples pulled from the internet and literature in favor of more comprehensive statistics. Furthermore, it calls into question the very terms of the argument, such as
75 what "proper language" truly is. The process by which languages evolve and change is a strange and often mysterious one, with elusive factors pushing and pulling the language in various directions. Perhaps the debate should not be centered on whether the language should
80 change. Instead, these researchers say, we should focus on what causes it to change.

The English language's fate will rely far less on the conventions and rules which have governed it in the past than on the influences which will mold it in the future.
85 Perhaps today's youth could be made to understand that the future of the language rests in their hands. This sense of responsibility and empowerment may be enough to drive these unwitting molders and shapers of language towards a more careful and considered use of English.
90 While education and outside factors have large roles in shaping a language, one must not disregard the roles of pride and respect. These are what cause us to mind our words more carefully around our elders, and to painstakingly choose our words when writing letters to
95 our sweethearts. If we could treat our everyday words with equal respect, regardless of who is receiving them, perhaps our language will enter a new age of measured change.

Reading | Practice

64

Which hypothetical approach is most similar to the author's proposal for the language?

A) Instilling in people a sense of duty to preserve the environment and stop littering
B) Teaching citizens of impoverished countries more efficient farming practices
C) Placing limits on gas usage to preserve fossil fuels
D) Funding bilingual signs in communities which have more than one commonly spoken language

65

Which choice provides the best evidence for the answer to the previous question?

A) Lines 40-53 ("Entire . . . languages")
B) Lines 78-81 ("Perhaps . . . change")
C) Lines 85-89 ("Perhaps . . . English")
D) Lines 92-95 ("These . . . sweethearts")

66

In the first paragraph (lines 1-23), the English language is portrayed most directly as

A) having a bleak future despite its rich past.
B) a static institution which has been wrongly portrayed as changing.
C) both honored and neglected by those who speak it.
D) heir to magnificence and history that cannot counterbalance its flaws.

67

As it is used in line 18, "brusque" most nearly means

A) civil.
B) lively.
C) final.
D) abrupt.

68

The author mentions "some linguists" (line 28) to suggest that the strict preservation of formal English is

A) unpopular with the general public because it fails to incorporate new conventions and idioms.
B) inadequate according to those who desire to keep the language in its purest state.
C) threatened by those who casually employ slang and "netspeak."
D) counterproductive because it intimidates those who would otherwise use it.

69

The aspect of the "debate" (line 46) that the author is most concerned with is

A) the optimistic belief that linguists can save the English language.
B) the validity of a language's adherence to convention as a measure of its health.
C) the greater linguistic flexibility of other languages as compared to that of English.
D) the potential to do more harm than good by altering a language's conventions.

70

The "other evidence" (line 67) serves primarily to

A) support a theory popularized by editors and professors.
B) substantiate the examples provided by 'netspeak.'
C) support the theories of linguists who disagree with preservation.
D) discourage the ambitions and goals of preservationists.

Reading I Practice

71

In lines 75-76 the author's discussion of "the process by which languages evolve and change" primarily suggests that

A) an academic setting is an ineffective place to study linguistic changes.
B) a focus on unimportant details have diverted linguists from their original goal.
C) more needs to be learned about the factors that contribute to linguistic changes.
D) linguistic research is essential to maintaining linguistic purity.

72

In lines 78-81, the researchers' observation about the focus of the debate about language is best described as

A) a misdirected narrative.
B) a conventional assessment.
C) a curt evaluation.
D) an unambiguous refusal.

73

Which choice provides the best evidence for the answer to the previous question?

A) Lines 46-50 ("The implications . . . encouraged")
B) Lines 55-58 ("While . . . time")
C) Lines 73-81 ("Furthermore . . . change")
D) Lines 90-92 ("While . . . respect")

74

As it is used in line 97, "measured" most nearly means

A) known.
B) rated.
C) quantified.
D) deliberate.

The passage is derived from an article published in a bioethics journal in 2000.

As a scientist, I find the conventional reaction to genetic engineering really riles me up —the belief that it is in some way "unnatural," a slap in the face of nature.

This is the argument: genetic engineering modifies
5 the natural characteristics of an organism. It is proof of man seeking to rule over nature rather than accepting it. Thus, we should ignore this emerging technology and its potential benefits and regress to an earlier, more natural state of existence, one that would exclude enhanced
10 organisms that benefit humanity.

There is an important assumption behind this idea that needs to be brought out and examined in order to be able to properly evaluate its downfalls. This assumption is that the genetic makeup of an organism, if left to itself,
15 will remain balanced (an "equilibrium of genetics") and the ethical role for us is to allow evolution to progress naturally. If one were to hold this belief, one would more than likely feel that scientific advancement since the successful production of insulin using genetically
20 modified bacteria represents a disastrous event—a wrong turn, akin to the use of eugenics by the Nazi party. Genetic engineering, more specifically the modification of an organism's genetic makeup ("DNA recombination"), is an instrument that destroys the balance of nature, and
25 hence is a destructive presence on the planet.

What rankles me most about this belief is that it implies that genetic modification, on the theoretical level, is not a natural process. A "natural process," to many non-scientists, is something that has not been
30 manipulated by scientists. As soon as we start changing genes and proteins, the "natural process" ceases to exist and something abnormal is created.

I think that this discussion of genetic engineering needs to begin with understanding that it isn't unnatural,
35 any more than bacteria or viruses are unnatural. Bacteria and viruses are both organisms that thrive on maintaining their natural processes. As part of these natural processes, they alter and manipulate their genetic makeup. There is nothing "unnatural" about this.

40 Nor is there anything unnatural about using this technology for our own benefit. Yes, many types of food have been genetically modified to yield larger crops and provide insect and viral resistances: today most crops have been genetically modified in some manner. But
45 this isn't really unnatural. There are plenty of organisms that can modify their own genetic makeup—think of a bacterium that becomes resistant to an antibiotic. From this point of view, genetic engineering is simply the exchange of useless traits for valuable traits.

50 Look at the consequences of manipulating an organism's traits. There is, obviously, the ability to produce more bountiful crops. Moreover, this process can create crops that are more nutritious than unmodified ones for the same resources. Indeed, "golden rice," a
55 genetically modified strain of rice, contains many times the vitamin A that regular rice does—a crop that can cure millions of people with vitamin A deficiency.

Gazing deeper into genetic engineering, in fact, shows that this process can be thought of as a natural
60 process on at least three levels. At the most fundamental level, although typically ignored, all organisms can manipulate their own genetic material. Genetic manipulation functions with similar patterns in all types of organisms, with their own specific "helper" proteins.
65 This approach to genetic manipulation has received highest academic praise—the creation of a subfield of biology, called "external genetic recombination," devoted to understanding it.

At a somewhat more introspective level, internal
70 genetic manipulation can serve as a model to aid in understanding how genetic engineering works. Both processes involve changes in an organism's DNA, and both enhance certain traits, allowing an organism increased chances of survival. Both require biological
75 methods to maintain the genetic manipulation, methods that are apparent and observable at all developmental stages: birth, maturity, and death.

Finally, genetic engineering is like any natural biological process; at the lowest level, it operates within
80 the well-defined laws of biology. There is, for example, a limit to how many genes can be manipulated within an organism's lifespan, set by different factors including the type and degree of the genetic manipulation. There is also a limit to how many genetic manipulations can be
85 introduced into an organism—a limit that is influenced by those same factors.

So let me explicitly state: Genetic engineering is a natural process and we can observe and use it in the same way we observe and use any other natural logical process.

Reading | Practice

2005 USA Poll: Should Food Manufacturers Label GMO Food?

(Pie chart showing: Yes, No, Unsure)

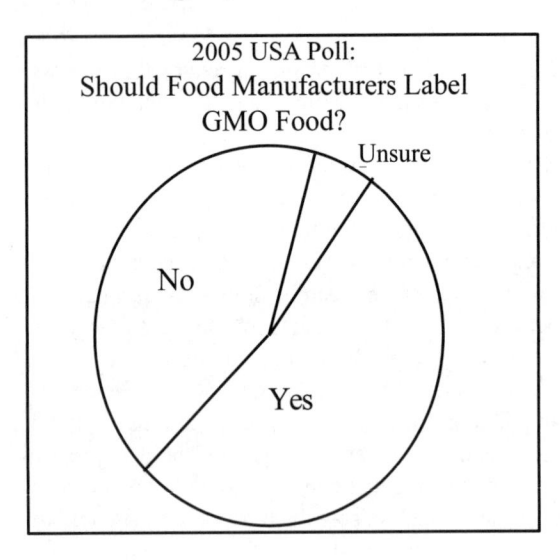

75

As it is used in line 2, "riles" most nearly means

A) alarms.
B) irritates.
C) infuriates.
D) muddies.

76

The author would most likely describe the more *"natural state"* (lines 8-9) as

A) a complicated conclusion.
B) a satisfactory solution.
C) an understandable argument.
D) a false supposition.

77

Which choice best provides the answer to the previous questions?

A) Lines 4-6 ("This . . . it")
B) Lines 26-28 ("What . . . process")
C) Lines 33-34 ("I think . . . unnatural")
D) Lines 74-77 ("Both . . . death")

78

According to the author, those who "hold this belief" (line 17) view the modification of bacteria as

A) the beginning of an unfortunate trend in science.
B) an example of science's double-edged potential.
C) a time when science was natural.
D) an example of an important scientific achievement.

79

The author would most likely characterize the views of the *"non-scientists"* (line 29) as

A) fallacious.
B) unintelligible.
C) legitimate.
D) logical.

80

The author compares genetic engineering to the processes of bacteria and viruses in the fifth paragraph (lines 33-39) in order to

A) explain how DNA recombination works.
B) point out the differences in genetic engineering.
C) imply that gene manipulation occurs even without human intervention.
D) suggest the potential obstacles to this process.

81

The author's attitude toward the "subfield" (line 66) is best characterized as one of

A) opposition.
B) approval.
C) uncertainty.
D) surprise.

Reading | Practice

82

Which choice best provides the answer to the following question?

A) Lines 58-60 ("Gazing . . . levels")
B) Lines 62-64 ("Genetic . . . proteins")
C) Lines 65-68 ("This approach . . . it")
D) Lines 87-89 ("Genetic . . . process")

83

In the tenth paragraph (lines 78-86), the author mentions limits to suggest that

A) genetic engineering is fixed by certain natural principles.
B) genetic engineering can change an organism's genetic makeup.
C) changes in an organism's genetic makeup must be self-regulating.
D) genetic engineering is often done unnecessarily and unethically.

84

As it is used in line 87, "explicitly" most nearly means

A) subtly.
B) unequivocably.
C) graphically.
D) lastly.

85

Does the accompanying pie graph enhance the author's point?

A) Yes, because the data insinuates mass distrust of GMO food products, therefore supporting the author's claim that people fear genetic modification on the whole.
B) Yes, because the data insinuates a split of opinion on the safety of GMO foods, indicating the author's position is widely supported.
C) No, because the data only provides information regarding opinions on food labeling, not on all genetic manufacturing.
D) No, because the data only represents Americans polled, leaving out other countries and cultures.

86

Based on the data in the pie graph, what percent of those polled do not believe genetically modified food products should be labeled?

A) 53%
B) 33%
C) 47%
D) 14%

Reading | Practice

Passage 1 is from Ulysses S. Grant's personal memoirs. Passage 2 is from letters written by the famous poet Walt Whitman to his mother during the Civil War.

Passage 1

    From an early period in the war I had been impressed with the idea that active and continuous operations of all the troops that could be brought into the field, regardless of season and weather, were
5 necessary to a speedy end of the war. The resources of the enemy and his numerical strength were far inferior to ours; but as an offset to this, we had a vast territory, and long lines of river and railroad communications to protect. Behind our own lines there were many bands
10 of guerillas and a large population disloyal to the government, making it necessary to guard every foot of road or river used in supplying our armies.
    In the South, a reign of military despotism prevailed, which made every man and boy capable
15 of bearing arms as a soldier; and those who could not bear arms in the field collected deserters and returned them. This enabled the enemy to bring almost his entire strength into the field.
    From the first, I was firm in the conviction that no
20 peace could be had that would be stable and conducive to the happiness of the people, both North and South, until the military power of the rebellion was entirely broken. I therefore determined to use the greatest number of troops against the armed force of
25 the enemy, thereby preventing him from using the same force at different seasons against first one and then another of our armies. My goal was to hammer continuously against the armed force of the enemy and his resources, until there should be nothing left.
30   These views have been kept constantly in mind, and orders given and campaigns made to carry them out. Whether they might have been better in conception and execution is for the people, who mourn the loss of friends fallen, and who have to pay the
35 financial cost, to say. All I can say is, that what I have done has been done conscientiously, to the best of my ability, and in what I conceived to be for the best interests of the whole country.

Passage 2

    I could not keep the tears out of my eyes.
40 Many of the poor young men had to be moved on stretchers, with blankets ove r them, which soon soaked as wet as water in the rain. Most were sick cases, but some badly wounded. I came up to the nearest hospital and helped. Mother, it was a dreadful
45 night -- pretty dark, the wind gusty, and the rain fell in torrents. One poor boy—this is a sample of one case out of the 600—he seemed to be quite young, he was quite small (I looked at his body afterwards), he groaned some as the stretcher bearers were carrying
50 him along, and again as they carried him through the hospital gate. They set down the stretcher and examined him, and the poor boy was dead. They took him into the ward, and the doctor came immediately, but it was all of no use. The worst of it is, too, that
55 he is entirely unknown—there was nothing on his clothes, or any one with him to identity him, and he is altogether unknown. Mother, it is enough to rack one's heart—such things. Very likely his folks will never know in the world what has become of him.
60 Poor, poor child, for he appeared as though he could be but 18.
    Things get worse and worse, as to the amount and sufferings of the sick, and as I have said before, those who have to do with them are getting more and
65 more callous and indifferent. Mother, when I see the common soldiers, what they go through, I get almost frightened at the world. I find my hands full all the time, with new and old cases—poor suffering young men, I think of them, and do try, mother, to do what I
70 can for them.
    Dearest mother, hope you and all are well— you must keep a good heart. Still, the fighting is very mixed, but it seems steadily turning into real successes for Grant. The news to-day here is very
75 good—you will see it N. Y. papers. I steadily believe Grant is going to succeed, and that we shall have Richmond—but O what a price to pay for it.

Chapter 2 Practice

Reading | Practice

87

Grant states that his armies had to "guard every foot of road or river" (lines 11-12) because

A) Both the land and water were under attack.
B) The guerrilla fighters fought primarily by boats and rafts.
C) Grant and his troops are protecting the U.S. government's land.
D) The land and rivers provide necessary resources for the soldiers.

88

In line 13, "despotism" most nearly means

A) obligation.
B) tyranny.
C) competence.
D) absence.

89

Which of the following statements most accurately expresses Ulysses' opinions about his decisions in the war?

A) Far too many soldiers died for an unjust war.
B) He is completely confident in all of his military decisions, believing them inscrutable.
C) With the information he had, he did his best under tumultuous circumstances.
D) This war was greatly expensive, and he feels lucky not to, personally, owe debt.

90

In Passage 2, the tone of the narrator's description of the "poor boy" in lines 46-57 can be best characterized as

A) dismal.
B) livid.
C) flummoxed.
D) alleviated.

91

In lines 64-65, the narrator suggests that "those who have to do with them are getting more and more callous and indifferent" in order to

A) express frustration that soliders don't care about one another.
B) implicate the actions of generals and other high ranking officials in the suffering of the soldiers.
C) reflect on the fact that he, too, used to be indifferent to the pain of injured.
D) blame the opposing rebel forces for all that have died.

92

The "price to pay" mentioned in lines 77 most likely refers to

A) The large number of lives lost in wartime.
B) The financial cost of weapons and food.
C) The emotional toll working at a hospital has taken on the narrator.
D) The many months the narrator must spend away from his mother.

93

In line 65, "callous" most nearly means

A) monotonous.
B) attentive.
C) insensitive.
D) violent.

94

The author's main purpose of Passage 2 is to convey

A) the intimate bond between Walt Whitman and his mother.
B) the tragedy of the young poor boy's death.
C) the exhausting nature of hospital work during a war.
D) the horrific amount of death and pain endured by soldiers in war.

Reading | Paired-Passages

95

Which of the following statements best accurately portray the prime distinction between the two perspectives on the Civil War?

A) The first passage regards soldiers and their deaths as battle strategy, whereas the second passage bemoans the amount of death inherent to war.
B) The first passage is told from the perspective of a lauded general, while the second passage is written from the perspective of a civilian.
C) The first passage is written in a letter to a family member, while the second passage is written in a personal diary.
D) The first passage is written by a General who is proud of the war, while the second passage is written by a poet who despised the Civil War.

96

The depictions of the Civil War battles in both passages led the reader to believe that

A) Grant was often in the news.
B) Grant was a reckless leader.
C) Grant was a successful general in the war.
D) Grant used Southern deserters in his armies.

97

Both of these passages are first person accounts of the Civil War. Which of the following does the author of Passage 2 use that the author of Passage 1 does not?

A) Memoir
B) Dialogue.
C) Imagery.
D) Historical details.

98

Which of the following statements from Passage 1 might the writer of Passage 2 disagree with?

A) "In the South, a reign of military despotism prevailed, which made every man and boy capable of bearing arms as a soldier..."
B) "My goal was to hammer continuously against the armed force of the enemy and his resources, until there should be nothing left."
C) This enabled the enemy to bring almost his entire strength into the field."
D) "Whether they might have been better in conception and execution is for the people, who mourn the loss of friends fallen, and who have to pay the financial cost, to say."

CHAPTER 3
Writing and Language

College Knowledge
Turning the Tables

Sample Students

	SAT Reading	SAT Math	SAT Writing	GPA	Misc.	AP & Honors Classes	Verdict
Max	600	510	570	3.4	Debate Team	Honors English	
Selena	470	490	460	3.3	n/a	Honors History	
Noreen	550	540	560	3.8	Yearbook Editor, Class Secretary, Track	AP English, Honors Math	
Emilia	550	420	380	2.8	n/a	n/a	
Kurt	530	590	510	3.3	n/a	Honors Physics, Honors Math	
Karina	600	590	580	3.0	Works Two Jobs, Hospital Intern	Honors Math	
Cody	720	700	700	2.7	Didn't Visit Any Colleges	n/a	
Lakisha	630	700	660	3.4	Father Is Cooper Union Alumnus	AP Calculus, AP Biology, AP English	
Benita	330	340	310	3.6	Expert Violinist, Tortolian	n/a	
Laura	480	470	490	2.9	Yearbook Staff, Political Volunteer, Drama Club	Honors History	

The Verdict

Which of the students above would you admit to your school? Which would you defer, waitlist, or reject? Why?

_____
_____
_____

Chapter 3

Writing and Language | Format

What is the Writing and Language Section?

The Writing and Language section asks you to revise and edit portions of passages using the conventions of standard written English. You will be tested not only on grammar rules, but also on the style and organization of the passage. You will not be tested on spelling or vocabulary specifically, though having a strong vocabulary may aid you in answering some questions.

What is the Format?

The Writing and Language section consists of 4 passages, each accompanied by 11 questions for a total of 44 questions. You will be given 35 minutes to complete the section. The passages cover a wide variety of subjects and literary styles. Below are examples of question types that will appear in this section.

Question: 1 . . . . 11 . . . . 22 . . . . 33 44

| Passage 1 | Passage 2 | Passage 3 | Passage 4 |

After days of no [41] improvement I removed, Joe from the group to speak to him.

41. A) NO CHANGE
    B) improvement, I removed,
    C) improvement, I removed
    D) improvement I removed

---

[15] Slowly, I too gained the confidence needed to solve the problem.

15. Which of the following true sentences, if inserted here, would best conclude the essay and maintain the tone established in this essay?
    A) Chelsea and I each learned a lot, but only the future will tell what happens next.
    B) I hope I don't meet anyone else who hates math as much as Chelsea did.
    C) Thank you Chelsea, for teaching me such an important lesson!
    D) I learned that tutoring is really hard work.

123

© 2016 Bell Curves, LLC

Writing and Language | Scoring

The Writing and Language Test composes 1/4 of your overall SAT total score, as it makes up half of the Evidence-Based Reading and Writing score.

The number of questions you get correct on this section will be converted into a test score, as is shown in the chart below. Remember, the exact conversion chart changes for each exam, but these scores are a reasonable approximation. The highest possible test score is a 40.

Raw Score	Test Score	Raw Score	Test Score	Raw Score	Test Score
0	10	15	19	30	29
1	10	16	20	31	30
2	10	17	21	32	30
3	10	18	21	33	31
4	11	19	22	34	32
5	12	20	23	35	32
6	13	21	23	36	33
7	13	22	24	37	34
8	14	23	25	38	34
9	15	24	25	39	35
10	16	25	26	40	36
11	16	26	26	41	37
12	17	27	27	42	38
13	18	28	28	43	39
14	19	29	28	44	40

Writing and Language | Overview

Pacing

The Writing and Language section consists of 4 passages and 44 questions that must be completed in 35 minutes. This works out to be a little under 9 minutes per passage or approximately 45 seconds per question. As you work your way through the section, be aware of how much time you have left for the remaining passages. If you are running out of time, attempt questions that can be done with the least amount of reading possible. Remember, you only score points from questions answered, not from reading the passage.

Literary Style

The passages will cover a diverse set of topics and will approach these topics with different formal styles. Make sure that as you are reading the passages, you are not only paying attention to not only what the author is saying but also to *how* the author is saying it. A passage about a new scientific breakthrough will likely have a much more serious tone than a passage about the author's grandparents, which is likely to be more personal. Keep in mind the style in which the passage is written, as this can help you answer some question types.

Context and Connotations

Context clues are key to answering many questions in the Writing and Language section. Questions that can seemingly be answered by reading just the underlined portion may actually require you to read sentences before and/or after, as well, in order to answer correctly. Ensure that you have read "around" that underlined portion to fully understand the context. It is also important to pick up on the connotations of words used by the author. Understanding the connotation of a word can be the difference between getting an answer right or wrong. If you do not know the connotation of a word, context clues in the sentence can be helpful in determining it.

Writing and Language | Question Types

The SAT will present you with questions from two general categories: grammar rules and style/organization.

GRAMMAR

> After days of no [41] improvement I removed, Joe from the group to speak to him.
>
> 41. A) NO CHANGE
>   B) improvement, I removed,
>   C) improvement, I removed
>   D) improvement I removed

Grammar questions refer to a specific underlined segment of the passage and may ask you to

- revise ineffective sentences
- determine the appropriate word or phrase in context
- fix errors in punctuation, word usage, and grammar

STYLE/ORGANIZATION

> [15] Slowly, I too gained the confidence needed to solve the problem.
>
> 15. Which of the following true sentences, if inserted here, would best conclude the essay and maintain the tone established in this essay?
>
>   A) Chelsea and I each learned a lot, but only the future will tell what happens next.
>   B) I hope I don't meet anyone else who hates math as much as Chelsea did.
>   C) Thank you Chelsea, for teaching me such an important lesson!
>   D) I learned that tutoring is really hard work.

Style/organization questions usually refer to a larger portion of the passage or to the passage as a whole and ask you to

- logically advance the passage
- organize ideas in a coherent manner
- maintain the proper tone and intent of the passage

Chapter 3

Grammar Rules

Writing and Language | Definitions

To effectively discuss the Writing and Language section, we must understand how words function in a sentence. Here is a quick review of parts of speech and grammar terms.

Part of Speech	Definition	Examples	Common Suffixes
Noun		*Nation, sadness, personality, justice, woman, Columbia, etc.*	-ness, -ity, and -tion
Pronoun		*I, we, you, thou, he, she, it, they, this, these, that, those, who, which, each, all, everyone, either, one, both, any, such, somebody, who, my, your, his, her, our, their, etc.*	
Verb		*to go, to be (was, were, are), to exist, to teach, to run, to decompose, to seem, etc.*	
Adjective		*Gracious, fastest, smarter, shy, blue, rotten, four, horse's, another, etc.*	-able, -ous, -er, and -est
Adverb		*so, very, truly, well, quite, more, deeply, rapidly, etc.*	-ly
Preposition		*at, by, in, on, of, to, for, into, with, from, in regard to, about, behind, toward, above, etc.*	
Conjunction		*and, but, as, or, because, etc.*	

Agreement
Agreement means grammatical correspondence in gender (i.e., male pronoun agreeing with male noun) or number (i.e., singular pronoun referring to singular noun).

Parallelism
Parallelism means the use of grammatically equivalent (structurally similar) constructions in corresponding clauses or phrases.
Example: SAT teachers generally like running and swimming. (The things that the teachers like are both activities that are expressed as -ing words.)

Phrase
A phrase is a group of words that does not contain a finite verb and its subject.

Clause
A clause is a group of words that contains a subject and a verb. Clauses form sentences and parts of sentences.

© 2016 Bell Curves, LLC

Chapter 3

Writing and Language | Grammar

The SAT Writing and Language section will require you to be familiar with the following grammar rules and how they are properly used.

- **Punctuation**
  (Commas, Periods, Semicolons, Colons, Apostrophes, Dashes)

- **Verbs**
  (Agreement, Tense, and Form)

- **Pronouns**
  (Number, Case, and Form)

- **Modifiers**
  (Misplaced, Comparative/Superlative)

- **Parallelism**
  (Lists)

- **Conjunctions**
  (Logical Connectors)

- **Run-ons and Fragments**
  (Subordinate/Dependent and Independent Clauses)

- **Redundancy**

- **Idioms**
  (Corresponding Verbs, Diction)

Writing and Language | Grammar Action Plan

The majority of questions in the Writing and Language section focus on grammar rules and errors. How you approach these questions will greatly impact your overall Writing and Language score. Use an approach that will keep you on the lookout for any violations of standard English conventions. Style and organization questions have their own individual Action Plans which we will look at later.

1. **Read and identify**
   Read the entire sentence containing an underlined portion of the passage. Look at the answer choices and let the differences between them tell you what the question is testing. Ask yourself what is changing in the answer choices. Are words changing? Are punctuation marks changing? The answer to these questions will help you determine the error tested. Actively think through the list of common errors and warning signs, and identify the type of error being tested.

2. **Try to find an error**
   If you do see an error, determine what rule is being broken (pronouns must be unambiguous, lists must be structurally similar, etc.). Eliminate all the answer choices that do not fix the error.

3. **Compare the remaining choices**
   Compare the remaining choices, two at a time, and find the differences between them. The differences will help you spot additional errors. Eliminate any choice that introduces a new error.

4. **Reread and choose**
   Take the remaining answer choice and plug it back into the sentence. Reread the entire sentence to ensure that there are not any errors you have overlooked.

5. **Repeat**
   Work your way through the rest of the passage using the Action Plan.

Writing and Language | Punctuation

Punctuation is one of the most important elements of writing a sentence and is one of the most frequently tested areas on the SAT. Let's review the most important punctuation.

Punctuation	Usage	Example
Period (.)	Used to end a complete sentence. A complete sentence must have a subject and a verb	My favorite teams are the New York Mets and the Duke Blue Devils.
Apostrophe (')	1. Used to show possession 2. Used in contractions	1. Grandma Betty is my dad's mother. 2. It's not my fault Peter can't come to the movie tonight.
Semicolon (;)	Used to connect two complete sentences that are closely tied in meaning * On the SAT, a semicolon and a period can be used interchangeably.	I love the Lord of the Rings trilogy; I have read all the books and seen all the movies.
Colon (:)	What comes before the colon must be a complete sentence What comes after a colon can be a word, phrase list, clause, etc. 1. Used to indicate that a list is to follow 2. Used to introduce a quote 3. Used to restate an idea within a sentence	1. I have three things to do today: fold the laundry, sweep the floor, and take a nap. 2. As the saying goes: "If you can't beat 'em, join 'em." 3. The team was poorly coached: it lacked cohesiveness and determination.
Comma (,)	1. Used in a list 2. Used in a compound sentence 3. Used to set off a phrase 4. Used to directly address someone 5. Used to tag questions 6. Used to set apart transition words 7. Used to set apart modifying phrases at the beginning of sentences 8. Used to set up contrasting phrases 9. Used to separate coordinate adjectives	1. My courses this year include history, math, science, and English. 2. After school I went to basketball practice, but I really wanted to go home and take a nap. 3. Jill, my best friend, has blonde hair. 4. "Wesley, fetch me that pitcher." 5. You don't mind, do you? 6. I am tired. However, I don't like to sleep. 7. After eating dinner, Bill did his homework. 8. Mary was ready to climb another mountain, while Jim was too tired. 9. In order to get home, we must travel over several narrow, winding, treacherous roads.
Dash (–)	Dashes and commas are basically interchangeable on this test. If a phrase is set off with a dash, it has to end with a dash or period.	1. Jimmy — a native of the area — expertly knew the local roads.

If one of the above punctuation marks is in the underlined portion of the sentence, double check that it is being used correctly.

Writing and Language | Punctuation Drill

Punctuation Review

Each of the sentences below has been written without any punctuation. Rewrite each sentence in the space provided using the appropriate punctuation.

1. Did you know that chocolate a favorite delicacy around the world is created from the cacao bean

2. Cacao beans are primarily grown in South and Central America especially in Mexico and Brazil

3. The beans grow on little shrubs in tropical areas these shrubs are actually relatives of North American evergreen trees

4. Once harvested the beans are cleaned dried and stored for future shipment

5. In many cases the cacao beans potency is enhanced through slow roasting

Writing and Language | Punctuation Drill

6. The cacao bean has a distinctive smell and taste, and is therefore used in both food and non-food products.

7. Although many people associate chocolate with dessert, chocolate is also found in unique dishes such as Mexican mole.

8. Nevertheless I prefer my chocolate in desserts my favorites are chocolate ice cream chocolate tortes and chocolate chip cookies

9. My mothers recipe for chocolate chip cookies has been handed down in my family for generations

10. Its incredible that some people dont like chocolate

Writing and Language | Punctuation Drill

11. In the United States, the two biggest chocolate companies are Mars, which makes M&Ms, and Hershey which makes Kisses.

12. Many people believe that the best chocolate in the world is found in European countries such as Belgium, Germany, France, and England.

    Maybe no ","

13. In England, Cadbury is the biggest candy company. It produces a number of excellent chocolate bars such as the Aero, the Double Decker, and the Toffee Crisp.

14. If you had to choose, what's your favorite use for chocolate?

Writing and Language | Punctuation Practice

Answer the questions below following the Grammar Action Plan on page 129 and the information in the Punctuation Chart on page 130.

Evaporation is the transformation of [1] matter – most commonly liquid water, from a liquid to a gaseous state. Although easy to forget, evaporation and the water cycle may very well be the most crucial part of our planet's ecosystem.

1. A) NO CHANGE
   B) matter, most commonly liquid water – from
   C) matter – most commonly liquid water – from
   D) matter, most commonly liquid water from

The fifth century B.C., known as the Golden Age, or High Classical Period, was [2] a period of cultural, artistic, and philosophical growth in Athens. Home to Plato and the Parthenon, this small, democratic city-state firmly entrenched Greece as the cornerstone of Western civilization thanks to its many achievements.

2. A) NO CHANGE
   B) a period of cultural artistic and philosophical growth, in
   C) a period of cultural, artistic, and philosophical growth, in
   D) a period of cultural artistic, and philosophical growth in

The consensus within the scientific community seems to be that eventually we will find intelligent and technologically advanced extraterrestrial life in distant parts of the galaxy. While the discovery of alien forms of life in other solar systems, [3] if not in our own seems likely; I find it most unlikely that myriad advanced technological civilizations are out there, waiting to be discovered.

3. A) NO CHANGE
   B) if not in our own seems likely. I find
   C) if not in our own, seems likely, I find
   D) if not in our own seems likely, I find

[4] Like the Chinese, the Mayans occasionally decorated their buildings with carvings made out of stone. Used on the exterior of the buildings, the carvings were placed on broad murals and ramps along stairs, as well as in the fronts of the [5] immensely, elaborate entrances.

4. A) NO CHANGE
   B) Like the Chinese the Mayans
   C) Like the Chinese – the Mayans –
   D) Like the Chinese, the Mayans,

5. A) NO CHANGE
   B) immense elaborate
   C) immense, elaborate
   D) immensely elaborately

Writing and Language | Punctuation Practice

The American [6] bison, an animal that typically symbolizes the Wild, West is actually the heaviest land mammal in North America. Also called the American buffalo, the bison has a large head with small, crescent-shaped horns and a shaggy coat of brown hair on its shoulders and legs.

Historically, the process of cutting trees to make paper products caused great harm to the environment. Since an area that has been cleared of trees can take more than 50 years to regrow, the ecosystem that relies on those trees will likely perish before the trees grow back. [7] Today, however, many woodcutters recognize the harm such practices cause, and thus the practice of reforesting is becoming increasingly commonplace.

With today's cloning technology, [8] its conceivable that a woolly mammoths' DNA could be injected into a living cell and perhaps an actual prehistoric woolly mammoth could be brought to life in a science lab. Science might soon be faced with the ethical question of whether to take a cell sample from a creature that has been dead for 20,000 years and use it to bring back an extinct species.

6. A) NO CHANGE
   B) bison, an animal that typically symbolizes the Wild West is
   C) bison, an animal that typically symbolizes the Wild, West is
   D) bison, an animal that typically symbolizes the Wild West, is

7. A) NO CHANGE
   B) Today, however
   C) Today however
   D) Today however;

8. A) NO CHANGE
   B) its' conceivable that a woolly mammoth's DNA
   C) it's conceivable that a woolly mammoth's DNA
   D) it's conceivable that a woolly mammoths DNA

Writing and Language | Subject-Verb Agreement

Subject-Verb Agreement

Nouns and verbs must agree in number. If the subject is singular, then the verb must be singular. If the subject is plural then the verb must be plural.

Incorrect Example: The committee *vote* on matters of policy and administration.
The "committee" is a singular subject (even though it may be made up of multiple members), whereas "vote" is a plural verb.

Note: Singular present tense verbs with third person singular subjects end in "s."
Example: The singer sings. The dancer dances. The doctor operates.

Corrected Example: The committee *votes* on matters of policy and administration.

The word committee is an example of a *collective noun*. A collective noun is a word that refers to a collection of things taken as a whole. Collective nouns are singular, even though they may be made up of multiple things.

Examples of Collective Nouns
Jury
Amount
Audience
Class
Group
Each
Every
Government
The number
(Note: numbers over one are plural)
The United States
(The name of any country)

The conjunctions used in a sentence can give you a clue as to whether you need to use a singular or plural verb. For example, the word *and* within the subject indicates that you must use a plural verb even if each item connected by the conjunction is singular.

Example: The cat *and* the dog **run** very quickly.

However, if the sentence has two subject nouns connected by *neither...nor* or *either...or*, the verb should agree with whichever subject noun is closest to it.

Incorrect Example: *Neither* those cats *nor* the dog run very quickly.
Example: *Neither* the cat *nor* the dog **runs** very quickly.

If the cat and the dog above had both been plural, then a plural verb must be used. If, as demonstrated, one noun is plural and one is singular, the item that comes after the "or" or the "nor" would determine whether to use a singular or plural verb.

<u>These are the warning signs of a Verb Agreement Error:</u>
1. A verb in the portion of the sentence you are asked to modify
2. A prepositional phrase between the subject and verb.

Ask: "Who or what is the noun doing this verb's action?"

SAT-R Workbook v. 1.5

Writing and Language | Verb Agreement Drill

Verb Agreement Review

Rewrite the sentences below, fixing any agreement errors.

1. The Netherlands ~~were~~ *was* part of the band of countries that signed the Treaty of Rome.

   Rewrite the sentence: _____

   _____

   _____

2. The newly elected President, to the dismay of her opponents, ~~have~~ *has* argued to phase out the electoral college.

   Rewrite the sentence: _____

   _____

   _____

Circle the word that best fits in each of the following sentences.

3. Neither my grandparents nor my mother (like / **likes**) rap music.

4. A witty, rapid-fire freestyle ability and a lyrically complex rhyming style (explains / **explain**) why Christopher Wallace is arguably one of the greatest freestyle rappers of all time.

5. An easy-to-understand yet complex flow (**was the trademark** / were the trademarks) of Christopher Wallace.

Writing and Language | Verb Agreement Practice

The Eiffel Tower was built in 1889 for the World Exhibition held in celebration of the 1789 French Revolution. The structure was meant to last only for the duration of the Exposition, but it still [1] stand today, despite not only protests from contemporary artists who feared that the tower would be the advent of structures without individuality, but also despite the many people who feared that this huge "object" would not fit into the architecture of Paris.

1. A) NO CHANGE
   B) was standing
   C) standing today
   D) stands today

Yoga [2] have served several mental and physical purposes for over 5,000 years.

2. A) NO CHANGE
   B) has served
   C) was served
   D) is serving

[3] Though no one know when or why the practice started, it certainly began before written history. Stone carvings of figures in Yoga positions have been found in Indus Valley archeological sites dating back 5,000 years or more.

3. A) NO CHANGE
   B) Though nobody know
   C) Though no one knows
   D) Though, no one knows

Imagine living during a time when the access to [4] constitutional rights were limited because of the color of your skin. For almost 300 years, such was the case for African Americans in America.

4. A) NO CHANGE
   B) constitutional rights is limited
   C) constitutional rights are limited
   D) constitutional rights was limited

Writing and Language | Verb Tense

Verb Tense

Verb tense refers to the time frame in which the sentence is taking place (past, present, or future). One easy way to maintain clarity in a sentence or paragraph is to make sure that all of the verb tenses reflect the appropriate time frames.

Incorrect Example: In the 1870s, the French sculptor Frederic Auguste Bartholdi *is commissioned* to design the Statue of Liberty.

The sentence took place in the 1870s, but the verb, "is commissioned" is in the present tense.

Corrected Example: In the 1870s, the French sculptor Frederic Auguste Bartholdi *was commissioned* to design the Statue of Liberty.

Below is a chart outlining the three tenses in the English language. Each tense has what is called a basic form, a progressive form, and a perfect form.

The *progressive form* of a verb shows an *ongoing action in progress*. To create the progressive form of a verb, we do the following:

helping verb "to be" + present participle (-ing form of the verb)

The *perfect form* of a verb is used to show a *completed action*. To create the perfect form of a verb, we do the following:

helping verb "have/had" + past participle

Tense	Basic Form	Perfect Form	Progressive Form
Present	I Eat	I Have Eaten	I Am Eating
Past	I Ate	I Had Eaten	I Was Eating
Future	I Will Eat	I Will Have Eaten	I Will Be Eating

These are the warning signs of a Verb Tense Error:
1. A verb in the portion of the sentence you are asked to modify
2. Phrases that indicate time.

Ask: "When does the action in this sentence take place?"

Writing and Language | Verb Tense Drill

Verb Tense Review

Rewrite the sentences below, fixing the errors that exist.

1. In March of 2006, Australian Nathan Deakes ~~becomes~~ *became* the first man to win both the 20km and 50km walks at consecutive Commonwealth Games.

   Rewrite the sentence: _____

   _____

   _____

2. In an interview last week, Sheik Reda Shata ~~discusses~~ *discussed* the challenges facing an Imam in America.

   Rewrite the sentence: _____

   _____

   _____

Circle the word that best fits in each of the following sentences.

3. Because a federal order restricts either party from commenting on the case, Mr. Smith (**is** / **will be**) unable to hold a press conference tomorrow.

4. John (**eats** / **ate**) his food with his hands and that annoyed his mother.

5. The police commissioner (**stated** / **states** / **will state**) that the bridge (**is** / **was**) closed yesterday.

Writing and Language | Verb Tense Practice

Wilbur and Orville Wright [1] was two of the most important figures in the history of aviation. In 1903, when the first airplane [2] will take off from a beach in Kitty Hawk, North Carolina, it was a Wright brothers design, over 10 years in the making, with Orville in the cockpit.

1. A) NO CHANGE
   B) are two of the most
   C) have been two of the most
   D) are being two of the most

2. A) NO CHANGE
   B) has taken off
   C) took off
   D) had been taking off

The Pyramid of Giza is aptly listed among the Seven Wonders of the Ancient World. [3] It is thirty times larger in volume than the Empire State Building, and its features are so large that they can be seen from the Moon.

3. A) NO CHANGE
   B) It was thirty times
   C) It has been thirty times
   D) It was being thirty times

The current availability of information, both from the Internet and from other sources, [4] have created a cosmopolitan society that is better informed than ever before. However, the way in which people consume information has made them value quantity over quality.

4. A) NO CHANGE
   B) had created a
   C) has created a
   D) had been creating

Writing and Language | Verb Forms

Verb Forms

In English, there are many different forms of one verb. Most regular verbs have up to six forms. These varying forms are often used to express tenses, but keep in mind that they are not the same as tenses.

Incorrect Example: We were *practiced* outside when it started to rain.

Corrected Example: We were *practicing* outside when it started to rain.

The -ing form of a verb cannot be the action in a full sentence unless it is accompanied by a helping verb, such as "were" in the corrected example above.

These are the warning signs of a Verb Form Error:
1. A verb in the portion of the sentence you are asked to modify.
2. The underlined verb is next to an auxiliary verb such as: do/does, is/are, was/were, has/have, and had.

Ask: "Does this verb have another form that would fit this context better?"

Writing and Language | Verb Forms Drill

Rewrite the sentences below, fixing the errors that exist.

1. Lisa had just began to relax when the fire alarm went off.

Rewrite the sentence: _____

_____

_____

2. Usain Bolt, an outstanding sprinter from Jamaica, has broke several world records during his Olympic career.

Rewrite the sentence: _____

_____

_____

Circle the word that best fits in each of the following sentences.

3. (**Believed / Believing**) to be over 2,000 years old, the Rosetta Stone helped linguists finally translate Egyptian hieroglyphs.

4. Right now, you are probably (**wonder / wondering**) how much longer this will take.

5. Does the team (**understood / understand**) the new plays that the coach is (**working / worked**) on?

Writing and Language | Verb Practice

Many experts believe that the rapid decline in CD sales, fueled by the demise of boutique record stores and the increase in digital downloads, [1] have permanently changed the music industry.

1. A) NO CHANGE
   B) has
   C) are
   D) having

The Inca trail was originally part of the Inca Empire's road system. The 43-kilometer trail, passing through cloud forest and alpine tundra, [2] leading to the Sun Gate on Machu Picchu Mountain.

2. A) NO CHANGE
   B) led
   C) has led
   D) would of lead

Edward Abbey is perhaps the best example of a writer using fiction to effect political change. His iconic stories of the desolate but beautiful American Southwest [3] documents a landscape under assault from the forces of development and industrialization.

3. A) NO CHANGE
   B) does document
   C) documenting
   D) document

A long time ago, I read that a single wrong turn could set a person's life onto a completely different path. A recent experience confirmed this to be true. One afternoon, I [4] will accidentally walk through the wrong door at my office building and into a completely unexpected situation that has reshaped how I think about the world.

4. A) NO CHANGE
   B) accidentally walk
   C) accidentally walked
   D) am accidentally walking

The novel Verne created, *Twenty Thousand Leagues Under the Sea*, became an instant science fiction classic. Writing decades before long distance undersea travel [5] had begun, Verne could fascinate readers with his portrayal of the enigmatic Captain Nemo.

5. A) NO CHANGE
   B) has begun
   C) have began
   D) had began

Writing and Language | Verb Practice

Microwave cooking is truly a modern marvel. Not since man's discovery of fire a million years ago has there been a new way to prepare food. Like most major inventions and new uses for currently existing technologies, the fact that we can use microwaves in a household appliance to cook [6] food is a completely accidental discovery.

6. A) NO CHANGE
   B) food was a
   C) food has been a
   D) food had been a

If Dr. Percy Spencer [7] has not unintentionally melted a chocolate bar by standing too close to radiation leaking through tubes in his lab, microwave ovens would not have become the staple kitchen appliance they are today.

7. A) NO CHANGE
   B) will not have
   C) was not
   D) had not

Scientists [8] had long debated the causes of global warming, but it has become increasingly clear that humans and their habits have played an important role. An increased burning of fossil fuels, for example, [9] leading to more carbon dioxide in the atmosphere; one of the three major contributors to the greenhouse effect and global warming in general.

8. A) NO CHANGE
   B) are debating long
   C) were long debating
   D) have long debated

9. A) NO CHANGE
   B) was leading
   C) leads
   D) have been leading

If the colonists [10] were not standing up for their beliefs by dumping tea into the Boston Harbor and renouncing King George III during the Revolutionary War, we would still be under the control of monarchic England. While it takes courage to perform such actions, they are at the very core of this country's national character.

10. A) NO CHANGE
    B) have not stood up
    C) had not stood up
    D) were not standing up

Writing and Language | Pronoun Agreement

Pronoun Agreement

Pronouns must agree in number, case, and gender with the nouns they replace.

Incorrect Example: One thing everyone knows about news is that *they* are biased.
    The pronoun "they" in this sentence is replacing "news." "News" is singular whereas "they" is plural.

Corrected Example: One thing everyone knows about news is that *it is* biased.

One popular pronoun question that the SAT likes to ask concerns whether to use the pronoun *you* or *one*. There is no "right" answer in simply comparing the two pronouns. However, in order to decide which one to use in any given situation, you must look at the surrounding information. If the passage has been using the word *you*, stick with it. If it has been using *one*, stick with that.

Another common type of question involves using the singular or plural possessive form for pronouns.

Incorrect Example: The travelers did not want to forget his or her tickets.
    The possessive pronouns "his" and "her" are singular, whereas "travelers" is plural.

Corrected Example: The travelers did not want to forget their tickets.

The following is the warning sign of a Pronoun Agreement Error:
1. Pronouns in the underlined part(s) of the sentence.

Ask: "What is the number and gender of the *pronoun*?"
    "Does it agree with the number and gender of the *noun*?"

Writing and Language | Pronoun Agreement Drill

Rewrite the sentences below, fixing the errors that exist.

1. Before boarding the boat, passengers must purchase his tickets at the counter so that they are allowed to board.

   Rewrite the sentence: _____

   _____

   _____

2. Because the chemical composition of wheatgrass juice is so similar to that of hemoglobin, people consume those to maintain good health.

   Rewrite the sentence: _____

   _____

   _____

Circle the word that best fits in each of the following sentences.

3. When you first go to college, (**you** / **one**) may think that banks are giving away money because of the plethora of credit card offers.

4. If one is diligent about studying for the SAT, (**they** / **one** / **he** / **she**) will be able to improve (**their** / **one's**) score significantly.

5. The tired puppy and the kitten collapsed on the pillows after playing in the yard all day with (**his** / **her** / **their** / **its**) rubber toys.

Chapter 3

Writing and Language | Pronoun Case

Pronoun Case and Form

Subject pronouns perform the action. Object pronouns receive the action. Below is a chart of the subject, object, and possessive pronouns.

Subject	Object	Possessive
I	Me	My/Mine
You	You	Your/Yours
He	Him	His
She	Her	Her/Hers
They	Them	Their/Theirs
We	Us	Our/Ours
Who	Whom	Whose
It	It	Its

Incorrect Example: Robert gave $100 to Malik and *I*.
  "I" is a subject pronoun, meaning that it does the action in a sentence. In the sentence above, the action is being done to the pronoun.

Corrected Example: Robert gave $100 to Malik and *me*.

Incorrect Example: For *who* am I buying this present?
  "Who" is a subject pronoun, meaning that it does the action in a sentence. In the sentence above, the action is being done to the pronoun.

Corrected Example: For *whom* am I buying this present?

One way to check whether you want to use who or whom in a sentence is to replace it with the words he/him. (If who/whom shows up in a question, answer the question with he/him.) If the replacement or answer uses the word *he*, then *who* is the correct word. If the replacement or answer uses the word *him*, then *whom* is the correct word.

Additionally, the SAT will ask you to ensure that the author is using the correct form of the pronoun. Make sure you are familiar with how the common pronouns are used.

Incorrect Example: The legends had been passed down to the children from *they're* grandparents.
  "They're" is a contraction for they are.

Corrected Example: The legends had been passed down to the children from *their* grandparents.

Incorrect Example: The dog didn't want to eat *it's* treat.
  "It's" is a contraction for it is. (The SAT will sometimes give *its'* as an answer choice. Never choose this option. It does not exist in the English language.)

Corrected Example: The dog didn't want to eat *its* treat.

The following is a warning sign of a Pronoun Case Error:
1. Pronouns in the underlined part(s) of the sentence.

Ask: "Who/what is actually doing the action, and who/what is being acted on?"

Writing and Language | Pronoun Case

Pronoun Case Review

Rewrite the sentences below, fixing the errors that exist.

1. Miss Fletcher gave the car keys to Mary and I.

   Rewrite the sentence: _____

   _____

   _____

2. Kyle and me waited for Matt to finish class so that we could all go to lunch.

   Rewrite the sentence: _____

   _____

   _____

Circle the word that best fits in each of the following sentences.

3. If you are interested in attending a particular university, (**your** / **you're**) best course of action would be to contact that school to find out its admission requirements.

4. John and (**I** / **me**) are going to the library to study for our midterm exam.

5. Ken wants to buy (**he and Tony** / **Tony and he** / **Tony and him**) a car.

Writing and Language | Pronoun Practice

It's easier to buy truffles at a gourmet market than it is to dig them out of the ground, but it's not as fulfilling. Once you find your first truffle nestled between the roots of an old oak or pecan tree, [1] <u>a person</u> will be hooked on truffle hunting for life.

1. A) NO CHANGE
   B) a truffle hunter
   C) you
   D) DELETE the underlined portion.

At first, Henry Ford made cars the traditional way, one at a time. However, he soon realized that the assembly line offered the potential to dramatically expand [2] <u>it's</u> production of automobiles.

2. A) NO CHANGE
   B) its
   C) their
   D) his

The Federal National Mortgage Association, known as Fannie Mae, was established in 1938 in the depths of the Great Depression. Over the years, Fannie Mae has been a great help to people of low or moderate income [3] <u>who</u> would otherwise be unable to qualify for a home loan.

3. A) NO CHANGE
   B) whom
   C) whose
   D) for whom

What vaulted Apple into the national spotlight and solidified its place as a legitimate competitor of Dell and Microsoft was not its software or even its ease of use, but rather the brightly-colored exteriors of the machines. Jobs seized upon the American public's desire for aesthetically-pleasing products, and in doing so, [4] <u>used their creativity</u> to get ahead.

4. A) NO CHANGE
   B) was using their creativity
   C) used his creativity
   D) will be using his creativity

Writing and Language | Pronoun Practice

In the early 1980s, the most popular guard dog in the U.S. was the German Shepherd, who is a fierce protector but a friendly pet. Today, however, the pit bull has become more popular. Pit bulls are known for their aggressive behavior [5] which makes it well suited for guard duty.

5. A) NO CHANGE
   B) which make them
   C) which makes them
   D) which make it

Many species of falcons are predatory and carnivorous. Rodents and rabbits are their primary source of food. A falcon's sight [6] is one of it's greatest assets, second only to it's speed.

6. A) NO CHANGE
   B) is one of its' greatest assets, second only to its' speed
   C) is one of their greatest assets, second only to their speed
   D) is one of its greatest assets, second only to its speed

The reptile's scales help to protect [7] it from its enemies and to conserve moisture in its body. Some kinds of lizards have fan-shaped scales that they can raise to scare away other animals. The scales can also be used to court a mate.

7. A) NO CHANGE
   B) them
   C) themselves
   D) themself

Oftentimes, you'll wake up in the middle of the night with random images and thoughts lingering in your head. You know that you never left your bed, [8] yet one feels like something has occurred; you have seen people and been to places. Dreams have intrigued scientists and psychoanalysts for centuries.

8. A) NO CHANGE
   B) yet you feel like
   C) yet one felt like
   D) yet you felt as though

Writing and Language | Modifiers

Modifying phrases describe other words or phrases. Modifiers are great for helping us provide accurate and informative descriptions.

When you add a modifying phrase to a sentence, you also add complexity, and with this complexity come additional chances for confusion. To avoid such confusion, we must make sure that modifiers clearly describe what they're supposed to describe, which means we must place a modifier as close as possible to the thing it's modifying.

Incorrect Example: Running to catch the train, *the heel* on Casey's shoe broke.
   The modifying phrase, "Running to catch the train" should be describing Casey. However, the way it is written here, it is describing the heel on Casey's shoe.

Corrected Example: Running to catch the train, *Casey broke the heel on her shoe.*

Additionally, the Writing and Language section may ask you to differentiate between comparative and superlative modifiers.

Comparative modifiers are used when comparing only two items.
Superlative modifiers are used when comparing three items or more.

Incorrect Example: Samantha was the *better* of her five siblings at playing soccer.
   The comparative modifier "better" can only be used when comparing two people. Since Samantha has five siblings, we must use the superlative modifier, *best*.

Corrected Example: Samantha was the *best* of her five siblings at playing soccer.

If a modifying phrase comes in the middle of a sentence, it must be separated from the rest of the sentence with a comma before the phrase and a comma directly after.

Incorrect Example: Harry's cat who was red and fat ate dinner.
   The modifying phrase *who was red and fat* is not separated with commas.

Corrected Example: Harry's cat, who was red and fat, ate dinner.

The following is a warning sign of a Modifier Error:
1. A phrase that describes another word or phrase, often set off by commas.

Ask: "What is the modifier describing, and is the modifier as close as possible to whatever it's describing?"

Writing and Language | Modifiers Drill

Rewrite the sentences below, fixing the errors that exist.

1. Dressed in an unappealing leather shirt and baggy jeans, it displayed the disrespectful and egotistical attitude of the musical artist as he took the microphone from Taylor Swift during her acceptance speech and began to rant about how great Beyonce's video was.

    Rewrite the sentence: _____

    _____

    _____

2. Walking into the café, a cup of coffee was immediately brought to Maggie's favorite table.

    Rewrite the sentence: _____

    _____

    _____

3. Between the two women, Linda was the most prepared to present at the meeting.

    Rewrite the sentence: _____

    _____

    _____

Writing and Language | Modifiers Practice

Work on The International Space Station began in 1998. Larger than any other manmade structure in orbit, [1] astronauts at this experimental facility are given a unique opportunity to do research in a microgravity environment.

1. A) NO CHANGE
   B) this experimental facility gives astronauts
   C) astronauts experimenting at this facility are given
   D) experimental astronauts at this facility are given

The [2] Amazons, a legendary tribe of warrior women appear often in Greek mythology. Tales of these female fighters and their warrior exploits frequently show up in legends throughout Antiquity.

2. A) NO CHANGE
   B) Amazons, a legendary tribe of warrior, women,
   C) Amazons a legendary tribe of warrior women,
   D) Amazons, a legendary tribe of warrior women,

Like many arts and sciences that are profound, beautiful, [3] and powerful, society continues to trivialize Yoga.

3. A) NO CHANGE
   B) and powerful society continues to trivialize.
   C) and powerful, society, continues to trivialize.
   D) and powerful, Yoga continues to be trivialized by society

Worn from all the time she'd spent at various friends' [4] weddings and parties, Erin's relief was enormous at having her summer free of social engagements.

4. A) NO CHANGE
   B) weddings and parties, Erin was enormously relieved to have
   C) weddings and parties, Erin's enormous relief at having
   D) weddings and parties, enormous relief was Erin's at having

Anxiously anticipating Christmas morning, [5] Tamika's presents were mainly what she was looking forward to.

5. A) NO CHANGE
   B) Tamikas presents mainly were what
   C) presents were mainly what Tamika was looking forward to
   D) Tamika was mainly looking forward to presents.

SAT-R Workbook v. 1.5

Writing and Language | Parallelism

Parallelism is the balancing of similar words, phrases, or clauses that have the same grammatical structure. This balancing can occur within a single sentence or over a paragraph. The SAT most often tests parallelism in the form of lists. A list is a series of two or more similar things in a sentence. A common mistake made when writing long sentences is the "inconsistent list" mistake. When writing a list, you must express all the objects, people, or actions in consistent form.

Incorrect Example: Abed loves hockey, *playing* football, and jogging.
                               In this list, "hockey" and "jogging" are nouns, while "playing football" is an action.

Corrected Example: Abed loves hockey, *football*, and jogging.

The following is a warning sign of a Parallelism Error:
1. A series of similar things, as well as commas and conjunctions.

Ask: "What are the different parts of the list and are they in the same form?"

Writing and Language | Parallelism Drill

Rewrite the sentences below, fixing the errors that exist.

1. *The Daily Show with Jon Stewart* first aired in 1996 under the name *The Daily Show*; each episode consists of an opening monologue, satirical sketches, and interviewing a celebrity.

   Rewrite the sentence: _____
   _____
   _____

2. It is clear that Alex doubts the proposal's fairness, Barney disputes its effectiveness, and my questions are its legality.

   Rewrite the sentence: _____
   _____
   _____

3. Everyone contributed to the charity breakfast: Larry cooked eggs; Ervin fried bacon, and Michael's job was to make the pancakes.

   Rewrite the sentence: _____
   _____
   _____

Writing and Language | Practice

I recently decided that a cell phone was the only phone I needed. Why bother with a home phone when a cell phone [1] is capable of taking pictures, play music, and download attachments?

1. A) NO CHANGE
   B) is able to take pictures
   C) is good at picture taking
   D) takes pictures

One of the world's leading architects, Frank Gehry is no stranger to controversy. Supporters admire his originality, his bold vision, and [2] there is a love of his willingness to take risks.

2. A) NO CHANGE
   B) they admire his willingness to take risks.
   C) the willingness for taking risks.
   D) his willingness to take risks.

Armstrong's pioneering style in scat singing popularized vocal jazz by incorporating syllabic improvisations reflecting rapid changes of [3] pitch articulation, tonality, and resonating.

3. A) NO CHANGE
   B) pitch articulation, tonality, and resonance.
   C) pitching articulation, tone, and resonating.
   D) articulating, toning, and resonating.

The PhD candidate's goals are usually threefold: [4] to find a great advisor, researching a compelling topic, and to pen an astute dissertation.

4. A) NO CHANGE
   B) to find a great advisor, researching a topic that compels and writing an astute dissertation.
   C) found a great advisor, researched a compelling topic, and penned an astute dissertation.
   D) to find a great advisor, to research a compelling topic, and to pen an astute dissertation.

She wasn't so much opposed [5] to the lecture as taking so much of class time.

5. A) NO CHANGE
   B) to lecturing as taking so much
   C) to the lecture as taken so much
   D) to the lecture as to it taking so much

Writing and Language | Conjunctions | Transitions

Just as paragraphs need transitions to flow smoothly and coherently, sentences also need correct and clear transitions in order to make sense. Conjunctions connect parts of a sentence, including clauses, and allow an author to clearly and effectively show the relationship between the parts being connected. (Independent clauses can stand on their own as complete sentences while dependent clauses need to lean on an independent clause.) Make sure that the conjunction or transitional phrase logically fits in the context of the sentence.

Incorrect Example: *Although* she always had a good time at the park, Heather wanted to go this afternoon. "Although" indicates a shift in direction between the two clauses. However, in the sentence above, it would build logically that *because* Heather has a good time at the park, she would want to go.

Corrected Example: *Because* she always had a good time at the park, Heather wanted to go this afternoon.

Warning signs of a Conjunction Error:
1. Conjunctions in the underlined portion(s) of the sentence.
2. Sentences that use multiple conjunctions or are composed of two independent clauses.

Ask: "Do the two parts connect clearly and logically?"

Common Conjunctions and Transition Words	
Or	...used to connect alternatives
If	...introduces a conditional clause
So	...therefore, in order to
Though	...despite, however
Thus	...as a result of
Nevertheless	...in spite of that, all the same
Until	...up to, as far as, till
Whereas	...when in fact, on the contrary
While	...during the time that, although
For	...with the object or purpose of
Moreover	...and further, besides
And	...connects clauses and sentences
But	...introduces a contrast
Because	...for the reason that
Furthermore	...in addition to
Although	...however, even though
Since	...for the reason that

Writing and Language | Conjunctions Drill

Rewrite the sentences below, fixing the errors that exist.

1. For many groups were vehemently opposed to the latest user interface changes to Facebook, many users expressed their support for the modifications.

    Rewrite the sentence: _____

    _____

    _____

2. Even though Dadius recently completed a merger with rival Beebox, yet the new company is still smaller than chief rival Syke.

    Rewrite the sentence: _____

    _____

    _____

3. Although Molasses McFadden has never donated to a charity because he doesn't believe in charity.

    Rewrite the sentence: _____

    _____

    _____

Writing and Language | Practice

Standing at the starting line of the Boston Marathon, Bill Rodgers was nervous. It had been a decade since he had run a marathon, [1] which he hoped he was adequately prepared for the event.

1. A) NO CHANGE
   B) and
   C) then
   D) DELETE the underlined portion.

[2] Before meeting at a volunteer event in the heart of Seattle, Eli has remained the object of Sara's affections.

2. A) NO CHANGE
   B) When meeting
   C) Since meeting
   D) After meeting

Johann Wolfgang von Goethe was a famous German writer born in the 18th century. [3] Because he was not always kind to the people in his life, he still issued the following advice: "Treat people as if they were what they ought to be and you help them to become what they are capable of being."

3. A) NO CHANGE
   B) Although he was not
   C) However he was not
   D) Therefore he was not

About an hour east of Santa Cruz, on the edge of California's Central Valley, lies the town of Gilroy. [4] However, most of the garlic grown in the United States comes from the farms that surround the town. Garlic is so important to Gilroy that the town holds an annual garlic festival.

4. A) NO CHANGE
   B) On the other hand, most
   C) Nevertheless, most
   D) Most

The new company, Kickstarter, has developed an innovative model for helping small businesses. Individuals make small contributions, which are bundled together and used to fund, [5] for example, a jeweler or woodworker who might have difficulty obtaining a more traditional loan.

5. A) NO CHANGE
   B) on the other hand,
   C) as a result,
   D) instead,

Writing and Language | Run-ons and Fragments

Sentence structure is one of the more commonly tested subjects on the SAT. Being able to recognize what constitutes a full sentence is a vital skill. A full sentence contains a subject and a verb. If it does not contain both of these elements, it is a sentence fragment. If a sentence consists of two independent clauses and is joined by only a comma or nothing at all, it is a run-on. A good way to test if a sentence is a run-on is to put a period between the clauses and see if they would be complete sentences on their own. If a clause cannot stand on its own as a complete sentence, it is known as a dependent clause.

Incorrect Example: Jawaharlal the first Prime Minister of an independent India.
"Jawaharlal" is the subject of the clause above, but because he is not doing an action, this is just a fragment.

Corrected Example: Jawaharlal *was* the first Prime Minister of an independent India.

These are the warning signs of a Run-on or Fragment Error:
1. Sentences that don't have a verb or that use the *-ing* form of the verb, such as "showing," without an accompanying form of the verb "to be," *i.e. is, was, were*, etc.
2. Sentences that sound incomplete
3. Clauses joined by a comma without a conjunction
4. Sentences with multiple subjects.

Ask: "What is the main verb and who is the subject? If I remove all modifiers, does the sentence still make sense?"

Writing and Language | Run-Ons and Fragments Drill

Rewrite the sentences below, fixing the errors that exist.

1. Robert Nester Marley, a music legend born in Jamaica, breaking music barriers with his activist lyrics.

   Rewrite the sentence: _____

   _____

   _____

2. We discovered the largest deposit of diamonds in the country it was amazing to see.

   Rewrite the sentence: _____

   _____

   _____

3. Andrew arrived at the party late he was delayed by the weather.

   Rewrite the sentence: _____

   _____

   _____

Writing and Language | Practice

People who use banter as a form of humor are usually agreeable companions that do not aim to hurt the target of their [1] teasing although their words may be provocative, the corners of their mouths are always turned up in a smile.

1. A) NO CHANGE
   B) teasing, because
   C) teasing; though
   D) teasing. Although

He added phrases to the works of others when it sounded right to [2] his ear, changed tempos, when it suited him.

2. A) NO CHANGE
   B) his ear and changed tempos
   C) his ear changed tempos,
   D) his ear, changed tempos

Every December, there's a contest in my village to see who can put up the most elaborate holiday [3] decorations, this year, I'm going to enter.

3. A) NO CHANGE
   B) decorations this
   C) decorations. This
   D) decorations. Because this

[4] We sat on the bluffs overlooking the water, we watched the waves roll in toward the shore, crash against the rocks, and dissolve into frothy pools.

4. A) NO CHANGE
   B) We had sat
   C) We were sitting
   D) As we sat

Coach Nadeau showed her lack of professionalism by walking out of the gymnasium in the middle of the [5] match. Leaving her student athletes at a time when they needed her.

5. A) NO CHANGE
   B) match leaving her
   C) match; leaving her
   D) match, leaving her

Writing and Language I Practice

Tasmanian Devils on average weigh 5 to 9 kilograms and measure 30 centimeters. [6] Found in nature only on the island of Tasmania, which is near Australia. Similar to the cartoon character, real Tasmanian Devils have thick strong bodies and short legs.

6. A) NO CHANGE
   B) Once found in nature
   C) Tasmanian Devils were found
   D) Tasmanian Devils are found

The only question left to be settled now is, "Are women persons?" And I hardly believe any of our opponents will have the boldness to say they are not. Being persons, then, [7] women are citizens no state has a right to make any law, or to enforce any old law, that shall abridge their privileges or immunities.

7. A) NO CHANGE
   B) women are citizens; no state
   C) women are citizens, no state
   D) women are citizens, and, no state

In addition to tool use, Goodall found evidence of other intellectual traits in chimpanzees once thought [8] uniquely human. Such as logical thinking and an idea of self.

8. A) NO CHANGE
   B) uniquely human, such as
   C) uniquely human. Things such as
   D) uniquely human. Like

Writing and Language | Redundancy

Redundancy means repeating a word, thought, or idea unnecessarily. Correct and clear grammar is concise and free of unnecessary repetition. You never want to repeat yourself, say the same thing twice, or be redundant.

Incorrect Example: After capsizing, the Titanic sunk *under the water* to a depth of several thousand feet *below sea level*.

By saying "under the water" and "below sea level," the sentence unnecessarily repeats the same information twice.

Corrected Example: After capsizing, the Titanic sunk to a depth of several thousand feet.

Warning signs of a Redundancy Error:
1. Synonyms for words that appear in the sentence.

Ask: "Is the additional word actually needed? Does the sentence make sense without the additional word?"

Writing and Language | Redundancy Drill

Rewrite the sentences below, fixing the errors that exist.

1. Telecommunications satellites orbit above the earth at distances in excess of 30,000 meters over the surface.

   Rewrite the sentence: _____

2. During the 2008 Summer Olympics, sprinter Usain Bolt ran the 100 meter dash, a distance of approximately 110 yards, in a time of 9.69 seconds, which broke his own world record of 9.72 seconds.

   Rewrite the sentence: During the 2008 summer olympics

3. The rising prices of fashionable clothing have increased dramatically over the past five years.

   Rewrite the sentence: _____

Writing and Language | Idioms

Idioms are phrases and combinations of words with meanings and structures that have become standardized through habit and usage. This basically means they are correct because, well, that's just the way it is. Often it is difficult to recognize the correct idiom in SAT questions because we repeatedly hear the incorrect form. An idiom can supplant an equally grammatically correct phrase simply through the virtue of being the common, accepted usage. There are no rules. Idioms are what they are.

Incorrect Example: The two men had a dispute *around* whose child was smarter.

Corrected Example: The two men had a dispute *as to* whose child was smarter.

The following is a warning sign of an Idiom Error:
1. Common idioms or underlined prepositions.

Ask: "Is an idiom in the sentence? If there is one, is the correct combination of words being used?"

Writing and Language | List of Common Idioms

Idioms	Examples
Argue … with (a person)	It is not wise to argue with your teacher the day before you ask him for a recommendation letter.
As … as	As immature as John is, he at least knows better than to drink and drive.
Between … and	There is no difference between a European size 36 shoe and an American size 6 shoe.
Capable … of	A determined and diligent student is capable of achieving any score on the SAT.
Comply … with	Jesse was able to comply with the rules once they were clearly explained.
Composed … of	The SAT is composed of three tests: the writing test, the critical reading test, and the math test.
Define … as	Many people define success on the SAT as getting the score needed to attend the school desired.
Different … from	The behavior of infant boys is different from the behavior of infant girls.
Dispute … over	The two men had a dispute over whose child was smarter.
Either … or	Martin will have either the tiramisu or the key lime pie for dessert.
In search … of	Since the beginning of time man has been in search of the meaning of life.
Intend … to	I intend to study six days a week for the SAT.
Mistake … for	People always mistake me for Janet Jackson.
Neither … nor	Neither the cat nor the dog liked staying home alone.
Not only … but also	Invisible Man is not only well written but it also tells the story of many men.
Plan … to	I often plan to study vocabulary but have neglected to and my SAT score is thus suffering.
Prior … to	Prior to the elections the mayor's ratings were incredibly high.
Prohibit … from	In New York people under the age of 21 are prohibited from consuming alcohol.
Regard … as	Michael Jordan is regarded as the undisputed king of basketball.
Responsible … for	Parents are responsible for their children.
Responsibility … to	Students have a responsibility to maintain good grades.
Superior … to	Joel's peach cobbler is far superior to any store bought one.
Try … to	Try to stay focused while taking the exam.
Used … to	Lucia used to only like science, now she likes math as well.

SAT-R Workbook v. 1.5

Writing and Language | Idioms

Rewrite the sentences below, fixing the errors that exist.

1. I'm going to try and find a new pair of shoes to go with these pants.

Rewrite the sentence: _____

_____

_____

2. If the convention had not been scheduled for the same week, there would of been enough rooms in the hotel for everyone.

Rewrite the sentence: _____

_____

_____

3. The epidemics in influenza and meningitis has paralyzed airline traffic for two weeks.

Rewrite the sentence: _____

_____

_____

Writing and Language | Diction

Diction means word choice. Many words in English sound alike, look similar, or even have similar meanings. When writing, we must be sure to consistently and correctly use the right words.

Incorrect Example: The biggest problem *effecting* our climate in the new millennium is the overproduction of polluting toxins caused by people's irresponsible and excessive consumption.

Effect can be used as a verb, but it is primarily used as a noun to signify "a change that took place."
Affect is a verb meaning "to change or influence something."

Corrected Example: The biggest problem *affecting* our climate in the new millennium is the overproduction of polluting toxins caused by peoples' irresponsible and excessive over-consumption.

Ask yourself, "Is the meaning of this word right for this sentence?"

<u>These are warning signs of a Diction Error:</u>
1. Words that are similar — in meaning or spelling — to other words we commonly use
2. A word you don't know, or whose meaning you are unsure of, in the underlined portion of the sentence.

Ask: "Is the meaning of this word right for this sentence?"

Writing and Language | Diction Drill

Rewrite the sentences below, fixing the errors that exist.

1. From Letta's prospective, politicians seemed far more interested in winning votes than in working for economic justice.

   Rewrite the sentence: _____

   _____

   _____

2. In order to participate in the tournament, Greendale High School had to field the full compliment of debaters.

   Rewrite the sentence: _____

   _____

   _____

3. The judge found no clear way to assess who's fault the accident was.

   Rewrite the sentence: _____

   _____

   _____

Chapter 3

Writing and Language | Practice

In the movie's opening scene, a missile [1] that is fired and consequently launched and projected from the deck of an aircraft carrier lands harmlessly in the ocean.

1. A) NO CHANGE
   B) fired
   C) fired and thereby projected
   D) fired and consequently propelled

My grandmother is five feet tall and weighs barely one hundred pounds. She doesn't exactly fit the stereotype [2] associated with that of a typical fan of death metal.

2. A) NO CHANGE
   B) that is often viewed as closely connected with that of
   C) that is linked to that for
   D) of

As Friday night draws near, my grandmother begins preparing for forty-eight hours of non-stop clubbing. She eagerly reads the weekly listing of concerts [3] that comes out once a week.

3. A) NO CHANGE
   B) that is published on a regular basis.
   C) that appears regularly.
   D) DELETE the underlined portion and end the sentence with a period.

Writing and Language | Practice

At the opening night of the hottest new musical on Broadway, the elaborate and flawless choreography [4] illicited uproarious applause.

4. A) NO CHANGE
   B) illicits
   C) elicits
   D) elicited

Throughout multiple conversations over the following months, Elyse did her best [5] to elude to her secrets without directly revealing them.

5. A) NO CHANGE
   B) towards eluding
   C) to allude
   D) try and elude

Some scholars believe a comprehensive look at US History must include [6] an acknowledgement about settler colonialism and imperialism.

6. A) NO CHANGE
   B) an acknowledgement of
   C) an acknowledgement that
   D) an acknowledgement around

My great grandfather Earl had [7] a tendency to overeat when there were jelly donuts available for breakfast.

7. A) NO CHANGE
   B) a tendency toward overeating
   C) a tendency for overeating
   D) a tendency of overeating

Although I repeatedly explained I had rear-ended her [8] car by accident, my mother did not believe me.

8. A) NO CHANGE
   B) car on accident,
   C) car, by accident,
   D) car and on accident,

Writing and Language | Argument Logic

The majority of style and organization questions will be Argument Logic questions. These questions will ask you to judge whether a phrase or sentence is appropriate in context, makes logical sense, or maintains the focus of the passage. Many times argument logic questions will test these concepts by asking you to insert text or delete it. Ask yourself if the phrase or sentence is logically consistent with the rest of the passage. The most important step when dealing with these questions is to make sure you really understand the question and what it is asking.

Argument Logic Action Plan

1. Identify the Question Type.
Many argument logic questions will begin with "Given that all the choices are true..." If you are asked to support a point, insert or delete specific text, conclude a paragraph, or answer a clearly non-grammatical question, you are most likely dealing with an argument logic question.

2. Determine Precisely What the Question is Asking.
Each argument logic question will be very specific in what it is asking. Figure out the particular piece of information the question wants.

3. Process of Elimination.
Once you have determined what the question is asking, eliminate any answer choice that does not satisfy it. Do not worry yet about the right answer; just get rid of the wrong answers.

4. Compare Remaining Choices.
You now know that if there is more than one answer choice remaining, every choice is wrong except one. Identify the differences between the remaining answer choices to determine which choice has the precise information needed.

Writing and Language | Argument Logic

Aunt Anna's Amazing Aptitude

My aunt Anna has a truly amazing <u>aptitude. The skill</u>[1] to advise people well. When I have a dilemma, I go to my aunt for advice. She listens attentively and somehow precisely knows my sentiments. Most people she knows bring her their problems and ask for her advice. [2] My aunt recognizes the importance of helping one another.

<u>My friend Stephanie says that her family is so busy that no one is ever home.</u>[3]

Her job requires her to go to social events and sometimes I go with her. I have watched her closely at these events; her eyes remain set on whoever is speaking, and she makes a note of every detail.

2. Which of the following true statements, if added here, would best strengthen the assertion that many people ask Aunt Anna for advice?

    A) Even my own brother takes his problems to her more readily than he does to our parents.
    B) Sometimes Aunt Anna asks for my advice.
    C) Lately, Aunt Anna has encouraged us to try to find our own answers to our problems.
    D) She always gives appropriate and helpful advice.

3. The writer is considering deleting the underlined sentence. Should the writer make this deletion?

    A) Yes, because the sentence doesn't further the writer's point about her aunt.
    B) Yes, because the sentence undermines the writer's point that people are too busy to help.
    C) No, because the sentence includes an important support to the writer's main point.
    D) No, because the sentence provides a necessary transition to the next paragraph.

Identify the Question Type
Question 2 asks us to strengthen an assertion. Question 3 asks us about deleting a specific piece of text. Therefore they are both Argument Logic questions.

Determine Precisely What the Question is Asking
Question 2 asks us to give additional evidence that "many people" seek Aunt Anna's advice. We need an answer that shows people seeking out her advice. Question 3 asks about deleting a sentence. This means we have to figure out what, if anything, that sentence adds to the passage.

Process of Elimination
In question 2, A shows someone who does not normally seek out advice, asking for Aunt Anna's, so we keep it. Choices B and C have nothing to do with asking for Aunt Anna's advice, so we eliminate them. Choice D tells us about the type of advice Aunt Anna gives, so we keep it. In question 3, we see the *yes or no* question format. The underlined sentence is about the author's friend Stephanie and her family. Since the rest of the passage has to do with Aunt Anna and advice, this sentence takes the focus away from its main point. Therefore, the writer should delete the sentence, and we can eliminate choices C and D.

Compare Remaining Choices
For question 2, we are choosing between A and D. D gives us no indication that "many people" are asking for advice. Choose **D**. For question 3, we still have A and B. Choice A matches our reasoning and choice B is not relevant to the passage. Choose **A**.

Writing and Language | Argument Organization

Argument Organization questions ask you to order the sentences or paragraphs of the passage so they present the most logical and coherent argument. Whenever you see numbers or letters before sentences or above paragraphs, you know there will be an Argument Organization question. Try to determine the main ideas of the sentences or the paragraphs and then order them so there is a logical bridge between the main ideas. You can use the answer choices to determine where to place the sentence or paragraph, and then rule out any choice that makes the passage incoherent.

Argument Organization Approach

1. Identify the Question Type
Argument Organization questions will always have numbers or letters above paragraphs or next to sentences. The question will ask you to move a piece of text that is already present in the passage.

2. Process of Elimination
Use the answer choices as your guide. Work your way through them, placing the text wherever each specifies. Eliminate any choice that does not flow coherently.

3. Reread and Choose
Take the remaining answer choice and reread the sentences or paragraphs to make sure the passage is coherent.

Chapter 3

Writing and Language | Argument Organization

Aunt Anna's Amazing Aptitude

My aunt Anna has a truly amazing aptitude. The₁ skill to advise people well. When I have a dilemma that I think is impossible to solve, I go to my aunt for advice. She listens attentively, inquires about certain details, and seemingly precisely knows my sentiments. Most of the people she knows bring their problems to her and ask for her advice. My aunt recognizes the importance of helping one another. My friend₂ Stephanie says that her family is so busy they are never home.

[1] Her job requires her to go to social events, and sometimes I go with her. [2] I have watched her at dinner; her eyes remain set on whoever is speaking, and she makes a note of every detail. [3] At her job, my aunt's [3] fellow workers and acquaintances benefit from her advice. [4] My aunt then demonstrates what a true counselor should be by giving advice that is helpful and beneficial. [5] Similarly, we make our friends.

3. For the sake of logic and coherence, Sentence 3 should be placed
   A) where it is now.
   B) before sentence 1.
   C) before sentence 2.
   D) after sentence 4.

Identify the Question Type
We have numbers next to sentences, and the question asks us where a specific sentence should be placed; therefore, we have an Argument Organization question.

Process of Elimination
Sentence 3 is about Aunt Anna giving advice to coworkers and acquaintances. It is preceded by a sentence in which the author describes her aunt speaking to someone at a social event and is followed by a sentence where the aunt dispenses advice. Sentence 3 does not logically fit here as sentences 2 and 4 flow coherently into each other, so we can eliminate answer choice A. When placed before sentence 1, sentence 3 connects the main idea that Aunt Anna gives good advice from the first paragraph with her workplace, which is mentioned in sentence 1. This placement makes the passage flow coherently. When placed before sentence 2, the paragraph loses the link between the author going with her aunt to the social event and the author observing her aunt at the social event. Therefore, we can eliminate C. Finally, when sentence 3 is placed after sentence 4, the paragraph loses any sort of logical flow, so we can eliminate choice D.

Reread and Choose
Rereading the paragraph before (without that last sentence that we removed previously), we see how the first paragraph now coherently flows into the second. Choose B.

© 2016 Bell Curves, LLC

Writing and Language | Practice

Westsider Marc Connelly
*Adapted from *100 New Yorkers of the 1970s*, **by Max Millard**

Eleven years ago, when I was in high school, I [1] had saw a movie just before Christmas that made a deep impression on me. It was a film of a stage play called [2] *The Green Pastures* — a fascinating look at life in biblical times, performed by an all-black cast.

[3] The memory of that film has remained in my consciousness like a religious experience although I never knew who wrote the play or when it was written. Therefore, it was a welcome surprise to learn that the playwright, Marc Connelly, lived just down the hall from me in my apartment building.

After speaking with him in person, my fascination with his life and career [4] continues to grow. Connelly was born in a small Pennsylvania town, the son of a pair of travelling actors.

1

A) NO CHANGE
B) have seen
C) seen
D) saw

2

A) NO CHANGE
B) The Green Pastures; a fascinating look
C) The Green Pastures. A fascinating look
D) *The Green Pastures*; which is a fascinating look

3

At this point, in order to incorporate specific information from the infographic below, the author wishes to add the following sentence:

> Although *The Green Pastures* is considered an American classic, it is now performed mostly by schools and amateur companies.

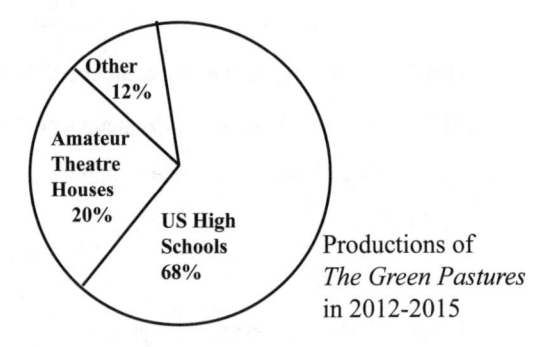

Other 12%
Amateur Theatre Houses 20%
US High Schools 68%

Productions of *The Green Pastures* in 2012-2015

Should the author make this addition?

A) No, because the sentence detracts from the main point of the passage.
B) No, because it does not make sense that an American classic would only be performed by schools and amateur companies.
C) Yes, because the sentence provides details about the significance of the play in American culture.
D) Yes, because the sentence explains why the film had such a profound impact on the author.

4

A) NO CHANGE
B) was continuing to grow
C) is continuing to grow
D) continued to grow

Writing and Language | Practice

He wrote *The Green Pastures* [5] in 1930; it won that year's Pulitzer Prize for drama. In his 70-year career, Connelly wrote dozens of plays.

However, Connelly was not simply a playwright. He was one of the most versatile talents in the American theater. He excelled [6] as an actor, director, producer, writing plays at Yale, and was even a very popular lecturer. He wrote musicals, stage plays, movie scripts and radio plays, which used to be a wildly popular form of entertainment prior to the explosive popularity of the television.

Connelly was one of the original staff members of the *New Yorker* magazine. One of the short stories he wrote for the magazine won an O. Henry, an award given to short stories of exceptional merit. Despite all of his success, his first novel wasn't published until he was 74 years old.

Some of the most interesting stories Connelly relayed to me were tidbits about his involvement in the Algonquin Round [7] Table, it was a group of celebrated New York writers who met for lunch daily for almost ten years. As Connelly tells it, the lunches were filled [8] by wisecracks, wordplay, and witticisms, the majority of which [9] end up in the newspaper columns of those involved.

5

A) NO CHANGE
B) in 1930. And it won that year's Pulitzer Prize
C) in 1930, it won that year's Pulitzer Prize
D) in 1930; it won that years Pulitzer Prize

6

A) NO CHANGE
B) as an actor, directing, producing playwriting professor at Yale,
C) as an actor, director, producer, and playwriting professor at Yale,
D) as an actor, director, producer, writing plays at Yale;

7

A) NO CHANGE
B) Table, a group of celebrated
C) Table; a group of celebrated
D) Table; which was a group of celebrated

8

A) NO CHANGE
B) through
C) of
D) with

9

A) NO CHANGE
B) had been ending up in the newspaper columns
C) would end up in the newspaper columns
D) will end up in the newspaper columns

Writing and Language | Practice

It was at the Round Table that Connelly met George Kaufman, [10] with who he teamed up to pen five comedies.

    One of the comments that Connelly made during our interaction really stuck with me, mainly because it was the first thing he said after he opened the door and welcomed me inside. "Theater is probably [11] the greater of all social instruments man ever invented. All religions have sprung from the theater."

10

A) NO CHANGE
B) who
C) with whom
D) whom

11

A) NO CHANGE
B) the greatest social instruments
C) the greatest social instrument
D) the greater social instruments

Writing and Language | Practice

The Galapagos Islands

[1]

[1] <u>Seeing as</u> many may have heard of the Galapagos Islands, most are not aware of the incredible importance of this archipelago. This chain of islands is comprised of nineteen individual islands located near the coast of Ecuador. It was named for the multitude of galapagos, or tortoises, that traverse the land. The islands [2] <u>were formed millions of years ago and was first discovered</u> by European explorers in the 1500s.

[2]

Darwin spent five weeks on the Galapagos Islands [3] <u>only</u>, gathering data and observing species. He spent the next twenty years, however, writing *The Origin of Species*, which was based on the theories of evolution and natural selection that he formulated based on these observations.

[3]

[4] <u>The tortoises on the Galapagos are the largest in the world.</u> The islands have remained a vast resource for scientists even today studying evolution, ecology, and geology.

1

A) NO CHANGE
B) Since
C) While
D) Because

2

A) NO CHANGE
B) was formed millions of years ago and was first discovered
C) formed millions of years ago and were first discover
D) were formed millions of years ago and were first discovered

3

The best placement for the underlined portion would be

A) where it is now.
B) before the word Galapagos.
C) after the word spent.
D) before the word Darwin.

4

Which choice is the most effective first sentence of paragraph 3?

A) NO CHANGE
B) Darwin was the first scientist to study the Galapagos Islands, but he was certainly not the last.
C) *The Origin of Species* sparked controversy in schools across the United States when it was published.
D) The Galapagos Islands were formed by a series of volcanic eruptions.

Writing and Language | Practice

[5] In fact, the Galapagos Islands are considered to be [6] the world's largest, most complex and diverse group of islands that have remained largely unaltered by human contact.

[4]
Beyond this diversity, which is invaluable to scientists, the rapid rate of [7] evolution, on the islands offers an opportunity found no where else in the world. Species on the islands are faced with many [8] difficulties: extreme variation in the climate, isolation from any mainland population, isolation between the islands themselves, and very low populations of species. The conditions that these plants and animals must [9] endure makes survival a challenge for any species. Therefore, the natural selection process is made evident in a much shorter time span. Evolution studies that elsewhere would take many decades to hundreds of years can be conducted in ten to twenty years on the Galapagos Islands.

[5]
It is this vital and unique characteristic of the Galapagos Islands that makes them so essential to conserve.

5
A) NO CHANGE
B) However,
C) In the other hand,
D) For a reason,

6
A) NO CHANGE
B) the world's largest, most diverse
C) the world's largest and biggest, most complex and diverse
D) one of the world's largest as well as one of the most complex and diverse

7
A) NO CHANGE
B) evolution on the islands offer,
C) evolution on the islands, offer
D) evolution on the islands offers

8
A) NO CHANGE
B) difficulties
C) difficulties;
D) difficulties,

9
A) NO CHANGE
B) endure make
C) endures makes
D) endures make

Writing and Language | Practice

[10] Under 75 percent of the land is protected as a national park, but the area is still threatened by the growing human population, the tourism industry, as well as the beautiful scenery. [11]

10

At this point in the passage, the author wishes to add statistical evidence to support the main idea.

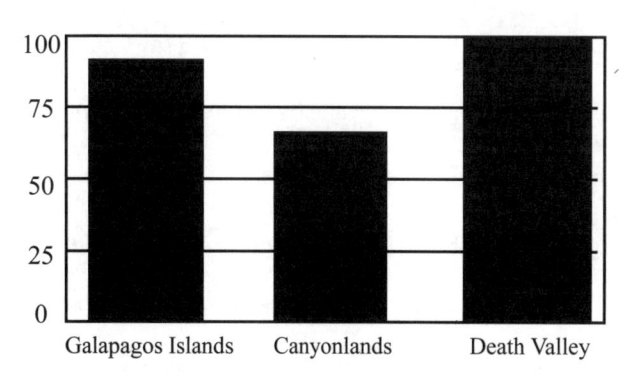

Percentage of Protected Land in National Parks

Judging by the information presented in the graph above, which of the following choices is best?

A) NO CHANGE
B) Over 95 percent of the land is protected as a national park, but the area is still threatened
C) Over 95 percent of the land is protected as a national park, but, the area is still threatened
D) Over 95 percent of the land is unprotected, nationally sanctioned land; still the area is

11

Upon reviewing this essay, the author realizes that he left out some important information. He wants to add the following sentence:

> Their worldwide fame, though, began in 1835 when Charles Darwin visited the islands.

The most logical and effective place to add this sentence would be after the last sentence of which Paragraph?

A) 1
B) 2
C) 3
D) 4

Writing and Language | Practice

How to Tell a Story
Adapted from How to Tell A Story and Others, **by Mark Twain**

I do not claim that I can tell a story as it ought to be told. I only claim to know how a story ought to be told, for I have been in the company of expert story-tellers for many years.

There are several kinds of stories, but only [1] one difficult kind—the humorous. I will talk mainly about that one. The humorous story is American; the comic story is English, and the witty story is French. The humorous story depends upon the manner of the telling for its effect; the comic story and the witty story [2] depends upon the matter.

The humorous story may be spun out at great length, may wander around as much as it pleases, and ultimately may arrive nowhere in particular. The comic and witty stories, [3] on the other hand, must be brief and end with a point. The humorous story bubbles gently along; the others burst.

1

A) NO CHANGE
B) one difficult kind; the humorous.
C) one difficult, kind, the humorous.
D) one difficult—kind, the humorous.

2

A) NO CHANGE
B) depends on
C) depend upon
D) depending on

3

Which of the following alternatives to the underlined portion would be LEAST acceptable?
A) however
B) on the contrary
C) despite
D) though

Writing and Language | Practice

The humorous story is strictly a work of art—high and delicate art—and only an artist can tell it. No art is necessary in telling the comic and the witty story; anybody can do it. The art of telling a humorous story [4] has been created in America, and has remained at home.

[1] The humorous story is told gravely; the teller [5] does their best to conceal the fact that he even dimly suspects that there is anything funny about it. [2] However, the teller of the comic story tells you beforehand that it is one of the funniest things he has ever heard, then tells it with eager delight, and is the first person to laugh when he gets through. [3] And sometimes, if he has had good success, [6] he is so glad and happy that he will repeat the punch line and glance around from face to face, collecting applause, and then repeat it again. [7] [4] It is a pathetic thing to see.

Very often, of course, the rambling and disjointed humorous story finishes with a point, a snapper, or whatever you may call it. At that point, the listener must be alert, for in many cases the teller will divert attention from that snapper by dropping it in a carefully casual and indifferent way, with the pretence that he does not know it is supposed to be funny.

4

A) NO CHANGE
B) have been created
C) was created
D) were created

5

A) NO CHANGE
B) does his best
C) do their best
D) do his best

6

A) NO CHANGE
B) he will have been so glad so
C) he is so happy that
D) he will be so glad and happy that

7

If the writer were to delete Sentence 4, the essay would primarily lose
A) an explanation of why the author feels a certain way about comic stories.
B) a description of the author's feelings towards a specific type of story-teller.
C) conflicting information about how the author feels about a story and how popular that type of story is.
D) a suggestion that comic story-tellers instead tell humorous stories.

Writing and Language | Practice

Artemus Ward used that trick a good deal; then when the audience belatedly caught the [8] innocent joke, he would look up with surprise as if wondering what they had found to laugh at. But the teller of the comic story does not gloss over [9] its [10] joke; he shouted it at you every time. And when he prints it in England, France, Germany, or Italy, he italicizes it, puts some whooping exclamation-points after it, [11] and sometimes explained it in parenthesis. All of this is very depressing and makes one want to renounce joking and lead a better life.

8

For the sake of logic and coherence of this sentence, the underlined portion should be placed
A) where it is now.
B) after the word *belatedly*.
C) before the word *surprise*.
D) before the word *wondering*.

9

A) NO CHANGE
B) its'
C) it's
D) their

10

A) NO CHANGE
B) joke; he shouts
C) joke. He shouted
D) joke as he shouts

11

A) NO CHANGE
B) and sometimes explains
C) and sometimes is explaining
D) and sometimes explain

Writing and Language | Practice

Westsider Craig Claiborne
Adapted from 100 New Yorkers of the 1970s, **by Max Millard**

"To be a good restaurant critic, you shouldn't have a conscience and you must accept that what you write may hurt [1] people's feelings," said Craig Claiborne, food editor of the *New York Times*. "I used to visit restaurants twice a day, frequently seven days a week [2] very often, and lie awake brooding about whether my reviews were honest — whether I was hurting somebody who didn't deserve to be hurt." [3] While being recognized throughout the United States as the father of modern restaurant criticism, Claiborne joined the *Times* in 1957 and shortly thereafter was given the go-ahead to write reviews based on a four-star system. "The *New York Times* made the decision. I was the instrument. It was the first newspaper that allowed a restaurant critic to say anything [4] he wants. It took a lot of guts, when a newspaper depends on advertising." [5] Claiborne, a native of Mississippi did not take himself or his work too seriously. He preferred to be called by his first name, [6] dressing in a particularly unfashionable manner, and to spend as little time as possible at his office.

1
A) NO CHANGE
B) peoples' feelings
C) people's feelings'
D) peoples' feeling's

2
A) NO CHANGE
B) very oftenly
C) more often than not
D) OMIT the underlined portion.

3
A) NO CHANGE
B) While being recognized throughout the United States as the father of modern restaurant criticism;
C) Recognized throughout the United States as the father of modern restaurant criticism,
D) After having been recognized throughout the United States as the father of modern restaurant criticism;

4
A) NO CHANGE
B) he wanted.
C) he has wanted.
D) you want.

5
A) NO CHANGE
B) Claiborne, a native, of Mississippi did
C) Claiborne, a native of Mississippi, did
D) Claiborne a native of Mississippi,

6
A) NO CHANGE
B) to dress in a particularly unfashionable manner, and spending as little time as possible at his office.
C) dressing in a particularly unfashionable manner, and spending as little time as possible at his office.
D) to dress in a particularly unfashionable manner, and to spend as little time as possible at his office.

Writing and Language | Practice

In spite of his earthiness, Claiborne unquestionably ranked as one of the leading food authorities of his time. His articles, which appeared in the *Times* each Monday, Wednesday, and Sunday, covered every subject from the particulars of a dinner in Washington for Chinese Vice-Premier Teng Hsiao-Ping to the [7] six most creative ways to preparing scallops. He wrote numerous best-selling cookbooks, and he traveled the world on fact-finding missions. Claiborne's rise from obscurity to obtaining the most [8] prestigious and distinguished food job in America astonished no one more than himself since his qualifications were a [9] principle B.A. in journalism and [10] one years' training at a hotel and restaurant school in Switzerland. However, the *Times* knew exactly what kind of person was needed, and Claiborne quickly proved

7
A) NO CHANGE
B) six most creative ways of
C) six more creatively ways of
D) six most creative ways by

8
A) NO CHANGE
B) prestigious and, distinguished, food job
C) prestigious and distinguished, food job
D) prestigious food job

9
The best placement for the underlined portion would be
A) where it is now.
B) after the word *his*.
C) after the word *in*.
D) after the word *qualifications*.

10
A) NO CHANGE
B) a years' training
C) one year's training
D) one years training

Writing and Language | Practice

to be that man. He threw himself into his work with [11] <u>boundless energy, he wrote no fewer than five</u> columns a week, but his relationship with the newspaper eventually became a love-hate affair.

As a result, Claiborne left the paper for almost two years. He agreed to return if the paper would have someone else do the local restaurant reviews; he also requested that his neighbor and cooking partner Pierre Franey share the Sunday byline. The conditions were immediately met.

11

A) NO CHANGE
B) boundless energy; writing no less than five
C) boundless energy, he was writing no less than five
D) boundless energy, writing no fewer than five

CHAPTER 3
Practice

Writing and Language | Practice

Westsider Cleveland Amory
Adapted from 100 New Yorkers of the 1970s, **by Max Millard**

[1] <u>Its impossible</u> to mistake the voice if you've heard it once — the tone of mock [2] <u>annoyance, the twangy, almost whiny drawl</u> that rings musically in the ear. It could easily belong to a cartoon character or a top TV pitchman, but it doesn't. It belongs to Cleveland Amory, an affable and rugged individualist who has been a celebrated writer for more than half of his 61 years.

[3] <u>Born, outside of Boston,</u> he showed his writing talent early, becoming the youngest editor ever at the *Saturday Evening Post*. His first book, *The Proper Bostonians*, was published in 1947. "Then I moved to New York," he mused, "because whenever I write about a place, I have to leave it." [4]

Amory's next career stop was writing for the *TV Guide*. It was here that Amory achieved his widest fame.

[5] <u>Moreover,</u> this was not fulfilling enough for him, and one of the chief reasons he gave for dropping his *TV Guide* column after 15 years was that "after years of

---

1

A) NO CHANGE
B) It is impossibly
C) Its' impossible
D) It's impossible

2

A) NO CHANGE
B) annoyance, the twangy almost whiny drawl
C) annoyance the twangy almost whiny drawl
D) annoyance, the twangy, almost, whiny drawl

3

A) NO CHANGE
B) Born outside of Boston
C) Born, outside of Boston
D) Born outside of Boston,

4

The author is considering deleting the following phrase from the preceding quote:

> because whenever I write about a place, I have to leave it.

If the writer were to make this deletion, the essay would primarily lose

A) a specific factor that led to Amory's success.
B) an example of a specific quality of Amory's personality.
C) an explanation of Amory's actions.
D) an elaboration on why Amory prefers New York to Boston.

5

A) NO CHANGE
B) Thus,
C) However,
D) In addition,

Writing and Language | Practice

trying to decide whether the Fonz is a threat to Shakespeare, I wanted to write about things that are more important [6] then that."

He was the magazine's star columnist from [7] 1963 to 1976; at which point he gave it up in order to devote his time to other projects, especially the Fund for Animals, a non-profit humane organization he founded in 1967. He has served as the group's president since the [8] beginning.

Amory's quest to protect animals from needless cruelty [9] began several decades ago when, as a young reporter in Arizona, he wandered across the border into Mexico and witnessed a bullfight. [10] Shocking that people could applaud the death agony of "a fellow creature of this earth," he began joining various humane societies. Today he is probably the best known animal expert in America.

6
A) NO CHANGE
B) then those.
C) than that.
D) than them.

7
A) NO CHANGE
B) 1963 to 1976, at which point he gave it up
C) 1963 to 1976: when, he gave it up
D) 1963 to 1976. When he gave it up

8
Here, the writer wishes to add a clause that conveys the immense popularity of Amory's Fund for Animals. Which of the following choices best accomplish this?

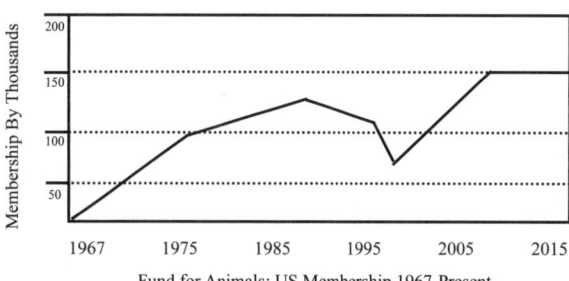

Fund for Animals: US Membership 1967-Present (graph showing membership by thousands from 1967 to 2015, rising from ~25 to ~150, with a dip around 1996)

A) beginning; group membership dropped sharply in 1996.
B) beginning; group membership dropped sharply in 1996, but has otherwise steadily climbed over the years.
C) beginning; now, they have 150,000 members across the United States.
D) beginning; now, they only have 150,000 members across the United States.

9
A) NO CHANGE
B) beginning
C) had began
D) have began

10
A) NO CHANGE
B) Shocked that people could applaud
C) It was shocking that people could applaud
D) Because he was shocked, that people could applaud

Writing and Language | Practice

"A lot of people ask me, 'Why not do something to help children, [11] and old people or minorities?'" he said, when asked about why he focuses his efforts particularly on animals. "My feeling is that there's enough misery out there for anybody to work at whatever he wants to. I think the mark of a civilized person is how you treat what's beneath you."

11

A) NO CHANGE
B) or old people, or minorities
C) nor old people, nor minorities
D) and old people; or minorities

Chapter 3 Practice

Writing and Language | Practice

The Zodiacal Light Mystery
Adapted from Curiosities of the Sky, **by Garrtt Serviss**

There is a singular phenomenon in the sky – one of the most puzzling of [12] all, that has long captured the attention of astronomers, defying their efforts at explanation. While very few, perhaps even none, of these scientists have ever seen it, [13] it's name is often spoken; when one is lucky enough to glimpse it, it exhibits a mystical beauty that charms and awes the beholder. This phenomenon is called *The Zodiacal Light*, and it marks the sun's annual path through the stars [14] that it completes on a yearly basis. The Zodiacal Light has given rise to many remarkable theories, and a true explanation of it would probably throw light on a great many other celestial mysteries.

If you are outdoors just after sunset – say, on an evening late in the month of February – [15] one may perceive, just after the angry flush of the dying day has faded from the sky, a pale ghostly presence rising above the place where the sun went down. The phenomenon brightens slowly with the fading of the twilight and soon distinctly assumes the shape of an elongated pyramid of pearly light, leaning toward the south. This is the Zodiacal Light.

12
A) NO CHANGE
B) all, which has
C) all – which has
D) all – that have

13
A) NO CHANGE
B) its → posessive
C) its'
D) their

14
A) NO CHANGE
B) that it completes yearly
C) that it has completed yearly
D) OMIT the underlined portion

15
A) NO CHANGE
B) you may perceive
C) one may be perceiving
D) you perceived

195

© 2016 Bell Curves, LLC

Writing and Language | Practice

[1] If the night is clear and the moon absent (and if you are in the country, [16] for city lights ruin the spectacles of the sky), you will be able to watch the apparition for a long time. [2] You will observe that the light is brightest near the [17] horizon, it gradually fades as the beam mounts higher. [18] [3] But when autumn comes it appears again, like a spirit of the morning announcing its reincarnation in the east. [4] It continues to be visible during the evenings of March and part of April, after which, ordinarily, it is seen no more, or if seen is relatively faint and unimpressive.

16

The writer is considering deleting the following phrase:

> for city lights ruin the spectacles of the sky

If the writer were to make this deletion, the sentence would primarily lose

A) an observation as to why city lights are damaging the Zodiacal Lights.
B) a reason the author personally prefers to watch the Zodiacal Lights from the country, as opposed to the city.
C) an example of why one location is better than another to view the Zodiacal Light.
D) a specific piece of evidence as to why many astronomers miss out on the phenomenon.

17

A) NO CHANGE
B) horizon; gradually fading
C) horizon; which gradually fades
D) horizon, gradually fading

18

For the sake of logic and coherence, Sentence 3 should be placed
A) where it is now.
B) before sentence 1.
C) before sentence 2.
D) after sentence 4.

Writing and Language | Practice

The Zodiacal Light truly is an incredibly beautiful sight. Its faint light requires the contrast of a background of dark sky in order to be easily seen. But within the tropics, where the Zodiac is always at a favorable angle, the mysterious light is more constantly visible. Nearly all observant travelers in the equatorial region have taken particular note of this phenomenon as it at once catches the eye and holds the attention as a novelty.

During a trip to South Africa [19] in 1909 an English astronomer E. W. Maunder found a remarkable difference between the appearance of the Zodiacal Light on his going and coming voyages. When crossing the equator going south, he did not see it at all. However, upon his return, when he was only one degree south of the equator, he had a memorable view of it. It was a bright, clear night, and the Zodiacal Light was [20] extraordinary, [21] brilliant; brighter than he had ever seen it before.

19

A) NO CHANGE
B) in 1909 an English astronomer, E. W. Maunder, found
C) in 1909 an English astronomer, E. W. Maunder found
D) in 1909, an English astronomer, E. W. Maunder, found

20

A) NO CHANGE
B) extraordinary,
C) extraordinarily
D) extraordinary

21

A) NO CHANGE
B) brilliant – brighter than he had ever seen it before
C) brilliant, brighter, than he had ever seen it before
D) brilliant; brighter then he had ever seen it before

Writing and Language | Practice

I recall my own personal favorite view of the Zodiacal Light from the summit of the cone of Mount Etna. There are few lofty mountains so favorably placed as Etna for observations of this kind. Rising directly from sea-level to an elevation of nearly eleven thousand feet, [22] observers on Mount Etna's summit at night feel lost in the midst of the sky. On this one particular occasion, the world beneath was virtually invisible in the moonless night. The blaze of the constellations overhead was astonishingly brilliant, yet amid all their magnificence, my attention was immediately drawn to a great tapering light that sprang from the place on the horizon where the sun would rise later and that seemed to be blown out over the stars like a long, luminous veil.

22

A) NO CHANGE
B) Mount Etna makes an observer on its summit
C) an observer on Mount Etna's summit
D) Mount Etna's observers on the summit

Writing and Language | Practice

The Best Lesson

Chelsea hated math with all the angst [23] which only a 14-year-old girl can muster.

I was volunteering as a peer tutor the summer before my senior year in high school, and Chelsea was assigned to me. She had failed her eighth grade pre-algebra class, which she needed to pass before starting her freshman year.

When Chelsea and I began to [24] study, she was reluctant to even try. She showed up late for appointments and did not complete her homework. I struggled to convince her that doing well in math was important to her future.

I wasn't going to give up on Chelsea, though. [25] With basic math skills, we started from fractions and decimals to organization. I kept our sessions light and fun but focused on encouraging her. Slowly, Chelsea started getting math problems right. We gradually increased the difficulty of the [26] work, Chelsea continued to improve.

I will never forget the day Chelsea walked into our session and said, "You know, this math stuff isn't so bad." I was floored. [27] She reluctantly admitted that she even sort of liked doing her math homework, which she had never liked doing before.

23

A) NO CHANGE
B) that
C) who
D) whom

24

A) NO CHANGE
B) study she, was
C) study, she, was
D) study, being

25

A) NO CHANGE
B) We started with basic math skills, from fractions and decimals to organization.
C) From fractions and decimals to organization, we started with basic math skills.
D) We started, from fractions and decimals to organization, with basic math skills.

26

A) NO CHANGE
B) work, and Chelsea continued
C) work and continued
D) work and Chelsea continued

27

A) NO CHANGE
B) She reluctantly admitted that she even sort of liked doing her math homework, especially if she was in the library where it was quiet.
C) She reluctantly admitted that she even sort of liked doing her math homework.
D) OMIT the underlined portion.

Writing and Language | Practice

Chelsea started showing up on time for appointments and consistently completing her homework. We even added in extra sessions before her big final. When she got her final grades, I was astounded; she had not only passed her course, but she had received an A on the final!

Later that year, Chelsea's mother told me what a difference [28] I will make in [29] her daughter's life. Not only was Chelsea earning a B+ in Algebra, [30] yet all of her other grades had also [31] risen and gone up. Chelsea was eager to do well in school for the first time in her life, and her mother could not thank me enough.

Chelsea affected me as much as I affected her. When I [32] felt overwhelmed [33] now I try to figure out what the fundamentals of the issue are in order to fix the situation. Slowly, I too gain the confidence needed to solve the problem.

28
A) NO CHANGE
B) had made
C) make
D) had make

29
A) NO CHANGE
B) her daughters' life
C) her daughters life.
D) hers daughter's life.

30
A) NO CHANGE
B) but
C) and
D) while

31
A) NO CHANGE
B) risen from the low grades they were before.
C) risen, this meant higher grades.
D) gone up.

32
A) NO CHANGE
B) will have felt
C) had felt
D) feel

33
A) NO CHANGE
B) now, I try to figure out, what are the fundamentals of the issue
C) now, I try to figure out what the fundamentals of the issue are
D) now, I try, to figure out, what the fundamentals of the issue are

Writing and Language | Practice

Directions: Give yourself 8 minutes and 30 seconds to complete the passage below. On the real SAT exam, you will have a little less than 9 minutes to complete each of the 4 passages (and 11 accompanying questions) in the allotted 35 minutes.

Chinese Americans

[1]
A Chinese proverb states, "When you drink the water, consider the source." It seems such obvious wisdom [34] now; an overused cliché for a generation in which everything insightful has already been said. [35] But all clichés are preserved by truth, and my ancestors were sending a simple, but powerful message to [36] their descendants: a people cannot succeed without their foundation in the past.

[2]
If a group of people is to survive, connections must be sustained between past and present generations. This is a truth that my grandfather clarified when he told me to "tell the others" about him, and it's a truth that generations of Chinese people in America have also understood.

[3]
Another Chinese proverb states, "We may visit friends but always return to our family." This is an adage that [37] reminded us of our instinctual need for our home and heritage. We long for self-identification and self-knowledge.

34

A) NO CHANGE
B) now, an overused cliché for a generation
C) now, an overused cliché, for a generation
D) now, an overused cliché, for a generation,

35

Which of the following alternatives to the underlined portion would NOT be acceptable?

A) However,
B) Nevertheless,
C) Although,
D) Yet,

36

A) NO CHANGE
B) its descendants, people
C) their descendants, a people
D) its descendants: a people

37

A) NO CHANGE
B) reminds
C) was reminding
D) had reminded

Writing and Language | Practice

[4]

For more than 150 years, the ties that have held Chinese Americans to their country of origin have thinned and frayed, and we find ourselves confused and lost, unsure of who we are and where we belong. Yet, with determined passion and unyielding devotion, Chinese Americans have managed to stay connected to the people who remain in China: parents send their children to learn a language fading from their own tongues; [38] families gathering from miles around to celebrate the traditional holidays, and Sunday mornings are filled with the clamor of dim sum carts.

[5]

There is an undeniable desire amongst Chinese Americans and their counterparts who have remained on the other side of the ocean to understand one another [39] more clearer. For generations [40] and hundreds of years, we have looked at one another like farmers gazing into a flowing stream. The image of the other is recognizably familiar [41] and distorted by the gentle movements of the water, and so what we could not discern from this distorted image, we have filled in for ourselves with everything we could imagine.

38

A) NO CHANGE
B) families gather from miles around to, celebrate the traditional holidays,
C) family is gathering from miles around to celebrate the traditional holidays,
D) families gather from miles around to celebrate the traditional holidays,

39

A) NO CHANGE
B) more clear
C) more clearly
D) the most clear

40

A) NO CHANGE
B) and many years
C) and one hundred years
D) OMIT the underlined portion

41

A) NO CHANGE
B) therefore
C) but
D) thus

Writing and Language | Practice

[6]

[1] Sometimes, when we finally meet, we are initially disappointed by the difference between our fabricated image and reality. [2] However, we are repeatedly reminded of our connection. [42]

[3] Shadowy ideals do not always reflect the real experience. [4] We wonder whether we had made a mistake, if the relationship we felt [43] might of not really been there, if the ties that held us together had not already broken. [5] The spirit of China is in each of us. [6] Through music, literature, and art, we make contact with one another, and the whole world is forced to take note. [44]

42

For the sake of logic and coherence of this paragraph, Sentence 2 should be placed

A) where it is now.
B) before Sentence 1.
C) after Sentence 3.
D) after Sentence 4.

43

A) NO CHANGE
B) might have
C) could
D) could of

44

The author is considering deleting the first sentence from Paragraph 4. If the writer removes this sentence, the essay would primarily lose

A) information about how Chinese Americans keep their culture alive.
B) details supporting the importance of family and self-identification.
C) the introduction of a concern many Chinese Americans feel today.
D) a transition from the importance of keeping in touch with Chinese origins to the reality that it is impossible to do so.

Writing and Language | Practice

Directions: Give yourself 8 minutes and 30 seconds to complete the passage below. On the real SAT exam, you will have a little less than 9 minutes to complete each of the 4 passages (and 11 accompanying questions) in the allotted 35 minutes.

Westsider George Balanchine
From 100 New Yorkers of the 1970s, **by Max Millard**

To some people he was known as the Shakespeare of dance — a title he probably deserves more than anyone else now living, but to his friends and colleagues, he was simply "Mr. B" — George Balanchine, the ageless Russian-born-and-trained choreographic genius whose zest for living was matched only by [45] his humility and his sense of humor.

[46] Mr. B, left his native St. Petersburg in 1924 spent the next nine years working as a ballet master throughout Europe, [47] after being persuaded by the American dance connoisseur Lincoln Kirstein to come to the United States in 1933. Following the move, Balanchine toured the world with the New York City Ballet. He always found the home crowd, however, to be the most appreciative.

45

A) NO CHANGE
B) his humility or his sense of
C) humility and his sense of
D) his humility and sense of

46

A) NO CHANGE
B) Mr. B who left his native St. Petersburg during 1924
C) Mr. B, who left his native St. Petersburg in 1924,
D) Mr. B, who left his native St. Petersburg in 1924

47

A) NO CHANGE
B) after persuasion
C) was persuaded
D) has been persuaded

Writing and Language | Practice

Balanchine almost single-handedly transplanted ballet to American soil and made it flourish. He played a [48] central and pivotal role in making New York the dance capital of the [49] world, since it undeniably is today for both classical and modern dance.

[50] Classical and modern dance were Balanchine's two areas of interest. He was a man passionate about his work, and there was no way to slow him down. Even during his 30th consecutive year serving as director of the New York City Ballet, Mr. B. continued to direct most of the dances for his 92-member company and to create new choreographic works of daring originality. He also taught at the School of American Ballet, which he cofounded in 1934 with Lincoln Kirstein. Balanchine thought of himself more [51] as a craftsmen than as creator, and often compared his work to that of a cook or cabinetmaker — two crafts, by the way, in which he was rather skilled.

48

A) NO CHANGE
B) central but pivotal
C) central
D) centrally pivotal

49

A) NO CHANGE
B) world, which it undeniably was
C) world; since it undeniably is
D) world, which it undeniably is

50

Which choice would most effectively and appropriately lead the reader from the topic of Paragraph 3 to that of Paragraph 4?

A) NO CHANGE
B) However, Balachine's success was not surprising.
C) Balanchine's family pleaded with him to take some time off from work.
D) Balanchine was lauded for his creativity and originality.

51

A) NO CHANGE
B) as a craftsman then as a creator
C) as a craftsman than as a creator
D) as craftsmen then as creator

Writing and Language | Practice

Balanchine did not write down his dances. [52] How then did he remember such works as *Prodigal Son*, which he had created almost 50 years prior to reviving it for the New York City Ballet in 1941? "How do you remember prayers?" he said in response to being asked this question. "You just remember. I remember everything."

Prodigal Son, in which the biblical story is danced out [53] extremely dramatic, is an example of a ballet with a plot, but the majority of Balanchine's works are based on music and movement [54] purely. Tchaikovsky and Stravinsky are the composers Balanchine most liked to use as inspiration for new dance works. The late Igor Stravinsky, a fellow Russian expatriate who was his longtime friend and collaborator, once described Balanchine's choreography as "a series of dialogues [55] perfectly complimentary to and coordinated with the dialogues of the music."

52

A) NO CHANGE
B) How then does he remember
C) How, then, does he remember
D) How, then, do they remember

53

A) NO CHANGE
B) extremely dramatically
C) extreme dramatically,
D) dramatically,

54

The best placement for the underlined portion would be
A) where it is now.
B) after the word *based*.
C) after the word *majority*.
D) after the word *works*.

55

A) NO CHANGE
B) perfectly complimenting to and coordinated with
C) a perfect compliment to in coordination with
D) in perfect compliments with the coordination of

Writing and Language | Practice

Directions: Give yourself 8 minutes and 30 seconds to complete the passage below. On the real SAT exam, you will have a little less than 9 minutes to complete each of the 4 passages (and 11 accompanying questions) in the allotted 35 minutes.

The Island of Krakatoa
Adapted from The Wonder Book of Volcanoes and Earthquakes by Edwin J. Houston

[1]

Krakatoa, located in the Straits of Sunda, is one of the many islands [56] which form the large island chain known as the Sunda Islands. It is not far from the equator, about 420 miles [57] south and is about thirty miles west of land of Java. The Straits of Sunda is an important piece of water that forms one of the great highways to the East.

[2]

Krakatoa is uninhabited and very small, measuring about five miles in length and less than three miles in width. This little piece of [58] land made itself famous by what took place on it during the month of August in 1883, when Krakatoa suffered a [59] tremendously, explosively volcanic eruption.

[3]

Krakatoa itself is a volcano. It is not surprising that Krakatoa is a volcanic island, [60] since it lies in one of the most active belts of volcanic islands in the world. The island of Java, small as it is, has nearly fifty volcanoes, [61] by which at least twenty-eight are active. Volcanic eruptions are so frequent that the island is seldom free from them.

56
A) NO CHANGE
B) which forms
C) that forms
D) that form

57
A) NO CHANGE
B) south, and
C) south -- and
D) south. And

58
A) NO CHANGE
B) land making
C) land makes
D) land could make

59
A) NO CHANGE
B) tremendously explosively
C) tremendous explosive
D) tremendously explosive

60
Which of the following alternatives to the underlined portion would be LEAST acceptable?
A) NO CHANGE
B) because
C) as
D) although

61
A) NO CHANGE
B) in which
C) from which
D) of which

Writing and Language | Practice

[4]

The long continued quiet of Krakatoa was broken on the 20th of May, 1883, when inhabitants of Java heard [62] noises; that sounded like the firing of guns. These noises were accompanied by the shaking of the ground and buildings. This happened during a season of the year known by the "dry monsoon." The island of Java greatly needed rain, as [63] they seldom rains during the months of the dry monsoon. When, therefore, the rumbling sounds of the approaching catastrophe of Krakatoa [64] were heard, the people, believing that the noises were due to [65] peals and gales of thunder, rejoiced. But when the rumbling sounds increased, it's clear that the sounds were the beginning of a volcanic eruption.

[5]

These disturbances were merely the forerunner of the terrible eruption soon to follow, and on Sunday, August 26th, 1883, without any further warnings, Krakatoa burst into terrible activity. [66] It began an explosive eruption that hasn't ever been equaled in severity in the memory of man. [67]

62
A) NO CHANGE
B) noises, that sounded
C) noises. That sounded
D) noises that sounded

63
A) NO CHANGE
B) it
C) it's
D) he

64
A) NO CHANGE
B) was heard
C) will be heard
D) would be

65
A) NO CHANGE
B) peals
C) peals, gales
D) peals, and gales,

66
A) NO CHANGE
B) It begins
C) It begun
D) Its beginning

67

Upon reviewing this essay, the author realizes that he left out some important information. He wants to add the following sentence:

> This was a phenomenon with which they were only too well acquainted.

The most logical and effective place to add this sentence would be after the last sentence of Paragraph
A) 2
B) 3
C) 4
D) 5

CHAPTER 4
The Math Test

Chapter 4

The Math Test | Overview

The Math Test on the SAT is broken down into two sections: the Non-Calculator section and the Calculator section. However, your score (on a scale of 200 to 800) is generated as a combination of these two sections. The Non-Calculator section is the third section on the exam, and you will have 25 minutes to complete it. The Calculator section is the fourth and final multiple choice section, and you will have 55 minutes to complete it.

The questions on the Math Test span a variety of topics, but they have one thing in common: They focus on real world scenarios. This means that the problems will rarely involve just one step. The topics on the SAT Math Test, in the language of the test-makers themselves, include the following:

Problem Solving & Data Analysis
These questions require quantitative reasoning about ratios, rates, and proportional relationships, particularly understanding and applying unit rate. You will also be expected to identify measures of center, overall patterns, and deviations from an overall pattern in data sets. You may be asked to perform any of the following:
Use ratios, rates, proportional relationships, and scale drawings to solve single and multistep problems
Solve single and multistep problems involving percentages, measurement quantities, units, and unit conversion
Analyze a scatterplot using linear, quadratic, or exponential models to describe how the variables are related and use this relationship to investigate key features of the graph
Compare linear growth with exponential growth
Use two-way tables to summarize categorical data and relative frequencies, and calculate conditional probability
Make inferences about population parameters based on sample data, including the use of confidence intervals and measurement error
Use statistics to investigate measures of center (mean, median, mode, range, standard deviation) of data and analyze shape, center, and spread
Evaluate reports to make inferences, justify conclusions, and determine appropriateness of data collection methods.
Heart of Algebra
These questions require analyzing, solving, and creating linear equations, inequalities and systems of equations. You may be asked to perform any of the following:
Create, solve, or interpret a linear expression/equation or a system of linear equations
Create, solve, or interpret linear inequalities or systems of linear inequalities
Build a linear function that models a relationship between two quantities using either an equation or function notation
Interpret variables and constants in expressions for linear functions within a context presented and make connections between a linear equation and the real-life meaning of a constant term, variable, or feature of a given equation
Understand connections between algebraic and graphical representations, including: selecting a graph described by a given linear equation, selecting a linear equation that describes a given graph, determining the equation of a line given a verbal description of its graph, determining key features of the graph of a linear function from its equation, and determining how a graph may be affected by a change in its equation.

The Math Test | Overview

Passport to Advanced Math
These questions require an understanding of the structure of expressions and the analysis, manipulation, and rewriting of these expressions. This includes reasoning with more complex equations, and interpreting and building functions. You may be asked to perform any of the following:

Create a quadratic or exponential function
Determine the most suitable form of an expression or equation to reveal a particular trait, given a context
Create equivalent expressions involving exponents and radicals, including simplifying or rewriting in other forms
Solve a quadratic equation having rational coefficients
Manipulate polynomial expressions and simplify the result
Solve an equation that contains radicals or contains the variable in the denominator of a fraction and identify when a resulting solution is extraneous
Solve a system of one linear equation and one quadratic equation
Rewrite rational expressions by adding, subtracting, multiplying, or dividing two rational expressions and simplify the result
Interpret parts of nonlinear expressions in terms of their context to describe the real-life meaning of a constant, a variable, or a feature of the given equation
Understand the relationship between zeros and factors of polynomials, and use that knowledge to sketch graphs
Understand a nonlinear relationship between two variables by making connections between their algebraic and graphical representations
Use function notation, and interpret statements using function notation to solve conceptual problems related to transformations and compositions
Rearrange an equation or formula to isolate a single variable.

Geometry
These questions require working with geometric figures. You may be asked to perform any of the following:

Solve problems using volume formulas (Any required volume formulas will be provided either on the formula sheet or within the question.)
Use the Pythagorean theorem to solve applied problems involving right triangles
Apply theorems about circles to find arc lengths, angle measures, chord lengths, and areas of sectors
Use concepts about congruence and similarity to solve problems about lines, angles, and triangles
Create or use an equation in two variables to solve a problem about a circle in the coordinate plane.

Trigonometry
These questions require working with trigonometric functions. You may be asked to perform any of the following:

Use trigonometric ratios to solve applied problems involving right triangles
Convert between degrees and radians and use radians to determine arc lengths
Use the relationship between similarity, right triangles, and trigonometric ratios
Use the relationship between sine and cosine of complementary angles.

The Math Test | Overview

Take a look at a sample conversion chart below showing the approximate raw scores and their corresponding scaled scores. Although the conversion chart is slightly different for each administration, these numbers can be used to give you a general idea of where you are currently scoring and how many more points you would need to reach your target score. When tackling the Math Test, keep your goal score in mind and make sure you are attempting enough questions in order to achieve this.

Math Test Conversion Chart					
Raw Score	Scaled Score	Raw Score	Scaled Score	Raw Score	Scaled Score
0	200	20	460	40	640
1	200	21	470	41	650
2	210	22	480	42	650
3	230	23	490	43	660
4	250	24	500	44	670
5	270	25	510	45	680
6	290	26	510	46	690
7	300	27	520	47	690
8	320	28	530	48	700
9	330	29	540	49	710
10	340	30	550	50	720
11	360	31	560	51	730
12	370	32	570	52	740
13	380	33	570	53	750
14	390	34	580	54	760
15	400	35	590	55	770
16	420	36	600	56	780
17	430	37	610	57	790
18	440	38	620	58	800
19	450	39	630		

Take a look at your first diagnostic exam. Find your math section score and circle that score on the chart above.

Use this to set a goal score for yourself for your next exam. For example, a reasonable goal would be to improve by 50 points on your next test. Put a star next to that goal score on the chart above.

How many raw points does this mean you will need to get in order to achieve your goal? _____

Keep this number in mind as you approach your prep. Realize that unless you are looking to achieve a perfect score, you may have some room to get questions wrong and still reach your target score. Therefore, you want to be careful not to spend too long on a question that is tripping you up if doing so ultimately means that you may not have enough time to attempt other questions that you may be more likely to answer correctly.

Chapter 4

The Math Test | Overview

Each question on the Math Test is worth a total of one raw point. You lose no points if you answer a question incorrectly, so even if you do not know how to do a particular problem, take a guess! Never leave a question blank.

There are two types of questions that you will see in each of the two math sections: Multiple Choice questions and Grid-In questions.

Multiple Choice Questions: Each multiple choice question has four possible answer choices, and you must select and bubble in the correct one.

Grid-Ins: Grid-In questions come at the end of each math section. For these, you will not be given any answer choices. You must generate the answer yourself and bubble it in the provided grid. The grids will look like this:

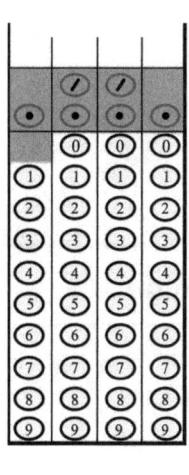

When gridding in your answer, there are a couple of things that you must remember:

1. You CANNOT round your answer prior to the last place in the grid. You can also choose not to round it at all.

For example, if your answer is 2/3 you can choose to either grid it in either its fractional form, or as .666 or .667. You will be marked INCORRECT if you bubble in .67.

2. Simply writing your answer in the provided spot is not enough. If you do not actually bubble in your answer, you will be marked INCORRECT.

3. You CANNOT grid in a mixed number.

For example, if your answer is one and a half, you must either grid it as a decimal (1.5), or as an improper fraction (3/2).

4. You CANNOT grid in a negative number. (There are no negative signs in the grid!)

5. You can grid your answer in any column. The placement does not matter.

www.bellcurves.com

The Math Test | Overview

As we mentioned, there are two math sections on the exam. They follow one another and comprise the third and fourth sections of the test. Take a look at the breakdown of each of these sections below so that you know exactly what to expect on test day:

Non-Calculator Section

Timing: 25 minutes

Multiple Choice	Grid-Ins
1 15	16 20

Calculator Section

Timing: 55 minutes

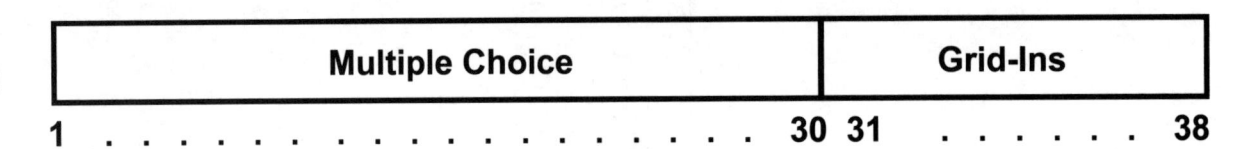

Multiple Choice	Grid-Ins
1 30	31 38

4a

TEST-TAKING STRATEGIES & BASICS:

DEFINITIONS, SUBSTITUTION, PLUGGING IN, FRACTIONS & DECIMALS

Problem Solving | Overview

It can be easy to become overwhelmed as you work through the Math Test, particularly because many of the problems involve taking multiple steps. It is important to keep yourself focused and to utilize all of the strategies that we will discuss in the coming chapters.

Therefore, as you approach each problem, ask yourself the following questions one at a time, until you find one that you are able to answer with a "Yes!" If you come across a problem for which you find yourself answering "No" to each of the questions, bubble in a guess and move on. There is no use spending time on a problem that you have no idea how to approach.

We will discuss each of these questions in further depth throughout the coming chapters:

1. Can I answer this mathematically?

2. Can I graph this on my calculator to get an answer?
   *This question only applies to the Calculator section

3. Can I plug in any of the answer choices?

4. Can I choose my own number to plug in?

Problem Solving | Overview

SAT questions test your ability to problem solve. In order to do this effectively, it is important to follow the steps below:

> **1. Read and Recognize**
> Read the *entire* question and identify/recognize the topic(s) being tested.
> Make note of particular areas of interest/trouble (i.e. positive and negative possibilities when variables are raised to even powers or the lack of the term "integer" to describe a variable).
>
> **2. Write Down Additional Information NOT Given in the Question**
> Write down any necessary formulas. If the problem does not require formulas, think clearly and systematically through the rules and steps you must follow to answer the question. Remember: Many of these questions will involve multiple steps.
>
> **3. Connect the Information Not Given to the Information Given**
> Reread the question and then write down and label each piece of information you are given. Integrate that information into the facts not given (i.e., put values given into the formulas).
>
> **4. Solve the Problem**
> Carefully solve the problem.
>
> **5. Reread the Question Asked and Select an Answer**
> Reread just the "question" (not the information leading up to it), to ensure that you have given the value requested.

Chapter 4

Definitions | Overview

Many SAT questions don't explicitly test your understanding of basic terminology, but answering them correctly ultimately requires an understanding of some terms. Fill in the chart below to review the meanings of a variety of these terms that may show up on the exam.

Term	Definition	Examples - Notes
Integer	a # w/ no decimal or fraction	**True** or False: -7 is an integer. **True** or False: 0 is an integer.
Digit	a # from 0-9	*Digit* is not the same thing as *number*.
Consecutive	a # in a sequence/order	This does not specify whether ascending order or descending order.
Distinct	different	If x and y are distinct, then $x \neq y$.
Even	#s or integers that are divisible by 2	**True** or False: 0 is even. **True** or False: -6 is even. **True** or False: 4.8 is even.
Odd	#s that aren't divisible by 2	3, 6, -1
Remainder	What is left over after division.	What is the remainder when 347 is divided by 6? 5
Multiple	a # that goes into another #	List some multiples of 7: 7, 14, 21, 28, 35, 42 A number is the smallest multiple of itself.
Least Common Multiple (LCM)	the smallest multiple between 2 numbers.	The LCM of 6 and 9 is 18. The LCM of $4xy$ and $7x^2$ is _____. You can use your calculator to find the LCM of two constants: 1. Press the MATH button. 2. Scroll over using the right arrow key until NUM is highlighted. 3. Select #8, lcm(. 4. Type in the two numbers, separating them with a comma, and press ENTER.
Absolute Value	the distance from zero that's always positive	$|-7| = $ 7 $|7| = $ 7 $|-4 + 2| = $ 2

Chapter 4

Definitions | Overview

Term	Definition	Examples - Notes
Factor	*what* 2 #'s that multiply into a larger #	What are all the factors of 24? 1, 2, 3, 4, 6, 8, 12, 24 Think of factors in pairs. 1 is a factor of every number. Any number is the largest factor of itself.
Greatest Common Factor (GCF)	the largest factor between 2 numbers	The GCF of 24 and 8 is _____. The GCF of $16xy$ and $8x^2$ is _____. You can use your calculator to find the GCF of two constants: 1. Press the MATH button. 2. Scroll over using the right arrow key until NUM is highlighted. 3. Select #9 from the list, gcd(. 4. Type in your two numbers, separating them with a comma. Press ENTER.
Prime	a # that has only 2 distinct, positive factors.	True or False: -7 is prime. True or False: 1 is prime. 2 is the least (and only even) prime number. 1 and 0 are not prime.
Factorial (n!)	multiply # w/ all numbers before that $\frac{8!}{3!} = \frac{8\cdot7\cdot6\cdot5\cdot4\cdot\cancel{3}\cdot\cancel{2}\cdot\cancel{1}}{\cancel{3}\cdot\cancel{2}\cdot\cancel{1}}$ ↑cancel out↑	$6! = 6\cdot5\cdot4\cdot3\cdot2\cdot1$ ←doesn't need You can use your graphing calculator to find the factorial of a number: 1. Type in the number in front of the factorial sign. 2. Press the MATH button. 3. Using the right arrow key, scroll over until PRB is highlighted. 4. Select #4 on the list, "!" and hit ENTER.
Reciprocal	fractional opposite of a #	The reciprocal of 4 is $\frac{1}{4}$.
Order of Operations	P → 1 E → 2 M ⎤ 3 D ⎦ → Right to left A ⎤ 4 S ⎦	Evaluate the expression: $4 + |-5 + 3| - (3-6)^2$
Scientific Notation	# from 1-10 · 10^ → $3\cdot10^1$	Write the following in scientific notation: $103{,}000 = 1.03\cdot10^5$

↓ 30

www.bellcurves.com

Definitions | Rules Review

1. What is the smallest positive integer?

   ~~0~~ 1

2. How many positive, even digits are there between -5 and 10?

   4

   *0 & 10 aren't digits or are neutral

3. Is 5 a factor of 5?

   yes

4. What is the remainder when 17 is divided by 3?

   $\frac{17}{3} = 5\ r\ 3$

   2 is the remainder

5. Is 1 a prime number?

   No

6. The smallest positive multiple of 12 is

   12

7. The smallest positive factor of integer y is

   ~~0~~ or 1

8. What is the value of 7.5×10^{-4}?

   .00075

9. For what value(s) of p is $|7-p| - 1 < 0$?

   7   $p \ne 7$

10. What is the value of $3! + 8!$?

    $3 \cdot 2 \cdot 1 + 8 \cdot 7 \cdot 6 \cdot 5 \cdot 4 \cdot 3 \cdot 2 \cdot 1$

    $6 + 8!$

11. What is the least common multiple of $10xy$, $6y^2$, $12x$?

    No solution

    $60xy^2$

12. Let p and q be numbers such that $-p < q < p$. Which of the following must be true?

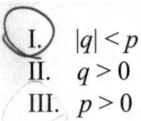

    I. $|q| < p$
    II. $q > 0$
    III. $p > 0$

    $-3 < J < 3$

Chapter 4

Substitution | Overview

On many SAT problems that seem like advanced algebra, you don't actually have to do any algebra at all! One of the best strategies for dealing with these questions is to simply replace the unknown values (variables) with real numbers.

There are three situations in which picking numbers will be helpful. The most common situation is when we see **variables in the answer choices.** When a problem contains variables in the answer choices, replace them with numbers and you will be able to solve it arithmetically instead of algebraically. Then compare the answer you get to the answer choices to see which matches.

Note: It is important that you plug the values you chose into ALL of the answer choices, just in case multiple choices work for a selected number. Should that be the case, select a new number, and just plug it into the choices that had worked the first time.

Let's try a practice question together:

> Michael is twice as old as Janet is and half as old as Tito is. If Janet is j years old, how old is Tito in terms of j?
>
> A) $\frac{j}{4}$
> B) $\frac{j}{2}$
> C) $2j$
> D) $4j$ *(circled)*

[Handwritten work: J = Janet = 8; M = 2j = 16; T = 2(2j) = 32 → (4j)]

What tells us that we can substitute our own numbers in the problem above? _____

Which variable should we substitute for? _____

What number should we choose and why? _____
_____

Using the number you chose, fill in the chart below for each of the people mentioned in the problem. How old is...

Janet (j):	Michael:	Tito:

Therefore, what is the numerical answer to the question asked above? _____

Compare the answer above to the choices by plugging in the value you chose for j. Which matches the numerical answer we got? Circle it above.

Rules for Picking Numbers
1. Pick easy numbers (usually integers): 2, 5, 10, etc.
2. Pick different numbers for different variables
3. Avoid 0, 1, and numbers in the question/answer choices.

Substitution | Overview

The second common situation in which we can pick numbers is when we are asked a **percent or fraction question with an unspecified starting value**.

Let's do a practice question together:

> If the liquid in a bucket, which is $\frac{3}{5}$ full, is emptied into an empty tub that is 8 times the size of the bucket, what percent of the tub will be filled?
>
> A) 0.48%
> B) 0.75%
> C) 4.8%
> D) 7.5%

What tells us that we can subsitute our own numbers in the problem above? _____

Notice that in this problem there are no variables to substitute for. In questions like this, we instead want to substitute for the starting amount (or full amount) that is not given. It is especially important to choose numbers that will be easy to work with for this type of substitution.

What might be a good number to choose here and why? _____

_____

What does that number represent in the problem? _____

So if the bucket is $\frac{3}{5}$ full, how much water is in it? _____

If the new bucket is 8 times the size of the original one, how large is that bucket? _____

Does the amount of liquid that we have change when we dump it into the new bucket? _____

So when that liquid is dumped into the new bucket, what fraction of the new bucket is full? _____

The final step is to convert this fraction into a percent:

Circle the correct answer above.

Chapter 4

$E-E=E$
$E-O=O$
$E+E=E$
$E+O=O$
$O+O=E$

$E \cdot E = E$
$E \cdot O = E$
$O \cdot O = O$

Substitution | Overview

The final common situation in which we can pick numbers is when we are given **"rules" about an unknown quantity**. Often, these have the words "must" or "could" in the question. It may take more than one set of substitution numbers to determine which answer is correct.

Let's do a practice question together:

> Which of the following statements must be true about odd and/or even numbers?
> A) The quotient of two even numbers is even. → division
> B) The product of three odd numbers is even.
> C) The sum of two even numbers is odd.
> D) The sum of an odd number and an even number is odd

What tells us that we can subsitute our own numbers in the problem above? _____

What is the given "rule?" _____

What might be a good number to choose here and why? _____
_____

Plug the number you just chose into each answer choice and eliminate any that does not work:

A) _____

B) _____

C) _____

D) _____

Since more than one option worked, what do we do? _____
_____

A) _____

B) _____

C) _____

D) _____

Circle the correct answer choice above.

www.bellcurves.com

Plugging In | Overview

Sometimes you may not be able to substitute your own number into a question. However, you may be able to plug one of the answer choices directly into the question. To decide whether or not a question is a good candidate for this strategy, ask yourself, "What do these answer choices represent in the question, and can I plug them in anywhere that will help me work backwards?"

This is a great strategy when the answers are numbers instead of variables and the question asks you to find a single unknown quantity, represented as a variable or as a "how much" or "how many" question. Because the answer choices given to you will always be in ascending or descending order, when plugging these in, start with either choice B or C and then move up or down from there as needed.

Here's an example: $S = x$ $B = 2x + 150$

> Barbara and Sharon share an apartment that has a monthly rent of $1,200. If Barbara pays $150 more than twice the amount that Sharon pays, how much does Barbara pay?
> A) $900
> B) $850
> C) $700
> D) $650

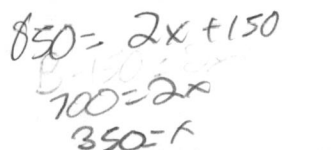

$850 = 2x + 150$
$700 = 2x$
$350 = x$

What do the answer choices represent in the problem above? _____

Let's start with answer choice C:

    C) Barbara = $700

        If Barbara pays $150 more than twice the amount Sharon pays, then Sharon would pay _____.

        Therefore, together they would be paying _____.

        Does that work? Why or why not? _____

So what should we try next? (Work out the calculations below) _____

1

A professional baseball player has a bonus structure built into his contract. He earns $235.60 each time he hits a homerun and $98.70 each time he hits a double. Which of the following expressions represents the amount of the bonus, in dollars, that the baseball player earns if he hits h homeruns and d doubles in a season?

A) $235.60h + 98.70d$
B) $(235.60 + 98.70)hd$
C) $235.60d + 98.70h$
D) $(235.60 + 98.70)(h + d)$

$235.6h + 98.7d$

2

$$s = 16.13 + 2.29t$$

The speed at which water flows downhill depends on the air temperature. The function above shows the relationship between s, the speed of the water, in centimeters per second, and t, the air temperature, in degrees Fahrenheit (°F).

Which of the following expresses the air temperature in terms of the speed of the water?

A) $t = \dfrac{s + 16.13}{2.29}$
B) $t = \dfrac{s - 16.13}{2.29}$
C) $t = \dfrac{2.29}{s + 16.13}$
D) $t = \dfrac{2.29}{s - 16.13}$

$t = \dfrac{16.13 - s}{2.29}$

3

Which of the following values is a solution of the inequality $10x + 2 < 3x - 12$?

A) -3
B) -2
C) -1
D) 0

$-8 < -15$

$-18 < -18$

$-6 - 12 = -18$

4

Luisa bought a stereo system at a store that gave a 30 percent discount off the original price. The total amount that she paid was d dollars, which included a 6 percent sales tax on the discounted price. Which of the following represents the original price of the stereo system in terms of d?

A) $\dfrac{0.76}{d}$
B) $\dfrac{d}{(1 - 0.30)(1 + 0.06)}$ ← answer
C) $\dfrac{d}{(1 - 0.06)(1 + 0.30)}$
D) $0.76d$

$d = x + 6\%$

HW = 7/9

5

A toll booth operator collects $2.25 each time a car passes through the toll. He began the day with d dollars, and did not spend any money. If he ended the day with a total of $128.25 after allowing 19 cars through the toll, what is the value of d?

A) $0
B) $38.00
C) $85.50
D) Cannot be determined from the information given.

6

On Tuesday morning, Giselle did s sit-ups per minute for a total of 16 minutes, and Tommy did p pull-ups per minute for a total of 7 minutes. Which of the following represents the total number of sit-ups and pull-ups completed by Giselle and Tommy on Tuesday morning?

A) $23ps$
B) $23 + ps$
C) $16p + 7s$
D) $16s + 7p$

7

$$D = \frac{6sl^3}{t}$$

The distance a baseball travels off a bat is modeled by a function of s, the speed of the pitch hit in miles per hour, t, the air temperature in degrees Fahrenheit (°F) and l, the length of the bat used, in meters.

Which of the following expresses the length of the bat in terms of the distance a baseball hit traveled, the air temperature and speed of the pitch?

A) $l = \sqrt[3]{\dfrac{6st}{D}}$

B) $l = \sqrt[3]{\dfrac{Dt}{6s}}$

C) $l = 6Dst$

D) $l = \sqrt[3]{\dfrac{6Dst}{3}}$

Chapter 4

HW = 7/9

1

If $\dfrac{x^2-5}{2} = y$ and $y = 10$, what is the value of x if $x < 0$?

A) -5
B) -4
C) -2
D) -1

$\dfrac{x^2-5}{2} = 10$

$25 - 5 = \dfrac{20}{2} = 10$

2

$$y = \dfrac{\left(\dfrac{r}{3,600}\right)\left(\dfrac{r}{3,600}+1\right)^t}{\left(\dfrac{r}{3,600}+1\right)^t - 1} M$$

The formula above gives the yearly payment y needed to pay off a mortgage of M dollars at r percent yearly interest over t years. Which of the following gives M in terms of y, r, and t?

A) $M = \dfrac{\left(\dfrac{r}{3,600}\right)\left(\dfrac{r}{3,600}+1\right)^t}{\left(\dfrac{r}{3,600}+1\right)^t - 1} y$

B) $M = \dfrac{\left(\dfrac{r}{3,600}\right)\left(\dfrac{r}{3,600}-1\right)^t}{\left(\dfrac{r}{3,600}+1\right)^t + 1} y$

Answer C) $M = \dfrac{\left(\dfrac{r}{3,600}+1\right)^t - 1}{\left(\dfrac{r}{3,600}\right)\left(\dfrac{r}{3,600}+1\right)^t} y$

D) $M = \dfrac{yrt}{3,600}$

3

If $\dfrac{x}{y} = 4$, what is the value of $\dfrac{8y}{x}$?

A) 0.5
B) 2
C) 4
D) 32

$x = 16$
$y = 4$

$\dfrac{32}{16} = 2$

4

$2x + 6y = 14$
$12y - 7x = -16$

What is the solution (x, y) to the system of equations above?

A) (-1, 4)
B) (2, -5)
C) (4, 1)
D) (-3, -6)

$2x = 14 - 6y$
$x = 7 - 3y$

$12y - 7(7 - 3y) = -16$
$12y - 49 + 21y = -16$
$33y - 49 = -16 + 49$
$33y = 33$
$y = 1$

5

If $x - 2y = 6$, what is the value of $\dfrac{4^x}{16^y}$?

A) 2^{14}
B) 4^6
C) 16^{-3}
D) The value cannot be determined from the information given.

$x = 12$
$y = 3$

$\dfrac{4^{12}}{16^3} = \dfrac{19}{4}$

227

www.bellcurves.com

6

If $x > 5$, which of the following is equivalent to $\dfrac{1}{\dfrac{1}{x-5} - \dfrac{1}{2x+6}}$?

A) $\dfrac{x+11}{2x^2 - 4x - 30}$

B) $\dfrac{2x^2 - 4x - 30}{x + 11}$

C) $\dfrac{2x^2 - 4x - 30}{x - 1}$

D) $\dfrac{x - 1}{2x^2 - 4x - 30}$

7

$$25a^2b^2 + 60ab^3 + 36b^4$$

Which of the following is equivalent to the expression shown above?
A) $(5a^2b^2 + 6b^3)^2$
B) $(5ab + 6b^2)^2$
C) $(6ab + 5ab^2)^2$
D) $(25ab + 6b^2)^2$

8

$$c = 246 + 75.25w$$
$$s = 189 + 89.50w$$

In the equations above, c and s represent the cost, in dollars, of maintenance on a convertible and sedan, respectively, w weeks after the purchase of each car. What was the cost of the convertible maintenance when it was equal to the sedan maintenance?
A) $480
B) $502
C) $547
D) $680

9

$$\sqrt{3a^2 + 6 + 40} = -b$$

If $a < 0$ and $b = -7$ in the equation above, what is the value of a ?
A) -7
B) -5
C) -3
D) -1

Chapter 4

Fractions & Decimals | Overview

When **adding or subtracting** fractions there are three options:

1. Create a common denominator → add/subtract
2. Convert to decimals → divide $\frac{n}{d}$
3. Use your calculator

Example:

What is the value of $\frac{1}{8} + \frac{3}{5}$?

Creating a common denominator:

What is the common denominator of the terms above? _____

$$\frac{}{40} + \frac{}{40} = \frac{}{40}$$

Converting to decimals:

What is $\frac{1}{8}$ as a decimal? _____

What is $\frac{3}{5}$ as a decimal? _____

The sum of those two decimals is _____

Using your calculator (TI graphing calculator):

Using the parenthesis button to separate each fraction, enter the fractions (using the division sign to create the fraction bar):

$$(\tfrac{1}{8}) + (\tfrac{3}{5})$$

Press ENTER.

To convert the resulting decimal answer back to a fraction, press MATH and then select the first item from the drop down list, FRAC.

Press ENTER.

Fractions & Decimals | Overview

When **multiplying fractions**, multiply across the top (numerator × numerator) and across the bottom (denominator × denominator). Do not cross-multiply, but you can cross-reduce where appropriate.

To **reduce** fractions, find a factor common to the numerator and denominator. Reducing can be helpful when multiplying and dividing fractions.

Again, this can all be done on your calculator if a question like this comes up in the calculator section.

Example:

What is the value of $\dfrac{5}{33} \times \dfrac{22}{7}$? $= \dfrac{10}{21}$

When **dividing**, we flip the second fraction and then multiply just as we did above.

Example:

What is the value of $\dfrac{2}{21} \div \dfrac{5}{14}$?

$\dfrac{2}{21} \cdot \dfrac{14}{5} = \dfrac{4}{15}$

Chapter 4

Fractions & Decimals | Rules Review

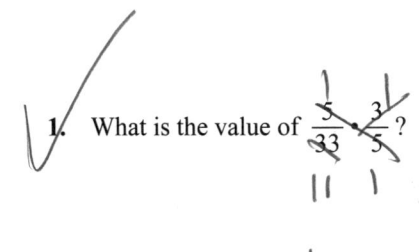

1. What is the value of $\frac{5}{33} \cdot \frac{3}{5}$?

$$\frac{\cancel{5}^1}{\cancel{33}_{11}} \cdot \frac{\cancel{3}^1}{\cancel{5}_1} = \frac{1}{11}$$

2. What is the value of $\frac{1}{9} - \frac{3}{5}$?

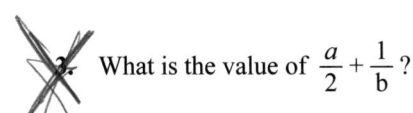

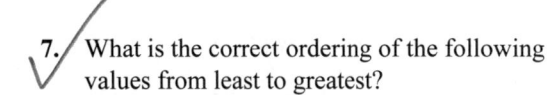

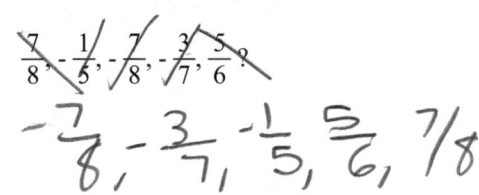

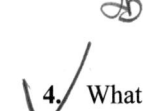

$$\frac{5}{45} - \frac{27}{45} = \frac{-22}{45}$$

$$\boxed{\frac{-22}{45}}$$

3. What is the value of $\frac{a}{2} + \frac{1}{b}$?

$$\frac{ab}{2b} + \frac{2}{2b} = \frac{ab+2}{2b}$$

4. What is the value of $\dfrac{\frac{1}{2} - \frac{1}{8}}{8}$?

$$\frac{4}{8} - \frac{1}{8} = \frac{3/8}{64/8}$$

$$\frac{3}{64}$$

$$\frac{\frac{3}{8}}{8} = \frac{3}{64}$$

$$\frac{3}{8} \cdot \frac{1}{8} = \boxed{\frac{3}{64}}$$

5. What is the value of $\frac{7}{8} \div \frac{14}{4}$?

$$\frac{7}{\cancel{8}_2} \cdot \frac{\cancel{4}^1}{\cancel{14}_2} = \frac{1}{4}$$

6. What is $(.4)(.8)$ as a fraction?

$$\frac{2}{5} \cdot \frac{4}{5} = \frac{8}{25}$$

7. What is the correct ordering of the following values from least to greatest?

$$-\frac{7}{8}, -\frac{1}{5}, -\frac{7}{8}, \frac{3}{7}, \frac{5}{6}$$

$$-\frac{7}{8}, -\frac{3}{7}, -\frac{1}{5}, \frac{5}{6}, \frac{7}{8}$$

8. What is the fraction $\frac{33}{121}$ in its most reduced form?

$$\frac{33}{121} \Rightarrow \frac{3}{11}$$

1, 3, 11, 33

$33/11 = 3$
$121/11 = 11$

231

www.bellcurves.com

Chapter 4

1

Larry's Lemonade Stand Sales

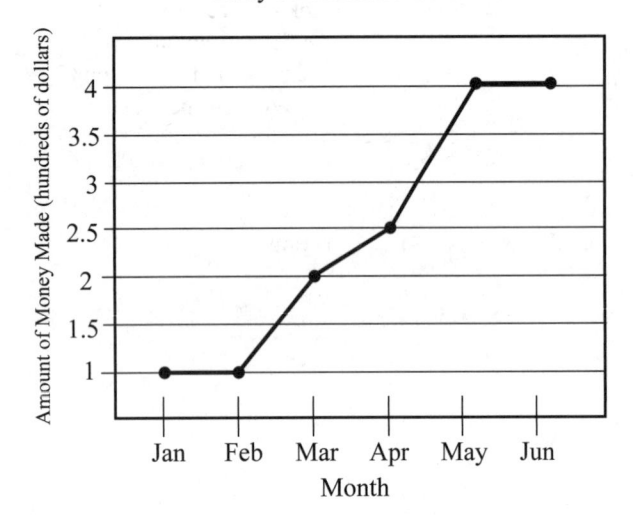

According to the line graph above, the amount of money that Larry made selling lemonade in April is what fraction of the amount he made in May?

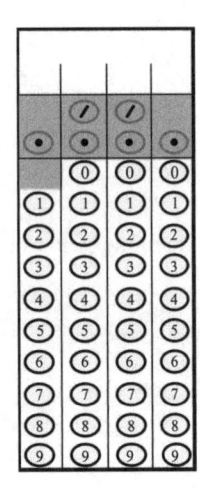

2

A ticket box office sells tickets to a rock concert for $24.50 each and to a wresting match for $17.25 each. The box office's revenue from selling a total of 121 tickets was $2,609.25. How many wrestling match tickets did the box office sell?

A) 35
B) 49
C) 63
D) 72

3

$$D = \frac{6sl^3}{t}$$

The distance a baseball travels off a bat is modeled by a function of s, the speed of the pitch hit in miles per hour, t, the air temperature in degrees Fahrenheit (°F) and l, the length of the bat used, in meters.

On Tuesday, Player A hit a ball that went 3.375 times the distance of one he hit on Monday. If the air temperature and speed of the pitch he saw remained the same, the length of the bat he used on Monday was what fraction of the length of the bat that he used on Tuesday?

A) $\frac{2}{5}$

B) $\frac{3}{7}$

C) $\frac{2}{3}$

D) $\frac{5}{8}$

4

If $\frac{3}{7}x = \frac{1}{9}$, what is the value of x?

A) $\frac{7}{27}$
B) $\frac{3}{63}$
C) $\frac{27}{7}$
D) $\frac{3}{16}$

5

The product of $\frac{a}{3} \times \frac{3}{4} \times \frac{4}{5} \times \frac{5}{6} \times \frac{6}{7} \times \frac{7}{8b}$ can be expressed as

A) $\frac{8b}{a}$
B) $\frac{a}{8b}$
C) $\frac{3ab}{2}$
D) $\frac{8a}{b}$

6

A subscription book service charges a monthly membership fee of $14.76, and includes a total of 5 books. For each additional book purchased, customers are charged $3.45 per book. For one month, Leslie paid a total of $80.31. How many books did Leslie get that month?

A) 17
B) 19
C) 21
D) 24

Chapter 4

1

The expression $\dfrac{7x+6}{x-2}$ is equivalent to which of the following?

A) $\dfrac{7+6}{2}$

B) $7 - \dfrac{8}{x-2}$

C) $7 + \dfrac{20}{x-2}$

D) $\dfrac{x+2}{7x-6}$

2

If $y + \dfrac{2}{5}y = \dfrac{4}{15} \times \dfrac{3}{4}$, what is the value of y?

3

A vineyard contains different types of grapevines. One-fourth of the number of white grapevines is one-tenth of the total number of grapevines in the vineyard. One-fifth of the number of red grapevines is one-fifteenth of the total number of grapevines in the vineyard. If there are 120 white grapevines in the vineyard, how many red grapevines are in the vineyard?

A) 20
B) 30
C) 100
D) 300

4

A one-meter-long wire is to be marked for cutting at intervals of fifths and thirds. How long is the shortest segment of the wire if the wire is cut at the marked intervals?

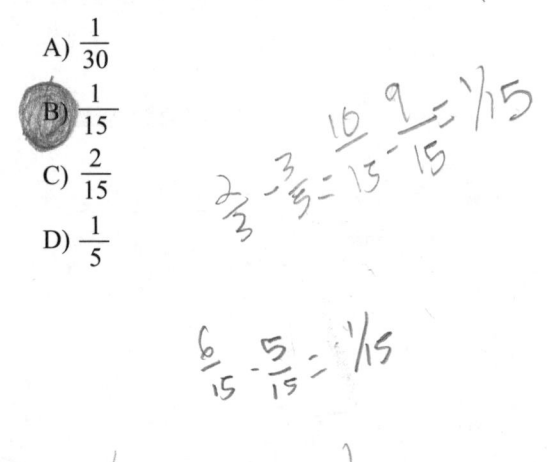

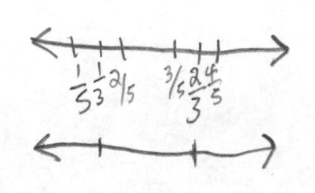

A) $\dfrac{1}{30}$

B) $\dfrac{1}{15}$

C) $\dfrac{2}{15}$

D) $\dfrac{1}{5}$

$\bar{5}r = 20$
$r = 100$

4b

PROBLEM SOLVING & DATA ANALYSIS:

RATIOS, RATES, PROPORTIONS, PERCENTS, SCATTERPLOTS, DATA ANALYSIS, MEASURES OF CENTER, DATA COLLECTION METHODS

Percents | Overview

Percent questions on the SAT are often multiple-step word problems. Therefore, it is essential to understand the basic building blocks and terminology related to percents before looking at more complex questions.

Example: 12 is what percent of 50?

Translate word for word:

When setting up a percent problem, think about slotting the information from the question into one of three possible equations. Any of these options will work; it is just a matter of which is easiest for you.

Option 1: $\text{Is} = \frac{\%}{100} \times \text{Of}$

In this option, "is" and "of" are taken directly from the words in the question. In the question above, "12 is". Therefore, 12, goes into the "is" slot. "What percent" indicates that we are looking to find the percent, which we can call variable x. Therefore, above the 100, we put an x. And then we see "of 50", so we can put 50 in the "of" slot.

$$12 = \frac{x}{100} \times 50$$

Option 2: $\text{Part} = \frac{\%}{100} \times \text{Whole}$

This option takes an understanding of which value in the equation is the part, and which is the whole. The percent will be denoted in the question as the percent. In the example above, we want to know what part of 50, 12 is. Therefore, 12 is the part, and 50 is the whole. When we set this particular equation up, we again use variable x for the percent, and we get the exact same answer as in Option 1.

⭐ Option 3: $\frac{\text{Part}}{\text{Whole}} = \frac{\%}{100}$

This is just a derivation of the equation above.

Sometimes questions will ask you to find the percent change that something experienced. To find this, use the formula below:

$$\frac{\text{New Value} - \text{Original Value}}{\text{Original Value}} \times 100 \qquad \frac{\text{New} - \text{old}}{\text{old}}$$

If the answer you get is positive, then it is a percent increase. If the value is negative, it is a percent decrease.

We will work with this formula more as we get into the practice questions.

$$\frac{Part}{Whole} = \frac{\%}{100}$$

Chapter 4

Percents | Overview

Percent problems often require multiple steps and may ask you to find either a percent increase or a percent decrease. Take a look at the example below:

> If a shirt normally priced at $30 has 20% deducted from its regular price, what is the new price?
> A) $6
> B) $14
> C) $16
> D) $24 *(circled)*

Handwritten work: $\frac{x}{30} = \frac{29}{100} \rightarrow \frac{x}{30} = \frac{1}{5} = \frac{x}{30} = \frac{6}{30}$

$30 - 6 = 24 = D$

$30 \times .8$

In order to find the new price, we must determine what 20% of the normal price is, then deduct that amount from the normal price.

Using the method you prefer from the previous page, find 20% of the regular price.

Once you have that amount, what should you do with it and why? _____

Therefore, the final sale price of the item is _____

This method will work everytime, but to save some time, you can calculate questions like this in one step.

If we take 20% of an item away from its original value, what percent are we left with? __80%__

Therefore, you can also solve for the sale price of something decreased by 20% by __× .8__

The same idea holds true for a percent increase. Take a look at the example below:

> If a shirt normally priced at $30 has a 7% sales tax added to the price, what is the price including tax?
> A) $31.07
> B) $32.10 *(circled)*
> C) $33.00
> D) $36.50

Handwritten work: $30 \times 1.07 = 32.1$

$\frac{x}{30} = \frac{7}{100} \rightarrow 210 = 100x$
$2.1 = x$
$+30$
32.1

If 7% sales tax is added to the item, what percent of the original item is the new cost? _____

Use the space below to calculate that percent of the original item:

237

www.bellcurves.com

Percents | Rules Review

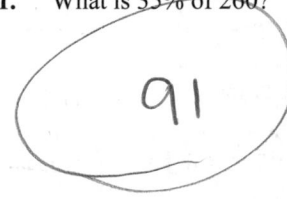

1. What is 35% of 260?

   91

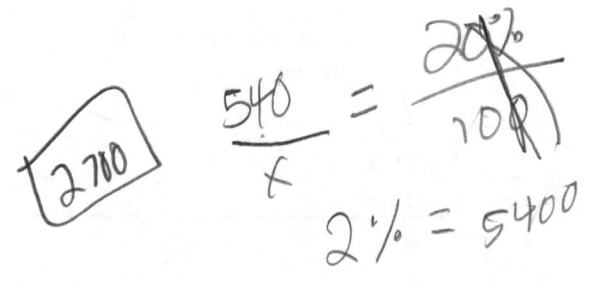

2. Twelve is what percent of 96?

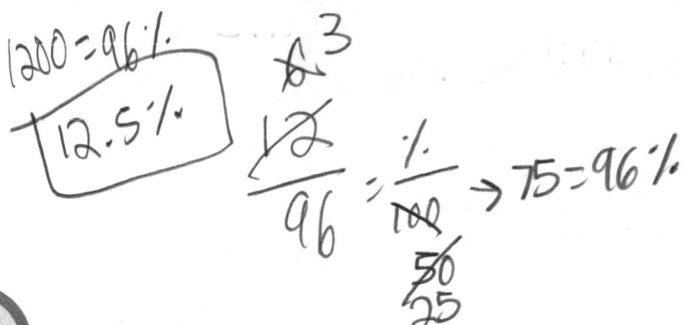

   $1200 = 96\%$
   12.5%

   $\dfrac{12}{96} = \dfrac{\%}{100} \rightarrow 75 = 96\%$

3. What percent of 75 is 15?

   $\dfrac{15}{75} = \dfrac{\%}{100} =$

   $75\% = 1500/75$

   20%

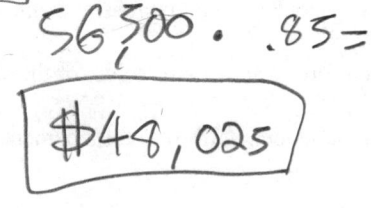

4. What is 25% of 25% of 25% of 32?

   $\dfrac{1}{4} \cdot \dfrac{1}{4} \cdot \dfrac{1}{4} \cdot 32$

   $\dfrac{1}{64} \cdot 32 = 50\%$

   0.5 → ½

5. Twenty percent of what number is 540?

   $\dfrac{540}{x} = \dfrac{20}{100}$

   $2\% = 5400$

   2700

6. If a stockbroker received a 52% bonus on his yearly $32,000 salary, what was his gross income after his bonus?

   $32,000 \cdot 1.52 =$

   $48,640

7. If a car, regularly priced at $56,500 is on sale for 15% off, what is the new price of the car?

   85%

   $56,500 \cdot .85 =$

   $48,025

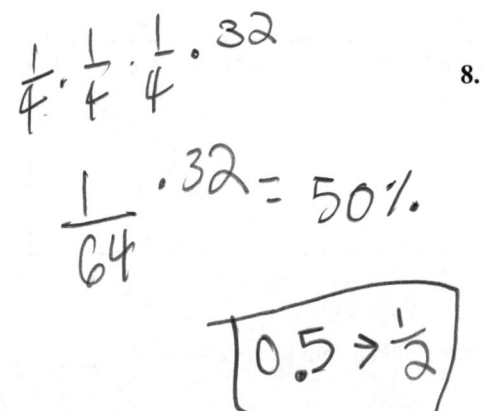

8. Julia can do 55 sit-ups in one minute in September. In June, she is able to do 66 sit-ups in one minute. By what percent did Julia's sit-up total increase?

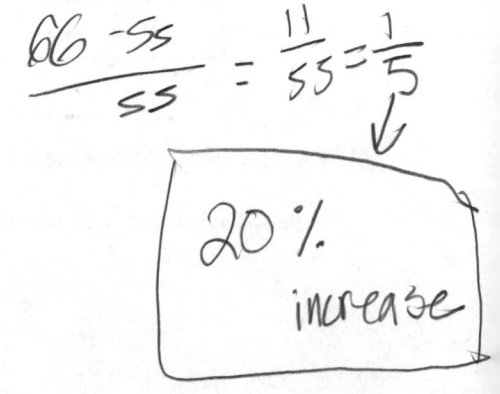

   $\dfrac{66-55}{55} = \dfrac{11}{55} = \dfrac{1}{5}$

   20% increase

Chapter 4

lol what oops?

1

The amount of money that an office supply company makes is directly proportional to the number of fax machines it sells. The company earns a total of $1,260 when it sells 18 fax machines.

70 per machine

The company spends 57% of its revenue on rent and employee salaries. The remaining portion of the revenue is the company's profit. What is the company's profit when it sells 18 fax machines?
A) $507.60
B) $541.80
C) $665.70
D) $718.20

1,260.

2

The combined weights of the women on the female wrestling team total 1,248 pounds, which is 36% less than the combined weights of the men on the male wrestling team. Which of the following best approximates the combined weights of the men on the male wrestling team?
A) 450
B) 800
C) 1,950
D) 2,050

$$\frac{1,248}{x} = \frac{36\%}{100} =$$

$$36\% =$$

3   CONFUSED

The sum of three integers is 1,357. The largest of the three numbers is 30% larger than the sum of the other two. What is the value of the largest number?
A) 486
B) 590
C) 688
D) 767

$$\frac{1}{3} = \frac{30\%}{100}$$

$$100 = 90\%$$

1357

$$\frac{688}{1357} = \frac{30\%}{100} = 100x =$$

4

Jessica surveyed a random sample of shoppers at the mall to determine whether they preferred shopping for clothing or electronics. Of the 360 shoppers surveyed, 52.5% preferred shopping for clothing. Based on this information, about how many of the total 1,025 shoppers who entered the mall that day preferred shopping for electronics?
A) 485
B) 515
C) 540
D) 600

189/360

47.5

47.5%

$$\frac{171}{360} = \frac{}{1025}$$

$$\frac{1025}{360} = 2.8472$$

× 171

486.815

239

www.bellcurves.com

5

Bacteria Present in Water

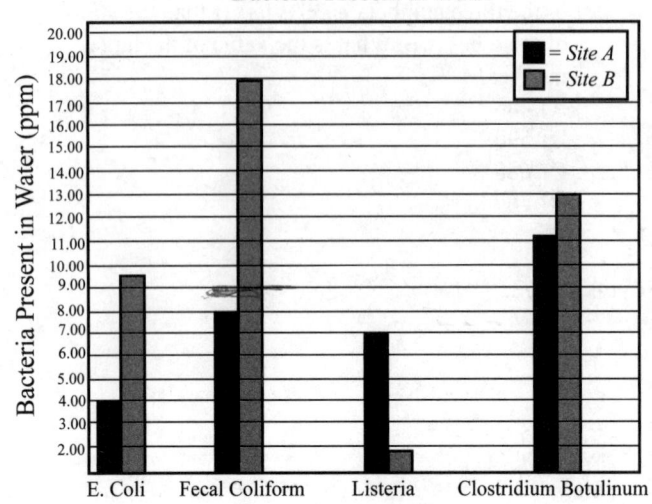

The bar graph above shows the bacteria present (in parts per million) in water at Sites A and B in 2014.

Of the following, which best approximates the percent decrease in the Fecal Coliform present from Site B to Site A?
A) 44%
B) 55%
C) 88%
D) 125%

6

The chart below shows the results of a survey conducted at Bramport Middle School.

Grade	Hair Color			
	Brown	Blonde	Red	Total
5	123	70	16	209
6	79	62	11	152
7	106	58	22	186
8	112	84	30	226
Total	420	274	79	773

Which of the following categories accounts for approximately 11 percent of all survey respondents?
A) 6th graders with red hair
B) 7th graders with blonde hair
C) 8th graders with blonde hair
D) 5th graders with brown hair

Chapter 4

Ratios & Proportions | Overview

Ratios and proportions are similar to one another and are similar to fractions. **Ratios** can be represented in three equivalent ways:

1. With words   A ratio of 4 to 5.

2. As "fractions" $\dfrac{4}{5}$

3. With a colon   4 : 5

For ratios with more than two parts, set up a grid. Take a look at the example below:

> A certain store carries three different items - *A*, *B* and *C* - in a ratio of 3 : 4 : 8. It has a total of 60 items in its inventory. How many of Item *C* does the store have in inventory?

To answer questions like these, we can set up a grid similar to the one below:

	Item *A*	Item *B*	Item *C*	Total
Ratio Values	3	4	8	√5
Multiplier	4	4	4	4
Real Values	12	16	32	60

Once you set up your grid, your next step is to fill it in based on the information given in the question. Let's fill in the one above with the information from this problem.

Now locate the column in which we have information from both categories and circle it. We can use this to find the multiplier, or the number we must multiply the ratio value by in order to reach the real value. The multiplier will be the same for each of the columns. Find the multiplier above and fill in the boxes in that row.

How would you use this to solve the question? _____

_____

www.bellcurves.com

Chapter 4

Ratios & Proportions | Overview

Proportions are pairs of ratios set across an equal sign. To solve a proportion, set up equal fractions and solve for the missing piece. Be sure to maintain consistency with the same unit on the top of each fraction and the same unit on the bottom of each fraction.

Let's take a look at an example:

> If it takes 5 bottles to hold a total of 30 gallons of juice, how many bottles will it take to hold 180 gallons of juice?

Since the ratio only has two parts, we can set up a proportion without needing to make a chart like the one on the previous page.

Fill in the proportion below, making sure to keep the same unit across the denominators and across the numerators, though it does not actually matter which unit you put first.

$$\underline{\quad 5:30 \quad} = \underline{\quad x:180 \quad}$$

Now that the proportion is set up, how do we go about solving for the missing value? __30__

$$\frac{1}{6} = \frac{x}{180}$$
$$6x = 180$$
$$x = 30$$

SAT-R Workbook v. 1.5

Ratios & Proportions | Overview

Questions on the SAT may utilize the terminology "directly proportional" or "inversely proportional."

Items that are **directly proportional** increase or decrease at the same rate as one another. For example, the number of hours a babysitter works and the amount of money she makes are directly proportional because as the babysitter works more hours, she earns more money at the same rate.

Items that are **inversely proportional** still vary at the same rate, but do so in opposite directions. As one variable increases, the other decreases at the same rate, and vice versa. For example, the number of miles a person drives and the amount of gas remaining in the tank are inversely proportional. As a person drives more miles, the amount of gas remaining will decrease.

To work with questions that ask about directly or inversely proportional items, we must memorize two equations:

The Equation of Direct Proportionality:

$$y = kx$$

where y represents one quantity (such as the amount of money a babysitter makes), x represents the other quantity (such as the number of hours the babysitter works) and k represents the constant of proportionality (the rate at which these quantities increase or decrease).

For example, if a babysitter works for a total of 12 hours, and we are told that the constant of proportionality is equal to 8, we can find out the total amount that the babysitter makes by plugging those numbers into the given equation:

$$y = (8)(12)$$

Therefore, the babysitter makes $96 when she works for a total of 12 hours.

The Equation of Inverse Proportionality:

$$y = \frac{k}{x}$$

where y represents one quantity (such as the number of miles driven), x represents the other quantity (such as the amount of gas in the tank) and k represents the constant of proportionality (or the rate at which these quantities increase or decrease).

Let's take a look at an example:

The number of miles driven in a car varies inversely with the amount of gas left in the car's tank. If a car that has been driven 90 miles has a total of 12 gallons remaining in the tank, how many gallons will be left in the tank if the car is driven 108 miles?

Step 1: Set up the equation and solve for the constant of proportionality.

$$90 = \frac{k}{12}$$

$$k = 1080$$

Step 2: Use that constant of proportionality to set up another equation and solve for the missing variable.

$$108 = \frac{1080}{x}$$

There would be 10 gallons of gas remaining in the tank.

www.bellcurves.com

Chapter 4

Ratios & Proportions | Rules Review

1. A ratio of 4 : 8 is the same as a ratio of

$$1:2$$

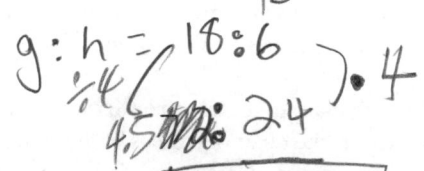

2. The ratio of $b : c$ is 2 : 7 and $b = 32$. What is the value of c?

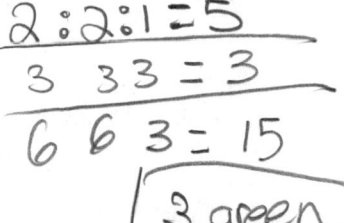

$$2:7 = 32:\boxed{112}$$

$$\frac{32}{2} = 16 \qquad 7 \cdot 16 =$$

3. What is the ratio of m to n if $13n = 39m$?

$$m:n = 39m:13n$$

$$\boxed{3:1 = m:n}$$

4. Every inch on a particular map represents 20 miles. Therefore, a distance of 170 miles is represented by how many inches on the map?

$$1:20 = 8.5:170$$

$$\boxed{8.5 \text{ in}}$$

5. Variables g and h vary inversely. When g is equal to 18, h is equal to 6. What is the value of g when h is equal to 24?

$$g:h = 18:6$$

$$\frac{18}{4} = 4.5 \qquad \boxed{g = 4.5}$$

6. If there are a total of 15 marbles in a bag in a ratio of 2 blue to 2 red to 1 green, how many green marbles are in the bag?

$$2:2:1 = 5$$
$$3 \quad 3 \quad 3 = 3$$
$$6 \quad 6 \quad 3 = 15$$

$$\boxed{3 \text{ green}}$$

7. The ratio of males to females at an event is 5 to 3. If 39 females are at the event, how many people are at the event?

$$5:3 = x:39$$

$$65 + 39 = \boxed{104 \text{ people}}$$
$$\uparrow \qquad \uparrow$$
$$m \qquad f$$

8. In a box with 156 markers, there is a ratio of 2 : 3 : 1 among the green, blue, and orange markers, respectively. How many green markers are in the box?

G	B	O	Total
2	3	1	6
26	26	26	26
52	78	26	156

$$\boxed{52 \text{ markers}}$$

244

SAT-R Workbook v. 1.5

Chapter 4

1

If x and y are directly proportional, and when $y = 96$, $x = 12$, what is the value of x when y is equal to 152?
A) 8
B) 14
C) 19
D) 23

2

The table below lists the average attendance at five conferences across the United States from 2009 to 2012.

	Year			
Conference	2009	2010	2011	2012
Farmers United	42,320	50,008	38,506	10,507
AutoClub USA	12,590	23,480	48,009	30,565
Educational Innovations	14,335	35,686	22,817	28,995
Artistic Expressions	68,900	74,578	62,304	59,002
Coding for the Future	13,568	39,903	21,445	54,257

Of the following, which conference has a ratio of its 2009 attendance to its 2012 attendance that is closest to the ratio of AutoClub USA's attendance in 2009 to its attendance in 2011?
A) Farmers United
B) Educational Innovations
C) Artistic Expressions
D) Coding for the Future

3

Callie can bake at least 22 sheets and at most 30 sheets of cookies per day. Each sheet contains 14 cookies. Based on this information, what is a possible number of cookies that Callie could bake in 2 weeks, if she works Monday through Friday?

4

A gardener plants tulips each spring. In one row, a total of 460 of the 1,200 bulbs bloomed. If the remaining tulips in the garden bloom at the same rate, about how many tulips out of the total 8,400 in the garden will bloom?
A) 209
B) 756
C) 2,900
D) 3,220

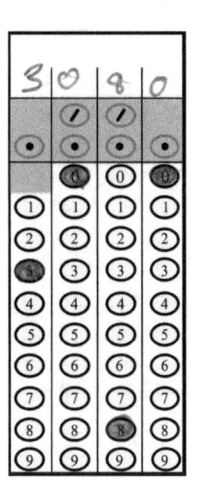

245

www.bellcurves.com

5

A scout estimates that a wide receiver sprints at a speed of 8.6 feet per second. According to the scout's estimate, how many feet would he expect the wide receiver to run in 25 seconds?

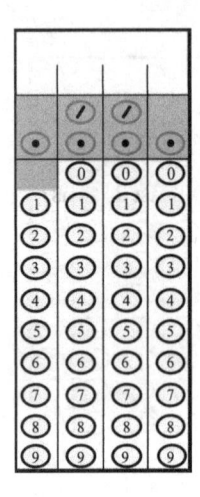

7

A contractor is estimating how many kilometers of PVC piping will be needed in the construction of a new apartment building. One kilometer of piping is needed to construct four apartments. If each apartment is identical in size and each is 390 square feet, approximately how many square feet could 8 kilometers of piping be used to construct?
A) 195
B) 780
C) 9,200
D) 12,500

6

1 kiloliter = 1,000 liters

1 deciliter = 0.1 liters

A water tank holds a total of 3 kiloliters of water. Based on the information given above, how many 1-deciliter bottles could be filled with the water in the tank, if the tank is filled to capacity?
A) 300
B) 3,000
C) 30,000
D) 300,000

8

The amount of money that an office supply company makes is directly proportional to the number of fax machines it sells. The company earns a total of $1,260 when it sells 18 fax machines.

How much money will the company make when it sells 306 fax machines?
A) $14,240
B) $18,960
C) $21,420
D) $32,480

Averages (Arithmetic Mean) | Overview

The term "arithmetic mean" often appears in average problems and means the same thing as "average." Use the Average T (below) to express the relationship between the parts of an average:

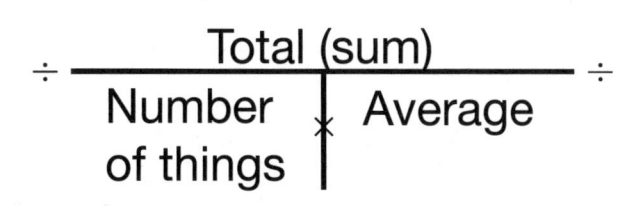

$$\div \frac{\text{Total (sum)}}{\text{Number of things} \quad | \quad \text{Average}} \div$$

Remember: To find the average of multiple averages, make a separate Average T for each set of information given and one for the combined average.

Let's work through a sample problem together:

> The average cost of 8 items is $40. Two more items are added, bringing the total cost of all 10 items to $370. What is the average cost of the last 2 items?
> A) $25
> B) $30
> C) $37
> D) $40

Remember that in order to work with multiple averages in the same question, we must set up separate Average T's. Let's start by setting up the Average T for the 8 items first:

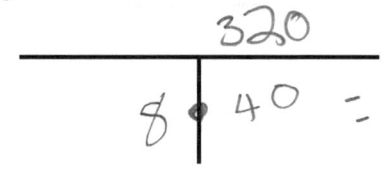

$$\frac{320}{8 \mid 40}$$

Now set up an Average T with the information we have regarding all 10 items.

$$\frac{370}{10 \mid 37}$$

How can we use this information to find the average of just the final 2 items?

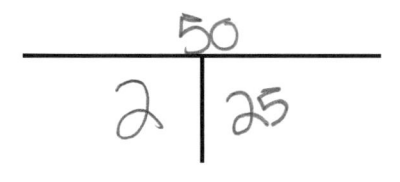

$$\frac{50}{2 \mid 25}$$

Chapter 4

Rates & Work | Overview

To do SAT word problems dealing with rates or work, find the relevant information in the problem and use the system below:

1. Use the Rate T (which is just a modified Average T, since rate is an average) to express the relationship between the parts:

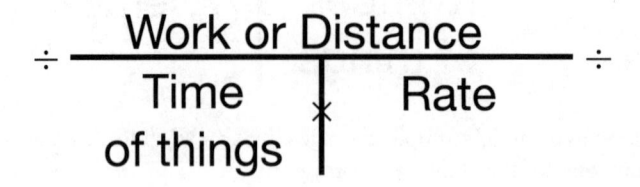

$$\div \frac{\text{Work or Distance}}{\text{Time} \quad \text{Rate}} \div$$
$$\text{of things}$$

2. For each new person or thing given, create a new chart.

3. If two people or things are *working together* (to complete a job or travel a distance), *add* their rates.

> John walks 3 miles in 30 minutes. How many minutes will it take him to walk 4.5 miles?
> A) 15
> B) 20
> C) 35
> D) 45

Let's start by creating a Rate T for John using the given information.

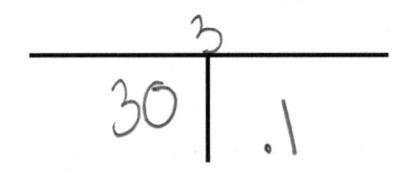

$$\frac{3}{30 \mid .1}$$

Using this, we can create a Rate T to solve for the time it would take him to walk 4.5 miles.

$$\frac{4.5}{45 \mid .1}$$

Averages, Rates, & Work | Rules Review

1. If the average (arithmetic mean) of eight numbers is 27, what is the sum of those numbers?

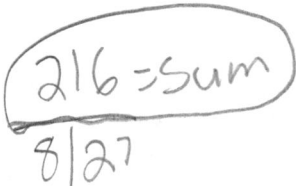

    216 = sum
    8 | 27

2. What is twice the sum of seven numbers with an average (arithmetic mean) of 13?

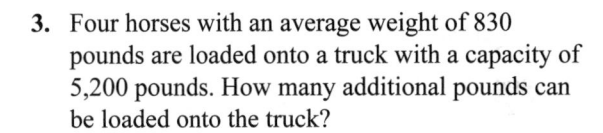

3. Four horses with an average weight of 830 pounds are loaded onto a truck with a capacity of 5,200 pounds. How many additional pounds can be loaded onto the truck?

4. If a student had an average (arithmetic mean) of 100 on his first 6 tests and a score of 85 on his next test, what will his new average be, to the nearest tenth?

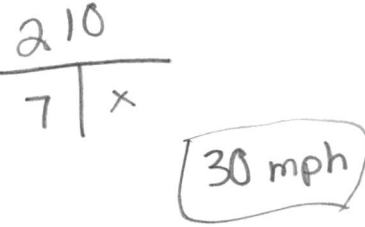

5. If Julian biked 210 miles in 7 hours, at what rate was he biking?

    210 / 7 × x

    30 mph

6. If Wilson paints 5 walls per hour, how many minutes will it take him to complete the 18 walls in his house?

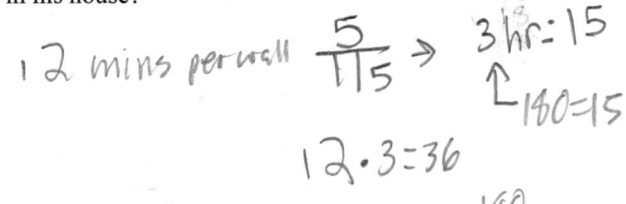

    12 mins per wall   5/15 → 3 hr = 15
                                   180 = 15
    12 · 3 = 36
                            180
                           + 36
    216 minutes   216

7. Jack climbs a hill in 5 hours at a rate of 2 miles an hour. If Jill climbs the same hill in 4 hours, what is her climbing rate?

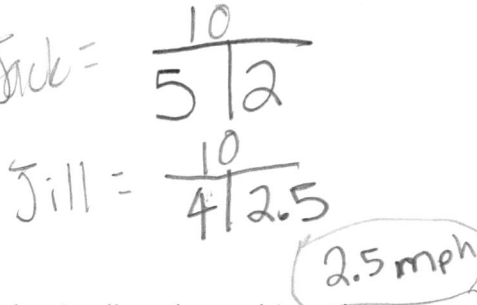

    Jack = 10 / 5 | 2
    Jill = 10 / 4 | 2.5

    2.5 mph

8. If Toya paints 5 walls per hour and Ava paints 3 walls per hour, working together, each at her respective pace, how many walls can they paint in 6 hours?

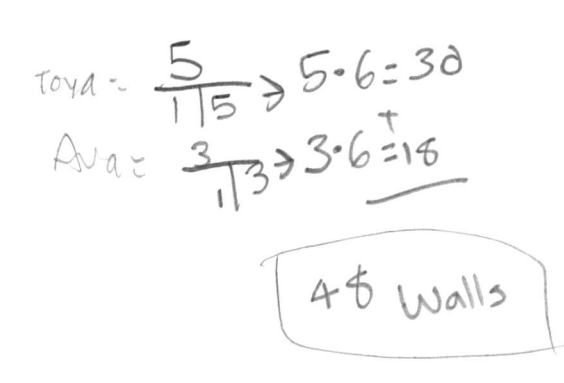

    Toya = 5/15 → 5·6 = 30
    Ava = 3/13 → 3·6 = 18

    48 walls

Chapter 4

1

The histogram below shows the grades on Mr. Simpson's social studies midterm.

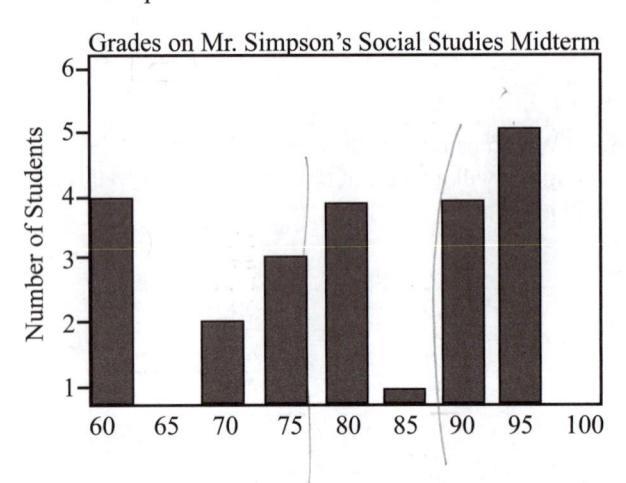

Grades on Mr. Simpson's Social Studies Midterm

Which of the following represents the approximate average (arithmetic mean) of the scores?

A) 70
B) 75
C) 80
D) 90

2

Sabrina can type 752 words in 10.8 seconds. If she continues to type at this rate, which of the following is closest to the number of words she will type in 6 minutes?

A) 11,750
B) 13.5003
C) 19,000
D) 25,000

3

Phillip is planning to travel from New York to Florida. The table below shows information about the route, the amount of time Phillip plans to travel each day, and the speed at which he travels.

Number of exits along the route	168
Number of highway miles	1,184
Number of tolls along the route	8
Number of hours per day Phillip plans to travel	6
Number of side-street miles	462
Phillip's average highway speed (miles per hour)	74
Phillip's average side-street speed (miles per hour)	33

If Phillip travels at the rates given in the table, which of the following is closest to the number of days it would take Phillip to travel the entire route?

A) 3
B) 5
C) 7
D) 8

4

The number of sprockets produced by a factory in one year is 4,665,600. It takes the factory five seconds to produce a sprocket. If the factory is open a full 24 hours on the day it is open, how many days of the year is the factory open?

A) 240
B) 256
C) 270
D) 289

5

Two beakers filled with equal amounts of aqueous solutions A and B were treated with a chemical to turn the solutions into solids. A scientist calculated the percentage of the liquid remaining in each beaker at 10 minute intervals. The data is displayed in the graph below.

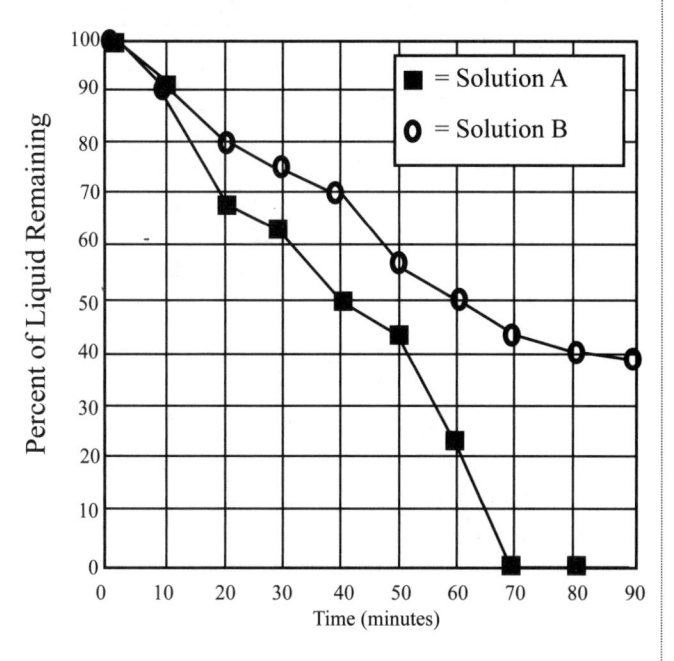

Which of the following statements correctly compares the average rates at which the two solutions become solid?

A) In every 10 minute interval, the magnitude of the rate of change of Solution A is greater than that of Solution B.
B) In every 10 minute interval, the magnitude of the rate of change of Solution B is greater than that of Solution A.
C) In the intervals from 10 to 20 minutes and from 50 to 60 minutes, the magnitude of the rate of change of Solution A is greater than that of Solution B.
D) In the intervals from 30 to 40 minutes and from 60 to 70 minutes, the magnitude of the rate of change of Solution B is greater than that of Solution A.

6

The table below shows the number of miles run by 14 professional sprinters in the year 2014.

Sprinter	Number of Miles
Savage	128
Dash	209
Silver	72
Cotter	211
Perlman	157
Daly	129
Barry	285
Lew	306
Schwartz	323
Oliver	245
McCurry	119
Luckert	409
Smith	292
Wright	311

According to the table, what was the mean number of miles run by each professional sprinter in 2014? (Round your answer to the nearest mile.)

7

Beatriz takes a total of 25 quizzes, scored 0 to 70 inclusive, in her calculus class. For her first 12 quizzes she receives an average (arithmetic mean) score of 57. What is the lowest score she can receive on her 13th quiz and still be able to have an average of a 63 on her 25 quizzes?

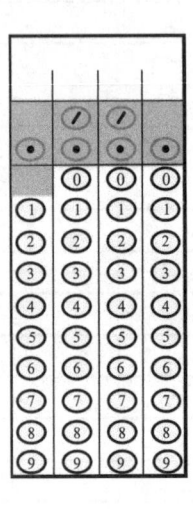

8

The table below lists the average attendance at five conferences across the United States from 2009 to 2012.

	Year			
Conference	2009	2010	2011	2012
Farmers United	42,320	50,008	38,506	10,507
AutoClub USA	12,590	23,480	48,009	30,565
Educational Innovations	14,335	35,686	22,817	28,995
Artistic Expressions	68,900	74,578	62,304	59,002
Coding for the Future	13,568	39,903	21,445	54,257

Which of the following best approximates the average rate of change in the attendance at the Farmers United Conference from 2009 to 2012?
A) Decreases by 4 people per year
B) Decreases by 10,600 people per year
C) Decreases by 15,800 people per year
D) Decreases by 31,000 people per year

Chapter 4

Measures Of Center | Overview

The SAT will test other measures of center in addition to the mean. The most common of these are listed below:

Mode – The number that appears most often in a set of numbers

    Set *A* includes: 1 1 3 4 4 4 6 7 10 11   The **mode** of Set *A* is ____4____.

Median – The middle of a set of numbers (after the numbers are put in consecutive order). To find the median of a set, first put the numbers in ascending order. The median of a set with an *odd* number of elements is the middle number. The median of a set with an *even* number of element is the average (arithmetic mean) of the two middle numbers.

    Set *A* includes: 1̶ 1̶ 3̶ 4̶ 4̶ 6̶ 6̶ 7̶ 1̶0̶ 1̶1̶ (5 written above)   The **median** of Set *A* is ____5____.

Range – The difference between the largest element in a set and the smallest element in the set. If the values of all the elements in a set increase or decrease by the same amount, the range does NOT change.

    Set *A* includes: 1 1 3 4 4 4 6 7 10 11   The **range** of Set *A* is ____10____.

                                        11−1=10

Standard Deviation – The Standard Deviation (SD) is a measure of how spread-out numbers in a set are. The more spread-apart the data, the higher the deviation. If the values of all the elements in a set increase or decrease by the same amount, the SD does NOT change.

    Ex: Set *B* includes: 1 3 4 4

To find the SD of a set of numbers, follow the three steps below:

1. Find the mean of the all of data points.

    The mean of Set *B* above is 3

2. Find the variance by finding the average of the squared distance of each data point from the mean.

    1 is a distance of 2 from the mean. 2 squared equals 4.
    3 is a distance of 0 from the mean. 0 squared equals 0.
    4 is a distance of 1 from the mean. 1 squared equals 1.

$$\frac{4+0+1+1}{4} = 1.5$$

3. Take the square root of the variance.

    The SD equals approximately 1.22.

Outlier – A value that is significantly smaller or larger than most of the other values in a data set.

253

www.bellcurves.com

Chapter 4

Measures Of Center | Rules Review

Set Q: {6, 2, 9, 14, 11, 10}

1. What is the median and mean of Set Q?

Median = 9.5
Mean = 8.6

2, 6, 9, 10, 11, 14

2. A group of students took a quiz. Six students scored a 4; five students scored a 5; eight students scored a 7; two students scored a 9, and one student scored a 10. What is the mode of the set of quiz scores for the class?

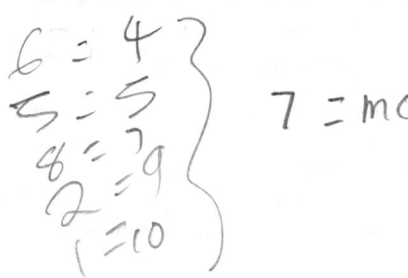

most frequent

6 = 4
5 = 5
8 = 7
2 = 9
1 = 10

7 = mode

Set N: {12, 3, 7, 5, x, 9}

3. If the median of Set N is 8, the value of x must be what?

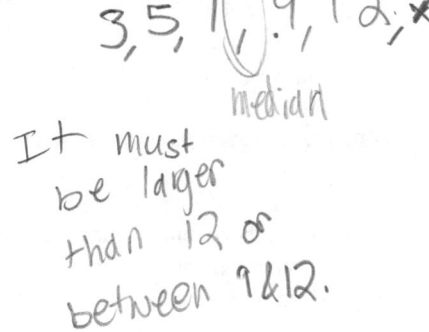

3, 5, 7, 9, 12, x
median

It must be larger than 12 or between 9 & 12.

x ≥ 9

Set N: {12, 3, 7, 5, x, 9}
Set M: {5, 3, 5, 7, 8}

4. If the mode of Set N is 4 greater than the mode of Set M, the value of x must be

9 = x

5. Of the 100 employees at a certain company, each of the 15 most experienced employees earned a salary of $41,000, and each of the 51 least experienced employees earned a salary of $21,000. If the other employees each earned a salary of $39,000, what was the median salary for the company?

15 = 41,000
51 = 21,000
34 = 39,000

39,000   21,000

Set A: {12, 11, 16, 11, 5, 17, 9}

6. If all of the elements in Set A were to be increased by 2, which of the following would not increase?

I. Median ≤ 11
II. Mode = 11
III. Range
IV. Mean
V. Standard Deviation

12 - 9 = 3
14 - 11 = 3

Chapter 4

1

A survey of the value of cars in a parking lot was taken, and it was found that the mean car value was $23,500 and the median car value was $27,900. Which of the following situations could explain the difference between the mean and median car values in the parking lot?

A) The cars have values that are close to one another.
B) There are a few cars that are valued much lower than the rest.
C) There are a few cars that are valued much higher than the rest.
D) Many of the cars are valued between $23,500 and $27,900.

2

A census taker interviewed 450 families at random from each of three towns. He asked each family how many people live the household. The results are shown in the table below.

Household Numbers Survey

Number in Household	Silvertown	Goldville	Copperton
1	25	80	50
2	75	140	60
3	115	30	190
4	160	80	40
5	30	60	80
6	45	60	30

There are a total of 1,800 residents in Silvertown, 2,220 residents in Goldville and 1,500 residents in Copperton.

What is the median number of household members for all the families surveyed?
A) 2
B) 3
C) 3.5
D) 4

3

The tables below give the distribution of test scores for Student A and Student B over the same 23 tests from September through June.

Student A

Test Score	Frequency
100	2
95	15
90	1
85	3
80	2

Student B

Test Score	Frequency
100	6
95	3
90	1
85	3
80	4
75	6

Which of the following is true about the data shown for these 23 tests?
A) The standard deviation of the test scores for Student A is larger.
B) The standard deviation of the test scores for Student B is larger.
C) The standard deviation of test scores for Student A is the same as that of Student B.
D) The standard deviation of test scores for these students cannot be calculated with the data provided.

4

The table below lists the weights, to the nearest pound, of a random sample of 30 African elephants.

Weights of African Elephants (in pounds)				
4,800	4,900	4,900	5,010	5,010
5,010	5,200	5,350	5,400	5,400
5,550	5,560	5,600	5,600	5,600
5,600	5,600	5,850	5,900	6,020
6,500	6,600	6,600	6,800	6,800
6,800	7,300	7,500	7,700	11,000

The outlier measurement of 11,000 pounds is an error. Of the mean, median, mode, and range of the values listed, which will change the most if the outlier is removed from the data set?

A) Mean
B) Median
C) Mode
D) Range

5

The table below shows the test scores for applicants to University X in 1990.

University X applicant pool data 1990				
Test scores	400	500	600	700
Number of applicants	15	30	55	40

What is the median of the test scores for applicants to University X in 1990?

A) 400
B) 500
C) 550
D) 600

6

A business consultant collects data from two different tech companies, each with four employees. The results of the study are listed in the tables below.

TechByte

Years of Employment	Salary in Dollars
1	58,000
3	60,000
6	72,000
12	83,000

CompUTech

Years of Employment	Salary in Dollars
1	44,000
2	57,000
4	71,000
15	84,000

Which statement is true about the data?

A) The median salaries for both companies are greater than $65,000.
B) The mean salary for CompUTech is greater than the mean salary for TechByte.
C) The salary range for CompUTech is greater than the salary range for TechByte.
D) The range in the years of employment for CompUTech is less than the range in years of employment for TechByte.

Data Collection | Overview

The SAT will sometimes ask you questions that involve no math at all. These questions may instead test your understanding of what makes a good sample population on which to conduct a survey or an experiment. When answering questions like these, keep a couple of things in mind:

> 1. **An experiment must contain as little bias as possible.**
>   Bias in an experiment will influence the results. For example, if you are conducting an experiment about how often students at a school work out, just interviewing students in the gym will cause your results to skew higher, since the students who do not go to the gym at all will not be counted.
>
> 2. **An experiment must contain as large a sample size as possible.**
>   Surveys conducted using only a small segment of a population will not necessarily be representative of the larger population. To increase the accuracy of a set of data, the number of people surveyed must represent a significant portion of the population.
>
> 3. **Just because the results of an experiment suggest something, that does not mean the suggestion always applies to all cases.**
>   For example, if an experiment suggests that if drivers take the Lincoln Tunnel rather than the Holland Tunnel from New York to New Jersey they will arrive quicker, it does not mean that EVERY single driver who takes the Lincoln Tunnel will arrive quicker. The experiment only suggests that this is likely to be the case.

Chapter 4

1

A researcher conducted a survey to determine whether people at a university prefer staying on campus over the weekend or going home. The researcher asked 198 students in their dorm rooms on Sunday morning, and 14 refused to respond. Which of the following factors makes it least likely that a reliable conclusion can be drawn about the weekend preferences of the students at the university?

A) The number of people who refused to answer
B) Population size
C) Where the survey was given
D) Sample size

2

A research study was conducted to determine if study technique Z is successful in raising test scores. From a large population of high school students, 400 students were chosen at random. Half of the participants were randomly assigned to prepare for an upcoming history test using technique Z, while the other half did not use technique Z. The resulting data showed that the participants who prepared using technique Z scored significantly higher than those in the control group. Based on the design and results of the study, which of the following is an appropriate conclusion?

A) Technique Z is likely to result in higher test scores for those who struggle in school.
B) Technique Z is likely to result in higher test scores than any other techniques available to students.
C) Technique Z will result in higher test scores for every student who uses it.
D) Technique Z will likely result in substantial increases in test scores nationwide.

3

A school newspaper will survey students about the quality of the school's theater department. Which method will create the least biased results?

A) Twenty-five actors are randomly surveyed.
B) Fifty students are randomly chosen from each grade level.
C) Students who dislike the school's theater department are chosen to complete the survey.
D) A booth in the auditorium is set up for students to voluntarily complete the survey.

4

A survey is being conducted to determine if a cable company should add another cooking channel to the schedule. Which random survey would be the least biased?

A) Surveying 50 women at a grocery store
B) Surveying 65 people at a mall
C) Surveying 55 men at a baseball game
D) Surveying 15 members of a cooking club

Scatterplots | Overview

A scatterplot is one way in which the relationship between two data sets can be expressed graphically. Each axis represents a different data set. Take a look at the example below:

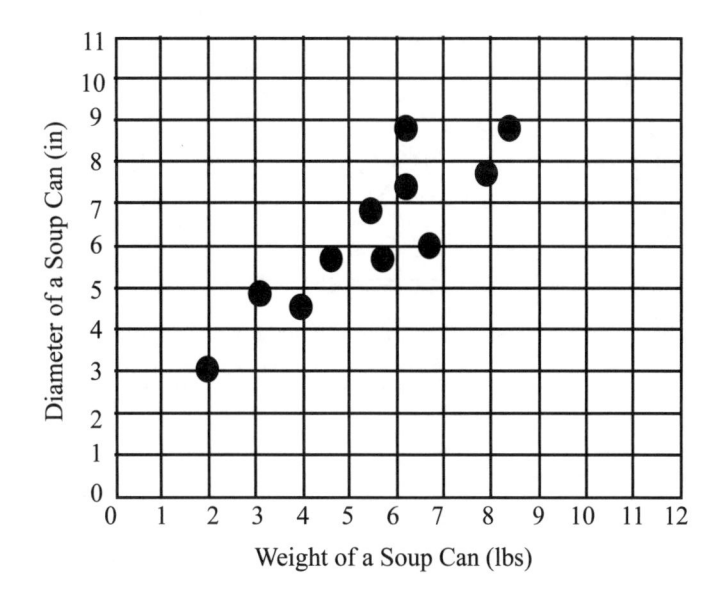

A scatterplot will tell us whether there is a positive correlation, a negative correlation, or no correlation between the data sets. In order to find this out, you must draw a Line of Best Fit onto the plot.

A Line of Best Fit drawn on a graph is a line that shows the general direction in which a group of points is heading. If we were to draw a Line of Best Fit onto the graph above, it would look like this:

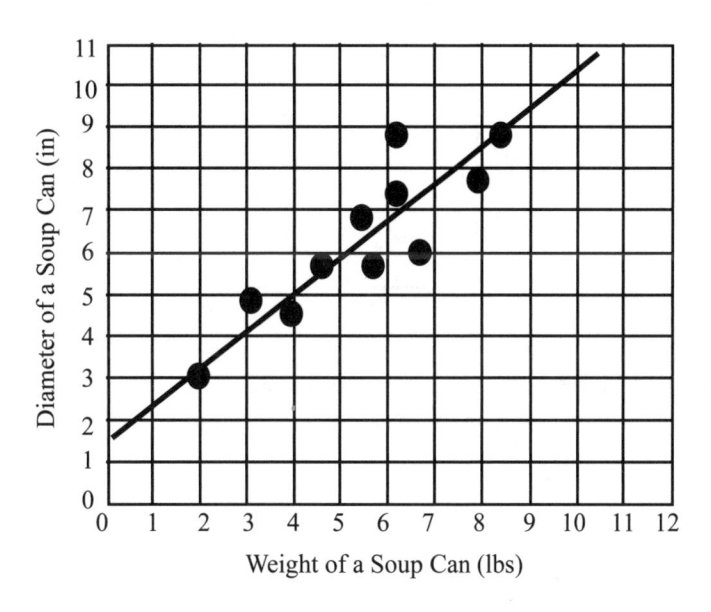

Scatterplots | Overview

The Line of Best Fit gives us information about the correlation. If the slope of the Line of Best Fit is positive, as in the previous example, the correlation between the data sets is positive.

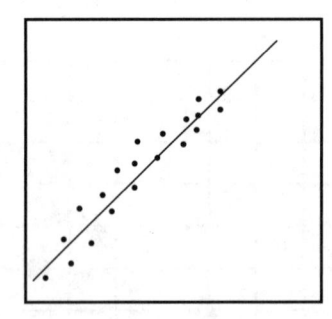

If the Line of Best Fit has a negative slope, then there is a negative correlation between the data sets.

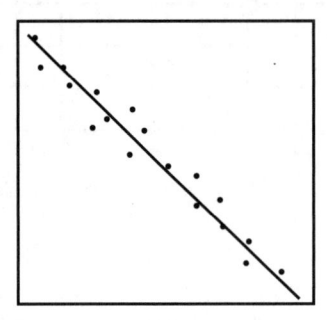

If no Line of Best Fit can be drawn, then there is no correlation between the data sets.

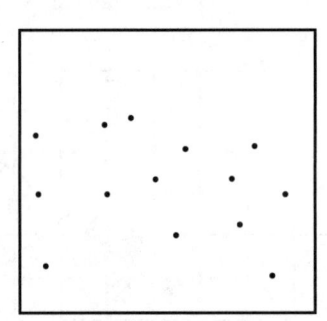

If the data points are tightly clustered around a Line of Best Fit, then the correlation is high. If they are more spread out, then the correlation between the sets is low.

Questions 1 and 2 refer to the following information.

A scientist created the scatterplot below to examine the relationship between wave height and seashell erosion rate at 11 beaches on the Pacific coast.

Seashell Erosion Rate versus Wave Height

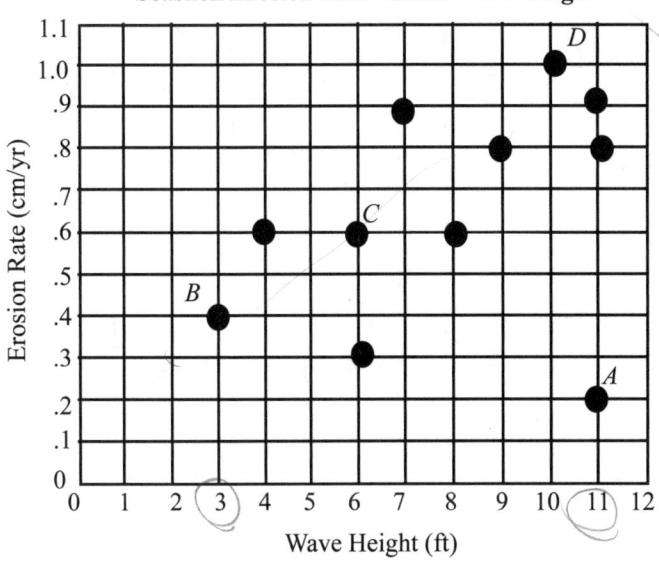

1

What is the erosion rate, in centimeters per year, of the beach with the shortest wave height?

A) 0.2
B) 0.4
C) 0.6
D) 0.9

2

Of the labeled points, which represents the beach for which the ratio of wave height to erosion rate is the greatest?

A) A
B) B
C) C
D) D

3

Which of the following scatterplots shows the relationship that is appropriately modeled with the equation $y = a^b x^b$, where a is a positive number less than 1 and b is a negative integer.

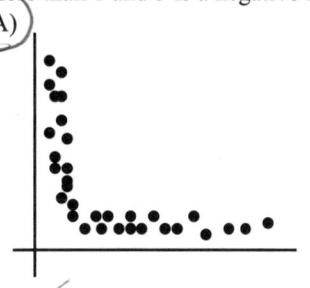

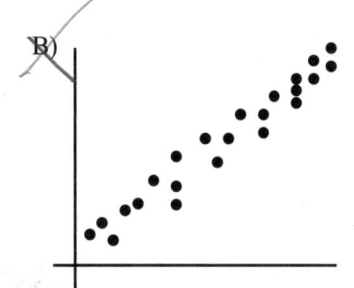

A)

B)

C)

D)

Chapter 4

HW=7/11

4

The relative speed of a car is defined as the ratio of $\frac{\text{average speed of a car model}}{\text{average speed of all car models}}$, expressed as a percent.

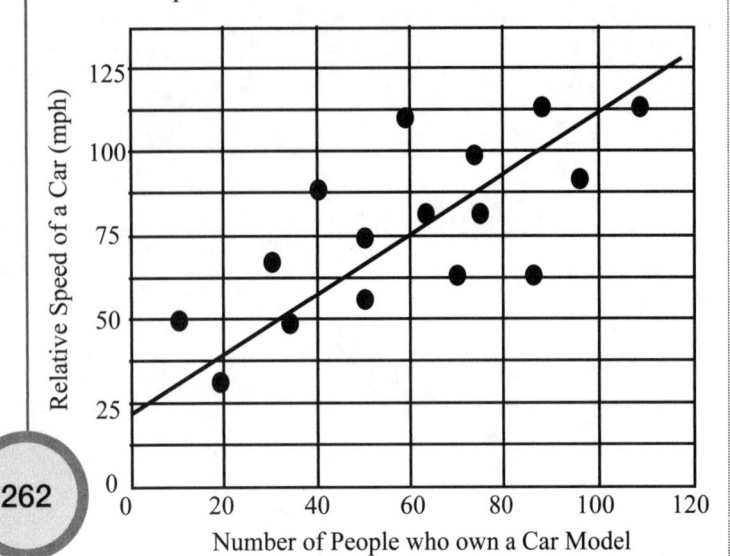

The scatterplot above shows the relative speed of a car and the number of people who own the car across the United States in 2008. The line of best fit is also shown and has the equation $y = .883x + 22$. Which of the following best explains how the number 22 relates to the scatterplot?

A) In 2008, the lowest car speed was about 22 mph.
B) In 2008, the lowest car speed was about 22% of the highest car speed.
C) In 2008, even in car models that were not popular with consumers, car speeds were never below 22% of the average across all models.
D) In 2008, even in car models that were not popular with consumers, car speeds were likely at least 22% of the average speed across all models.

5

Kelly was training for a marathon on each of 11 days. The scatterplot below shows her running time each day and the number of steps taken.

Running Time versus Steps Taken

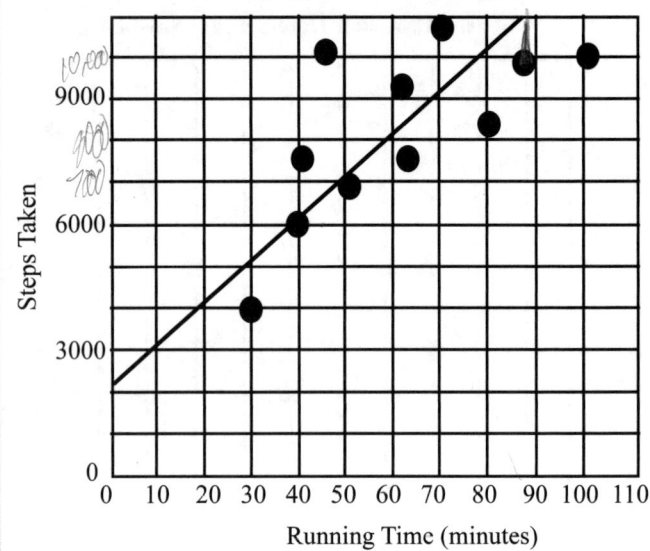

The line of best fit for the data is also shown. For the run that took 1 hour and 28 minutes, Kelly's steps taken were about how many less than the number predicted by the line of best fit?

A) 750
B) 1,100
C) 1,900
D) 2,300

6

The scatterplot below shows the number of dollars spent (in millions) on sporting events in various years.

Money Spent on Sporting Events, 1980 - 2010

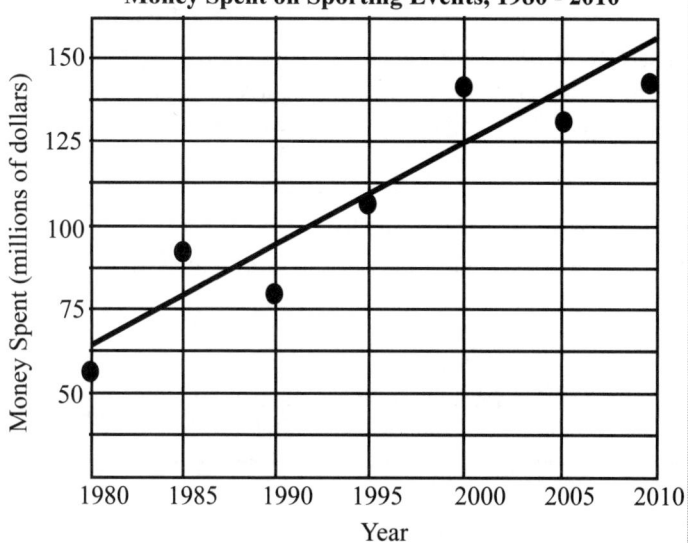

According to the line of best fit in the scatterplot above, which of the following best approximates the year in which the amount of money spent on sporting events was estimated to be 119 million dollars?

A) 1986
B) 1994
C) 1998
D) 2003

7

Which of the following graphs best shows a strong positive association between rate (r) and time (t)?

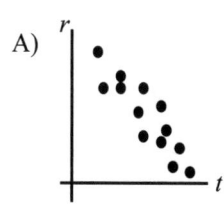

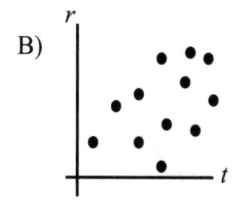

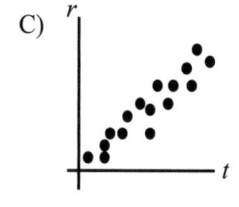

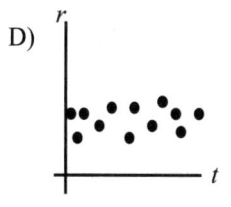

A)

B)

C)

D)

Chapter 4

Analyzing Tables & Graphs | Overview

Scatterplots are not the only way that the SAT will test data analysis. The exam will also test your ability to interpret graphs, tables, and charts.

When a question gives you a set of data represented in one of these ways, follow the steps below:

> 1. **Identify what the axes represent and the units in which they are expressed.**
> Make sure you understand what each axis (or column/row heading if you are dealing with a chart) represents. It is easy to get confused and read data from the wrong axis, so take steps to avoid making a silly mistake like that.
>
> 2. **Identify the data that the question is referencing and circle it.**
> This step will help you avoid falling into the trap of looking at data that is not necessary to answer a specific question.
>
> 3. **Carefully read the information and use it to answer the question.**
> Once you have identified what you are looking for, find that specific information and use it to answer the question.

Chapter 4

Analyzing Tables & Graphs | Overview

Sometimes the SAT will take these questions one step further by asking you to calculate the probability of something being selected from all of the potential data points in a set. To calculate the probability, use the formula below:

$$\text{Probability} = \frac{\text{Successful Outcomes}}{\text{Total Outcomes}}$$

Things to remember:

1. Probabilities are always going to be between 0 and 1, inclusive.
2. A probability of 0 means the action, event, or outcome will not happen.
3. A probability of 1 means the action, event, or outcome will definitely happen.
4. To find the combined probability of two or more independent events, multiply the probabilities of all events.

Take a look at the example below:

The data in the table below were gathered by a teacher who is studying the amount of money spent on school supplies by students in her 8th grade math classes.

	$0 - $25	$26 - $45	$46 - $100	Total
Class 1	5	8	12	25
Class 2	3	12	5	20
Class 3	6	9	4	19
Total	14	29	21	64

Class 1 consists of 25 students; Class 2 consists of 20 students, and Class 3 consists of 19 students. If a student is chosen at random from those who spend at least $26, what is the probability that the student is in Class 3?

A) $\frac{3}{16}$

B) $\frac{6}{19}$

C) $\frac{6}{25}$

D) $\frac{13}{50}$

Probability is just the number favorable outcomes over all possible outcomes.

How many favorable outcomes do we have in the question above? _____

How many possible outcomes are there? _____

Therefore, the probability of selecting a student in Class 3 from those who spent at least $26 is _____

www.bellcurves.com

Chapter 4

1

The number of dorm rooms with air conditioning units across six residence halls on Campus X is shown in the graph below.

Number of Dorm Rooms with Air Conditioning Units

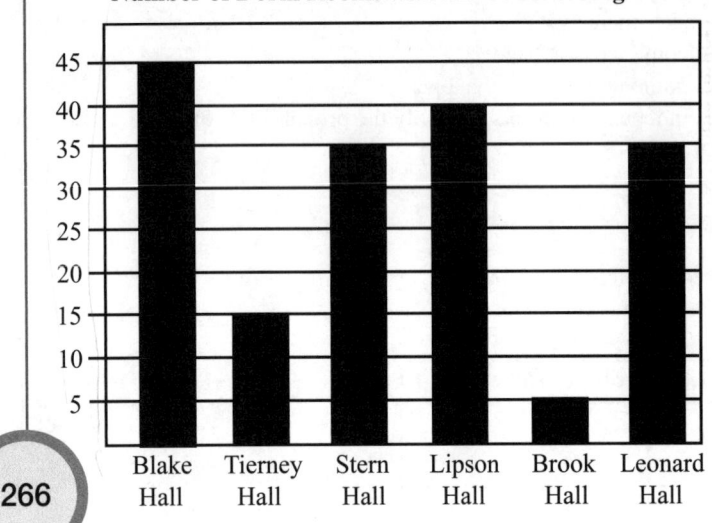

Blake Hall	45
Tierney Hall	15
Stern Hall	35
Lipson Hall	40
Brook Hall	5
Leonard Hall	35

If the total number of rooms with air conditioning units equals 1,750, what is an appropriate label for the vertical axis of the graph above?
A) Rooms with Air Conditioning Units
B) Rooms with Air Conditioning Units (in tens)
C) Rooms with Air Conditioning Units (in hundreds)
D) Residence Halls on Campus X

Questions 2 and 3 refer to the following information.

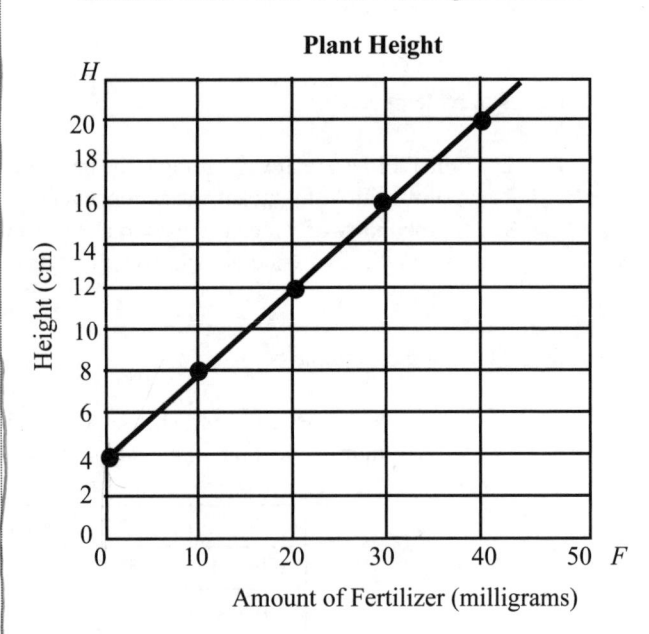

Plant Height

(Graph: Height H (cm) vs. Amount of Fertilizer F (milligrams); line passes through (0, 4), (10, 8), (20, 12), (30, 16), (40, 20))

2

What does the H-intercept represent in the graph?
A) The height of the control group in the experiment
B) The combined heights of all plants tested
C) The total amount of fertilizer needed to make a plant grow
D) The increase in height from one plant to another correlated with the amount of fertilizer provided

3

Which of the following represents the relationship between the height of a plant and the amount of fertilizer provided?
A) $H = 0.4F$
B) $H = 2.5F$
C) $H = 0.4F + 4$
D) $H = 2.5F + 4$

4

The table below shows the distribution of gender and height for professional basketball players.

Gender	Height Under 6'2"	6'2" or Taller	Total
Male	8	29	37
Female	17	6	23
Total	25	35	60

If one of the players surveyed is chosen at random to appear in a commercial, what is the probability that the player will either be a female 6'2" or taller, or a male under 6'2"?

A) $\frac{2}{15}$

B) $\frac{7}{30}$

C) $\frac{23}{30}$

D) $\frac{13}{15}$

5

The graph below shows Sarah's distance from her house during a 4-hour bike ride.

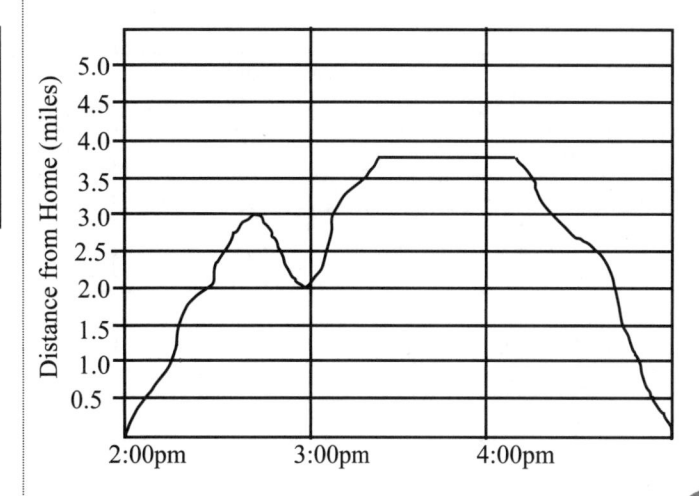

Along the route, Sarah was forced to backtrack for one mile to pick up her water bottle that had fallen out of its holder. Sarah also stopped for 45 minutes during the bike ride to stretch her hamstring before she headed home. Based on the graph, which of the following is closest to the time she retrieved her water bottle and continued on her ride?

A) 2:12 pm
B) 2:55 pm
C) 3:20 pm
D) 4:08 pm

6

The table below shows the 75 sporting events that had the highest attendance in 2014, categorized by sport and by level.

Level	Type of Sport				
	Basketball	Baseball	Football	Tennis	Total
Professional	11	4	21	3	39
College	10	2	12	2	26
High School	3	2	4	1	10
Total	24	8	37	6	75

What proportion of the sporting events are college basketball games?

A) $\frac{2}{75}$

B) $\frac{11}{75}$

C) $\frac{2}{15}$

D) $\frac{24}{75}$

7

The graph below shows the total number of flowers purchased on Valentines Day each year from 1998 through 2006.

Valentines Day Flower Sales

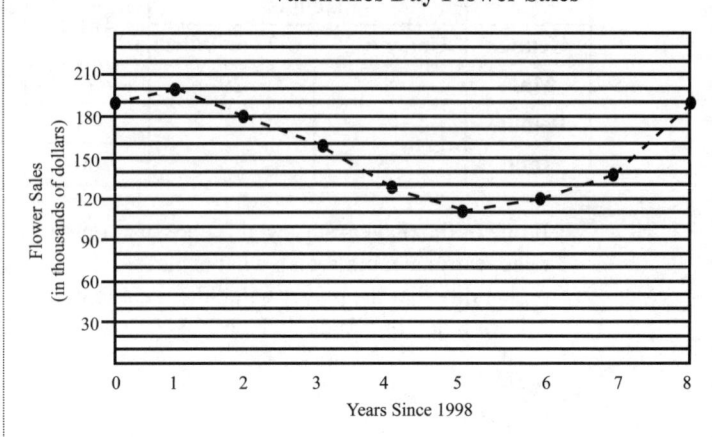

Based on the graph, which of the following best describes the general trend in Valentines Day flower sales from 1998 through 2006?

A) Sales generally decreased each year since 1998.
B) Sales generally increased each year since 1998.
C) Sales increased between 1998 and 1999, and then again between 2003 and 2006.
D) Sales generally remained steady between 2000 and 2003.

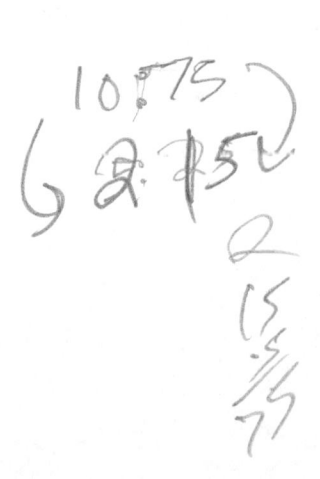

8

The data in the table below were gathered by an economist who was studying the amount of money saved on a monthly basis by teenagers in high school.

	$0 - $50	$51 - $100	$101 - $150	Total
Group 1	20	33	37	90
Group 2	22	35	33	90
Total	42	68	70	180

Group 1 consisted of 90 student who held part-time jobs and Group 2 consisted of 90 students who received an allowance from their parents. If a teenager is chosen at random from those who saved at least $51, what is the probability that the teenager belonged to Group 2?

A) $\frac{34}{69}$

B) $\frac{35}{69}$

C) $\frac{35}{138}$

D) $\frac{35}{68}$

4c

HEART OF ALGEBRA:

MANIPULATING & TRANSLATING EQUATIONS, INEQUALITIES, SYSTEMS OF EQUATIONS, FUNCTIONS

Chapter 4

Manipulating Equations | Overview

Working with algebraic expressions requires knowledge of the terms, names, and definitions of common algebraic components. The most important aspects of algebraic expressions for the SAT are given in the table below. Some of these concepts may look familiar as they are concepts we have already dicsussed.

Term	Definition	Examples – Notes
Equation	*Something that has an = sign*	$5x + 6 = 11$
Inequality	*comparison of things < > ≤ ≥*	$5x + 6 < 11$ or $1.21 \geq 5y + 9$
Square	*# times itself*	25 is the square of 5.
Square Root		The square root ($\sqrt{}$) of 36 is 6.
Absolute Value	*distance from zero # positive*	Absolute value of a is represented as $|a|$.
Exponent	*how many times a # is multiplied by itself.*	5^3 is a term where 5 is the base, and it is raised to the 3rd power (i.e. $5 \times 5 \times 5$). 3 is the exponent.
Direct Variation	*↑ & ↑*	$y = 2x$ Here the value of y will always be twice the value of x. So when x is 2, y is 4; when x is 3, y is 6, and so on.
Inverse Variation	*↑ & ↓*	$xy = 2$ Here the value of y will decrease in proportion to x as x increases. So when x is 2, y is 1; when x is 4, y is $\frac{1}{2}$, and so on.

www.bellcurves.com

Chapter 4

Manipulating Equations | Overview

Now that you know the lingo, let's talk about how to solve algebra problems. To solve an algebraic expression you must do three things:

1. Combine like terms and then isolate the variable

2. Do the opposite math operation

3. Do the same thing to both sides of the equal (or inequality) sign

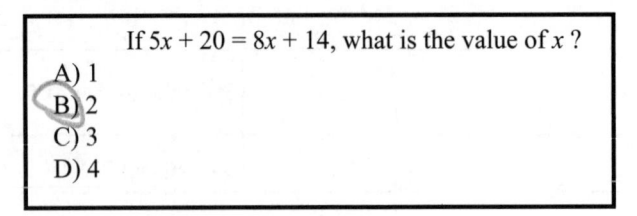

> If $5x + 20 = 8x + 14$, what is the value of x?
> A) 1
> B) 2
> C) 3
> D) 4

What is the first step in solving the equation above?

$10 + 20 = 16 + 14$
$30 \quad 30$

When you isolate the variable, the value of x is equal to _____2_____.

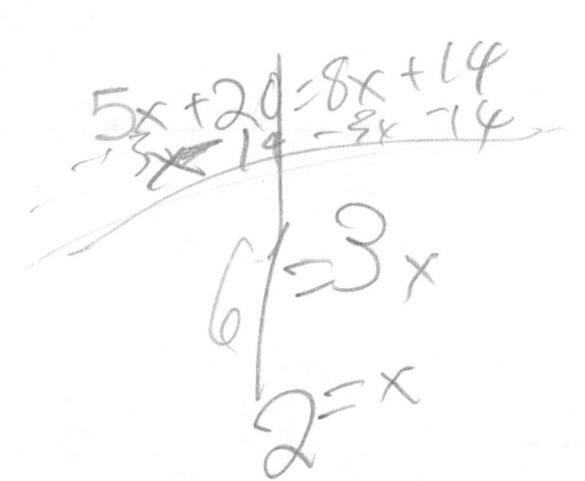

$5x + 20 = 8x + 14$
$-5x \quad -14 \quad -5x \quad -14$

$6 = 3x$

$2 = x$

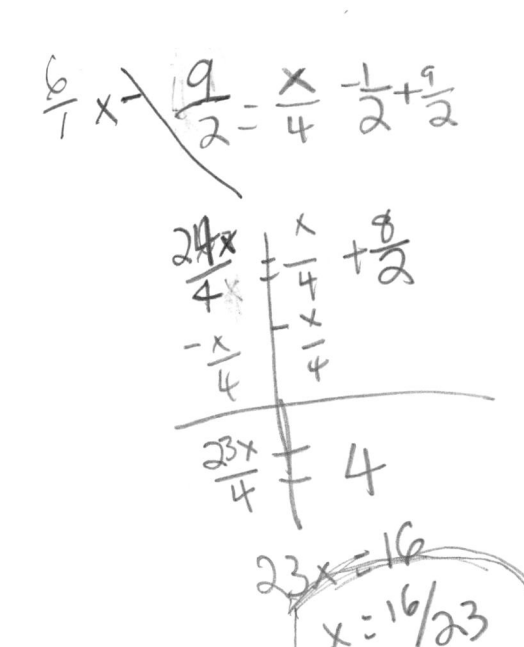

Manipulating Equations | Rules Review

1. $x + 2 = 7$

    $x = 5$

2. $3x + 6 = 27$

    $3x = 21$
    $x = 7$

3. $4x = 20 + 5x$

    $-x = 20$
    $x = -20$

4. $\dfrac{x}{5} = \dfrac{3}{7}$

    $x = \dfrac{15}{7}$

5. $\dfrac{2}{3}x = 6$

    $2x = 18$
    $x = 9$

6. $19 = 17 - 2x + 5x$

    $2 = 3x$
    $\dfrac{2}{3} = x$

7. $\dfrac{3}{5}x = \dfrac{4}{3}$

    $3x = \dfrac{20}{3} \cdot \dfrac{1}{3}$

    $x = \dfrac{20}{9}$

8. $6x - 4.5 = \dfrac{x}{4} - \dfrac{1}{2}$

    $6x - 4.5 = x - 2$

    $5x = 2.5$

    $\boxed{x = \dfrac{1}{2}}$

    $3 - 4.5 = -1.5$

    $\dfrac{1/2}{4/2} = \dfrac{1}{4} - \dfrac{1}{2} = \dfrac{1}{4} - \dfrac{2}{4} = -\dfrac{1}{2}$

$\dfrac{6}{1}x - \dfrac{9}{2} = \dfrac{x}{4} - \dfrac{1}{2} + \dfrac{9}{2}$

$\dfrac{24x}{4} = \dfrac{x}{4} + \dfrac{8}{2}$

$-\dfrac{x}{4} \quad -\dfrac{x}{4}$

$\dfrac{23x}{4} = 4$

$23x = 16$

$x = 16/23$

Chapter 4

1

Which of the following expressions is equal to 0 for some value of y?
A) $|y + 7| - 8$
B) $|y + 8| + 8$
C) $|y - 7| + 8$
D) $8 + |y + 7|$

2

If $\dfrac{x+y}{2x} = \dfrac{4}{9}$, which of the following must also be true?
A) $\dfrac{y}{x} = 9$
B) $\dfrac{x}{y} = 9$
C) $\dfrac{x}{y} = \dfrac{1}{9}$
D) $\dfrac{x}{y} = -9$

3

If $5y = 40$, what is the value of $8y - 6$?
A) 32
B) 49
C) 58
D) 70

4

If $\dfrac{x}{12} = \dfrac{2x+3}{-12}$, what is the value of $\dfrac{x}{4}$?
A) -4
B) -1
C) $-\dfrac{1}{4}$
D) $\dfrac{1}{4}$

5

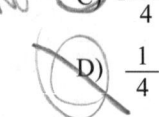

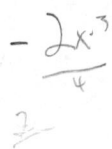

If $7x + 11 = 25$, what is the value of $14x + 8$?
A) 28
B) 32
C) 36
D) 50

6

If $\dfrac{x-2}{x+2} = 18$, what is the value of x?
A) $-\dfrac{17}{25}$
B) $\dfrac{38}{17}$
C) $\dfrac{7}{36}$
D) $\dfrac{21}{39}$

274

SAT-R Workbook v. 1.5

Translating Equations | Overview

You must memorize a few terms and know what their math equivalents are in order to attack algebra word problems. Let's review a few key terms.

Term	Math Equivalent
Of, by	Multiply
Is added to, more than, greater than	Added to another number
Less than, taken from	Subtracted from another number
Percent	Divided by 100
Is, are, were, results in	Equals
Goes into, divided by, out of	Division
What, a number	Variable (like w, x, y, or a)

Translating Equations | Rules Review

Translate the following into mathematical expressions.

1. A number decreased by 13

   $x - 13$

2. John has 5 times as many shirts as Pam.

   $5p = j$

3. Two times the sum of *x* and *y*

   $2(x+y)$

4. Larry bought 5 hotdogs and 6 bottles of water for a total cost of 12 dollars.

   $5h + 6b = 12$

5. What is 12 divided by the quantity 4 less than 10?

   $12 \div (10-4)$

6. A number subtracted from 5 is 4 times the sum of 2 and 3.

   $5 - x = 4(2+3)$

Chapter 4

1

If $5x + 17$ is 18 more than 24, what is the value of $10x + 4$?

A) 5
B) 27
C) 38
D) 54

2

Amy wants to purchase a dress. To find the best deal, she searches two stores. At Store A the dress costs 30% more than at Store B. If the dress costs $150 at Store B, how much more does it cost at Store A?

A) $45
B) $80
C) $170
D) $195

3

To ship a package, the weight of it must be under 850 pounds. A pencil manufacturer wants to ship pencils to a university. The shipping materials weigh 125 pounds, and the manufacturer is including an extra box of erasers that weighs 70 pounds. If each box of pencils weighs 11 pounds, how many boxes of pencils can the manufacturer fit in the package?

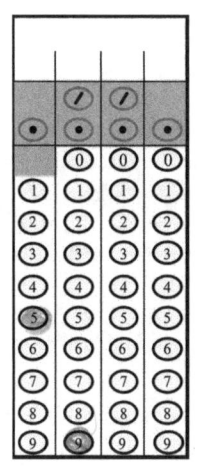

4

When 6 times an integer y is subtracted from the sum of 22 and 49, the difference is equal to 23. What is the value of the sum of 3 and 7 times y?

A) 48
B) 56
C) 59
D) 72

5

George has to pay his cell phone bill every month. The monthly cost is a fixed charge of $40 plus $0.50 for every 10 sent text messages. In a particular month, he sent 500 text messages. How much did he have to pay for his phone bill that particular month?

A) $25
B) $42.50
C) $65
D) $250

6

A chef has c ounces of cookie batter in his kitchen, and plans to use it to create cookies that weigh 5 ounces each, which will result in 2 ounces of leftover batter. If he were going to make the same number of cookies but instead create ones that weighed 7 ounces, he would need an additional 18 ounces of batter. How many ounces of batter does the chef have in his kitchen?

A) 45
B) 50
C) 52
D) 62

7

To make the track team, a sprinter must be able to run at a speed of 32 feet per second. Miguel currently runs at a speed of 23 feet per second, but believes that with practice, he can increase his speed by 0.1 feet per second per day. Which of the following represents Miguel's speed w weeks from now?

A) $23 + 0.1w$
B) $32 - 0.7w$
C) $23 - 0.1w$
D) $23 + 0.7w$

Chapter 4

1

The fixed cost of manufacturing couches is $1,725.00 per week. The cost for extra fabric is $23.75 per couch and the cost to make one pillow is $14.23. Which of the following expressions can be used to model the cost of manufacturing p couches in one month, each requiring extra fabric, and two pillows?

A) $1,725p + 23.75p + 2(14.23)p$
B) $4(1,725p) + 4(23.75p) + 2(14.23p)$
C) $1,725p + 23.75p + 14.23p$
D) $4(1,725) + 23.75p + 2p(14.23)$

2

The number of flowers that bloomed in a nursery from March through June is four times the number of flowers that bloomed from July though October. If 64 flowers bloomed in March, 18 bloomed in April, 20 bloomed in May, 26 bloomed in June, and f flowers bloomed between July and October, which of the following equations is true?

A) $4f = (64 + 18 + 20 + 26)$
B) $f = 4(64 + 18 + 20 + 26)$
C) $\dfrac{f}{4} = (64 + 18 + 20 + 26)$
D) $\dfrac{f}{4} = 4(64 + 18 + 20 + 26)$

3

Malnati's Pizzeria charges a base price of $9 per pizza plus $2 per topping. Gigio's Pizzeria charges a base price of $11 per pizza plus $1.50 per topping. If x represents the number of toppings on a pizza, which of the following equations could be used to determine the number of toppings for which the price of a pizza at Malnati's would equal the price of a pizza at Gigio's?

A) $9x + 1.5 = 11x + 2$
B) $9 + 1.5x = 11 + 2x$
C) $9x + 2 = 11x + 1.5$
D) $9 + 2x = 11 + 1.5x$

4

Two entrepreneurs started their businesses at the same time. John's business started with 600 employees and increased by 300 employees each year. Jack's business started with 1,400 employees and increased by 200 employees each year. If y represents the number of full years the businesses have been running, which of the following equations could be used to determine the number of years until the number of Jack's employees equals the number of John's employees?

A) $200y + 300y = 600$
B) $600 + 300y = 1,400 + 200y$
C) $200y + 300y = y$
D) $200y + 300y = 1,400 + 300y$

Chapter 4

5

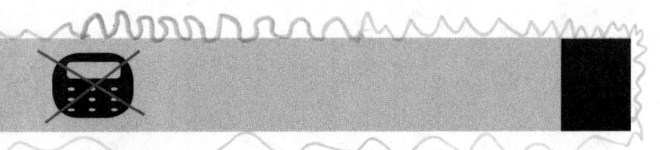

A taxi company charges its passengers $1.50 as a base price with an additional $0.75 per quarter mile that the taxi travels. Which of the following expressions represents the cost, in dollars, of taking a taxi m miles?

A) $1.5 + m$
B) $1.5 + .75m$
C) $15 + 75m$
D) $1.5 + 3m$

6

A moving company charges customers $3.25 per box and $62.50 per 100 pounds of furniture. Which of the following expressions represents the price of hiring the moving company, in dollars, to move b boxes and f hundred pounds of furniture?

A) $b + 625f$
B) $3.25(100)b + 62.5f$
C) $3.25(100)b + 62.5(100)f$
D) $3.25b + 62.5f$

Chapter 4

Systems Of Equations | Overview

Systems of equations involve two (or more) equations that have the same two (or more) variables. When given a system, you have two options for working with the equations:

Option 1 (Substitution Method): Solve for one variable in terms of the other.

    1. Isolate one variable (using the manipulating rules we already discussed).
    2. Plug this value into the other equation.

> What is the value of x if $5y = 20$ and $3x + 11y = 20$?
> A) 16
> B) 8
> C) 4
> D) -8

Handwritten work:
$y = 4$
$3x + 44 = 20$
$3x = -24$
$x = -8$

(D is circled)

Which of the two given equations should we solve first, and why? _____

_____

Now we can take the value of y and plug it into the second equation to solve for x:

Systems Of Equations | Overview

Option 2 (Elimination Method): Align the equations and manipulate them.

1. Arrange the equations one above the other so that the variables line up.
2. Add or subtract the equations to isolate the desired variable or quantity.

> If $3x - 2y = 6$ and $3y - 2x = 4$, then $x + y =$
> A) 24
> B) 10
> C) 2
> D) 1

The first step is to stack the two equations on top of one another so that the common variables are lined up:

Then take a look at the expression we are asked to solve for. Ask yourself if there is anything we can do with the two given equations (add or subtract them) to give us the expression.

If we had not been able to add or subtract the equations to get the given expression, you should add or subtract the given equations so that one variable cancels out, and then solve the remainder of the problem using substitution.

Chapter 4

Systems Of Equations I Rules Review

1. What is the value of x if $10y = 50$ and $-4y - 3x = 10$?

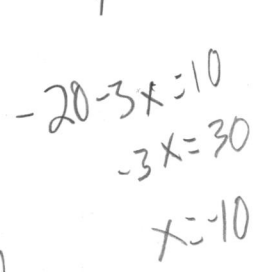

   $y = 5$
   $-20 - 3x = 10$
   $-3x = 30$
   $x = -10$

   $\boxed{x = -10}$

2. If $52 - 2y = 46$ and $4x + 3y = 19$, then the value of x is

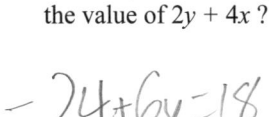

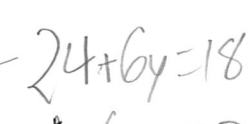

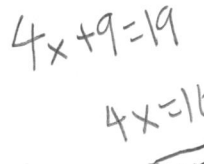

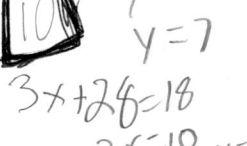

   $-2y = -6$
   $y = 3$
   $4x + 9 = 19$
   $4x = 16$
   $\boxed{x = \frac{5}{2}}$

3. If $3x + y = 13$ and $x + 2y = 1$, then what is the value of $4x + 3y$?

   $3x + y = 13$
   $x + 2y = 1$
   $4x + 3y = 14$
   $\boxed{14}$

4. If $x + y = 13$ and $2x + y = 26$, then the value of $3x + 2y$ is

   $13 + 26$
   $\boxed{39}$

5. What is the value of $2x$ if $22y + 4x = 50$ and $11y + 3x = 40$?

   $22y + 4x = 50$
   $-(11y - 3x = 40)2$
   $11y + x = 10$
   $\boxed{30}$

6. If $3x + 4y = 18$ and $2(y + 2) - x = 12$, then what is the value of $2y + 4x$?

   $2y + 4 - x = 12 \to 2y - x = 6$
   $-x = 6 - 2y$
   $x = -6 + 2y$

   $-24 + 6y = 18$
   $6y = 42$
   $y = 7$
   $3x + 28 = 18$
   $3x = -10$ $x = -\frac{10}{3}$

   $3x + 4y = 18$
   $-x + 2y = 8$

   $2x + 2y = 10$
   $\frac{20}{3} + 28$

7. Jennie and Helena went to the amusement park and purchased ride tickets and hot dogs for their friends. Jennie spent a total of $16.40 on two hot dogs and three ride tickets. Helena spent a total of $29.20 for four hot dogs and two ride tickets.

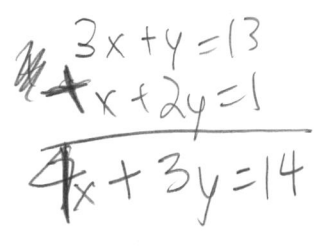

   Write a system of equations that can be used to find the price of one ride ticket and the price of one hot dog.

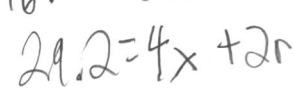

   $\boxed{16.4 = 2x + 3r}$
   $\boxed{29.2 = 4x + 2r}$

Chapter 4

1

After pooling the money in their wallets, Danny and Claire had a total of $325. If Danny had $65 more than Claire, how much money did Claire have?

A) $130
B) $135
C) $195
D) $205

2

Last month Jessica walked 17 more miles than Samantha. If they walked a combined 123 miles, how many miles did Jessica walk?

A) 53
B) 61
C) 70
D) 89

3

The total price of three copies of book X and two copies of book Y is $19.00. The total price of 5 copies of book Y is $16.00 more than 3 copies of book X. What is the total price of one copy of book X and two copies of book Y?

A) $8
B) $11
C) $13
D) $16

4

The incomplete table below shows the number of soccer players and basketball players in Lamborg High School, broken down by gender.

	Sport Played		
Gender	Basketball	Soccer	Total
Male			85
Female			68

The number of female soccer players is 3 times the number of male soccer players, while the number of male basketball players is 6 times the number of female basketball players. If a student were to be selected at random, what would be the approximate probability the student would be a female soccer player?

A) 0.37
B) 0.44
C) 0.48
D) 0.56

$$5x + p = 7x - 10$$
$$5y + q = 7y - 10$$

In the equations above, p and q are constants. If $p - q$ equals $\frac{1}{8}$, which of the following is true?

A) x is y plus $\frac{1}{8}$
B) x is y minus $\frac{1}{4}$
C) x is y plus $\frac{1}{16}$
D) y is x minus $\frac{1}{2}$

SAT-R Workbook v. 1.5

Chapter 4

1

$$2x + 3y = 15$$
$$2x + y = 29$$

What is the solution (x, y) to the system of equations above?

A) $(7, 18)$
B) $(18, -7)$
C) $(-18, -7)$
D) $(18, 7)$

2

$$3x + 6y = 24$$
$$2x + 3y = 18$$

According to the system of equations above, what is the value of x?

3

In the system of equations below, p and q are constants.

$$px - qy = 4$$
$$-6x + 14y = 24$$

If the system has infinitely many solutions, what is the value of $\frac{p}{q}$?

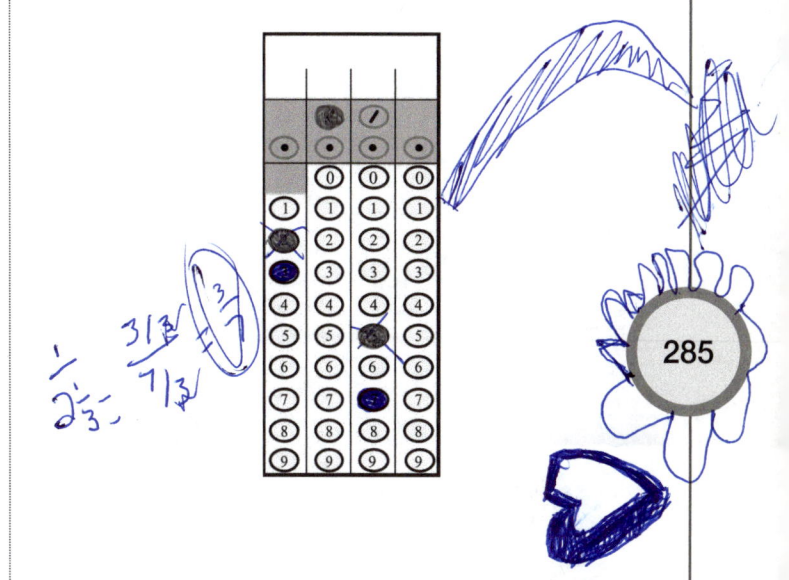

4

$$3x + 4y = 14$$
$$-6y + 9x = -12$$

If (x,y) is a solution to the system of equations above, what is the value of $x + y$?

A) $\frac{3}{11}$
B) $\frac{4}{9}$
C) $\frac{7}{5}$
D) $\frac{11}{3}$

5

$$kx - 4y = 12$$
$$\frac{1}{2}x - 7y = 16$$

In the system of equations above, k is a constant and x and y are variables. For what value of k will the system of equations have no solution?

A) $-\frac{2}{7}$

B) $-\frac{3}{5}$

C) $\frac{2}{7}$

D) $\frac{3}{5}$

6

In a school supply store, each spiral notebook has 80 more sheets of paper than a marble notebook has. If Luisa bought 4 spiral notebooks and 3 marble notebooks which totaled 1,930 sheets of paper, how many sheets of paper are in a marble notebook?

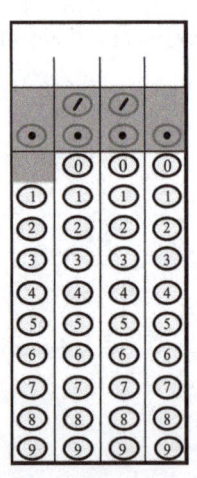

7

$$\frac{a}{b} = 7$$
$$2(b + 10) = a$$

If (a,b) is the solution to the system of equations above, what is the value of a?

A) 4
B) 7
C) 12
D) 28

8

$$3y = x - 6$$
$$y = (4x^2 - 5)(x + 3)$$

How many ordered pairs (x,y) satisfy the equations shown above?

A) 1
B) 2
C) 3
D) Infinitely many

Inequalities | Overview

Solving inequalities is just like solving equations. **However,** if you multiply or divide by a negative number, you must flip the inequality sign.

> If $-7p - 11 > 52$, which of the following must be true?
> A) $p > 9$
> B) $p > -9$
> C) $p = 9$
> D) $p < -9$

[handwritten: $-7p > 63$, $p < -9$, D circled]

Remember that solving an inequality is very similar to solving a regular equation:

To solve an inequality with two inequality signs, perform operations on all three parts of the inequality.

> If $6 < 3y < 30$, which of the following must be true?
> A) $2 < 3y < 10$
> B) $6 < y < 5$
> C) $2 < y < 10$
> D) $3 < 3y < 15$

Start by finding the GCF of all parts of the inequality. In the example above, the GCF is _____.

Then divide each of the parts by that GCF. Use the space below to complete the work.

Therefore, the answer to the problem above is _____.

www.bellcurves.com

Inequalities | Overview

Another unique type of inequality is one containing an absolute value.

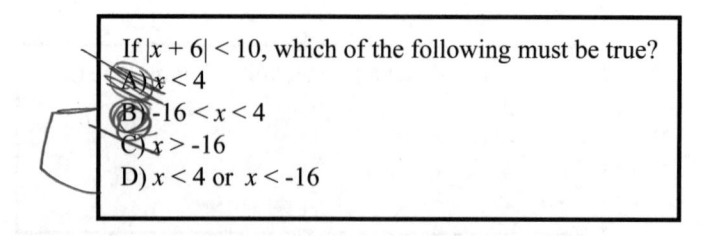

> If $|x + 6| < 10$, which of the following must be true?
> A) $x < 4$
> B) $-16 < x < 4$
> C) $x > -16$
> D) $x < 4$ or $x < -16$

Step 1: Drop the absolute value bars and rewrite the equation. Then solve as normal.

Step 2: Create a second equation in which you drop the absolute value bars, switch the inequality sign and negate the value on the opposite side. Then solve as normal.

Step 3: Combine the two inequality answers.

Inequalities I Rules Review

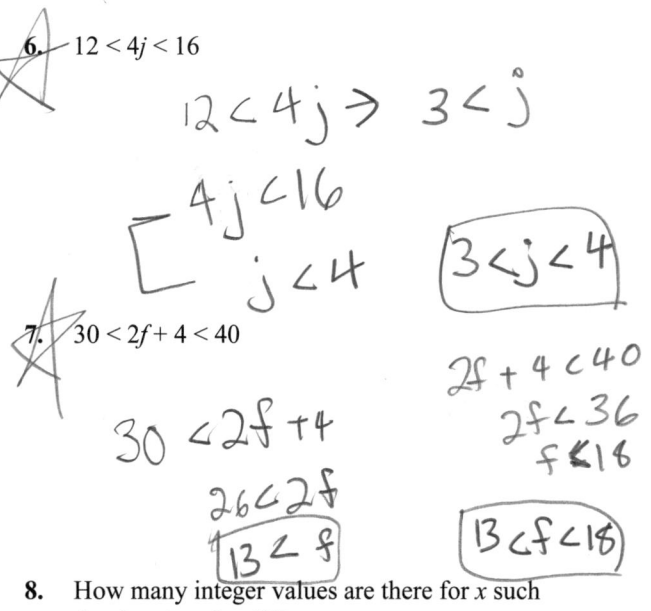

1. $x + 2 > 7$

    $x > 5$

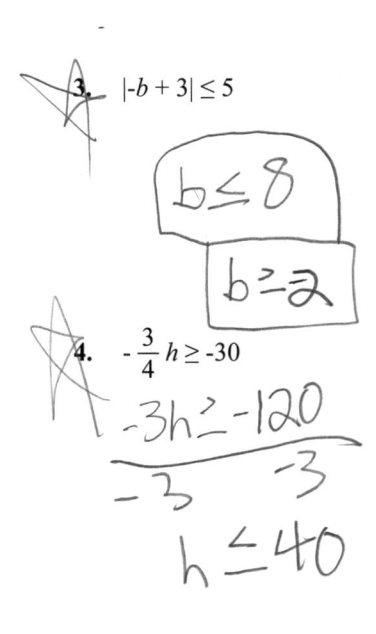

2. $4 - r \geq 1$

3. $|-b + 3| \leq 5$

    $b \leq 8$

    $b \geq -2$

4. $-\frac{3}{4}h \geq -30$

    $\dfrac{-3h \geq -120}{-3 \quad -3}$

    $h \leq 40$

5. $6 - 6x < 30 + 4x$

6. $12 < 4j < 16$

    $12 < 4j \Rightarrow 3 < j$

    $4j < 16$
    $j < 4$

    $3 < j < 4$

7. $30 < 2f + 4 < 40$

    $30 < 2f + 4$
    $26 < 2f$
    $13 < f$

    $2f + 4 < 40$
    $2f < 36$
    $f < 18$

    $13 < f < 18$

8. How many integer values are there for x such that $0 < 4x + 8 < 12$?

9. If $-4 \leq 2x + 6 < 10$, what is the least possible value of $4x^2 - 1$?

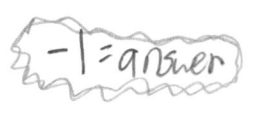

    $-4 \leq 2x + 6$
    $-10 \leq 2x$
    $-5 \leq x$

    $2x + 6 < 10$
    $2x < 4$
    $x < 2$

    $-5 \leq x < 2$

    zero ≠ x

    -1 = answer

Chapter 4

1

$x < k - y$
$-y > x + g$

In the xy-plane, if (0,0) is a solution to the system of inequalities above, which of the following relationships between g and k must be true?

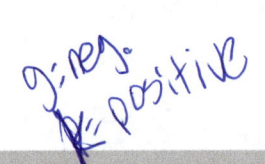

A) $|g| < |k|$
B) $g < k$
C) $-g = k$
D) $|g| = |k|$

2

A farmer harvests wheat and corn each fall. A bag of corn, c, weighs a total of 355 pounds and a bag of wheat, w, weighs 405 pounds. The farmer harvests at most 7,500 pounds each fall, or a maximum of 18 bags. Which of the following systems of inequalities represents this relationship?

A) $\begin{cases} 355c + 405w < 7{,}500 \\ c + w > 18 \end{cases}$

B) $\begin{cases} 355c + 405w > 7{,}500 \\ c + w < 18 \end{cases}$

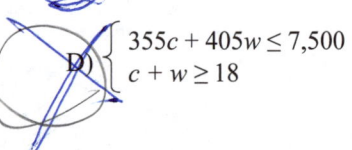

C) $\begin{cases} 355c + 405w \leq 7{,}500 \\ c + w \leq 18 \end{cases}$

D) $\begin{cases} 355c + 405w \leq 7{,}500 \\ c + w \geq 18 \end{cases}$

3

As of June 1, 2015, Ken's bank account holds a total of $23,450. Each month he deposits an additional $330. If Ken is saving up to purchase a car that costs $56,000, which of the following inequalities describes the set of months in which he will have at least enough money to purchase the car if m represents the number of months since June 1, 2015?

A) $56{,}000 - 23{,}450 \geq +330m$
B) $23{,}450 + 330m \geq 56{,}000$
C) $23{,}450 \geq 56{,}000 + 330m$
D) $23{,}450 + 330m \leq 56{,}000$

4

Faye wants to attend the county fair. The price of admission is $12.50, and each ride costs an additional 50 cents. If she can spend at most $23.00 at the fair, which inequality can be used to solve for r, the number of rides Faye can go on?

A) $0.50 + 12.50r \leq 23.00$
B) $12.50 + 0.50r \leq 23.00$
C) $0.50 + 12.50r \geq 23.00$
D) $12.50 + 0.50r \geq 23.00$

5

A track coach bets his runners that he can guess the times it will take them to complete a race within 5 minutes of their official time. When the first runner begins, the coach writes his guess and labels it g. If the runner completes the race in t minutes, which of the following inequalities represents the relationship between the actual time and the coach's correct guess?

A) $g \geq 5 + t$
B) $g < 5 < t$
C) $-5 < g + t < 5$
D) $-5 < g - t < 5$

7

Which of the following is equivalent to $|x - k| < 5$?

A) $x - k < 5$ or $x + k < 5$
B) $x - k < 5$ and $k - x < 5$
C) $x - k < -5$ or $x - k > 5$
D) $x - k > -5$ or $x - k < 5$

6

Which of the following is the solution set for the system of inequalities below?

$$2x \leq 10$$
$$3x + 17 \geq 29$$

A) $x \leq 2$
B) $x \leq 5$
C) $4 \leq x \leq 5$
D) $-4 \leq x \leq 5$

Functions | Overview

What is a Function?
A function is a relation between a set of inputs and a set of allowable outputs such that each input is related to exactly one output. A function is generally denoted like this: $f(x)$, where f represents the output when we use x as the input. Take a look at the example below:

> A company produces t televisions per week. The profit, p, the company makes on the televisions is represented by the following function: $p(t) = 120t - 36$.

In the example above, the profit a company makes (or the output) is dependent on the number of televisions produced (or the input).

Understanding the Pieces of a Function
Many SAT questions require you to understand what each part of a function represents. Take a look at how the function above has been broken down:

$$p(t) = 120t - 36$$

$p(t)$ represents the profit, p, that the company will make, depending on how many televisions, t, it produces.

The number attached to the variable is how much the function increases or decreases by depending on how many televisions are produced. Since we are looking for the profit, 120 represents the amount of money that the company makes per television. Although the amount it makes per television (120) remains constant, the total amount the company makes depends on whether it sells 3 televisions or 3,000 televisions.

The number NOT attached to a variable, in this case 36, represents a fixed quantity that is NOT affected by the number of televisions sold. Since this value of 36 is subtracted in the example above, we know that 36 must represent a cost, or something that takes away from the profit. It may represent something like the fixed monthly cost of producing televisions.

Functions I Overview

Evaluating Functions

Sometimes questions will ask you to evaluate functions, or find the values of functions based on different inputs. Take a look at the example below:

> A company produces t televisions per week. The profit, p, it makes on the televisions is represented by the following function: $p(t) = 120t - 36$, where $120 is the amount of revenue the company makes per television, and $36 is the fixed monthly cost of producing televisions. To the nearest dollar, what is the difference in profit between producing 6 televisions and 9 televisions?

What is it that we are trying to find? _____

How can we find the profit when the company produces 9 televisions?

How can we find the profit when the company produces 6 televisions?

What is the difference between the two scenarios?

Chapter 4

Functions | Overview

Translating Functions

Sometimes instead of giving you the actual function equation, a question will ask you to create an equation based on information given. Take a look at the example below:

> Halifax Tuna Wholesale Company charges restaurants a fixed price of $4.75 per tuna up to 3 pounds, and then an additional $0.40 for each additional pound the tuna weighs. Which function would determine the cost, $c(t)$, in dollars that a restaurant would pay to purchase a tuna weighing t pounds, where t is an integer greater than 3?

What is the function input in the question above? _____

What is the function output value? _____

What factors affect the output? _____

_____

How can we put this information into the form of a mathematical function? Flip back to page 292 if you are not sure where to start.

Chapter 4

Functions | Overview

Composite Functions

Composite functions require you to put two functions together and to evaluate them one step at a time to get a final answer. To work with composite functions, we must remember to always work our way from inside the parentheses outward.

Take a look at an example below:

> The function $f(x)$ is defined as $f(x) = x + 2$ and the function $g(x)$ is defined as $g(x) = 2x$. What is the value of $f(g(5))$?

Step 1: Evaluate the function in the parentheses.

Step 2: Take the value you just found and use it to evaluate the function outside of the parentheses.

Functions | Rules Review

1. If $f(x) = 3x^3$, what is $f(2)$?

   8·3 = 24

   $f(2) = 24$

2. If for all real numbers x, $f(x) = \dfrac{\sqrt{x^2} + 1}{\sqrt{x^2} - 1}$, what is the value of $f(3)$?

   $\dfrac{\sqrt{9} + 1}{\sqrt{9} - 1} = \dfrac{4}{2} = 2$ ✗

3. If for all values of x, $f(x) = \dfrac{5x + 2}{4}$, then what is the value of $f(7) + f(5)$?

   $f(12)$

   $60 + 2 = 62$

   $\dfrac{62}{4} = 15.5$

   15.5

   16

4. For all real numbers p, $f(p) = \dfrac{1}{2}(p + 2)$. What is the value of p such that $f(p) = 18$?

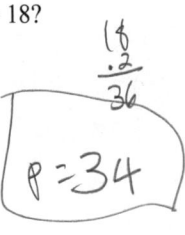

   $\dfrac{18}{\cdot 2}$
   36

   $p = 34$

   $36 \cdot \dfrac{1}{2} = 18$

5. The owner of a tutoring business has one employee, who is paid an hourly rate of $35. The owner estimates his weekly profit using the function $P(x) = 1780 - 35x$. In this function, x represents the number of:

   hours

6. The value in dollars, $d(t)$, of a certain car after t years is represented by the equation $d(t) = 22{,}000(0.73)^t$. To the nearest dollar, how much more is the car worth after 2 years than after 3 years?

   306

   2 yrs = 32,120
   3 yrs = 48,180

   $16,060

7. In 2015, Tourist Taxi charged $1.50 for any ride up to 3 miles and $0.70 per mile for each additional mile. Create a function that would determine the cost, $c(m)$, in dollars of a cab ride of m miles where m is an integer greater than 3?

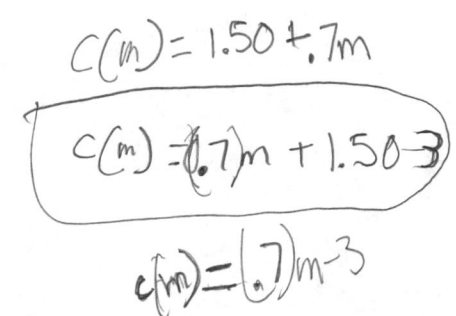

   $c(m) = 1.50 + .7m$

   $c(m) = (.7)m + 1.50$

   $c(m) = (.7)m - 3$

Chapter 4

1

A telemarketing firm began selling and marketing a new product. The total number of sales, S, generated by the firm is defined by the function

$$S(c) = \frac{\frac{4}{5}c}{10} + 275$$

where c is the total number of consumers the firm attempted to call. If the firm attempted to call 3,000 people, what was the total number of sales?

A) 120
B) 240
C) 465
D) 515

2

When Sam studies for a math exam, the grade she receives, g, can be expressed as a function of the time in hours she spends studying, t, and the amount of other homework in hours, h, she has to complete. The grade can be expressed as $\frac{h^2}{t}$. For Sam's final exam, she spent 15 hours on other homework and scored a 75. How many hours did Sam spend studying for her math exam?

A) 3
B) 4
C) 5
D) 6

3

The function f satisfies f(5) = 7 and f(8) = 12. The function g satisfies g(4) = 5 and g(9) = 10. What is the value of f(g(4))?

A) 5
B) 7
C) 10
D) 12

4

$$h = 36 + 2.3b$$

The height of a new building being constructed can be modeled by the expression above, where h is the height of the building in feet and b is the number of bricks added to the foundation. How many bricks have been added to the foundation when the building reaches a height of 700.7 feet?

A) 242
B) 280
C) 289
D) 304

5

x	2	4	6	8
f(x)	4	14	24	34

The table above shows values of the linear function f. Which of the following defines f?

A) f(x) = 5x − 6
B) f(x) = x + 10
C) f(x) = 2x + 10
D) f(x) = 4x + 6

6

$$D = F + \frac{ST}{R}$$

The distance, D, traveled by a Go-Cart at the Ridgeway County Fair can be calculated by adding the force applied to the pedal, F, to the quotient of the highest speed reached, S, multiplied by the time spent driving in minutes, T, and divided by the resistance level of the track, R.

At which of the following times, in minutes will the distance be closest to 1,200 miles if the highest speed reached is 45 miles per hour, the force applied to the pedal is 3.8 newtons, and the resistance level of the track is 1.2?

A) 27
B) 32
C) 41
D) 55

7

$$s(w) = 24 + 12w$$

Katia took over her sister's stamp collection and each week added a fixed number of stamps to the collection. The function above models the number of stamps, s, in Katia's collection after w weeks. According to the model, how many stamps were in Katia's collection when she took it over from her sister?

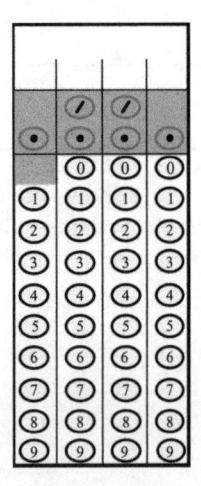

8

An engineer is studying the effects of utilizing robots to mechanize a factory's system of computer manufacturing. He currently has a total of 1,200 computers in inventory. The number of computers he expects the robots to produce next month, $C_{\text{next month}}$, can be estimated by finding the number of computers present in inventory this month, $C_{\text{this month}}$, using the model below.

$$C_{\text{next month}} = C_{\text{this month}} + 0.6(C_{\text{this month}}) \left[1 + \frac{k(C_{\text{this month}})}{k + 10} \right]$$

The constant, k, in this model is the amount of time, in minutes, the robot can run without requiring repairs.

According to the function, what will be the number of computers in inventory at the end of next month if $k = 1{,}550$? (Round your answer to the nearest whole number.)

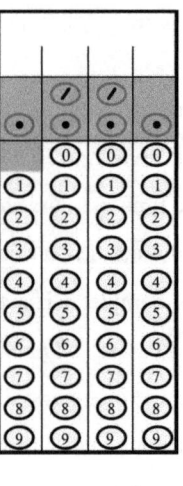

1

A catering company estimated the price, p, of job x, in dollars, using the function $p(x) = 1{,}450 + 90wh$, where w is number of waiters needed and h is the number of hours the waiters must work. Which of the following is the best interpretation of the number 1,450 in the function?

A) The company pays the waiters a total of $1,450.
B) The company is charged a fee of $1,450 by the venue.
C) The company charges a fixed price of $1,450 for working an event.
D) Each waiter works a total of 1,450 hours per year.

2

$$h = 11 + 57.8m$$

An architect uses the model above to estimate the height, h, in feet, of a building, in terms of the months, m, spent constructing it, between 6 and 18. Based on the model, what is the estimated increase, in feet, of the building each month?

A) 11
B) 40.6
C) 57.8
D) 68.8

3

$$h(x) = 15 + jx^3$$

For the function h defined above, j is a constant and $h(3) = 123$. What is the value of $h(-2)$?

A) -17
B) -49
C) 32
D) 49

4

A company that manufactures printers first pays a start-up cost, and then spends a fixed amount to manufacture each printer. If the cost of manufacturing p printers is given by the function $c(p) = 5.25p + 125$, the value 5.25 best represents

A) the fixed cost to manufacture printers each month
B) the profit earned from the sale of one printer
C) the amount spent to manufacture each printer
D) the average number of printers manufactured

5

A cable television company charges a one-time installation fee and a monthly service charge. The total cost is modeled by the function $y = 60 + 106x$. Which statement represents the meaning of each part of the function?

A) y is the total cost, x is the number of months of service, $106 is the installation fee, and $60 is the service charge per month.
B) y is the total cost, x is the number of months of service, $60 is the installation fee, and $106 is the service charge per month.
C) x is the total cost, y is the number of months of service, $60 is the installation fee, and $106 is the service charge per month.
D) x is the total cost, y is the number of months of service, $60 is the installation fee, and $106 is the service charge per month.

6

If $g(x) = -7 - 3x^2$, what is the value of $g(-2x)$?

A) $-7 - 12x^2$
B) $12x^2 - 7$
C) $-7 - 12x^4$
D) $-7 - 6x^2$

4d

PASSPORT TO ADVANCED MATH:

EXPONENT, RADICAL AND QUADRATIC EQUATIONS, QUADRATIC & EXPONENTIAL FUNCTIONS, GRAPHING FUNCTIONS, POLYNOMIAL EXPRESSIONS & FACTORING, IMAGINARY NUMBERS

Chapter 4

Exponents I Overview

When working with exponents on the SAT, it is important to memorize and understand the rules in the table below:

You can only ADD or SUBTRACT expressions with exponents if they have the **same base AND the same exponent**.		
$x^2 + y^2$ remains $x^2 + y^2$	$x^2 + x^3$ remains $x^2 + x^3$	$x^2 - x^3$ remains $x^2 - x^3$
$5y^2 - y^2$ becomes __$4y^2$__	$y^2 + y^2$ becomes __$2y^2$__	$15y^2 - 7y^2$ becomes __$8y^2$__
You can multiply expressions with exponents if they have the **same base**. To multiply expressions with the same base, add the exponents and keep the base the same.		
$x^5 \cdot y^4$ remains $x^5 \cdot y^4$		$y^2 \cdot y^3$ becomes __y^5__
You can divide expressions with exponents **only** if they have the **same base**. To divide numbers with the same base, subtract the exponents and **keep the base**.		
$\dfrac{x^5}{y^3}$ remains $\dfrac{x^5}{y^3}$	$\dfrac{y^5}{y^3}$ becomes __y^2__	$\dfrac{3^8}{3^6}$ becomes __3^2__
You can rewrite expressions with different bases **only** if they have the same exponents		
$x^2 \cdot y^2$ can be written as x^2y^2 or as $(xy)^2$	$3^2 \cdot 5^2$ can be written as $(3 \cdot 5)^2$ or as $(15)^2$	$\dfrac{12^5}{3^5} = \left(\dfrac{12}{3}\right)^5 = 4^5$
When raising an expression with exponents to another exponent, multiply the exponents, **but keep the base**.		
$(x^3)^5$ becomes __x^{15}__	$(2^4 x^5)^3$ becomes __$2^{12} x^{15}$__	$(3x^4 y^5)^2$ becomes __$9x^8 y^{10}$__
You **cannot** distribute exponents around addition/subtraction signs.		
$(5^3 + 2^2)^2 \neq 5^6 + 2^4$	$(x^3 + y^2)^2 \neq x^6 + y^4$	$(x^3 + y^2)^2 = (x^3 + y^2)(x^3 + y^2)$
To work with values that have different bases, try using the **change of base formula** to get the values in terms of a similar base.		
$2^{3x+3} = 8^{6x}$ 8 can be rewritten as 2^3 $2^{3x+3} = 2^{3(6x)}$ $2^{3x+3} = 2^{18x}$ $3x + 3 = 18x$ $x = 5$	$3^{5x-2} = 9^{4x}$ $3^{5x-2} = (3^2)^{4x}$ $x =$ _____	$4^{3x+6} = 64^{2x}$ $x =$ _____

301

www.bellcurves.com

Exponents | Overview

There are some other things to keep in mind when dealing with exponents:

1. A fractional exponent is another way to express a root: $3^{\frac{2}{3}} = \sqrt[3]{3^2}$

2. To eliminate a negative exponent, put the number under 1 and change the exponent to positive:

    $3^{-2} = \dfrac{1}{3^2}$ or $x^{-3} = \dfrac{1}{x^3}$

3. Positive fractions get smaller when raised to powers: $\left(\dfrac{1}{2}\right)^2 = \dfrac{1}{4}$

4. A negative number raised to an even power will become positive: $\left(-\dfrac{1}{2}\right)^2 = \dfrac{1}{4}$

5. A negative number raised to an odd power will stay negative: $(-3)^3 = -27$

6. One raised to any power = one. $1^{40} = 1$

7. Zero raised to any power = zero. $0^{40} = 0$

8. Anything raised to the zero power = one. $x^0 = 1$

9. If $x^2 = 16$, then $x = 4$ or -4. Whenever you see even exponents, always consider negative values for the base as well.

10. Keep in mind that $(-2)^2 = 4$, but $-2^2 = -4$

Example:
If $8^3 = 2^x$, what is the value of x?
A) 3
B) 4
C) 8
D) 9

Explanation:
The variable in this problem is in the exponent place. Thus, in order to solve for x, we are going to have to use some exponent rules.

Which rule(s) of exponents would could we use here?

_____

How would you rewrite the equation?

Therefore, the answer to the problem above is _____.

Exponents | Rules Review

1. $x^5 + x^5 =$

   x^{10}

2. $(x^5)(x^4) =$

   x^{20}

3. $\dfrac{y^{16}}{y^7} =$

   y^9

4. $(3x^3)^4 =$

   $3^4 x^{12}$

5. $9x^5 - 3x^5 =$

   $6x^5$

6. $\dfrac{9^{13}}{9^3} \cdot 9^{5-12} =$

   $9^{10} \cdot \dfrac{1}{9^7} =$ 9^3 $(3^2)^3 = 3^6$

7. $(a^4)(a^4)(a^4) =$

   a^{64}

Chapter 4

Roots | Overview

Like exponents, roots have several rules. Memorize these rules to increase your speed and accuracy with root-related problems.

The square root of a number asks what number, when squared, gives the value under the root. (The square root operation **always** yields a positive value!)		
$\sqrt{16} =$ _4_	$\sqrt{x^2} =$ _x_	$\sqrt{4y^4} =$ _$2y^2$_

If there is addition or subtraction to be done underneath the root then those operations must be completed first.		
$\sqrt{9+9} =$ _$\sqrt{18}$_	$\sqrt{x^2 + x^2} =$ _$\sqrt{x^4}$_	$\sqrt{a-b} \neq \sqrt{a} - \sqrt{b}$

When adding or subtracting, the number under the root must be the same.		
$3\sqrt{2} + 4\sqrt{2} =$ _$7\sqrt{2}$_	$9\sqrt{7} - 14\sqrt{7} =$ _$-5\sqrt{7}$_	$3\sqrt{2} + 4\sqrt{3} = 3\sqrt{2} + 4\sqrt{3}$

When multiplying or dividing roots, multiply or divide the numbers outside of the root, and then separate or combine the items under the root.		
$\sqrt{(36)(16)} =$ _24_	$\sqrt{\frac{25}{4}} =$ _5/2_	$4\sqrt{2} \cdot 2\sqrt{3} =$ _____

When the result under the root is not a perfect square you should look for ways to simplify the root. You can do this by factoring out perfect squares.		
$\sqrt{75} =$ _$5\sqrt{3}$_	$\sqrt{48} =$ _$4\sqrt{3}$_	$\sqrt{a^2 b} =$ _$a\sqrt{b}$_

Typically, roots will not be left in the denominator; the fraction will be re-expressed to remove the roots.		
$\frac{1}{\sqrt{3}} = \frac{1}{\sqrt{3}} \cdot \frac{\sqrt{3}}{\sqrt{3}} = \frac{\sqrt{3}}{3}$	$\frac{10}{\sqrt{5}} =$ _____	$\frac{x}{\sqrt{y}} =$ _____

If there is a negative number under a square root sign, the answer is an imaginary number, a topic we will discuss later in the chapter.

SAT-R Workbook v. 1.5

Roots | Rules Review

1. $5\sqrt{5} + 4\sqrt{5} =$

2. $\sqrt{3} \cdot \sqrt{12} =$

3. $7\sqrt{3} - \sqrt{108} =$

4. $\sqrt{\dfrac{147}{3}} + \sqrt{\dfrac{64}{9}} =$

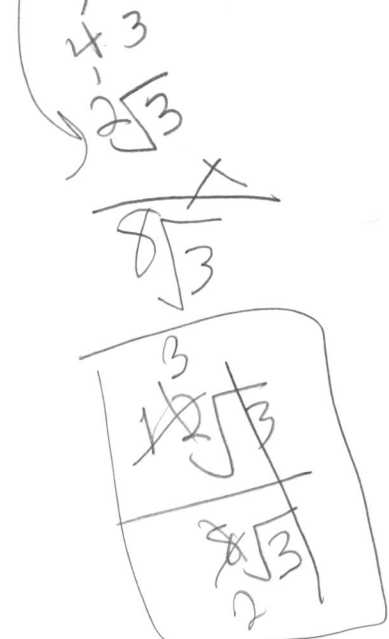

5. $\sqrt[3]{343} =$

6. $\dfrac{\sqrt{\dfrac{36}{12}}}{\sqrt{\dfrac{12+4}{5+7}}} =$

Chapter 4

1

If g and h are positive real numbers, in the equation below, what is g in terms of h?

$$\sqrt{g} + 4\sqrt{h} = 7\sqrt{h}$$

A) $3h$
B) $9h$
C) $9\sqrt{h}$
D) $49\sqrt{h}$

2

In the equation $A = b^x$, b is a constant and $x > 0$. If the value of A decreases as the value of x increases, which of the following must be true?

A) $-1 < b < 0$
B) $b = 0$
C) $0 < b < 1$
D) $1 < b$

3

If $g = 3\sqrt{3}$ and $2g = \sqrt[4]{16x}$, what is the value of x?

4

Which of the following is equal to the expression $b^{\frac{5}{4}}$, for all values of b?

A) $\sqrt[\frac{4}{5}]{b^{\frac{5}{4}}}$
B) $\sqrt{b^{\frac{4}{5}}}$
C) $\sqrt[4]{b^5}$
D) $\sqrt[5]{b^4}$

5

Which of the following could be the value of $\sqrt{x^4}$ for some integer x?

A) 2
B) 5
C) 6
D) 9

6

If $\dfrac{27x^k}{9x^4} = 3x^{18}$ and $2x^{a^2} \cdot 5x^{b^2} \cdot x^{ba} \cdot 3x^{ba} = 30x^{49}$ what is the value of $k(a + b)$?

A) 67
B) 140
C) 154
D) The value cannot be determined from the information given.

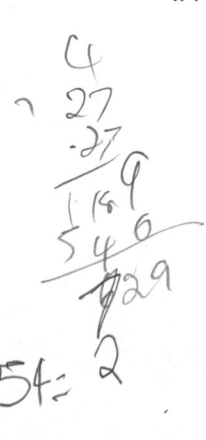

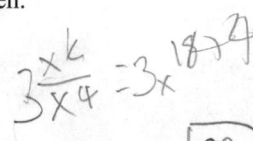

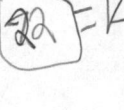

SAT-R Workbook v. 1.5

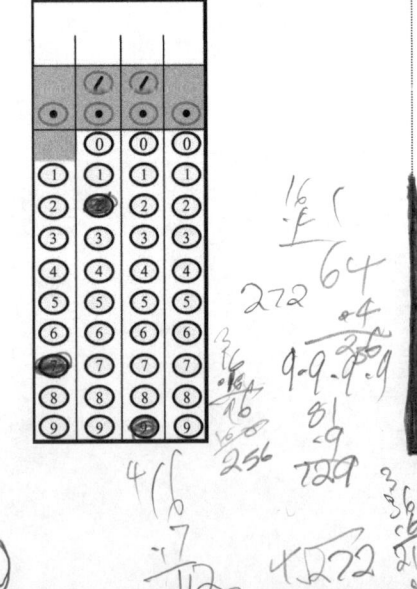

Chapter 4

Working With Polynomials | Overview

What is a Polynomial?
A polynomial is an algebraic expression consisting of more than 2 algebraic terms, particularly terms that contain different powers of the same variable.

Adding/Subtracting Polynomials
You can only add or subtract values with the same variables that are raised to the same exponents (like terms). For example

$$4x + 5x = \underline{9x}$$

$$4x + 5y = \underline{4x+5y}$$

$$4x - 5x^2 = \underline{}$$

$$4x^3 + 5x^2 - 10x^3 = \underline{-6x^3 + 5x^2}$$

When you subtract polynomials, it is important to pay attention to any parentheses you may see. For example

$$(5x^2 - 10x^3) - (-3x^2 + 8x^3)$$

The first step in subtracting polynomials is to rewrite the polynomials, without the parentheses, switching the signs in the second polynomial. Therefore, the equation would look like this:

Now combine like terms as we did above to get the final answer:

Multiplying Polynomials
Any time you multiply numbers with variables, follow traditional exponent and fraction rules. For example

$$6x(5x^3) = \underline{}$$

If you are multiplying something by a polynomial, use the FOIL (First-Outer-Inner-Last) Method. For example

$$(5x + 6)(4y - 2) =$$

First: _____

Outer: _____

Inner: _____

Last: _____

$$(5x + 6)(4y - 2) = \underline{}$$

www.bellcurves.com

Working With Polynomials | Overview

Fractional Polynomials: Addition/Subtraction
To add fractions with polynomials, add or subtract following the same rules as those for working with normal fractions. This means that the first thing we must always do is find a common denominator. Let's work through an example below:

$$\frac{x+2}{11} + \frac{5}{3x} =$$

Step 1: Find the common denominator. To do so, multiply both fractions by what one denominator is "missing" but that the other one has. Remember to use FOIL if necessary.

Step 2: Add the numerators, keeping the denominator the same. Combine like terms if possible.

Fractional Polynomials: Multiplication
Multiplying fractional polynomials is easier than adding fractions. To do so, multiply straight across the numerator and straight across the denominator. Remember to use FOIL.

$$\frac{x+2}{11} \times \frac{5}{3x} =$$

Fractional Polynomials: Division
Dividing fractions is very similar to multiplying them. There are two steps to follow. First, we switch the division sign to a multiplication sign, and then we switch the numerator and the denominator of the second fraction.

$$\frac{x+2}{11} \div \frac{5}{3x} =$$

Chapter 4

1

$(4x^2y^2 - 2x^2 + 3xy^2) + (-xy^2 + 3x^2 + 7x^2y^2)$

Which of the following is equivalent to the expression above?
A) $3x^2y^2 - x^2 - 4xy^2$
B) $5x^2y^2 + x^2 + 2xy^2$
C) $-3x^2y^2 + x^2 + 4xy^2$
D) $5x^2y^2 - x^2 - 4xy^2$

2

The expression $9xy - 4x(5x + 2y)$ is equivalent to
A) $-19xy$
B) $xy - 20x^2$
C) $9xy - 20x^2$
D) $17xy - 20x^2$

3

$(7x^2 - 5x + 2) - (1 - 4x + 3x^2)$ is equivalent to
A) $4x^2 - x + 1$
B) $4x^2 - x - 1$
C) $10x^2 - 9x + 1$
D) $4x^2 - x^2 - 1$

4

$(x - 2)(x^2 + 3x - 2)$

Which of the following is equivalent to the expression above?
A) $x^3 + x^2 - 8x + 4$
B) $x^3 + x^2 + 2x - 4$
C) $x^3 + x^2 + 8x - 4$
D) $x^3 + 5x^2 + 2x + 4$

5

$4x^2 + 2x - 6$
$-7x^2 + 5x - 11$

Which of the following is the difference of the two polynomials shown above?
A) $3x^2 - 7x - 5$
B) $11x^2 - 3x - 5$
C) $-3x^2 + 7x - 17$
D) $11x^2 - 3x + 5$

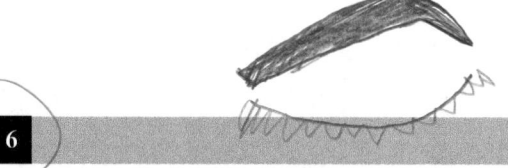

6

$-3(2x^2 - 7x + 3) - 4(-x^2 - 2x + 4)$

If the expression above is rewritten in the form of $ax^2 + bx + c$, where a, b, and c are constants, what is the value of $a + b$?

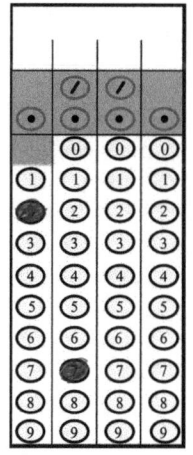

309

Chapter 4

Quadratic Functions | Overview

Quadratic Equations are polynomials that have variables raised to the 2nd power or greater. The standard form for a Quadratic Equation is $ax^2 + bx + c = 0$.

Foiling, as we discussed in the previous section, is used to turn binomials into a complete quadratic expression. However, to turn a quadratic expression into binomials, we must factor. There are three main types of factoring you may encounter on the SAT exam.

Greatest Common Factor (GCF) Method: To use this method, you must find a common factor to pull out of each element of the expression.

Example:
$$8x^3 + 4xy^3 - 24xz$$

What is the GCF of the three terms in the expression above? _____

When we pull this GCF out of each term, what are we left with? _____

Difference of Perfect Squares Method: The second type of factoring is the Difference of Perfect Squares method. To use this method, one perfect square must be subtracted from another in the given expression.

Example:
$$16x^2 - 100$$

Step 1: Set up two sets of parentheses, one with an addition sign in the middle and the other with a subtraction sign in the middle.

(−   )(+   )

Step 2: Find the square root of the first element in the expression and put it st the beginning of each set of parentheses. Find the square root of the second element in the expression and put it at the end of each set of parentheses.

(_____ − _____)(_____ + _____)

SAT-R Workbook v. 1.5

Quadratic Functions | Overview

Quadratic Factoring Method:
The third type of factoring is the Quadratic Factoring method. In order to use this method, a quadratic equation must be in standard form.

Example: $x^2 + 2x - 24 = 0$

To factor this, we must find a pair of numbers that multiply to equal the constant term and that also add to equal the coefficient of the *x* term. Set up those numbers in a pair of parentheses:

( )( )

If the question had asked you not simply to factor the quadratic equation, but to find the roots (or zeroes), we would set each root equal to 0 and solve.

( ) = 0   ( ) = 0

x = _____   x = _____

If there had been a coefficient in front of the x^2 term, we could not have used the method above. If you see a coefficient in front of the x^2 term, first ask yourself if there is a GCF that you can pull out from all of the terms.

Example:

$4x^2 + 20x + 16 = 0$

Step 1: Since we see a number in front of the x^2 term, we see if we can factor out a GCF.

Step 2: Factor the expression inside the parentheses in the same way as in the example above.

Chapter 4

Quadratic Functions | Overview

Quadratic Formula
Another way to algebraically solve quadratic equations when they don't factor into integers is to use the Quadratic Formula. The Quadratic Formula is:

$$\frac{-b +/- \sqrt{b^2 - 4ac}}{2a}$$

a is the coefficient of the x^2 term. If there is no coefficient written, a is equal to 1, NOT 0.
b is the coefficient of the x term. If there is no coefficient written, b is equal to 1, NOT 0.
c is the value of the third term.

Let's work out an example together:

Find the roots of $4x^2 - 2x - 5 = 0$

a is equal to _____

b is equal to _____

c is equal to _____

Now plug these values into the formula:

The **discriminant** in a quadratic equation, $b^2 - 4ac$, provides us with a lot of information about the roots, or zeroes, of an equation.

If $b^2 - 4ac < 0$ then the two roots are imaginary (complex)
If $b^2 - 4ac = 0$ then there is only one real root
If $b^2 - 4ac > 0$ then there are two distinct, real roots
If $b^2 - 4ac =$ a positive perfect square then there are two distinct real, rational roots

Quadratic Functions | Overview

Factoring by Grouping

We can use the *factoring by grouping* technique to factor a wide variety of equations, even ones that are not in the standard Quadratic Formula. Take a look at the example below:

For what real value of x is the following equation true: $2x^3 - 12x^2 + 5x - 30 = 0$

Step 1: Pull out the GCF from the first two terms. (If there is no GCF, switch the order of the terms so that you are able to pull out a GCF from the first two.)

Step 2: Pull out the GCF from the last two terms.

Step 3: Combine the GCF from the first two terms with the GCF from the last two terms to create a binomial.

Step 4: Multiply the binomial from Step 3, by the common binomial in Steps 1 and 2 and then set the product equal to 0 to solve for the roots.

Quadratic Functions | Overview

Another option if you are unable to factor out a GCF from all of the terms is to factor using the Rainbow Technique. To do so, follow the steps below:

Example: $4x^2 + 20x + 21 = 0$

Since we are unable to factor out a common factor that would leave a coefficient of 1 in front of the x^2 term, we know that we may be able to use the Rainbow Technique.

Step 1: Multiply the leading coefficient by the constant term.

Step 2: For the value you just found, find a set of factors that add together to give you the coefficient of the x term.

Step 3: Rewrite the equation separating the x term into a sum of the factors from the previous step.

Step 4: Factor by grouping. (See the previous page if you need a reminder.)

No matter which technique we may use to factor a quadratic equation, the format is always the same:

$$a(x^2 - (\text{sum of the roots})x + (\text{product of the roots}))$$

where *a* is the leading coefficient of the x^2 term and has been factored out of each of the other terms.

Another way to think about finding the sum of the roots of a quadratic equation is by solving for it using: $\frac{-b}{a}$

Quadratic Functions | Overview

1. If $x > y$, $x^2 - y^2 = 63$, and the sum of x and y is 9, what is the value of x?

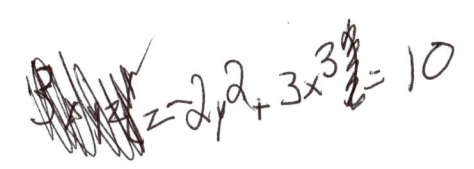

2. If $(2x - 4)(x + 3) = 0$, what are all possible values of x?

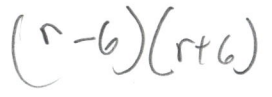

3. If $x^2 + 4x + 4 = 0$, what are all possible values of x?

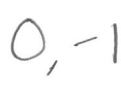

    $8x^2 + 16x + 24 = 0$

4. In the quadratic equation above, what is the value of the sum of all the roots?

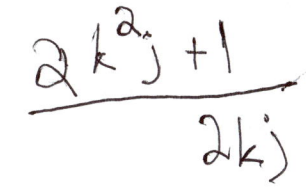

5. Factor the following equation:
   $3xyz^2 - 6xy^3z + 9x^4yz = 30xyz$

6. Factor the equation $r^2 - 36 = 0$

7. Simplify the equation $\dfrac{16k^4j^3 + 4kj}{8k^2j^2}$

    $2x^2 + 5x - 11 = 0$

8. In the quadratic equation above, what are the values of the roots?

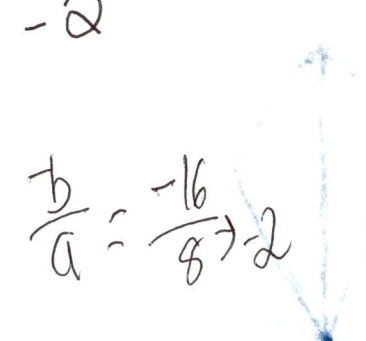

Chapter 4

1

What is the sum of all values of p that satisfy $4p^2 + 8p + 24$?

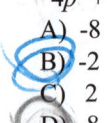

A) -8
B) -2
C) 2
D) 8

2

If $p < 0$ and $p^2 - 16 = 0$, what is the value of p?

A) -16
B) -4
C) -2
D) -0.5

3

$$5x(2x + 6) - 2(4x - 1) = ax^2 + bx + c$$

In the equation above, a, b, and c are constants. If the equation is true for all values of x, what is the value of c?

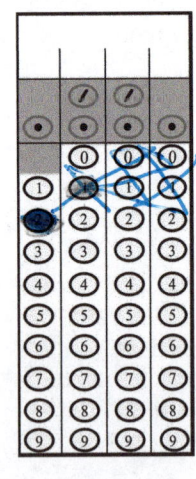

4

What are the zeroes of the equation

$$3x^2 + 4x - 10 = 0$$

A) $x = \dfrac{-2 \pm \sqrt{34}}{6}$

B) $x = \dfrac{-2 \pm \sqrt{34}}{3}$

C) $x = \dfrac{-4 \pm \sqrt{34}}{3}$

D) $x = \dfrac{-2 \pm \sqrt{136}}{3}$

5

What is the sum of the solutions of $x^2 + x - 20 = 0$?

A) -9
B) -1
C) 1
D) 4

6

$$6x^3 - 24x^2 + 8x - 32 = 0$$

For what real value of x is the equation above true?

SAT-R Workbook v. 1.5

Exponential Functions | Overview

What is Exponential Growth?
Exponential growth happens when the rate of growth increases more rapidly in proportion to a growing total. Therefore, the larger the total you have, the larger the rate of growth. Exponential growth is NOT a linear function, as the number does not increase by the same amount each time.

A commonly tested type of exponential growth is the amount of interest accrued on a bank account over time.

The formula for interest is

$$P = C \left(1 + \frac{r}{n}\right)^{nt}$$

where:

P = Future Value
C = Initial Deposit
r = Interest Rate
t = Number of years invested
n = Number of times per year the interest is compounded

If you are told that the interest is compounded "annually," this means that the interest is added to the total only one time per year. Therefore, a simpler way to think about that equation would be

$$P = C(1 + r)^t$$

What is Exponential Decay?
Exponential decay is the opposite of exponential growth. Instead of the rate of growth increasing as time passes, the rate of decay increases as time passes. Therefore, instead of the quantity increasing, it is decreasing.

The general formula for exponential decay is very similar to the formula for growth. However, instead of adding the rate of change, you must subtract it:

$$P = C(1 - r)^t$$

Chapter 4

1

A radioactive substance being studied in a lab decays at an annual rate of 7%. If the initial amount of the substance was equal to 428 milligrams, which of the following functions models the amount remaining after a total of 8 years?

A) $f(8) = 428(1.07)^8$
B) $f(8) = 428(1.7)^8$
C) $f(8) = 428(.93)^8$
D) $f(8) = 428(8)^{.07}$

Questions 2 and 3 refer to the following information.

Nina opened a bank account that earns 6% interest compounded annually. Her initial deposit was $250. She uses the model $250(x)^t$ to assess the value of the account after t years.

2

What is the value of x in the expression above?

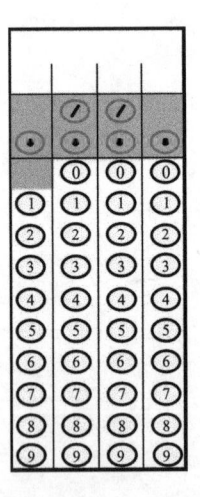

3

Nina's sister Lisa opened an account at a bank next door and deposited $250 on the same day that Nina did. Lisa's bank offers a 4.5% interest rate compounded annually. After 25 years, how much more money will Nina have in her account than Lisa? (Round your answer to the nearest dollar and ignore the dollar sign when gridding your response.)

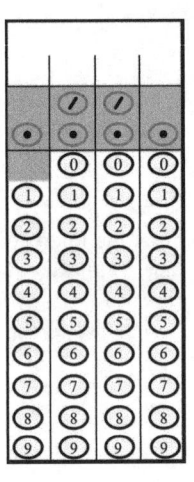

4

Of the following four types of radioactive decay schedules, which option would yield exponential decay?

A) Each successive year, 15 milligrams of the substance decays.
B) Each successive year, 2.5% of the original amount of the substance decays.
C) Each successive year, 3.6% of the current amount remaining of the substance decays.
D) Each successive year, 1.5% of the current amount is added to the remaining substance.

5

A city planner estimates that, starting from the present, the population of the city will increase by 6% every 15 years. If the current population of the city is 76,000, which of the following expressions represents the city planner's estimate of the population t years from now?

A) $76{,}000(.06)^{15t}$

B) $76{,}000(1.06)^{15t}$

C) $76{,}000(.94)^{\frac{t}{15}}$

D) $76{,}000(1.06)^{\frac{t}{15}}$

7

Tara was given $2,700 by her grandparents when she turned 5 years old. Her parents invested it for her at a 3% interest rate compounded annually. No deposits or withdrawals were made. Which expression can be used to determine how much money Tara had in the account when she turned 18?

A) $2700(1 + 0.03)^{13}$
B) $2700(1 - 0.03)^{13}$
C) $2700(1 - 0.03)^{18}$
D) $2700(1 + 0.03)^{18}$

6

The population of bacteria in a laboratory study is calculated over the course of 50 days, as shown in the table below.

Time (Days)	Bacteria Population
0	20
10	60
20	180
30	540
40	1,620
50	4,860

Which of the following best describes the relationship between time and the bacteria population during the 60 days?
A) Exponential growth
B) Exponential decay
C) Increasing linear
D) Decreasing linear

8

$$P = 750\left(1 + \frac{r}{52}\right)^{52t}$$

The expression above models the amount of money, in dollars, accrued in a year after an initial $750 deposit in an account that pays an annual inerest rate of r compounded weekly. Which of the following expressions represents the difference between the amount of money accrued in this account, versus one offering the same interest rate but compounded daily?

A) $750\left(1 + \frac{r}{52}\right)^{52t} + 750\left(1 + \frac{r}{365}\right)^{365t}$

B) $750\left(1 + \frac{r}{52}\right)^{52t} - 750\left(1 + \frac{r}{365}\right)^{365t}$

C) $750\left(1 + \frac{r}{52}\right)^{52t} - 750\left(1 + \frac{r}{52}\right)^{365t}$

D) $750\left(1 + \frac{r}{52}\right)^{52t} - 750\left(1 - \frac{r}{365}\right)^{52t}$

Chapter 4

Function Graphs | Overview

Functions can be represented graphically on a coordinate plane, with the values on the *x*-axis representing the *inputs*, or those numbers in the *domain*, while the *y*-axis represents the outputs, or the values of *f*(*x*) that compose the *range*.

The SAT may test your understanding of this concept by giving you a graph and asking you to use the graph to evaluate a function. Take a look at the example below:

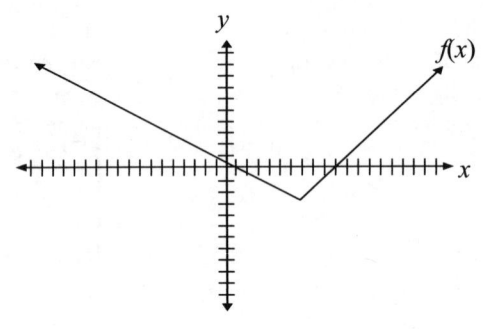

In the graph above, what is the value of *f*(10) ?
A) -2
B) 0
C) 1
D) 2

Is *f*(10) the input or the output of the function above? _____

Does this mean we will get our answer from the *x*-axis or the *y*-axis? _____

Therefore, the value of *f*(10) is equal to _____.

Chapter 4

1

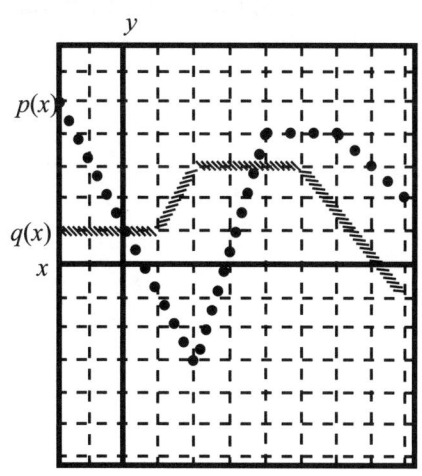

Graphs of functions p and q are shown in the xy-plane above. For which of the following values of x does $p(x) + q(x) = 0$?

A) -3
B) 2
C) 3
D) 7

2

The complete graph of the function f is shown below. Which of the following is/are equivalent to 0?

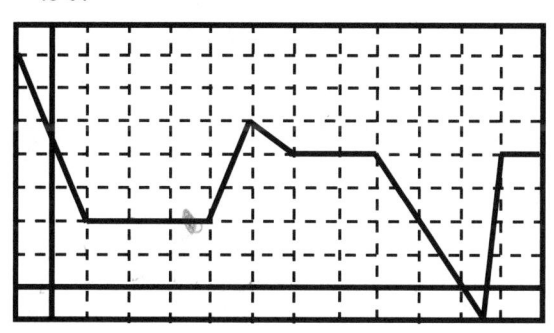

I. $f(10)$
II. $f(1) - f(4)$
III. $f(3.5)$
IV. $2f(5) - f(10)$

A) I only
B) III and IV only
C) I and II only
D) I, III and IV only

3

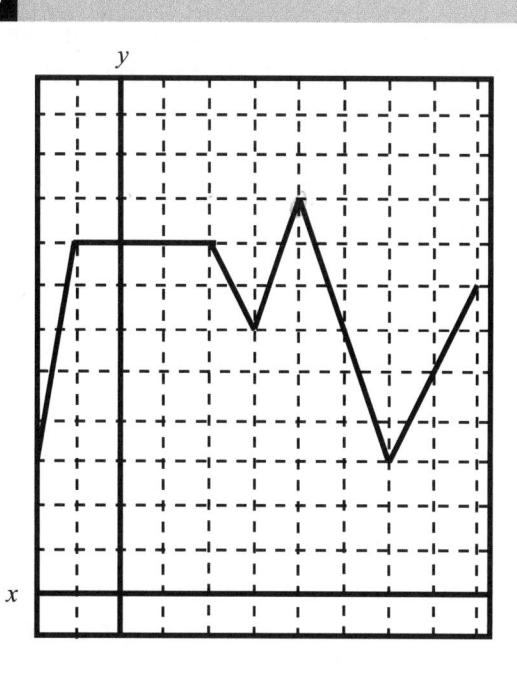

The complete graph of the function f is shown in the xy-coordinate plane above. For what value of is the value of the function at its maximum?

A) 1
B) 4
C) 8
D) 9

4

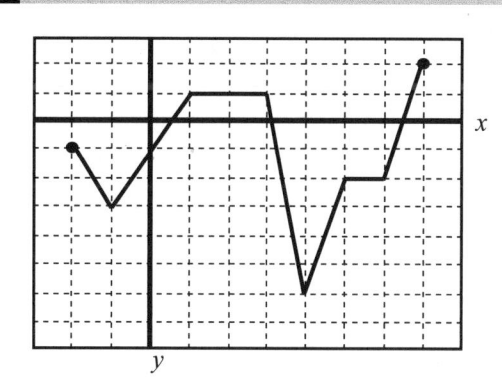

The complete graph of the function f is shown in the xy-plane above. For what two values of x, will the sum of their $f(x)$ values be equal to 0?

A) -1 and 1
B) -1 and 0
C) 2 and 4
D) 7 and 5

Quadratic Function Graphs | Overview

Many times you may not be given a graph to accompany a function equation in a question. In these situations, on the calculator section of the exam, you can actually graph these functions as opposed to using algebra to solve them.

Prior to taking the exam, make sure that you are completely comfortable with how to graph on your calculator. Below is a step-by-step guide as to how to graph using a Texas Instrument graphing calculator.

$$\text{Graph the following expression: } 2f(x) = 4x + 6$$

Step 1: Manipulate the equation to put it in terms of $f(x)$ or y, depending on which format you are given in the question, and then simplify it if you're able.

Step 2: On the upper right corner of your calculator click the Y = button.

Step 3: On the first line, where it says \Y$_1$ = , enter your equation: $2x + 3$. (Use the X,T,θ,N button to get the x variable.)

Step 4: Press the GRAPH button located on the upper right side of the calculator.

When working with the graphs of quadratic functions, we can add to this basic plan a couple of steps that will help us solve for the roots or turning point (vertex) of a particular function.

Quadratic Function Graphs | Overview

The graph of a quadratic equation is a parabola:

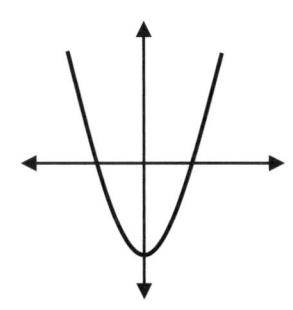

The solutions to a quadratic equation (also called roots or zeroes) on a graph are the locations at which the graph crosses the *x*-axis. Therefore, instead of solving for the solutions algebraically, which involves a lot of factoring, you can simply graph on your calculator. (This holds true for algebraic equations raised to any degree: The number of roots an equation has is equal to the number of times the graph crosses the *x*-axis.)

To graph a quadratic equation on the calculator, the equation MUST be set equal to 0. If it is not, first manipulate the equation to move everything to one side so that it is equal to 0.

Step 1: Follow Steps 1 – 4 on page 322.

Step 2: To find the exact points at which the graph crosses the *x*-axis, click 2ND, TRACE (CALC), and select number 2: zero.

Step 3: This will take you back to the screen with the graph, and you will see a blinking cursor on the parabola. Choose the leftmost location where the parabola crosses the *x*-axis, and using the left arrow button, move the cursor so that it is anywhere to the left of that point. Then press ENTER.

Step 4: Now move the cursor so that it is to the right of that point, and press ENTER again. Make sure that the cursor is only to the right of the first intersection, and is NOT also to the right of the second point of intersection.

Step 5: The calculator will prompt you to Guess. Press ENTER again. It will then display your first zero as the *x* value on the lower left corner of the screen.

Step 6: Repeat steps 2 – 5 to calculate the second point of intersection.

Chapter 4

Quadratic Function Graphs | Overview

Turning Point (Vertex)
The turning point (vertex) is the point on a parabola at which the curve changes direction. In the example below, the dotted arrow is pointing to the turning point.

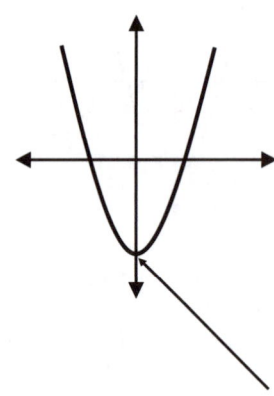

There are two ways to find the turning point of a graph: algebraically and graphically.

Algebraically
To solve algebraically, you can use the formula below to find the x-coordinate of the turning point, and then plug that value back into the given equation to find the corresponding y-coordinate.

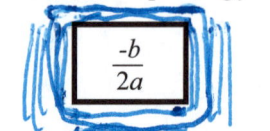

$$\frac{-b}{2a}$$

where a is the leading coefficient in a quadratic equation and b is the coefficient of the x term.

Graphically

Step 1: Follow Steps 1 – 4 on page 322.

Step 2: Click 2ND, TRACE (CALC), and select number 3 or 4, maximum or minimum. If the graph opens upward, choose minimum, and if it opens downward, choose maximum.

Step 5: This will take you back to the screen with the graph, and you will see a blinking cursor on your graph. Using the left arrow button, move the cursor anywhere to the left of the turning point. Press ENTER.

Step 6: Move the cursor to the right of that point, and press ENTER again.

Step 7: The calculator will prompt you to Guess. Press ENTER again. It will then display the x and y coordinates of the turning point.

Quadratic Equations in Vertex Form
The vertex form of a quadratic equation is as follows:

$$f(x) = a(x - h)^2 + k$$, where (h,k) is the vertex of the parabola, and a is the coefficient of the x^2 term.

SAT-R Workbook v. 1.5

1

$$y = x^2 - 14x - 32$$

The equation above represents a parabola in a standard *xy*-coordinate plane. Which of the following equivalent forms of the equation displays the roots of the equation as constants or coefficients?

A) $y + 32 = x^2 - 14x$
B) $y = x(x - 14) - 32$
C) $y = (x - 16)(x + 2)$
D) $y + 14x = x^2 - 32$

2

$$a(x + 7)(x - 3)$$

In the quadratic equation above, *a* is a nonzero constant. The graph of the equation in the *xy*-coordinate plane is a parabola with vertex (*p*, *q*). Which of the following is equal to *pq*?

A) $75a$
B) $50a$
C) $25a$
D) $2a$

3

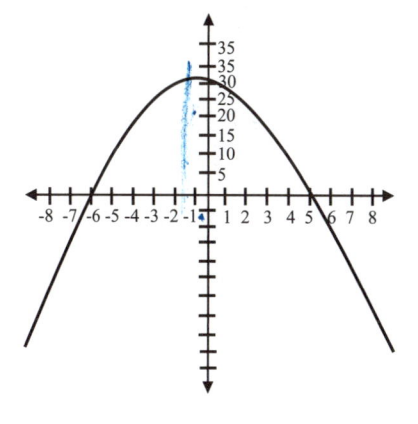

Which of the following is the equation for the graph shown above?

A) $-(x^2 - x - 30) = 0$
B) $x^2 - x - 30 = 0$
C) $-(x^2 + x - 30) = 0$
D) $x^2 + x + 30 = 0$

4

In the *xy*-coordinate plane, the graph of function *g* has *x*-intercepts at -5, -2, and 7. Which of the following could define *g*?

A) $g(x) = (x - 7)(x - 5)(x - 2)$
B) $g(x) = (x - 7)(x + 5)(x + 2)$
C) $g(x) = (x - 7)(x + 5)(x - 2)$
D) $g(x) = (x + 7)(x - 5)(x - 2)$

5

$$g(x) = -(x+3)(x-8)$$

Which of the following is an equivalent form of the function g above in which the maximum value of g appears as a constant or coefficient?

A) $g(x) = (x-32)^2 + 2.5$
B) $g(x) = -(x-2.5)^2 + 32$
C) $g(x) = -(x+2.5)^2 + 30.25$
D) $g(x) = -(x+30.25)^2 + 2.5$

6

If the function g has six distinct zeroes, which of the following could represent the complete graph of g in the xy-coordinate plane?

A)

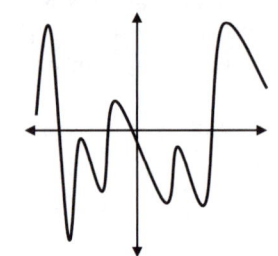

B)

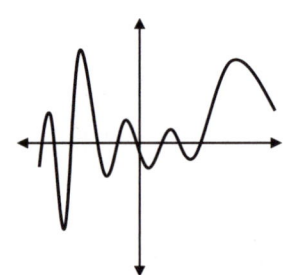

C)

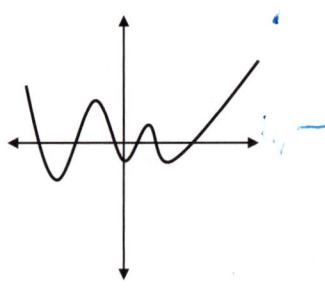

D)

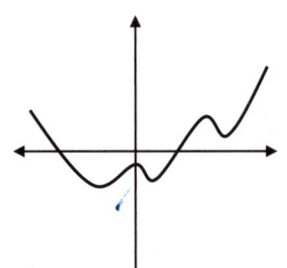

Chapter 4

Inequality Function Graphs | Overview

Inequality functions can also be graphed on a standard (x, y) coordinate plane. The only difference between graphing an inequality and graphing a normal line or quadratic equation, is that after graphing the inequality, we must shade in the area containing the range of values that satisfy the equation.

Check out the example below to see how we can use a calculator to graph inequalities:

$$\text{Graph the inequality: } f(x) \geq x + 2$$

Step 1: Follow Steps 1 – 3 on page 322.

Step 2: Once you enter an equation, on the left side next to Y_1 you should see a slash, or \
Scroll over until you are on top of that slash and it is blinking. Press ENTER until you see ◥.
This symbol means $\geq$. If the equation is $\leq$ press ENTER one more time and you will see ◣.

Step 3: Press GRAPH, which is located in the top right corner of your calculator.

The graph of the inequality function above is below:

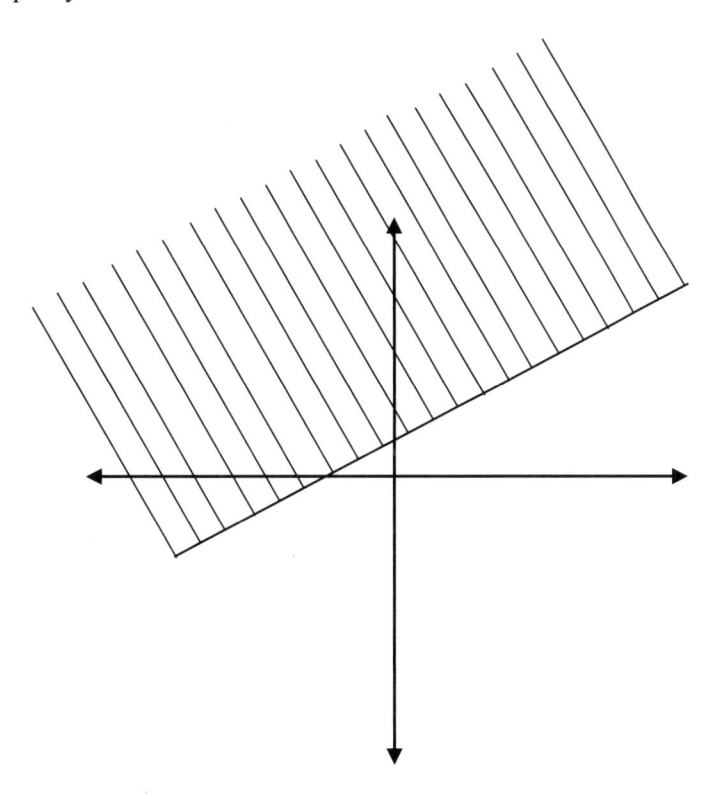

Chapter 4

Systems Of Equations Graphs | Overview

Just as we solved systems of equations earlier algebraically, we can also solve them graphically.

To solve a sytem of equations graphically, the first step is to graph each equation. Then to find the solution that satisfies both equations, follow the steps below:

Step 1: Follow Steps 1 – 4 on page 322 for each equation.

Step 2: Click 2ND - TRACE (CALC).

Step 3: Select 5: intersect.

Step 4: The cursor will show up on the first curve and you will be asked "First curve?" Press ENTER. Then do the same for the second curve. The calculator will then ask you to GUESS. Press ENTER again.

Your answer will be displayed as the x and y coordinates at the bottom of the screen.

Systems of Inequalities

To graphically find the solution to a system of inequalities, first graph each inequality. Then to find the solution set, locate the area on the graph where the shading from both inequalities overlaps.

Exponential Function Graphs | Overview

Exponential Growth
On a graph, exponential growth looks like this:

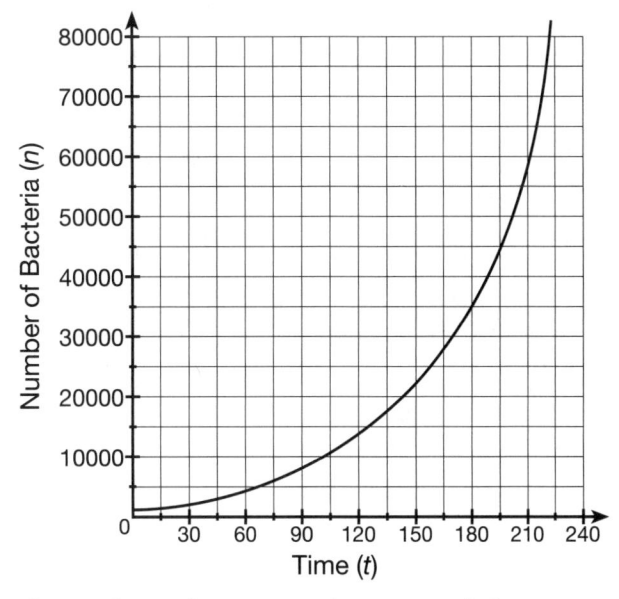

Notice that this graph is not linear. The *y*-axis represents the amount of what we are measuring, and the *x*-axis represents the time.

What information does the *y*-intercept of the graph tell us? _____

Exponential Decay
On a graph, exponential decay looks like this:

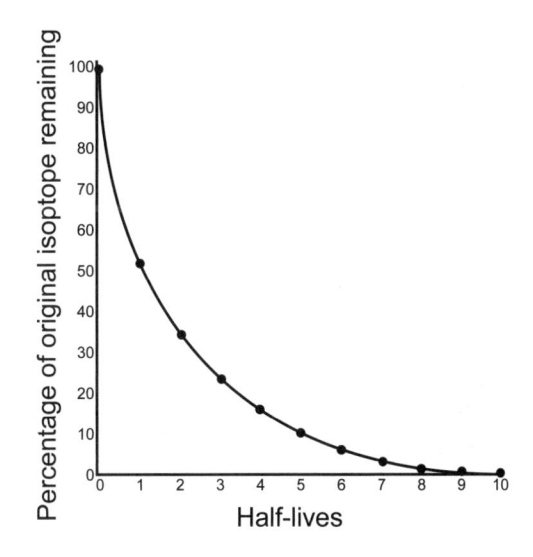

Notice that again, this graph is not linear. As with the growth graph, the place where the line crosses the *y*-axis is equal to the initial amount of the substance.

Chapter 4

1

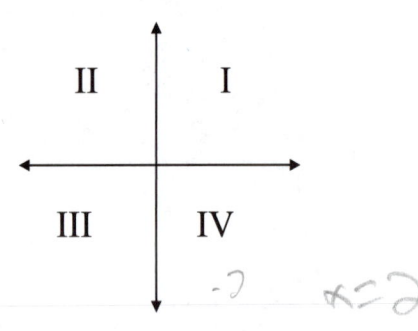

If the system of inequalities $y < 3x + 6$ and $y \geq (x-4)^2 + 3$ is graphed on the xy-coordinate plane shown above, which quadrant would contain the solutions to the system?

A) Quadrant I
B) Quadrant II
C) Quadrant III
D) Quadrant IV

2

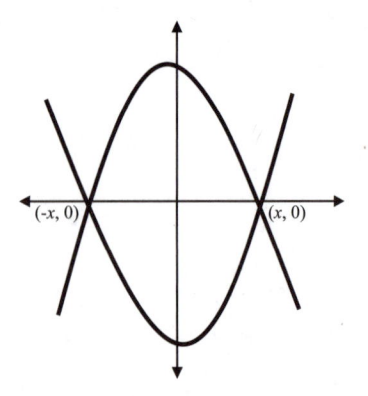

The functions p and q, defined by $p(x) = 3x^2 - 9$ and $q(x) = -3x^2 + 9$, are graphed in the xy-coordinate plane shown above. The graphs of p and q intersect at points $(x, 0)$ and $(-x, 0)$. What is the value of x?

A) 1
B) $\sqrt{3}$
C) 3
D) $2\sqrt{3}$

3

The number of bricks at a construction site triples every month during the building period. Which of the graphs below could model the number of bricks present at the site throughout the building period?

A) 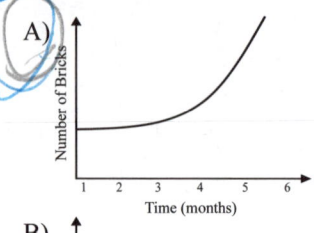
B) 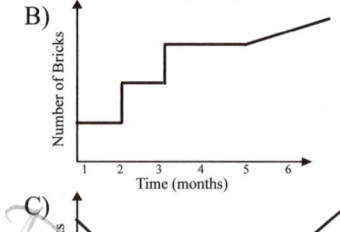
C)
D)

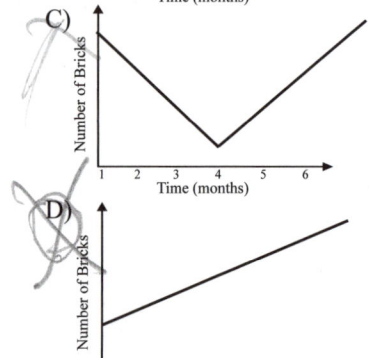

4

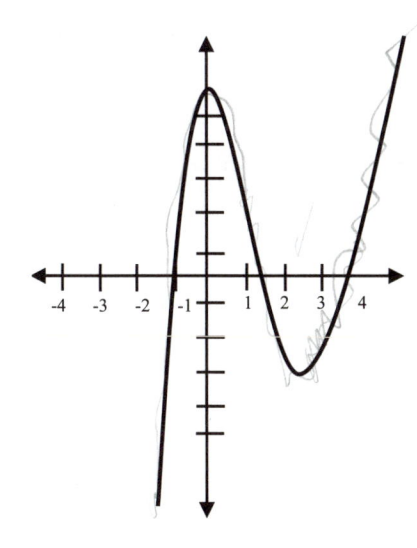

The function $g(x) = x^3 - 4x^2 - .25x + 6$ is graphed in the *xy*-coordinate plane shown above. If *k* is a constant and $f(x) = k$ has two real solutions, which of the following could be the value of *k* ?

A) -4
B) -1
C) 3
D) 6

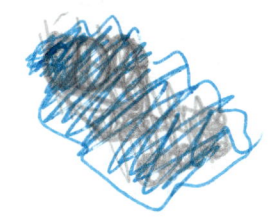

Imaginary (Complex) Numbers | Overview

Imaginary numbers (denoted by *i*) are the opposite of real numbers. They are formed as a result of finding the square root of a negative number.

Example:

$$\sqrt{-16} = 4i$$
$$\sqrt{-25} = 5i$$

Working with imaginary numbers is similar to working with any other variable, with a couple of exceptions:

1. The most commonly tested rule is that $i^2 = -1$.

    Example:
    $$(7i)(10i) = 70i^2 = 70(-1) = -70$$

2. Imaginary numbers raised to other exponents have meanings as well.

$$i = \sqrt{-1}$$
$$i^2 = -1$$
$$i^3 = -\sqrt{-1}$$
$$i^4 = 1$$

Following i^4, the values continue to cycle in loops of 4.

$i^5 =$ _____

$i^6 =$ _____

$i^7 =$ _____

$i^8 =$ _____

3. When imaginary numbers are in the denominators of fractions, they must be treated as if they were radicals, and the fraction must be *rationalized*. In order to rationalize a denominator, an imaginary binomial expression must be multiplied by its *conjugate*.

    Example: $\dfrac{3}{i-7}$

    Step 1: Multiply both the numerator and denominator by the conjugate.

    Step 2: Simplify using your knowledge of imaginary numbers raised to exponents.

4. If complex numbers show up on the calculator section, you can find the answer using the calculator. To type in *i*, hit 2ND and then the period (.) button.

SAT-R Workbook v. 1.5

Chapter 4

Imaginary (Complex) Numbers | Rules Review

1. Evaluate: $\sqrt{-121}$

    $11i$

2. $(6 + 2i)(3 - 4i) =$

    $18 - 24i + 6i - 8i$

    $18 - 26i$

    $26i, 18$

3. $(4 + 7i)^2 =$

    $16 + 49i^2$

    $16 - 49$

    -33

    $56i - 33$

    $\downarrow$

    $16 + 28i + 28i + 49i^2$

    $16 + 56i - 49$

    $-33 + 56i$

4. Simplify: $\dfrac{11 + 4i}{1 - 3i} \cdot \dfrac{1+3i}{1+3i} = \dfrac{11 + 33i + 4i - 12}{1 + 3i - 3i - 9i^2}$

    $\dfrac{11 + i}{11 + 5i}$

    $\dfrac{-1 + 37i}{10}$

5. $(2 + 3i)(2 - 3i) =$

    $4 - 6i + 6i - 9i^2$

    $4 - 9i^2$

    $4 + 9 = 13$

6. $11 + i(7 - i) =$

    $11 + 7i - i^2$

    $7i + 12$

www.bellcurves.com

Chapter 4

1

If $i^2 = -1$, which of the following is equivalent to $(2 + i)^2 - (2 - i)^2$?

A) 0
B) 2
C) $4i$
D) $8i$

2

If x is a positive real number, which of the following expressions represents $x + \sqrt{-36x^2}$ as a complex number?

A) $6xi$
B) $7xi$
C) $6xi + x$
D) $12xi + x$

3

For all pairs of nonzero real numbers x and y, the product of $yi - x$ and which of the following expressions is a real number?

A) $-yx$
B) $xi - y$
C) $xi + y$
D) $yi + x$

4

Which of the following complex numbers is equivalent to $\dfrac{5i + 6}{3i - 4}$?

A) $\dfrac{38i + 9}{-25}$

B) $\dfrac{38i - 9}{-25}$

C) $\dfrac{38i - 9}{16}$

D) $\dfrac{38i + 9}{16}$

5

For the complex number i and an integer b, which of the following is a possible value of $1 + i^b$?

A) -1
B) 0
C) 1
D) 1.5

6

For $i = \sqrt{-1}$, what is the difference of $(9 - 4i)$ and $(-6i - 5)$?

A) $14 - 2i$
B) $4 + 2i$
C) $4 - 10i$
D) $14 + 2i$

4e GEOMETRY & TRIGONOMETRY:

LINES & ANGLES, TRIANGLES, CIRCLES, POLYGONS, COORDINATE GEOMETRY, 3D GEOMETRY, TRIGONOMETRY

Chapter 4

Geometry | Overview

Geometry is not a very big topic on the SAT. However, the questions in this topic often rely on your knowledge of formulas and rules dealing with a limited number of shapes. The majority of the formulas you need are provided at the beginning of each math section. The reference information you are given looks like this:

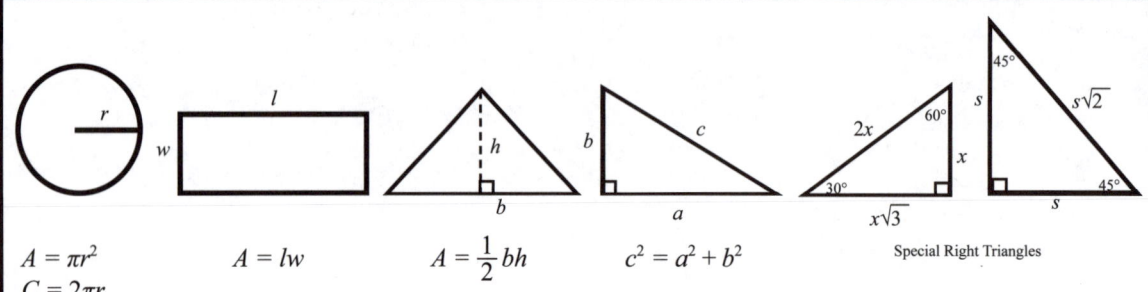

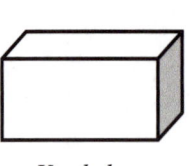

$A = \pi r^2$
$C = 2\pi r$

$A = lw$

$A = \frac{1}{2}bh$

$c^2 = a^2 + b^2$

Special Right Triangles

$V = lwh$

$V = \pi r^2 h$

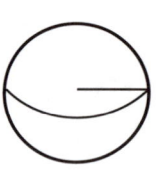

$V = \frac{4}{3}\pi r^3$

$V = \frac{1}{3}\pi r^2 h$

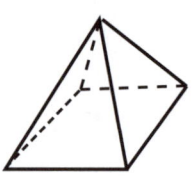

$V = \frac{1}{3}lwh$

The number of degrees of arc in a circle is 360.
The number of radians of arc in a circle is 2π.
The sum of the measures in degrees of the angles of a triangle is 180°.

SAT-R Workbook v. 1.5

Geometry | Overview

Use the following approach to attack geometry questions:

1. Draw the figure and write in the necessary information.
Not all geometry problems give you a figure. When they do not, draw your own so you can visualize the problem. The figure is a great place to begin solving by writing in all the information from the problem as well as any information you can deduce.

2. Write down all the formulas you may need.
Many geometry problems require the use of one formula or another. Make sure you write down the ones that you will need for any given problem.

3. Plug numbers into the appropriate formula.
Plug the information from your figure and from the problem into the formulas you have written down.

4. Solve for the values that you can solve for.
While you may not get the answer from one formula, the value you can solve for in that formula may be pivotal in another that will lead you to the final answer.

The most commonly tested type of geometry is coordinate geometry, a topic that is not covered in the given reference information.

Chapter 4

Coordinate Geometry | Overview

Term	Definition
Equation of a Line	__$y = mx + b$__, where m is the __slope__ and b is the __y-intercept__. This is also known as slope-intercept form.
y–intercept	The y-intercept of a line is point _____ where the line crosses the y-axis
x–intercept	The x-intercept of a line is point _____ where the line crosses the x-axis.
Slope	_____ or _____ **Vertical** lines have a(n) _____ slope. **Horizontal** lines have a slope equal to _____. **Perpendicular** lines have slopes that are _____. **Parallel** lines have slopes that are _____.
Midpoint Formula	The midpoint of a line segment in the coordinate plane can be found by taking the averages of the x coordinates and y coordinates of two endpoints: $x_{av} = \dfrac{x_1 + x_2}{2}$ $\quad$ $y_{av} = \dfrac{y_1 + y_2}{2}$
Distance Formula	$\sqrt{(x_1 - x_2)^2 + (y_1 - y_2)^2}$ where (x, y) is one endpoint and (x_1, y_1) is the other.
Equation of a Circle	_____ where h and k represent _____ respectively and r represents the _____.
Quadrants	The quadrants in a coordinate plane are numbered as shown in the diagram to the right. II I III IV

Coordinate Geometry | Overview

Equation of a Circle

As we saw in the chart on the previous page, the equation of a circle on a coordinate plane is as follows:

$$(x-h)^2 + (y-k)^2 = r^2$$

Sometimes a question may ask us to find out information about the center of a circle or the length of the radius but will give us an equation that looks very different from the above equation of a circle. Look at the example below:

> $$x^2 + y^2 - 4x + 6y = 4$$
>
> The equation of a circle in the xy-coordinate plane is shown above. What is the radius of the circle?

On first glance it may seem like the radius is equal to 2 since the number to the right of the equal sign is the radius squared in the equation of a circle. However, that is only true when the equation is in the standard form. Our example is not. Therefore, in order to solve this equation, we must manipulate it to put it in standard form.

To handle questions like these, we can use a technique called **Completing the Square**.

$$x^2 + y^2 - 4x + 6y = 4$$

Step 1: Move the constant to the side of the equal sign opposite the rest of the terms if it is not there already. In this case, the constant is already there so we do not need to worry about that.

Step 2: Rearrange the terms so that all of the terms with x's are next to one another and all of the terms with y's are next to one another.

Step 3: Find half of the coefficient of the x term and square it. Then add that term to both sides. Then repeat this process for the y terms.

Step 4: Factor the left side of the equation to get it in "squared form."

Step 5: Now that the equation is in standard form, we can identify the center or the radius, depending on what the question is asking for.

The center of the equation above is _____

The radius of the equation above is _____

www.bellcurves.com

Coordinate Geometry | Rules Review

1. What is the slope of a line that passes through points (4, 6) and (9, 7)?

2. What is the length of a line segment with endpoints at the origin and (5, 12)?

3. What is the y-intercept of the line with the equation $10y = 5x - 12$?

4. What is the equation of a circle with a center at (8, 5) and a radius of 4?

5. If a line with slope $\frac{4}{3}$ also passes through point (15, 4), what is the equation of that line?

6. What is the slope of a line with a y-intercept of 5 and an x-intercept of -4?

7. Line r is perpendicular to the x-axis and passes through point (-6, 12). What must be the equation of line r ?

1

In the *xy*-coordinate plane, the line determined by the points (3, *b*) and (*b*, -14.5) passes through the point (5, 3). Which of the following could be the value of *b* ?

A) -2
B) 4
C) 7
D) 10

2

If line *p* contains points in Quadrants III and IV, but no points from Quadrants I or II, which of the following must be true?

A) The slope of line *p* is positive.
B) The slope of line *p* is negative.
C) The slope of line *p* is zero.
D) The slope of line *p* is undefined.

3

In the *xy*-coordinate plane, square *DEFG* has a center at point *H*. The coordinates of points *D* and *H* respectively, are (5, 9) and (2, 5.5). What is the slope of the diagonal connecting points *E* and *G* ?

A) $-\dfrac{6}{7}$

B) $-\dfrac{9}{5.5}$

C) $\dfrac{7}{6}$

D) It cannot be determined from the given information.

4

Chef Liam is catering a dinner party. In order to decide where to purchase the food and rent waiters and silverware from, he created the table below.

Company Name	Cost of Food, *F* (dollars)	Rental Cost of Waiters, *W* (dollars per hour)	Rental Cost of Silverware, *S* (dollars per hour)
X	1,250	22	19
Y	1,625	14	16
Z	1,420	31	15

The total cost, *y*, for buying the food and renting the waiters and silverware in terms of the number of hours, *x*, is modeled by the equation $y = (W + S)x + F$.

If the relationship between the total cost, *y*, of buying the food and renting the waiters and silverware for *x* hours is graphed on the *xy*-coordinate plane, what does the slope of the line represent?

A) The cost of buying food
B) The total cost of catering the dinner party
C) Chef Liam's profit from catering the dinner party
D) The cost of renting the waiter and silverware

5

Which of the following represents a circle in the *xy*-coordinate plane with a center at (-2, 5) and a diameter with endpoint (-6, 14)?

A) $(x + 2)^2 + (y + 5)^2 = \sqrt{97}$
B) $(x - 2)^2 + (y + 5)^2 = 97$
C) $(x + 2)^2 + (y - 5)^2 = \sqrt{97}$
D) $(x + 2)^2 + (y - 5)^2 = 97$

6

The graph of line g on an xy-coordinate plane has an x-intercept at a and a y-intercept at b. If b − a is equal to 0 and a = b, which of the following is true about the slope of line g ?
A) It is positive.
B) It is negative.
C) It is undefined.
D) it equals zero.

7

A line in the xy-coordinate plane passes through the point (1,5) and has a slope of -4. Which of the following points lies on the line?
A) (5, -9)
B) (7, -19)
C) (9, -22)
D) (11, -32)

8

$$x^2 + y^2 + 8x - 12y = 11$$

The equation of a circle in the xy-coordinate plane is shown above. What are the coordinates of the center of the circle?
A) (6, 4)
B) (-4, -6)
C) (-4, 6)
D) (6, -4)

Chapter 4

1

The line $y = kx - 3$, where k is a constant, is graphed in the xy-coordinate plane. If the line contains the point (a, b), where $a = 0$ and $b = 0$, what is the slope of a line perpendicular to the given one in terms of a and b?

A) $\dfrac{a}{3 + b}$

B) $\dfrac{3 + b}{a}$

C) $\dfrac{a}{-3 - b}$

D) $\dfrac{-a}{-3 - b}$

2

The graph of a line in the xy-coordinate plane has a slope of -5 and contains the point (2, 7). The graph of a second line passes through the points (2, 10) and (9, -11). If the two lines intersect at the point (m, n), what is the value of $n - m$?

A) -16
B) -5.5
C) 5
D) 16

3

Which of the following equations has a graph in the xy-coordinate plane for which y is always less than or equal to 4?

A) $y = -|2x| - 8$
B) $y = (-x)^2 + 4$
C) $y = |x| + 4$
D) $y = -|2x| - 4$

4

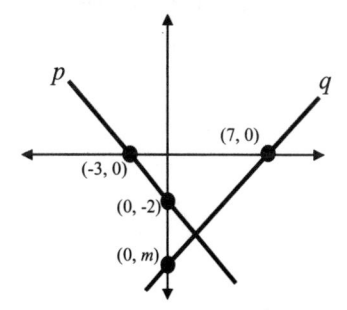

In the xy-coordinate plane shown above, line p is perpendicular to line q. What is the value of m?

A) -7.75
B) -9
C) -10.5
D) -12

5

In the standard xy-coordinate plane, the line $2y - 14x = -24$ is perpendicular to a line with the equation

A) $y = 7x + \dfrac{1}{12}$

B) $y = \dfrac{1}{7}x + 15$

C) $y = -\dfrac{1}{7}x - 21$

D) $y = -7x + 16$

Lines And Angles | Overview

Below is a chart with the important terms and concepts you will need to know about lines and angles.

Term/Concept	Definition
Parallel	
Perpendicular	
Bisect	
Midpoint	
Vertical Angles	
Supplementary Angles	
Complementary Angles	

Chapter 4

1

If $y = 2x = 3z$, what is the value of z in the six segments that intersect as shown below?

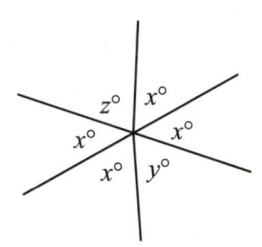

Note: Figure not drawn to scale.

A) 27°
B) 36°
C) 54°
D) 60°

2

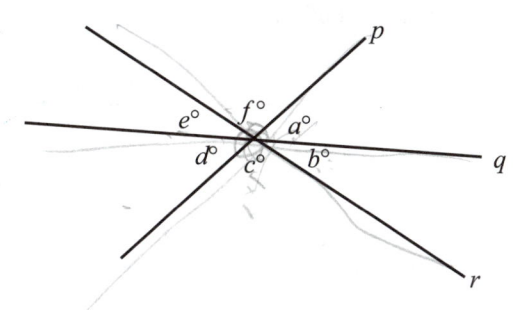

Note: Figure not drawn to scale.

In the figure above, lines p, q, and r intersect at a point. Which of the following must be true?

A) $a + b + c = a + b + d$
B) $f - e = c - b$
C) $f + c = a + d$
D) $a + c = b + d$

3

In the figure below, parallel lines j, k and l are cut by transversal, h. What is the value of $(x + y) - (z + q)$?

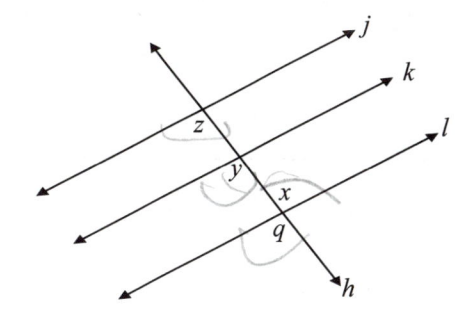

A) 0°
B) 90°
C) 180°
D) 360°

4

In the figure below, E and B are on line GH and AB and CD are parallel to one another. Points J and K lie on line EF. The measure of angle CKF is 27° and the measure of angle HBJ is 120°. What is the measure of angle GEJ?

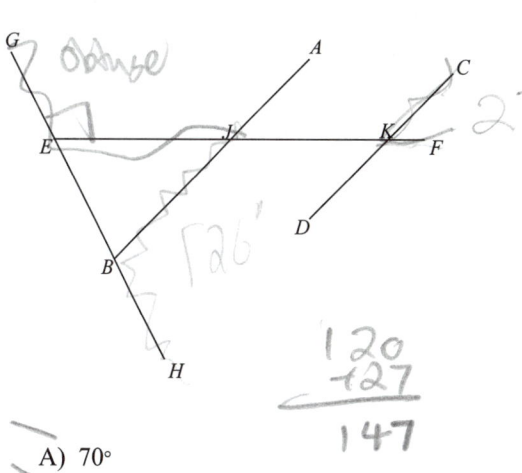

A) 70°
B) 83°
C) 87°
D) 93°

Triangles | Overview

What is a Triangle?
A triangle is defined as a plane figure with three straight sides and three angles.

Important Triangle Definitions and Formulas

Term	Definition and Formula
Congruent ($\cong$)	Equal
Similar Triangles ($\sim$)	Triangles are similar if they have the same shape, but they can be different sizes. The sides of similar triangles are in proportion to one another. Two triangles can be proven similar by proving that _____.
Degrees	There are _____ in any triangle.
Right Triangle	A right triangle has one right (90°) angle.
Isosceles Triangle	An isosceles triangle has two congruent sides and two congruent angles. The congruent angles are opposite (directly across from) the congruent sides.
Equilateral Triangle	An equilateral triangle has three congruent sides and three congruent angles. Each angle in an equilateral triangle measures _____.
Scalene Triangle	A scalene triangle has no congruent sides.
Obtuse Triangle	An obtuse triangle is one in which one angle measures greater than 90°.
Acute Triangle	An acute triangle is one in which all three angles measure less than 90°.
Third Side Rule	The Third Side Rule states that the third side of any triangle will always be **greater** than the **difference** of the other two sides, but **less** than the **sum** of the other two sides.
Pythagorean Theorem	_____, where c is the hypotenuse of the right triangle.

Side - Angle Relationships

In any triangle, the largest angle is always directly opposite the largest side, and the smallest angle is always directly opposite the smallest side. Any angles across from equal sides are also equal to one another.

Take a look at the triangle below:

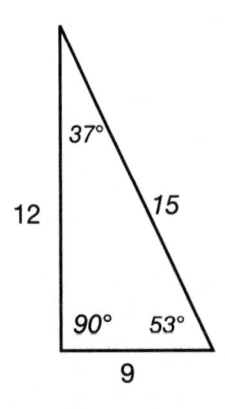

```
       37°
      /|
     / |
   15  12
   /   |
  /53° |90°
 ------
    9
```

The largest side (15) is directly opposite the largest angle 90°. The smallest side (9) is directly opposite the smallest angle, 37°.

Chapter 4

Triangles I Overview

Similar Triangles

Triangles are *similar* if they have equal angle measures as well as sides that are in proportion to one another. Similar triangles differ from *congruent* triangles in that congruent triangles must have equal angle measures AND equal side measures.

The two triangles in this picture are similar:

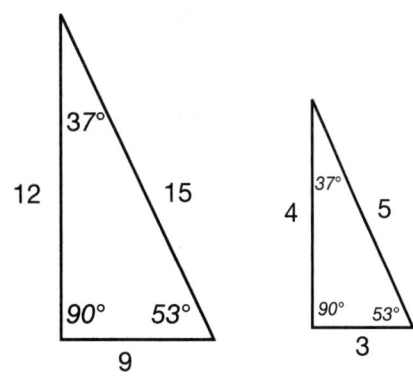

When working with similar triangles, you must know which side or angle from Triangle *A* corresponds directly with which side or angle from Triangle *B*.

Whenever one triangle is inscribed via a parallel line, inside another triangle (as in the example below), the two resulting triangles are similar.

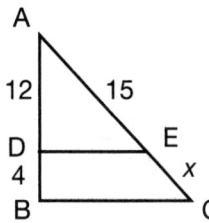

You are able to prove two triangles congruent using the Angle-Angle Theorem. This theorem states that as long as two triangles have two angle measures in common, they are similar.

Which angles in the triangles ADE and ABC are congruent to one another? _____

_____

Knowing that they are similar, we are able to solve for the missing piece, *EC*. Since we know that the sides of similar triangles are in proportion with one another, we can set up a ratio that follows the pattern:

$$\frac{\rule{2cm}{0.4pt}}{\rule{2cm}{0.4pt}} = \frac{\rule{2cm}{0.4pt}}{\rule{2cm}{0.4pt}}$$

When we solve for *x*, we find that it is equal to

www.bellcurves.com

Triangles | Rules Review

1. What is the area of a triangle with a height of 5 and a base of 8?

2. What is the height of a triangle with base 6 and area 30?

3. If the area of a right triangle with integer sides is 30, what could be the lengths of its legs?

4. An isosceles triangle has sides of lengths of x, y, and z. If the length of x is 6 and the perimeter of the triangle is 20, what are the possible lengths of each of the sides of the triangle?

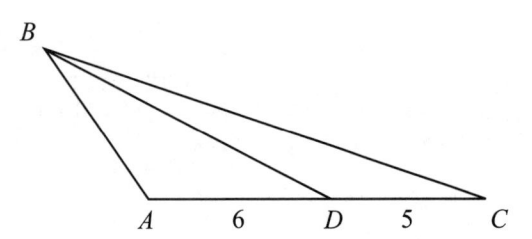

5. What is the area of triangle ABC in the figure above if the area of triangle ABD is 12?

6. If in triangle ABC, $AB = 9$ and $BC = 7$, what is the range of possible values for AC?

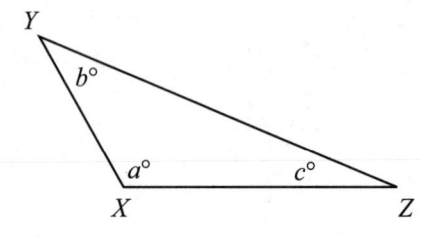

Note: Figure not drawn to scale.

7. If $XY < XZ < YZ$, then what is the proper angle ordering, from least to greatest, in triangle XYZ?

8. Triangle A has a height of 10 and a base of 4. If triangle B and A have equal areas and the height of triangle B is half that of triangle A, what is the base of triangle B?

Chapter 4

1

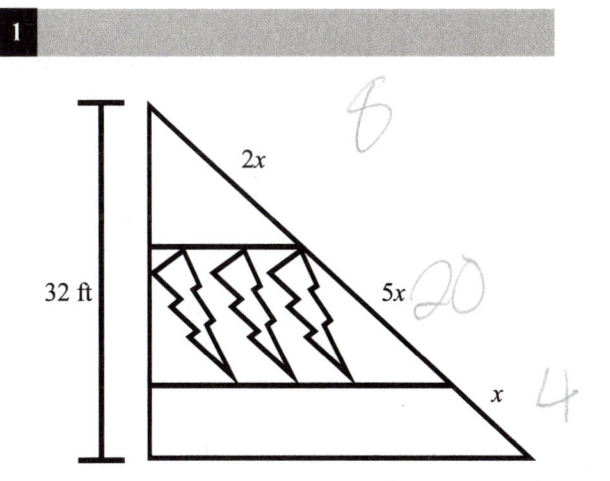

For their upcoming homecoming game, the Rockford High Bolts are creating a right-triangular flag measuring 32 feet in height. The flag is cut into three sections by two parallel lines, as shown above. What is the maximum vertical height, in feet, of the lightning bolts they can paint in the middle section?

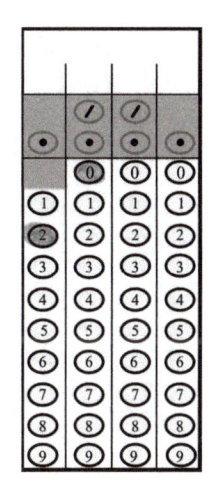

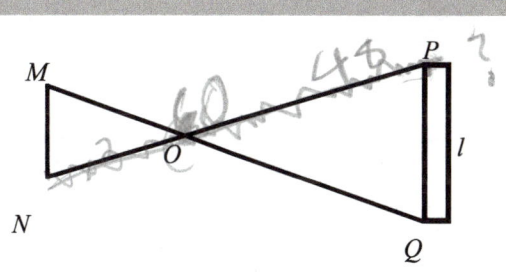

2

An architect wants to find the length l, in feet, of the front desk in a hotel lobby, as represented in the blueprint above. The lengths represented by PO, NO, QO and MN are 48 feet, 12 feet, 52 feet, and 17 feet, respectively. Segments MQ and PN intersect at point O, and angles OQP and OMN are congruent. What is the length of the front desk?

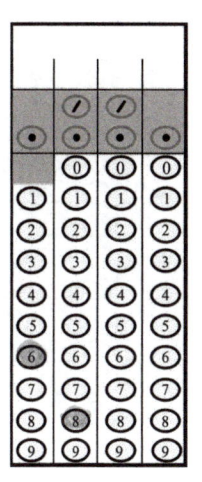

Chapter 4

3

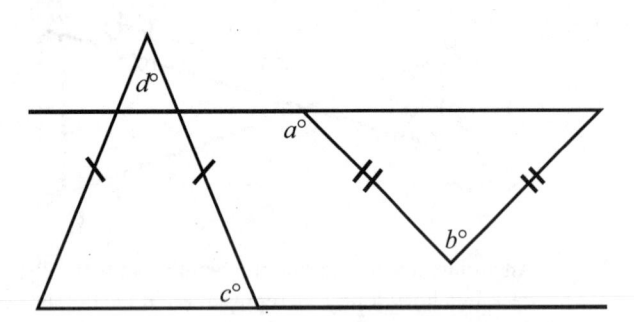

Two isosceles triangles are shown above. If $2c + b = 180$ and $d = 40$, what is the value of a?

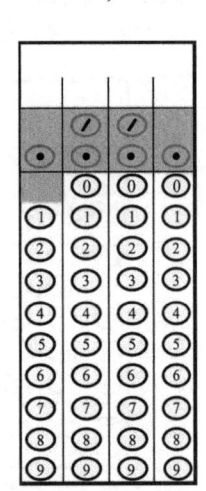

4

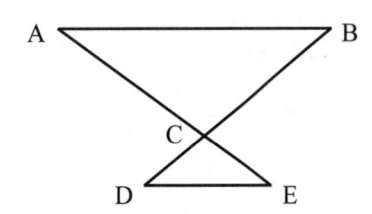

In the figure above, line segments AB and DE are parallel to one another and segments BD and AE intersect one another at point C. If CE, AC and CD measure 7, 28, and 5 respectively, what is the difference in the length of AE and the length of BD?
A) 10
B) 12
C) 15
D) 20

5

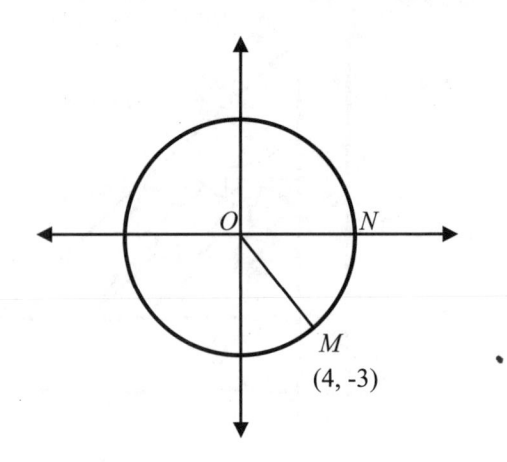

M (4, -3)

A perpendicular line (not drawn) from point M to the x-axis is called point P. What would be the perimeter of triangle OPM?

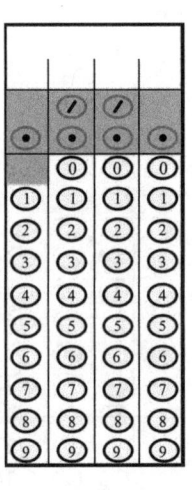

Circles | Overview

Memorize the following terms, rules, definitions, and formulas, and familiarize yourself with how they are applied to circles.

Term/Rule	Definition/Formula
Diameter	A line from one point on the circle through the center to another point on the circle Twice the radius
Radius	A line drawn from the center to any point on the circle Half the diameter
Area	πr^2, where r is the radius
Circumference	The distance around the perimeter of the circle $2\pi r$, where r is the radius and d is the diameter
Degrees in a Circle	There are 360° in a full circle and 180° in a semi-circle.
Arc	A portion of the circumference
Sector	A portion of the area that extends from the center of a circle to the edge, bound by 2 radii.
Chord	A line from one point on the circle to another. The diameter is the longest chord.
Central Angle	An angle within a circle formed by two radii, with the center of the circle as a vertex The measure of the central angle is equal to the measure of the arc it intercepts. Sometimes the measure of the central angle is given in radians instead of degrees. To convert the radians into degrees, replace π with 180.
Arc, Sector and Central Angle Proportions	Arcs, Sectors, and Central Angles have proportionality with the circle as a whole: $$\frac{}{360°} = \frac{}{\text{circumference of circle}} = \frac{}{\text{total area}}$$
Tangent Line	A line tangent to a circle touches a circle at just one point. When a tangent line meets a radius, the two lines form a right angle.
Triangle Inscribed in Semi-Circle	A triangle inscribed in a semi circle is always a _____.
Square Inscribed in a Circle	When a square is inscribed in a circle, the diagonal of the square is equal to the diameter of the circle. The diagonal of a square cuts it into two 45-45-90 triangles, and there is a special side relationship for those triangles.
Circle Inscribed in a Square	When a circle is inscribed in a square, the diameter of the circle is equal to the side length of the square.

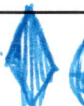

Circles I Overview

Example:

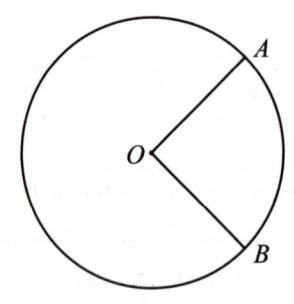

If in the circle shown above with center O the area of the sector AOB is 36π and the radius is 12, what is the measure of the angle AOB?
A) 24°
B) 30°
C) 45°
D) 90°

Which two parts of the circle proportions given on the chart on the previous page can we use here?

_____

Plug the given information into the proportion:

Therefore, angle AOB is equal to _____.

Circles I Rules Review

1. The area of a circle with a diameter of 10 is

2. The circumference of a circle with a radius of 12 is

3. What is the radius of a circle with an area of 169π?

4. What is the circumference of a circle with an area of 625π?

5. Two segments are drawn from the center of the circle to two distinct points on the edge of the circle. If the sum of the two segments is 26, what is the area of the circle?

6. What is the radius of circle A, if a 60° sector in circle A has an area of 7π?

7. A circle has center O and a radius of 5. Angle AOC has a measure of 40°, and arc ABC is a minor arc. What is the perimeter of sector $ABCO$?

Chapter 4

1

In a circle with center O, central angle AOB has a measure of $\frac{6\pi}{5}$ radians. The length of minor arc AB is what percent of the circle's circumference?

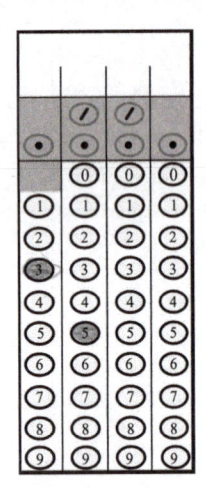

2

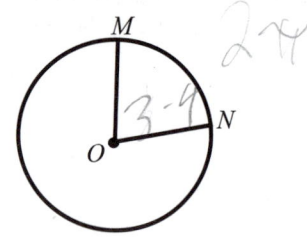

In the figure above, the circle has a center at O; the length of radius NO is between 3 and 4, and the length of minor arc MN is 2π. If the measure of angle z is an integer value, what is one possible value for z?

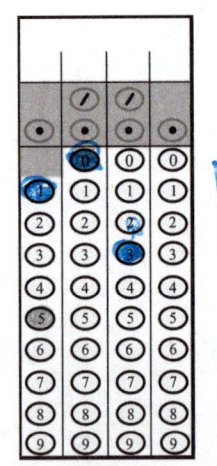

3

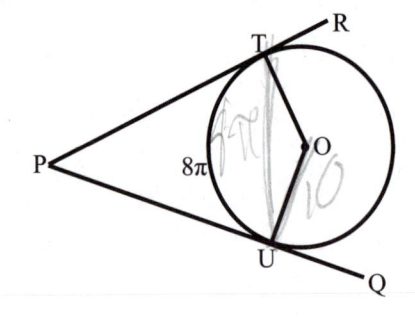

In the figure above, point O is the center of the circle; line segments PQ and PR are tangent to the circle at points U and T respectively, and the segments intersect at point P as shown. If the measure of minor arc TU is equal to 8π and the measure of the radius is 10, what is the measure, in degrees, of angle UPT?

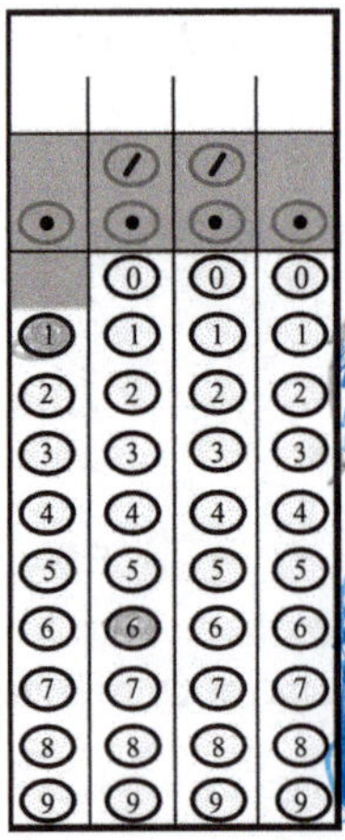

4

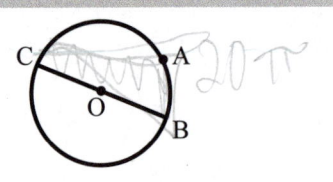

In the circle above, segment BOC is the diameter. If the length of arc CAB is equal to 20π, what is the length of the diameter of the circle?

A) 10
B) 15
C) 20
D) 40

Other Polygons & 3D Geometry | Overview

Below is a chart with information about common quadrilaterals (shapes with four sides).

Figure	Sides	Angles	Perimeter	Area
Quadrilateral	4 sides	Total 360°	Sum of exterior sides	bh
Parallelogram	4 sides. Opposite sides are parallel and equal.	Total 360°. Adjacent angles =180°. Opposite angles are equal.	Sum of exterior sides	bh *where h is the vertical height, NOT the slant height*
Rectangle	4 sides. Opposite sides are parallel and equal.	Total 360°. All angles are 90°.	$2l + 2w$. Sum of exterior sides	bh or lw
Square	4 sides. All sides are equal. Opposite sides are parallel.	Total 360°. All angles are 90°.	$4s$. Sum of exterior sides	bh or lw or s^2
Rhombus	4 sides. All sides are equal. Opposite sides are parallel.	Total 360°. Adjacent angles =180°. Opposite angles are equal.	$4s$. Sum of exterior sides	$\dfrac{d_1 d_2}{2}$ *where d_1 and d_2 are the diagonals*
Trapezoid	4 sides. 2 parallel bases	Total 360°. Adjacent angles =180°.	Sum of exterior sides	$\dfrac{b_1 + b_2}{2} h$

Additional Polygon Information

The measure of the interior angles in any polygon can be found using the formula: $180°(n - 2)$, where n represents the number of sides of the polygon.

To find the measure of one interior angle in a polygon, divide the result from the equation above by the number of sides in the polygon.

The sum of the measure of the exterior angles of any polygon = 360°

Chapter 4

Other Polygons & 3D Geometry | Overview

The SAT tests knowledge of volume and surface area, otherwise known as 3D or solid geometry. Relevant information for both volume and surface area can be found in the charts below. Familiarize yourself with this information prior to test day.

Rectangular Prisms

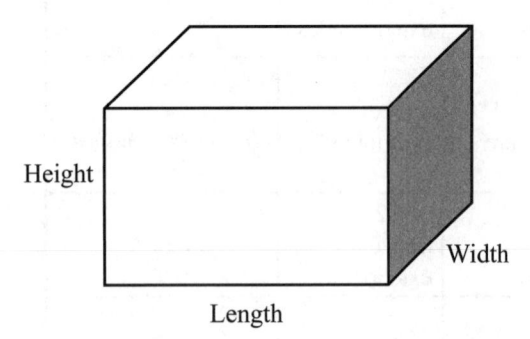

Cubes

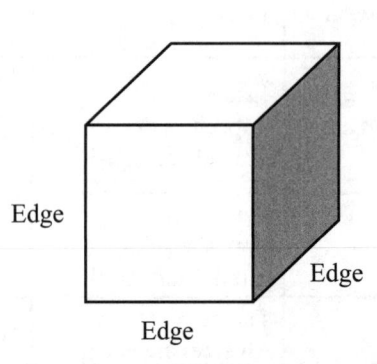

Term	Definition and Formula
Edge	Refers to the length along any "side" of a cube. All edges of a cube are equal.
Volume	(length)(width)(height)
Surface Area	Sum of the areas of the individual faces. All rectangular solids consist of 3 pairs of faces, each pair with equal areas. A cube has 6 faces, all equal in area. Surface Area of a Rectangular Box = $2lw + 2lh + 2hw$ Surface Area of a Cube = $6s^2$
Longest Distance in a Rectangular Solid	$\sqrt{height^2 + length^2 + width^2}$ 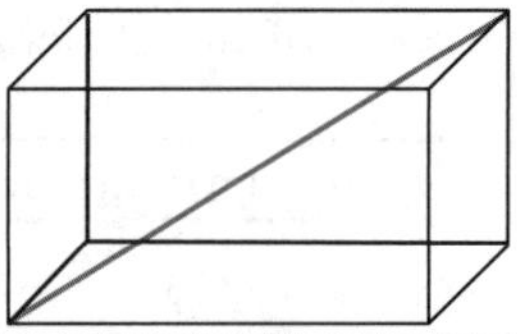

Cylinders

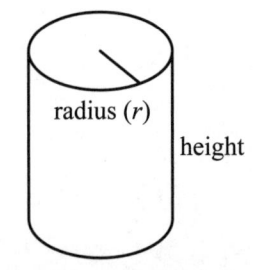

Spheres

Cones

Term	Formula
Volume	$\pi r^2 h$
Surface Area	$2(\pi r^2) + 2\pi rh$ (2 circle areas + area of the "wrapper")

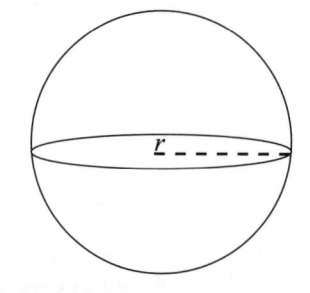

Term	Formula
Volume	$\frac{4}{3}\pi r^3$

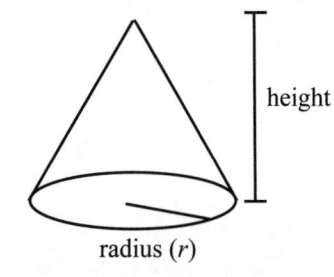

Term	Formula
Volume	$\frac{1}{3}h\pi r^2$

SAT-R Workbook v. 1.5

Other Polygons & 3D Geometry | Rules Review

1. A square with a side of 5 will have a perimeter of

2. What is the distance around a square path that encloses an area of 121 square feet?

3. What is the perimeter of a rectangle with area 10 and length 4?

4. A rectangle with an area of 60 and a diagonal of 13 has a perimeter of

5. If a square cloth of area 625 square inches has a square of area 144 square inches cut from its edge, what is the largest perimeter of the larger cloth that can be created?

6. What is the volume of a cube with an edge of 6?

7. What is the length of the edge of a cube with a volume of 1,331?

8. What is the volume of a 10 inch high cylinder with a circular top that has a circumference of 12π?

Chapter 4

1

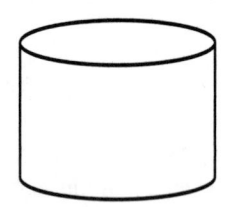

The jar of peanut butter above is in the shape of a right circular cylinder. The volume of the peanut butter in the jar is 108π cubic inches. If the area of the bottom of the jar is equal to 16π inches, what is the measure of the height of the jar?

2

Cindy uses a garden hose to fill a one-quart jug of water. She plans to use that water to fill identical spherical water balloons to half of their total capacities. Each balloon has a diameter of 2.5 inches. How many balloons will Cindy be able to fill entirely using just the water in the jug? (Note: There are 231 cubic inches in 1 gallon.)

A) 7
B) 13
C) 14
D) 15

3

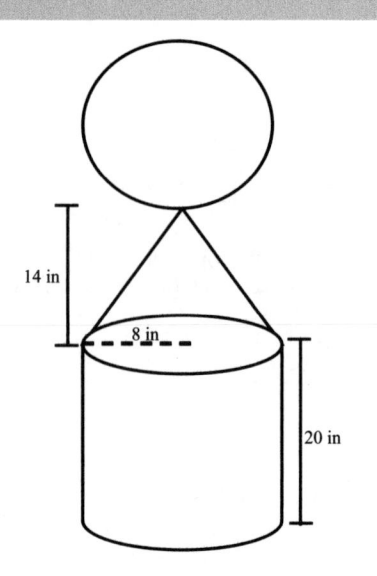

A basketball trophy is constructed with a right circular cylinder topped with a right circular cone. The cone is then topped with a sphere that has the same diameter as the cylinder. The internal measurements are shown in the figure above. Of the following, which is closest to the volume of the trophy, in cubic inches?

A) 5,560
B) 6,000
C) 6,516
D) 7,100

4

A square has the same perimeter as a regular octagon (an 8-sided polygon with all sides congruent and all interior angles congruent). If the area of the square is 289 square inches, how long, in inches, is each side of the octagon?

A) 7.5
B) 8
C) 8.5
D) 9

5

Which of the following variable expressions represents twice the area of a rectangle with a length of $y + 3$ and a width of $y - 6$?

A) $2y^2 - 6y - 18$
B) $2y^2 - 3y - 18$
C) $y^2 - 6y - 36$
D) $2y^2 - 6y - 36$

6

A rectangle was altered by decreasing its length by 15 percent and increasing its width by 25 percent. The area of the new rectangle is what percent of the area of the original rectangle?

A) 10
B) 36.25
C) 63.75
D) 106.25

7

$$A = \frac{180°(n-2)}{n}$$

The measure of an interior angle, A, in any polygon is related to the number of sides, n, of the polygon by the formula shown above. If the measure of an interior angle of a polygon is greater than 140°, what is the smallest number of sides the polygon can have?

A) 9
B) 10
C) 11
D) 12

8

Leslie has two cans of soup, both of which which are right circular cylinders. The diameter of the base of the chicken noodle soup can is 3 times the diameter of the base of the tomato soup can, and the height of the tomato soup can is 3 times the height of the chicken noodle soup can. The volume of the chicken noodle soup can is how many times the volume of the tomato soup can?

A) 0
B) 3
C) 4
D) 8

9

The mass of an object is equal to the product of the object's density and its volume. What is the density, in grams per liter, of an object with a mass of 16 grams and a volume of 64 liters?

A) 0.25
B) 6
C) 256
D) 1,024

10

Cheryl built a rectangular soccer field with a width of 11 feet and a length of 24 feet. She wants to increase the area of the field to 150% of its current size, without changing the length. What will be the new width, in feet?

A) 5.5
B) 16.5
C) 24
D) 396

Trigonometry | Overview

Trigonometry is the branch of math dealing with the relations of the sides and angles of triangles and with the relevant functions of any angles.

Term	Definition
Sine	A trigonometric function equal to the ratio of the side _____ to a specified angle (in a right triangle) to the _____ $$\text{Sine} = \frac{}{}$$ Sine is an *odd function,* since sin(x) ≠ sin(-x)
Cosine	A trigonometric function equal to the ratio of the side _____ to a specified angle (in a right triangle) to the _____ $$\text{Cosine} = \frac{}{}$$ Cosine is an *even function,* since cos(x) = cos(-x)
Tangent	A trigonometric function equal to the ratio of the side _____ to a specified angle (in a right triangle) to the side _____ to the specified angle $$\text{Tangent} = \frac{}{}$$ Tangent can also be expressed in terms of sine and cosine using the following ratio: $$\text{Tangent} = \frac{\text{Sine}}{\text{Cosine}}$$
Cosecant	Cosecant is the reciprocal of *sine* and can therefore be thought of as _____ or $\frac{1}{\text{Sine}}$
Secant	Secant is the reciprocal of *cosine* and can therefore be thought of as _____ or $\frac{1}{\text{Cosine}}$
Cotangent	Cotangent is the reciprocal of *tangent* and can therefore be thought of as _____ or $\frac{1}{\text{Tangent}}$ or $\frac{\text{Cosine}}{\text{Sine}}$
Trigonometric Identity	$\sin^2 x + \cos^2 x =$ _____
Inverse Sine, Cosine, and Tangent	Inverse sine, cosine, and tangent are used when we know the measures of the sides, but not of the angles. These operations are denoted by $\cos^{-1}$, $\sin^{-1}$ and $\tan^{-1}$. You can use your calculator to find these inverses by hitting the 2nd button, and then either sin, cos or tan, depending on what you are looking to find.
Radians	Radians are another way (in addition to degrees) to measure an angle. π radians = _____ °

SOHCAHTOA is the commonly used acronym to help you remember the sine, cosine, and tangent ratios.

Trigonometry | Overview

We can use our knowledge of what sine and cosine mean in a triangle to help us derive an important rule.

To do so, let's take a look at the sample triangle below:

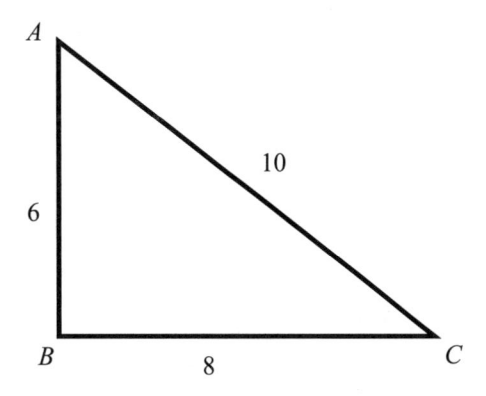

Triangle with vertices A (top), B (bottom left), C (bottom right). AB = 6, BC = 8, AC = 10.

What is the sine of Angle A? _____

What is the cosine of Angle C? _____

What is the relationship between sine A and cosine C ? _____

This information can be used to help us understand a basic trigonometric rule:

$$\text{sine(Angle } A) = \text{cosine}(90° - \text{Angle } A)$$

Since Angle B is equal to 90°, Angle A + Angle C must add up to _____° because a triangle has a total of _____°.

Therefore, in the equation above, **90° – Angle A** is equivalent to _____.

And as we proved above, the sine of Angle A is equal to the _____.

Chapter 4

1

In a right triangle, the cosine of angle A measuring $x°$ is equal to $\frac{15}{7}$. What is the measure of $\sin(90° - x°)$?

2

Angles a and b are acute angles and the cosine of angle a is equal to the sine of angle b. If $a = 3x + 16$ and $b = 2x - 11$, what is the value of x?

A) 7
B) 11
C) 13
D) 17

3

Triangles MNO and PQR are similar, where vertices M, N, O correspond to P, Q, R. The measure of angle N is 90°, the measure of side MN is 10, and the measure of side MO is 26. The measure of each side of triangle PQR is three times the measure of its corresponding side in triangle MNO. What is the value of sine R?

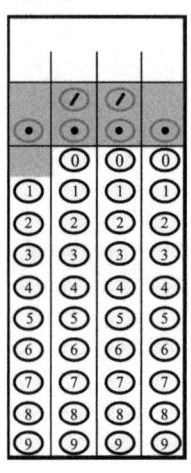

4

For angle B in $\triangle ABC$, which of the following trigonometric expressions has the value $\frac{25}{20}$?

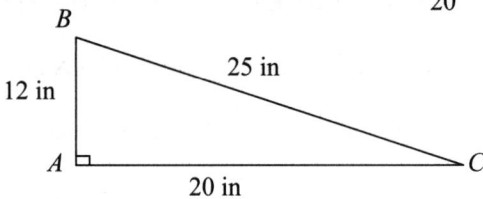

(triangle with B at top, A at bottom-left with right angle, C at bottom-right; AB = 12 in, BC = 25 in, AC = 20 in)

A) tan B
B) csc B
C) sin B
D) sec B

5

In right triangle *JKL* below, the sine of angle *K* is equal of 0.2. What is the cosine of angle *L* ?

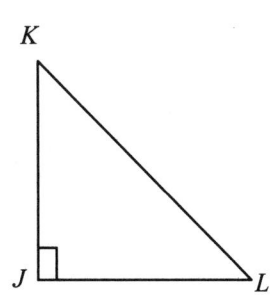

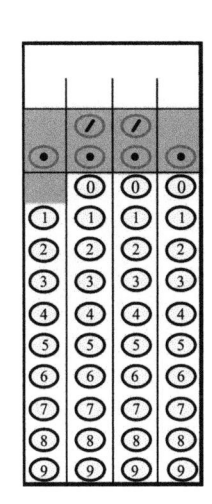

CHAPTER 4
Practice

Chapter 4 Practice

SUBSTITUTION | PLUGGING IN

1

The monthly fee for docking a boat at Spring Lake is $50 per boat and $20 for each tube attached to the boat. Last year, monthly fees were paid for b boats and t tubes. Which of the following expressions gives the total amount, in dollars, collected for monthly fees last year?
A) $50b + 20t$
B) $50(b + t) + 20t$
C) $70(b + t)$
D) $(50 + 20)(b + t)$

2

Ring-A-Ding Phone Company charges each customer $160 for telephone installation, plus $40 per month for service. Dial Tone Phone Company charges $210 for telephone installation, plus $30 per month for service. A customer who signs up for Dial Tone will pay the same total amount for his or her telephone as a customer who signs up for Ring-A-Ding if each pays for installation and service for how many months?
A) 4
B) 5
C) 7
D) 9

3

Karen is participating in a Math Quiz Challenge Bowl. After the first six rounds, Karen leads all participants with an average of 80.5. After everyone else but Karen competes in the seventh round, Karen is in second place, and the leader has an average of 82. What is the minimum score Karen needs in the seventh round in order to finish alone in first place?
A) 88
B) 90
C) 91
D) 92

4

A cell phone company charges $85.00 per month for up to 300 sent text messages. The cost for any additional text message is $0.08 per message. If t represents the total number of text messages sent and b represents the bill at the end of the month, which linear equation can be used to determine a user's monthly bill?
A) $b = 85 + 300(.08)t$
B) $b = 85 + (t - 300)(.08)$
C) $b = 85 + (300 - t)(.08)$
D) $b = 85t + (300)(.08)$

SUBSTITUTION

PLUGGING IN

5

Maggie has $9 less than does her brother Ron, who has d dollars on Tuesday. If Ron gives Maggie $6 on Wednesday, and she does not spend any of her money, which of the following is an expression for the amount of money, in dollars, that Maggie has?

A) $2d + 6$
B) $2d - 3$
C) $d + 15$
D) $d - 3$

6

In a basketball game, some shots are worth 2 points each and some are worth 3 points each. J.J. scored a total of 73 points in one game, taking a total of 35 shots, missing only 8. How many 3-point shots did J.J. make during the game?

A) 11
B) 13
C) 16
D) 19

Chapter 4 Practice

SUBSTITUTION

1

Last year, Greta made S sales at a car dealership. For each sale, she took home D dollars, and gave C dollars back to the dealership management company. What percentage of the money earned from all of Greta's sales last year went back to the dealership management company?

A) $\dfrac{SD}{S(D+C)} \times 100$

B) $\dfrac{SD}{(D+C)}$

C) $\dfrac{S}{(D+C)} \times 100$

D) $\dfrac{SC}{S(D+C)} \times 100$

2

A tailor makes a profit of $18 for each alteration he does. If he made $216 dollars on Monday, $234 on Tuesday and $396 on Wednesday, how many alterations did he make for those three days?

A) 47
B) 30
C) 22
D) 13

PLUGGING IN

3

If a, b, and c are distinct nonzero numbers and $a = \dfrac{bc}{b+c}$, which of the following must be equal to b?

A) $\dfrac{c}{ac-1}$

B) $\dfrac{c}{ac+1}$

C) $\dfrac{ac}{c-a}$

D) $\dfrac{ac}{c+a}$

4

Which of the following expressions is equivalent to $-x^3 + 2x^2$?

A) $-x(x - x^2)$
B) $-x^2(x - 2)$
C) $-x^2(2x + 2)$
D) $x^2(2x + 1)$

SUBSTITUTION ❌ PLUGGING IN

5

$$x^2 - (\sqrt{4x}) - 104 = (2y)^2$$

If $x > 0$, and $y = 6$, what is the value of x?
A) 12
B) 14
C) 16
D) 18

6

Martin and Eddie shared a hotel room at a conference. The price of the room for the one night was x dollars per person. Martin had purchased a soda through room service and owed an additional $4. However, they decided to split the bill evenly. If they each left a 15% tip for the cleaning staff, which of the following expressions represents the amount, in dollars, each of them paid? (Assume there is no sales tax.)
A) $x + 1.0$
B) $5x + 1.2$
C) $1.15x + 2.3$
D) $2.25x + 1.8$

Chapter 4 Practice

FRACTIONS

1

What is the least common denominator when subtracting the fractions $\frac{2}{12}$, $\frac{7}{10}$, $\frac{1}{5}$ and $\frac{2}{3}$?

A) 24
B) 30
C) 60
D) 120

2

A 12-pound ball of cookie dough is sliced into quarters and each quarter is sliced into eighths. What is the weight, in ounces, of each final slice? (16 ounces = 1 pound)

A) 4
B) 6
C) 18
D) 43

3

The cost of membership to a Book Of the Month Club is a one-time fee of $38.50, plus a monthly fee of $5.75. Jasmynne wrote a check for $130.50 to pay for her membership for a certain number of months, including the one-time fee. How many months of membership did she pay for?

A) 4
B) 8
C) 16
D) 22

DECIMALS

4

The Center City Zoo offers group rates for tickets to view the new penguin exhibit. For groups with fewer than 40 people, the cost is $12.65 per person. For groups with 40 people or more the cost is $10.75 per person. Freeport Junior High purchased tickets in advance for 32 students. However, the morning of, an additional 12 people joined the group. Assuming that Freeport Junior High was granted the group ticket rate for all students, how much additional money do they owe when they arrive to view the exhibit?

A) $23.40
B) $68.20
C) $83.90
D) $129.00

5

Discount tickets to a concert went on sale at midnight and were available until 4:00am. Amber bought 23 tickets at 2:00am for a total of $1,293.75. When Carmen purchased 7 tickets at 10:00am, she paid a total of $510.30. What was the difference between the price of one discount ticket and one ticket at full price?

A) $16.65
B) $42.30
C) $56.25
D) $72.90

Chapter 4 Practice

FRACTIONS

6

Marissa is a babysitter who charges $17.25 per hour. She babysits Timmy for 7 hours each day for a total of 92 days each year. However, this year, Marissa was sick for a total of 16 days and had her friend Monique fill in for her. Monique only charges $15.70 per hour. How much money will Timmy's family save this year by paying Monique each time that Marissa is sick?

A) $65.10
B) $173.60
C) $576.90
D) $1,758.40

DECIMALS

7

At a school, 180 female and 102 male students were selected at random to receive an iPad. If the school decided to give iPads to 72 more female students, how many more male students would they also have to give iPads to if they wanted $\frac{5}{7}$ of the students with ipads to be male?

Chapter 4 Practice

FRACTIONS

1

If $7\frac{5}{9} = y + 4\frac{1}{4}$, then $y = ?$

A) $2\frac{1}{9}$

B) $2\frac{11}{36}$

C) $3\frac{7}{36}$

D) $3\frac{11}{36}$

2

What number can be added to the numerator and denominator of $\frac{7}{37}$ to get $\frac{1}{4}$?

A) -3
B) 2
C) 3
D) 5

3

Given that $x = \frac{2}{7}$ and $y = \frac{2}{3}$, what is the value of $\frac{11}{42} + xy$?

A) $\frac{8}{42}$

B) $\frac{19}{42}$

C) $\frac{15}{52}$

D) $\frac{44}{882}$

DECIMALS

4

What is the value of n, if $\dfrac{1}{1-\frac{1}{5}} = n$?

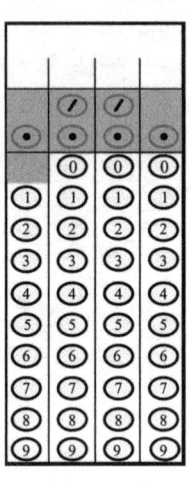

5

The graph below shows the number of laptops made in 6 factories in China.

Manufacturer	Laptops Produced
Factory 1	80,000
Factory 2	50,000
Factory 3	30,000
Factory 4	25,000
Factory 5	75,000
Factory 6	40,000

Using the information in the table, what fraction of the total laptops were made in factory 5?

A) $\frac{1}{8}$

B) $\frac{1}{5}$

C) $\frac{1}{4}$

D) $\frac{3}{10}$

PERCENTS

1

The calcium saturation level of tap water is found by dividing the amount of calcium the water currently has per ounce by the calcium capacity per ounce of the water and then converting to a percent. If the tap water at Marni's house currently has 6.9 milligrams of calcium per ounce of water an the calcium capacity is 10.6 milligrams per ounce, what is the calcium saturation level, to the nearest tenth of a percent?
A) 37.1%
B) 57.9%
C) 65.0%
D) 65.1%

2

If 123% of a number is 629.76, what is 60% of the number?
A) 307.2
B) 315.69
C) 333.46
D) 368.012

PERCENTS

3

The table below shows the monthly sales totals (in millions of dollars) for 4 departments at Save-All Department Store during the most recent 3 months.

Department	Month Number		
	1	2	3
Clothing	23.4	42.3	36
Makeup	52.5	61.6	62.1
Furniture	11.6	17.5	12.8
Jewelry	34.1	14.5	42.8

Which of the following is closest to the percent increase in jewelry sales from Month 1 to Month 3?
A) 23%
B) 26%
C) 28%
D) 31%

4

Mrs. Golden's class was constructing a circle graph to show the favorite types of music of all the students in the school. According to their poll, 41% of the students said that rap was their favorite; 12% said pop was their favorite; 32% said rock was their favorite; 9% said house music was their favorite and 6% said that they did not have a favorite genre. Rounded to the nearest degree, what will be the measure of the sector representing those who said that house music was their favorite?
A) 9°
B) 14°
C) 32°
D) 41°

PERCENTS

5

Daria's biology grade increased by 15% from her first test to her second test, and by 20% from her second test to her third test. By what percent did Daria's grade increase from her first test to her third test?
A) 29%
B) 31%
C) 35%
D) 38%

PERCENTS

6

Marcus wants to buy a $135 baseball glove. However, he knows that in two weeks the glove will go on sale for 15% off. Marcus also has a coupon for an additional 8% off any sale item. Rounded to the nearest percent, what percent of the original price of the glove would Marcus pay if he waits two weeks to purchase it?
A) 22%
B) 23%
C) 68%
D) 78%

Chapter 4 Practice

RATIOS | PROPORTIONS

1

At a factory, 350,000 cogs are required to produce 5,000 swingsets. How many cogs would be required to produce 32,500 swingsets?
A) 22,750
B) 2.275×10^5
C) 3.436×10^5
D) 2.275×10^6

2

On planet Lexicon, the standard measure of volume is called a *jipton*. It is approximately equal to 4.68 milliliters. It is also equivalent to one-fourth of a larger unit called a *keegon*. Based on these relationships, 116 keegons is equivalent to how many liters, rounded to the nearest hundredth?
(1,000 milliliters = 1 liter)

3

An architect is creating a scale drawing for a new home. The basement measures 23 feet wide by 16 feet long. He is using a scale of .3 inches = 1 foot for the scale drawing of the house. What will be the dimensions, in inches, of the basement in the scale drawing?
A) 2.3 by 1.6
B) 3.9 by 5.0
C) 5.6 by 8.3
D) 6.9 by 4.8

4

On a certain map a distance of 16 miles is represented by 0.125 inches. If the map indicates that the distance from Casey's home to her Aunt Carol's home is 2.25 inches, how many total miles will Casey drive in a round trip visit to Aunt Carol's home?

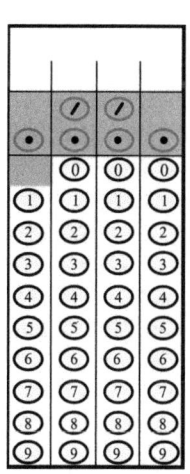

375

www.bellcurves.com

Chapter 4 Practice

RATIOS

5

Principal Wiley polled the students in his school and asked each of the 425 students which one of six school-branded clothing items they would purchase. The principal's survey results are displayed in the table below.

Clothing Item	Number of Students
Hat	82
Sweatshirt	98
T-Shirt	154
Pajama Pants	50
Sandals	24
Gloves	17
Total	425

Principal Wiley will order a total of 2,975 school-branded clothing items in the proportions dictated by the students in the table above. How many sweatshirts will he order?

A) 98
B) 105
C) 476
D) 686

6

One apple tree can produce about 30 apples each year. An apple orchard has 40 rows of 100 trees each. The orchard owner needs an estimate of how many apples he can harvest, so he takes a count of the apples from row 1. There are 2 good apples for every rotten apple in row 1. If the ratio remains true for the rest of the orchard, how many good apples can the orchard owner expect?

A) 80,000
B) 95,000
C) 115,000
D) 120,000

PROPORTIONS

7

If a and b are inversely proportional for $a = 24$ and $b = 6$, what is the value of b when $a = 36$?

Chapter 4 Practice

AVERAGES

1

Throughout a marking period, Sydney has earned the following grades on six 100-point tests: 72, 83, 91, 73, 92, and 88. What score must she receive on her final exam in order to earn an average grade of 85 for the marking period?

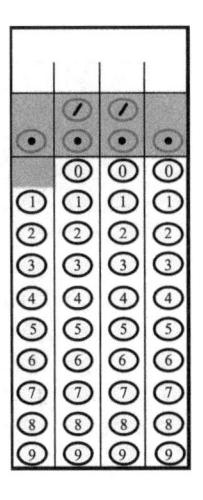

2

The following chart shows the total attendance (in thousands) at various events taking place in Central Park across four months.

Event	Month			
	July	August	September	October
Pop Concert	125	75	83	69
Movie	38	29	25	18
Rock Concert	90	82	79	44
Rap Concert	80	100	75	82
Triathlon	16	21	8	5

What is the average monthly attendance to a concert in the months of July and August?
A) 86,000
B) 88,000
C) 90,000
D) 92,000

RATES

3

A survey of members of a football team asked the 60 players how many hours (rounded to the nearest hour) they had spent practicing last week. The 60 responses are summarized by the histogram below.

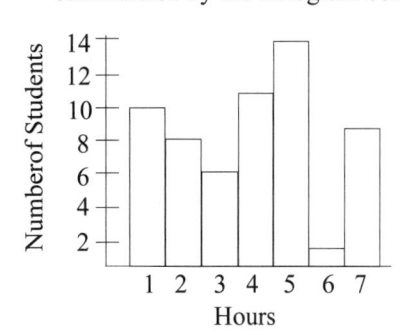

To the nearest hundredth, what is the average number of hours for the 60 survey responses?
A) 2.95
B) 3.88
C) 5.81
D) 6.92

4

Esmerelda and Josephine left for the mall at 2:45pm. When Esmerelda checked her watch at 3:25pm, they had traveled a distance of 60 miles. At this rate, what time would they arrive at the mall if it was a total distance of 180 miles away?
A) 4:15 pm
B) 4:30 pm
C) 4:40 pm
D) 4:45 pm

377

www.bellcurves.com

Chapter 4 Practice

AVERAGES

5

Calvin drove 880 miles in 16 hours of actual driving time. By driving an average of 15 miles per hour slower for the same distance, it would have taken Calvin how many additional hours to complete the trip?

6

If a is equal to the average (arithmetic mean) of x and 7, b is the average of $4x$ and 7, and c is the average of $7x$ and 28, what is the average of a, b, and c in terms of x?
A) $2x + 19$
B) $2x + 7$
C) $3x + 15$
D) $4x + 18$

RATES

7

A water cooler in an office currently holds 138 liters of water. If employees drink the water at a rate of 4.8 liters per hour for a total of 8 hours each day, how many liters will remain after 2 days?

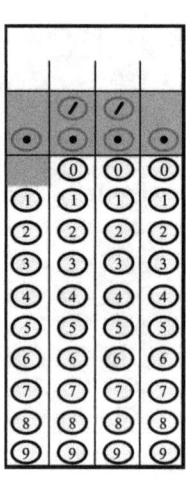

8

A model train travels at a constant rate of 8 inches every 10 seconds. At this rate, which of the following is closest to the number of feet the train travels in 5 minutes?
A) 17
B) 20
C) 24
D) 40

MEASURES OF CENTER

1

Cynthia looked at her exam scores shown below for the first and second semester of her history class.

Semester 1: 80, 93, 90, 85, 96
Semester 2: 88, 93, 77, 74, 85, 82, 89

Which statement about Cynthia's performance is correct?
A) The range of scores for semester 1 is greater than the range of scores for semester 2.
B) The median score for semester 2 is greater than the median score for semester 1.
C) The mean score for semester 2 is greater than the mean score for semester 1.
D) The third quartile for semester 1 is greater than the third quartile for semester 2.

2

Mrs. Simmons raised all her students' scores on a recent quiz by seven points. How were the median and the range of the scores affected?
A) The median increased by seven and the range increased by seven.
B) The median remained the same and the range remained the same.
C) The median remained the same and the range increased by seven.
D) The median increased by seven and the range remained the same.

3

Hailey created a list of her 16 test grades from chemistry class. She then divided each grade by 5 to produce a second list of numbers. She then took each of the numbers in the second list and added 4 points to each score to create a third list of numbers. The median of this third set is x. Which of the following expresses the median of Hailey's original chemistry test scores?
A) $5(m + 4)$

B) $5m + 4$

C) $5(m - 4)$

D) $\frac{m}{5} + 4$

4

The table below shows the annual salaries for the 18 lawyers at a firm in terms of thousands of dollars

65	68	71	79	80	82
82	96	101	101	101	112
120	123	126	137	138	166

The firm hires an additional lawyer and pays him a salary of $172,000 per year. Which statement about the median and mean is true?
A) Both the median and the mean will increase.
B) Only the mean will increase.
C) Only the median will increase.
D) Neither the median nor the mean will change.

MEASURES OF CENTER

5

The median of a set of data containing 7 items was found. Six data items were added to the set. Four of these items were greater than the original median, and the other 2 items were less than the original median. Which of the following statements must be true about the median of the new data set?
A) It is the mean of all data items in the set.
B) It is the average of the original median and the new items in the set.
C) It has not changed from the original median.
D) It is greater than the original median.

6

A florist has an end of season sale on rose bushes, tulips, and daisies. There are 8 rose bushes, 9 tulips and 17 daisies. Before the sale, roses are $22, tulips are $13, and daisies are $15.50. If all the flowers are marked down by the same amount, what will happen to the range of the flower prices?
A) Range will decrease
B) Range will increase
C) Range will not change
D) Cannot be determined from given information

DATA COLLECTION

1

The mayor of Greenville wants to upgrade the playground equipment in the town square. Which random survey group would be the most biased?

A) 75 working men and women from the town
B) 150 of Greenville's taxpayers
C) 100 of the families living in Greenville
D) 40 stay-at-home moms from Greenville

Questions 2 and 3 refer to the following information.

A scientist conducted a survey of eye color from three towns in northern Norway. The scientist had 400 members of each town participate in his survey and the results are indicated in the chart below.

Eye Color	Town A	Town B	Town C
Brown	83	77	62
Green	96	101	124
Blue	133	160	143
Hazel	88	62	71

2

Which of the following is a reliable conclusion from this survey?

A) The most common eye color for people in Norway is blue.
B) The most common eye color for northern Norway is blue.
C) The least common eye color for the people of Scandinavia is brown.
D) The least common eye color for northern Norway is green.

3

If the scientist wanted to make a conclusion about the eye color of all Norwegians, which of the following changes to his survey would produce the best results?

A) Surveying a fourth town in northern Norway
B) Surveying a larger number of people from his original three towns
C) Surveying a total of six towns in eastern Norway
D) Surveying three additional towns in southern Norway

4

A survey of people exiting a museum was conducted every week for six weeks.

If true, which of the following makes the survey results less reliable?

A) The survey was conducted every Tuesday for six weeks
B) The survey was conducted at both exits for the museum
C) The survey was conducted on a different day of the week each week
D) The survey questions were asked of adults and children

5

Mrs. Twig decided to survey three high schools in her city to find out which type of math was the favorite of students. She sent out one survey for each of the 6,200 students at the three schools and received 4,800 replies. She found out that 2,200 students prefer algebra, 1,200 prefer geometry, and 1,400 prefer algebra 2. Which of the following is a reliable conclusion from Mrs. Twig's survey?

A) The students in her city prefer algebra over other mathematics
B) The students in her city dislike geometry
C) The students in her city's high schools most likely prefer algebra
D) The students in her city haven't taken calculus

Chapter 4 Practice

SCATTER PLOTS

1

Bacteria Present in Water

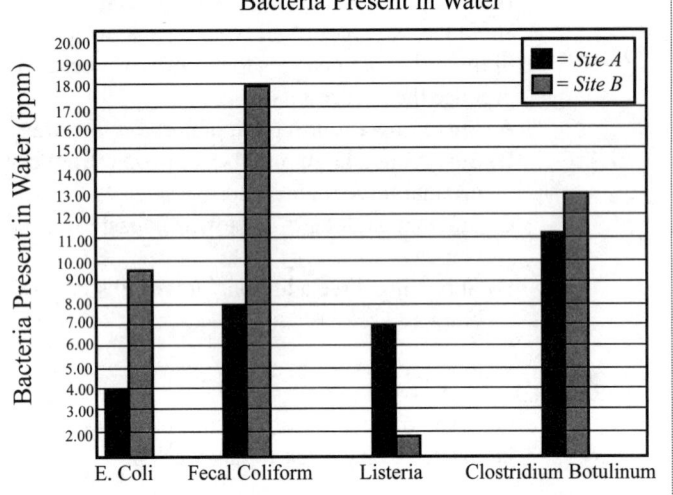

The bar graph above shows the bacteria present (in parts per million) in water at Sites A and B in 2014.

If a scatterplot were to be created to represent the data above, where bacteria present in water in 2014 for site A is plotted on the x-axis, and bacteria present in water for site B is plotted on the y-axis for each of the given bacteria types, how many data points would fall below the line $y = x$?

A) 1
B) 2
C) 3
D) 4

Questions 2 and 3 refer to the following information.

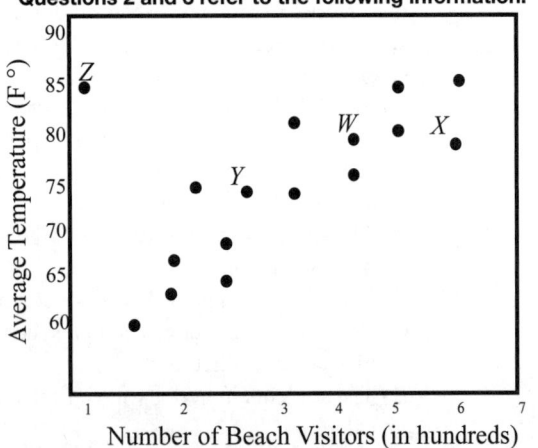

2

What is the correlation between the average daily temperature and the number of beach visitors in the graph above?

A) Negative correlation
B) Positive correlation
C) No correlation
D) Can't be determined

3

Which of the labeled points could be considered an outlier?

A) W
B) X
C) Y
D) Z

4

The scatterplot below shows the amount of money Tim invested (in thousands) for retirement over a number of years.

Amount of Money Tim Invested

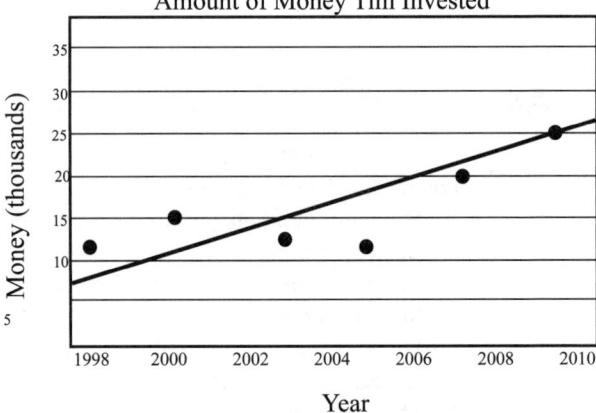

According to the line of best fit, in which year did Tim invest $15,000 for retirement?

A) 1998
B) 2003
C) 2005
D) 2009

SCATTER PLOTS

Questions 5 and 6 refer to the following information.

The scatter plot below shows the relationship between the number of hours slept and the grade point average (GPA) for 11 students.

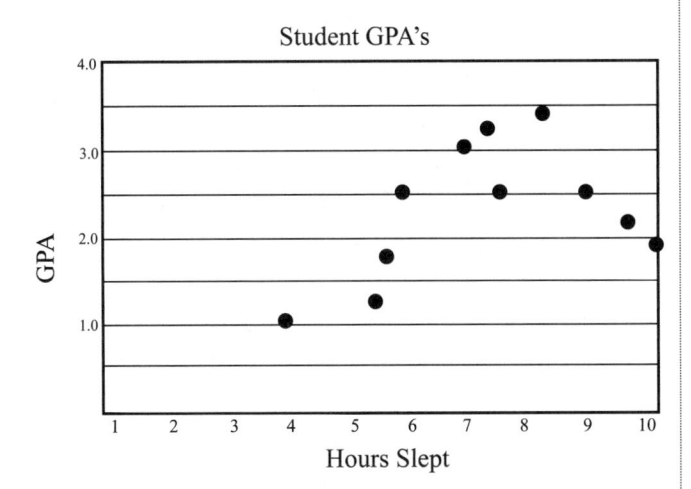

Student GPA's

5

What is the ratio of sleep to GPA for the student who sleeps the fewest hours each night?
A) 2.25
B) 4
C) 4.4
D) 7.33

6

Which of the following can be concluded from this scatter plot?
A) The students who sleep the most have the highest GPA
B) The students who sleep the least have the highest GPA
C) The students who sleep approximately eight hours each night have the highest GPA
D) The students who sleep exactly 7 or 9 hours will get a 4.0 GPA

Chapter 4 Practice

TABLES

1

Chef Liam is catering a dinner party. In order to decide from where to purchase the food, rent waiters, and rent silverware, he created the table below.

Company Name	Cost of Food, F (dollars)	Rental Cost of Waiters, W (dollars per hour)	Rental Cost of Silverware, S (dollars per hour)
X	1,250	22	19
Y	1,625	14	16
Z	1,420	31	15

The total cost, y, of buying the food and of renting the waiters and silverware in terms of the number of hours, x, is modeled by the equation $y = (W + S)x + F$.

What is the smallest number of hours, x, for which the total cost of food and of renting waiters and silverware from Company X will be greater than the total cost of food and of renting waiters and silverware from Company Y?

A) 34
B) 35
C) 38
D) 42

2

The table below summarizes the results of 325 high school seniors who applied to college.

	Took 3+ AP Classes	Took < 3 AP Classes
Accepted Early Decision	72	29
Deferred Early Decision	66	83
Rejected Early Decision	17	58

If one of the surveyed seniors who was accepted early decision is chosen at random to receive a scholarship, what is the probability that he or she took 3 or more AP classes?

A) .22
B) .36
C) .40
D) .71

GRAPHS

3

A census taker interviewed 450 families at random from each of three towns. He asked each family how many people live in the household. The results are shown in the table below.

Household Numbers Survey

Number in Household	Silvertown	Goldville	Copperton
1	25	80	50
2	75	140	60
3	115	30	190
4	160	80	40
5	30	60	80
6	45	60	30

There are a total of 1,800 residents in Silvertown, 2,220 residents in Goldville and 1,500 residents in Copperton.

Based on the survey data, which of the following most accurately compares the expected total number of Silvertown families having 3 household members with that of Goldville?

A) The total number of families with 3 people in the household in Silvertown is 85 more than in Goldville.
B) The total number of families with 3 people in the household in Goldville is 75 more than in Silvertown.
C) The total number of families with 3 people in the household in Silvertown is 312 more than in Goldville.
D) The total number of families with 3 people in the household in Silvertown is 118 more than in Goldville.

Chapter 4 Practice

TABLES | GRAPHS

Questions 4 and 5 refer to the following information.

Electronics Plus is measuring their video game sales during the holiday season. Their data is collected in the chart below.

Platform	Dec 1	Dec 8	Dec 15	Dec 22
YBox	54,000	25,000	33,000	76,000
Funstation	36,000	?	?	?
Wheeee	81,000	13,000	55,000	12,000

4

The store believes it will sell 50,000 Ybox games per week, between December 1st and December 30th. How many games does it have to sell between December 22nd and December 30th in order to meet that goal?

A) 22,000
B) 55,000
C) 62,000
D) 78,000

5

The marketing team predicts that every week, Funstation sales will increase by 20% from the previous week. About how many Funstation games will Electronics Plus sell on the week of December 15th?

A) 7,200
B) 14,440
C) 43,000
D) 51,840

6

The table below shows the number of college athletes, in hundreds, across 4 NCAA conferences.

Conference	Sport			Total
	Soccer	Football	Basketball	
ACC	42	56.5	32.8	131.3
SEC	39.9	78.6	43	161.5
Big East	36.7	49	37.5	123.2
Big 10	46.6	67.7	27.4	141.7
Total	165.2	251.8	140.7	557.7

Based on the table, if a basketball player is chosen at random, which of the following is closest to the probability that he or she was in the ACC?

A) 0.06
B) 0.23
C) 0.30
D) 0.46

7

The histogram below shows how many chocolate chips are in a certain number of cookies.

Number of Chocolate Chips in a Cookie

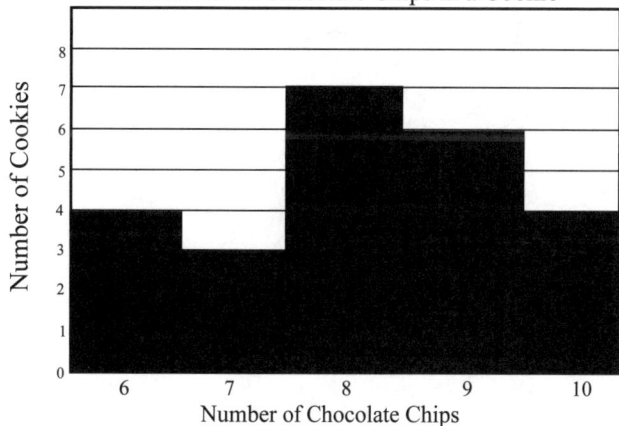

How many cookies are represented by the graph?

A) 5
B) 18
C) 24
D) 40

Chapter 4 Practice

MANIPULATING EQUATIONS

1

When $(p - r)$ is equal to 12, what is the value of $\dfrac{p-r}{4} + (p-r)^2 - \dfrac{(p-r)^3}{24}$?

A) 24
B) 48
C) 60
D) 75

2

If $15(x + 3) = -4(-x - 14)$, then $x = ?$
A) 0.25
B) 1
C) 1.5
D) 2.2

3

What is the value of $x(2x - 4)^2$ for $x = 5$?
A) 60
B) 80
C) 120
D) 180

4

The expression $5(3x - 6) - 4(-x - 2)$ is equivalent to
A) $11x - 22$
B) $19x - 22$
C) $11x + 38$
D) $19x + 38$

5

If $\dfrac{x^2 + 5}{y} = 29$, then which of the following is also true?

A) $y = 20(x^2+5)$

B) $x = \dfrac{29}{y}$

C) $x = \sqrt{(29y - 5)}$

D) $y = 5 - x^2$

6

If $\dfrac{18 - x^2}{x^2 - 14} = 1$, what is the value of $\sqrt{x}$?

A) 2
B) 4
C) 16
D) 22

TRANSLATING EQUATIONS

1

The cost of using a prepaid cellphone is $1.15 per minute. Kathy needs to buy a phone preloaded with t hours of talking time, which of the following equations represents the cost, c, of a prepaid cellphone with t hours of talk time?

A) $c = \dfrac{1.15t}{60}$

B) $c = \dfrac{60t}{1.15}$

C) $c = \dfrac{1.15(60)}{t}$

D) $c = 1.15(60t)$

2

Kaitlin has some cherries. If she makes 5 cherry pies, she will have 15 leftover cherries, but if Kaitlin wants to make 8 cherry pies, she has 45 too few cherries. How many cherries does Kaitlin have?
A) 90
B) 115
C) 140
D) 200

3

Theo just joined the wrestling team and is starting to gain muscle mass. Each week that he works out with the wrestling team he gains 0.9 pounds of muscle. If Theo weighs 134 now, which of the following equations represents Theo's weight in k weeks?
A) $.9k + 134$
B) $134(.9k)$
C) $.9 + 134(k)$
D) $134 - .9k$

4

X and Y are positive integers. Four less than three times the larger number is equivalent to eight times the smaller number. If $X + Y = 16$, what is the value of X?
A) 4
B) 5
C) 12
D) 13

5

Hannah needs new basketball shoes. The pair she wants is on sale for 30% off. She has a coupon for an additional 15% off the sale price and she has a $25 gift card for the store where the shoes are sold. How much money, aside from her gift card, will Hannah have to take to the store in order to buy the shoes if they originally cost $80?
A) $12.50
B) $15.00
C) $22.60
D) $38.10

6

Jackson is moving to college and wants to take some of his book collection with him. He has one box big enough for 25 novels but not for his atlas, and another box big enough for his atlas and 18 novels. However, Jackson is concerned about the weight of the box. He decided he will take whichever box weighs the least. If the atlas weighs eight pounds and each novel weighs 2 pounds, what is the weight of the box Jackson takes to college with him?
A) 52
B) 49
C) 44
D) 40

TRANSLATING EQUATIONS

1. The smaller of two numbers is less than the larger by 6. The difference of three times the larger and twice the smaller is 72. If x is the larger number, which equation below determines the correct value of x?
A) $3x - (2x + 12) = 72$
B) $3x - (2x - 6) = 72$
C) $3x - (2x + 6) = 72$
D) $3x - (2x - 12) = 72$

2. In order to study for her finals, Julie created a study plan for herself. She plans to increase the number of minutes she will study each week by 75 minutes. If she plans to budget a total of 1,305 minutes for studying the week prior to the exam, for how many minutes will she plan to study 16 weeks prior to the test?
A) 105
B) 180
C) 255
D) 330

3. Leslie and Manny have ages that are consecutive even integers. The product of their ages is 2,024 Which equation could be used to find Manny's age, m, if he is the older of the two?
A) $2m^2 + 1 = 2{,}024$
B) $m^2 - 2m = 2{,}024$
C) $3m = 2{,}024$
D) $m^2 + 2m = 2{,}024$

4. Stephen has six more quarters than pennies in his pocket, for a total of $3.84. Which equation could be used to determine the number of pennies, p, in his pocket?
A) $2.50(6p) + 1.0(p) = \$3.84$
B) $2.50(6 + p) + 1.0(p) = \$3.84$
C) $0.25(6 + p) + 0.01(p) = \$3.84$
D) $0.25(6p) + 0.01(p) = \$3.84$

5. For her niece's birthdays, Aunt Greta gave gifts of either $85 or $120. This year, Aunt Greta spent a total of $1675 giving her sixteen nieces birthday gifts. How many gifts of $120 did she give?

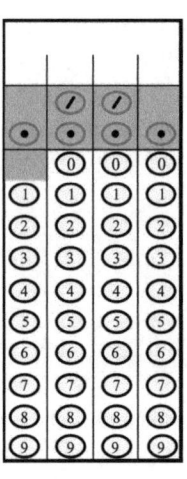

SYSTEMS OF EQUATIONS

1

The cost of an order of french fries and an order of onion rings together is $6.50. The cost of 3 orders of french fries and 1 order of onion rings is equal to $15.00. What is the cost of 5 orders of onion rings and an order of french fries?

A) $11.25
B) $12.75
C) $15.50
D) $16.25

2

A flower shop owner was buying flowerpots and shovels for his store. A flowerpot and shovel cost $9.00 in total. If the shop owner buys 8 flowerpots and 5 shovels for a total of $63.00, how much does a flowerpot cost?

A) $3.00
B) $3.50
C) $4.00
D) $6.00

3

$$y = -7$$
$$y = cx^4 + d$$

In the system of equations above, c and d are constants. For which of the following values of c and d is there exactly one real solution to the system of equations?

A) $c = 3, d = 7$
B) $c = -3, d = 10$
C) $c = 5, d = -10$
D) $c = 5, d = -7$

4

Michael and Kristen went out to a restaurant with a group of their friends and they split the bill. Michael spent a total of $217.00 on four appetizers and six entrees. Kristen spent a total of $89.00 for one appetizers and three entrees. If each entree costs the same amount and each appetizer costs the same amount, what is the price of one entree and one appetizer?

A) $17.25
B) $23.50
C) $42.66
D) $62.20

SYSTEMS OF EQUATIONS

5

Rob is in charge of buying food for the company picnic. He decides to spend all of his money on Mystery Burgers and Veggie Dogs. Mystery Burgers cost $2.40 and Veggie Dogs cost $1.75. If Rob bought 30 items and spent a total of $60.30, how many Mystery Burgers did Rob buy for the company picnic?

A) 6
B) 8
C) 10
D) 12

6

Stew's Grocery Store sold a total of 328 apples and bananas. He sold apples for $0.65 each and bananas for $1.06 each. If he made $299.71 from the sale of apples and bananas, how many fewer apples than bananas did Stew sell?

SYSTEMS OF EQUATIONS

1

For what value b would the following system of equations have infinitely many solutions?

$$3x - 7y = 12$$
$$6x - 14y = 4b$$

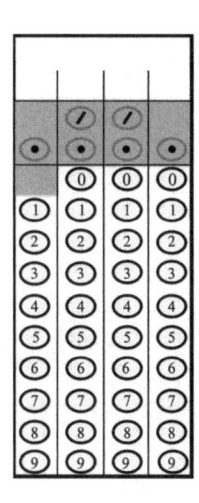

2

During the 2013 baseball season, the centerfielder Perez earned, p, which was 2.6 million dollars more than the shortstop Simmons earned, s. Together, the two players earned a total of 9.9 million dollars. Which system of equations could be used to determine the amount each player earned, in millions of dollars?

A) $p + s = 9.9$
   $p + 2.6 = s$
B) $p + s = 9.9$
   $s + 2.6 = p$
C) $p + s = 2.6$
   $s + 2.6 + p = 9.9$
D) $p + s = 9.9$
   $s + 9.9 + p = p + 2.6$

3

Which system of equations has the same solution as the system below?

$$8x + y = 21$$
$$7x - 2y = 35$$

A) $8x + y = 21$
   $21x - 14y = 35$
B) $8x + y = 21$
   $14x - 4y = 70$
C) $16x - 2y = -32$
   $7x - 2y = 35$
D) $x + 2y = 32$
   $7x - 2y = 35$

4

$$(px + 6)(12 - qx) = 6x^2 + rx + 72$$

If the equation above is true for all values of x, and $p + q = -5$, what are the two possible values for r?

A) 24 and 66
B) -84 and 76
C) -78 and 48
D) 24 and 114

Chapter 4 Practice

INEQUALITIES | INEQUALITIES

1

The pounds of garbage, p, generated by Centerville in the month of May satisfies the inequality $|p - 75| \geq 49$. Which of the following could NOT be the amount of garbage, in pounds, generated by Centerville in the month of May?

A) 14
B) 26
C) 120
D) 124

2

If the inequality $a - b > b$, then which of the following *must* be true?

A) $a = b$
B) $a > b$
C) $b < 0$
D) $a > 0$

3

If $3q + 7 \leq 1$, what is the greatest possible value of $5q - 11$?

A) -24
B) -21
C) -18
D) -16

4

$$Y < -3x - 2$$
$$Y > 6x + 4$$

Which of the following could be a solution to the above inequalities?

A) (-1, 3)
B) (3, 5)
C) (-4, 2)
D) (2, 1)

4

Kim plans to sell four times as many boxes of cookies as Hallie. If Kim and Hallie need to sell a total of at least 160 boxes of cookies in order win a free trip, which inequality could be used to determine how many boxes, h, Hallie needs to sell?

A) $5h \geq 32$
B) $5h > 32$
C) $5h < 160$
D) $5h \geq 160$

6

Natalie is planning a birthday party and wants to have a live band and dinner for everyone who attends. She has found a band that will charge her $1,250 and a catering service that will provide a full three-course dinner for $17.50 per person. If her goal is to keep the average cost per person between $30.85 and $67.50, how many people, p, must attend?

A) $22 \leq p \leq 94$
B) $25 < p < 95$
C) $25 \leq p < 94$
D) $15 \leq p < 95$

7

If $24 < 6f - 19$, what is the least possible value of $11f$?

A) 80
B) 77
C) 65
D) 42

Chapter 4 Practice

FUNCTIONS | FUNCTIONS

1

When Dana throws a ball, the height of the ball, y meters, is modeled by $y = 3 + 12x - 5x^2$, where x is the time in seconds the ball has been in the air. According to this model, which of the following times, in seconds, allows the ball to reach the greatest height?

A) 0.6
B) 0.8
C) 1.0
D) 1.2

2

The period T, in seconds, of a pendulum is given by the equation $T = (6.3)\sqrt{\frac{L}{9.8}}$, where L is the length of the pendulum in meters. What length, in meters, must the pendulum be for the pendulum's period to be 3.15 seconds?

A) 0.55
B) 2.45
C) 3.57
D) 4.90

3

An oak tree is 2 feet tall at week 0 and grows 0.75 feet each month. Which function(s) below can be used to determine the height, $f(m)$, of the oak tree in m months?

I. $f(m) = 2m + 0.75$
II. $f(m) = 2m + 3(m - 1)$
III. $f(m) = f(m - 1) + 0.75$ where $f(0) = 2$

A) I only
B) III only
C) I and II only
D) I and III only

Questions 4 and 5 refer to the following information.

$$B(p) = \frac{1}{3}p + 25$$

$$C(p) = 190 - p$$

The quantity of coffee beans bought by a roaster and the quantity of coffee beans bought by coffee shops are functions of the price of coffee beans. The functions above show the relationship between beans available from the roaster and beans purchased by coffee shops. The function $B(p)$ shows how many bushels of coffee beans are bought by the roaster at P dollars, and the function $C(p)$ shows how many bushels of coffee beans are bought by coffee shops when each bushel costs P dollars.

4

How will the number of coffee bean bushels purchased by the roaster change if the price of one bushel is increased by $18?

A) The quantity supplied will increase by 6 bushels
B) The quantity supplied will decrease by 6 bushels
C) The quantity supplied will increase by 12 bushels
D) The quantity supplied will increase by 18 bushels

5

The roaster has to obtain the coffee beans before the coffee shops can purchase them. Ideally, the roaster would like to purchase a certain quantity of bushels and then sell all of its coffee bean stock to coffee shops. What price per bushel of coffee beans would allow the roaster to buy and then sell the same amount?

A) $88.50
B) $99.00
C) $115.40
D) $123.75

393

www.bellcurves.com

FUNCTIONS / FUNCTIONS

1
If $f(x) = 2x^3 + 3x^2 - 12x$, then $f(-5) = ?$
A) -385
B) -265
C) -175
D) -115

2
If $f(x) = x^3 + 6x$, and $g(x) = 2x^2 + \sqrt{x}$, then what is the value of $f(5) + g(9)$?
A) 10
B) 45
C) 295
D) 320

3
If $f(x) = x^2 + 6$, then $f(x - y) = ?$
A) $x^2 + 2xy + y^2 + 6$
B) $x^2 - 2xy + y^2 + 6$
C) $x^2 - 2xy + y^2$
D) $x^2 - 12xy + y^2$

4
The cost of airing a radio spot is modeled by the function $C(n) = 320n + 780$, where n is the number of times the spot is aired. Based on this model, which statement is true?
A) The radio spot costs $0 to produce and $320 per airing up to $780.
B) The radio spot costs $320 to produce and $780 each time it is aired.
C) The radio spot costs $780 to produce and $320 each time it is aired.
D) The radio spot costs $1100 to produce and can air an unlimited number of times.

5
$$H = -.34t^2 + vt + k$$

The above equation estimates the path of a soccer ball after a goalie kick where H is the height in feet t seconds after the kick from an initial height of k with an initial speed of v feet per second. Which of the following equations represents v in terms of H, k and t?

A) $v = \dfrac{.34(H-k)}{t}$

B) $v = \dfrac{H + k - 16}{t}$

C) $v = .34t + \dfrac{H-k}{t}$

D) $v = .34t - \dfrac{H+k}{t}$

FUNCTIONS | FUNCTIONS

6

A t-shirt company produces t units of a product per week, where $C(t)$ represents the total cost and $R(t)$ represents the total revenue for the week. The functions are modeled by $C(t) = 120t + 135$ and $R(t) = -0.75t^2 + 520t - 80$. If the profit is calculated by finding the difference between revenue and cost where $P(t) = R(t) - C(t)$, what is the total profit, $P(t)$, for any given week?

A) $P(t) = -0.75t^2 + 400t - 215$
B) $P(t) = 0.25t^2 + 640t - 215$
C) $P(t) = -0.75t^2 + 640t + 215$
D) $P(t) = 0.75t^2 - 400t + 215$

7

When Tatiana goes to the gym, she spends a total of 15 minutes stretching, filling her water bottle, and tying her shoes. The equation $t = 5e + 15$ models the time, t minutes, Tatiana budgets for a trip to the gym during which she will do e exercises. Which of the following statements MUST be true according to Tatiana's model?

A) She budgets 5 minutes per exercise.
B) She budgets 10 minutes per exercise.
C) She budgets 15 minutes per exercise for cardio and 5 minutes per exercise for strength-building.
D) She budgets a 15 minute water break after each 5 exercises she completes.

Chapter 4 Practice

EXPONENTS | ROOTS

1

$4x^3 \cdot 6x^2y^4 \cdot 5x^5y^2$ is equivalent to which of the following?
A) $15x^{10}y^6$
B) $15x^{30}y^8$
C) $120x^{10}y^6$
D) $120x^{30}y^8$

2

If p is a real number such that $p^4 = 6561$, then $p^3 + 2\sqrt{p} = ?$
A) 30
B) 450
C) 729
D) 735

3

The expression $\sqrt{125a^{15}b^6}$ is equivalent to
A) $25a^5b$
B) $25ab^2$
C) $5a^5b^2$
D) $5ab$

4

If $x^5 = 32$, $y^3 = 216$, and $z^2 = 121$, what is the value of $x+y+z$?
A) 2
B) 11
C) 17
D) 19

5

Which of the following expressions, if any, are equal for all real numbers r ?

I. $\sqrt{r^4}$
II. $-|r^2|$ -1
III. $|-r^2|$

A) I and II only
B) I, II and III
C) I and III only
D) II and III only

6

The normal amount of sodium in the water in a fish tank is 2.3×10^{-7} milligrams per liter. Yesterday, when the water was tested, the sodium level was exactly 1,000 times less than the usual amount. What concentration of sodium, in milligrams per liter, was in the water tested yesterday?
A) $2.3 \times 10^{-7,000}$
B) 2.3×10^{-10}
C) 2.3×10^{-9}
D) 2.3×10^{-4}

7

Which of the following is equivalent to $\left(\frac{1}{4}a + 8ab\right)^2$?

A) $\frac{1}{16}a^2 + 64ab^2$

B) $a\left(\frac{a}{16} + 4ab + 64ab^2\right)$

C) $a\left(\frac{a}{16} + 64b^2\right)$

D) $a\left(\frac{a}{16} + 64ab^2\right)$

POLYNOMIALS — POLYNOMIALS

Chapter 4 Practice

1

$(x^3 + 4x^2 - 13) - (-5x^2 - 14x + 11)$ is equivalent to:
A) $x^3 + 9x^2 + 14x - 24$
B) $x^3 - x^2 - 14x - 2$
C) $x^3 - x^2 + 14x - 2$
D) $x^3 + 9x^2 - 14x + 2$

2

$$C(x) = -(1.3x - 3)^2 + 16$$

The above equation represents the projectile path of a catapult launched from a height of 29 meters. Which of the following is an equivalent equation?
A) $C(x) = 1.69x + 13$
B) $C(x) = -1.69x^2 + 7.8x + 7$
C) $C(x) = -1.69x^2 - 3.9x - 9$
D) $C(x) = 1.69x^2 + 7.8x + 16$

3

What is the value of $4x^2 + 7x - 3$ subtracted from $2x^2 + 9x - 1$?
A) $-2x^2 + 2x + 2$
B) $-2x^2 - 2x - 2$
C) $-2x^2 + 16x - 4$
D) $2x^2 - 2x - 2$

4

If $A = 9x^2 + 7x - 2$ and $B = -6x^2 - x + 12$, then $A - B$ equals
A) $23x - 14$
B) $3x^2 + 8x - 4$
C) $3x^2 + 6x + 10$
D) $15x^2 + 8x - 14$

5

What is the product of $9x^3 + 2x - 4$ and $x + 3$?
A) $9x^4 - 27x^3 - 2x + 12$
B) $11x^4 + x + 7$
C) $9x^4 + 27x^3 + 2x^2 + 2x - 12$
D) $9x^3 + 3x - 1$

6

What is the result when $(x - 3)^2$ is subtracted from $(2x - 7)^2$?
A) $4x^2 - 28x + 49$
B) $x^2 - 6x + 9$
C) $5x^2 - 34x + 58$
D) $3x^2 - 22x + 40$

397

www.bellcurves.com

POLYNOMIALS

7

$$(x^3 - y^3)(z^3 + y^3)$$

Which of the following expressions is equivalent to the above equation?

A) $(xyz)^3 - y^6$
B) $(yx)^3 + (xz)^3 - (yz)^3 - y^6$
C) $x^3 - y^3 + xz^2 + zy^3 + y^6$
D) $x^3y^3 + z^3 - y^3$

POLYNOMIALS

8

When $9x^2 - 7x + 1$ is subtracted from $3x^2 - 2x + 14$, the result is equivalent to:

A) $(2x - 3)(3x + 5)$
B) $-6x^2 + 5x + 13$
C) $12x^2 + 9x + 15$
D) $6x^2 - 5x - 13$

QUADRATIC FUNCTIONS

1

Which of the following quadratic equations has solutions $x = 4p$ and $x = -2q$?
A) $x^2 - 8pq = 0$
B) $x^2 - 2x(q + 2p) + 8pq = 0$
C) $x^2 + 2x(q + 2p) - 8pq = 0$
D) $x^2 + 2x(q - 2p) - 8pq = 0$

2

What are the values for y that satisfy the equation $(y - 2g)(y + 3h) = 0$?

A) $-2g$ and $-3h$

B) $-2g$ and $3h$

C) $2g$ and $-3h$

D) $\frac{1}{2}g$ and $-3h$

3

If $(x + 4)$ is a factor of $2x^2 + kx - 24$, what is the value of k ?
A) -1
B) 2
C) 4
D) 6

4

What is the sum of the 2 solutions of the equation $x^2 - 4x - 21$?
A) -7
B) -4
C) 0
D) 4

5

If $(6x + 4)^2$ is written in the form $ax^2 + bx + c$, where a, b, and c are integers, $(a + b) - c$ is equal to what value?
A) 4
B) 28
C) 68
D) 72

6

For all $x > 8$, $\dfrac{(x^2 + 2x - 8)(x + 6)}{(x^2 + 10x + 24)(x + 2)} = ?$

A) $\dfrac{(x + 6)}{(x + 4)}$

B) $\dfrac{1}{(x + 2)}$

C) 1

D) $\dfrac{(x - 2)}{(x + 2)}$

399

www.bellcurves.com

QUADRATIC FUNCTIONS

7

$$\sqrt{x+j} = x+7$$

If j is equal to 19, what is the solution set of the equation above?

A) {-10, -3}
B) {-10, 0}
C) {0}
D) {3, 10}

9

$$\frac{1}{4}x^2 = \frac{1}{2}fx - \frac{3}{2}g$$

In the equation above, f and g are constants. What are the solutions for x?

A) $x = f \pm \sqrt{f^2 - 6g}$
B) $x = -f \pm \sqrt{f^2 - 24g}$
C) $x = 2f \pm \sqrt{4f^2 - 6g}$
D) $x = -2f \pm \sqrt{4f^2 - 6g}$

8

$f(x)$	x
-2	0
0	-3
2	-5
4	-11

The function f is defined by a polynomial. The chart above shows some values of $f(x)$ and x. Which of the following must be a factor of $f(x)$?

A) $x + 3$
B) $x + 2$
C) $x - 3$
D) $x - 2$

10

Jesse and Priscilla are each saving money to buy an apartment. The total amount of money Jesse will save is modeled by the function $j(m) = 70 + 10m$. The total amount of money Sarah will save is modeled by the function $p(m) = m^2 + 46$. After how many months, m, will they have the same amount of money saved?

EXPONENTIAL FUNCTIONS

1

A landlord charges a late fee on rent payments that are overdue. The equation $r = 2650(0.76)^d$ represents the value, r, of rent owed when it is d days past due. What is the y-intercept of this equation and what does it represent?

A) 0.76, the percent the landlord increases the rent by each day it is past due
B) 2650, the maximum amount the landlord can charge for rent
C) 2650, the regular monthly cost of rent without any late fees
D) 2014, 76% of the regular montly cost of

2

Sylvia deposited $7,650 in an account at Livingstone Banking Center, earning 3.6% interest, compounded annually. If she has made no additional deposits or withdrawals, what equation can be used to find S, her account balance after t years?

A) $7,650(1.36)^t$
B) $7,650 + (1.036)^t$
C) $7,650 + (.036)^t$
D) $7,650(1.036)^t$

3

The current population of Tinytown is 23,040. If the population, P, increases by 16% each year, which equation could be used to find the population after t years?

A) $23,040 + (1.16)^t$
B) $23,040(1.016)^t$
C) $23,040(1.16)^t$
D) $23,040 + (0.84)^t$

4

The breakdown of a radioactive chemical compound is represented by the function $f(t) = 189(0.29)^t$ where $f(t)$ represents the number of milliliters remaining of the substance and t represents the time, in years. In the function $f(t)$, what do 189 and 0.29 represent?

A) 189 represents the initial amount of the substance, and 0.29 represents the rate of decay of 29%
B) 189 represents the number of years the substance has been decaying, and 0.29 represents the rate of growth of 29%
C) 189 represents the amount of the substance remaining, and 0.29 represents the initial amount of the substance
D) 189 represents the initial amount of the substance, and 0.29 represents the rate of decay of 71%

5

Joesphine invested $725 in a savings account at a 2.8% annual interest rate, compounded annually. She made no additional deposits or withdrawals on the account for 7 years. What is the value, to the nearest dollar, of the balance in the account after 7 years?

Chapter 4 Practice

FUNCTION GRAPHS

1

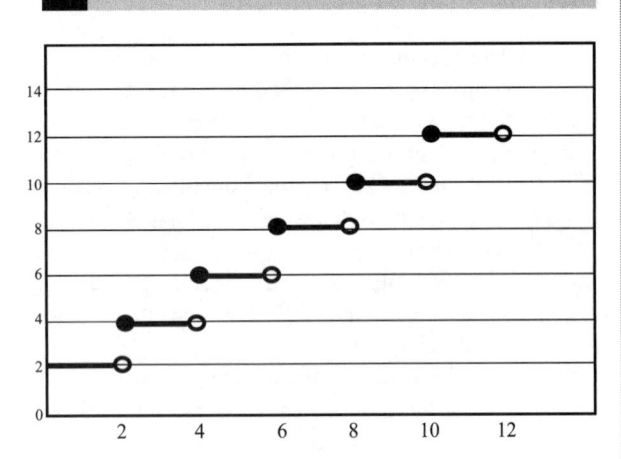

In the function h, shown above, what is the value of $h(2) + h(4) + h(8)$?

A) 20
B) 18
C) 16
D) 14

Questions 2 and 3 refer to the following information.

The complete graph of functions f and g are shown in the graph below.

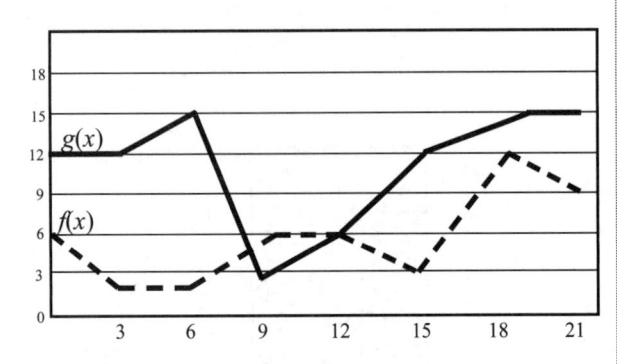

2

What is the value of $f(g(15))$?

A) 4
B) 6
C) 8
D) 12

3

Which of the following is true about functions f and g?

I. Function g is greater than function f over the interval $0 \leq x \leq 21$
II. Function f is less than function g over the interval $15 \leq x \leq 21$
III. Function g is equal to function f at exactly two points

A) I only
B) II and III only
C) I, II, and III only
D) None

4

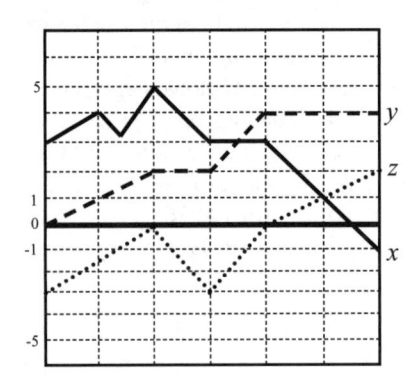

Where does the sum of the functions of x, y and z equal 0?

A) $x = 0$
B) $x = 5$
C) $x = 2$ or 4
D) $y = 3$

QUADRATIC FUNCTION GRAPH

1

In the *xy*-coordinate plane, the point (5, -2) lies on the graph of the function $f(x) = 0.5x^2 - 12x + c$. What is the value of c?

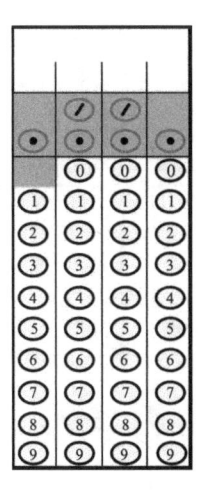

2

What is the vertex of the parabola represented by the equation $y = -6x^2 + 24x + 16$?

A) -2
B) -0.5
C) 0.5
D) 2

3

$$f(v) = 3x^2 - 25x - 88$$

The path a wrecking ball swings on at the end of its chain can be represented by the equation above. Which of the following equations is equivalent to the one given above?

A) $f(v) = (x + 9)(x - 7)$
B) $f(v) = x^2 - 24x - 26$
C) $f(v) = (x + 8)(3x - 11)$
D) $f(v) = (x^2 + 8)(3x - 12)$

4

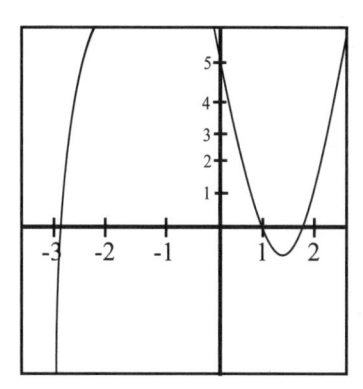

Which of the following equations could be the equation for the graph shown above?
A) $y = x^3 - 6x + 5$
B) $y = x^3 - x^2$
C) $y = 10x(x^2 - 3)$
D) $y = x^4 - x^2 + 3$

5

The function $f(x) = -4x^4 - 3x^3 + 5x^2$ is graphed in the *xy*-plane below.

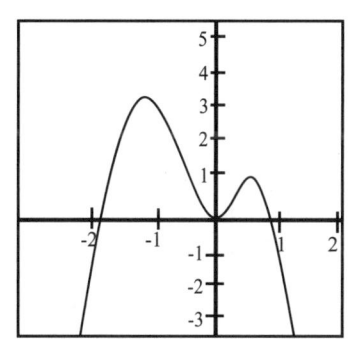

If the answer set for $f(x) = m$ has four possible solutions, which of following could be m?
A) 1
B) 0.5
C) -1
D) -2

Chapter 4 Practice

ADVANCED FUNCTION — GRAPHS

1

What is the x-coordinate of the point in the standard (x,y) coordinate plane at which the 2 lines $y = 3x + 1$ and $y = 4x + 5$ intersect?

A) -11
B) -4
C) -1
D) 6

2

The equations $y = x^3 - 9x + 16$ and $y = 7x + 16$ intersect at three points. Which of the following is the solution set for the intersection of these two equations?

A) (0,16), (-4, -44), (-12, 0)
B) (0,16), (-4, -12), (4, 44)
C) (4, 12), (8, 10), (0, 0)
D) (-4, 12), (0, 24), (44, 4)

3

In the xy-coordinate plane, the parabola with the equation $y = x^2 - 2x$ intersects the line with the equation $y = 63$ at two points, C and D. What is the length of the line segment that connects C and D?

A) 2
B) 7
C) 9
D) 16

4

Which of the following systems of inequalities is represented by the shaded region of the graph below?

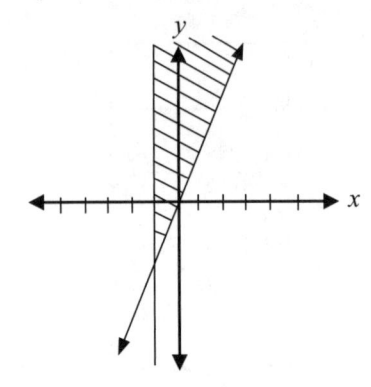

A) $y \geq 3x$ and $x \geq -1$
B) $y \leq 3x$ and $x \leq -1$
C) $y \leq 3x$ and $x \geq -1$
D) $y \geq 3x$ or $x \geq -1$

5

$$y \leq 3x$$
$$y \geq 12x - 885$$

In the xy-coordinate plane, if a point with coordinate (x, y) lines in the solution set of the system of inequalities above, what is the maximum possible value of y?

Chapter 4 Practice

IMAGINARY NUMBERS

1

In the complex numbers, where $i^2 = -1$, what is the value of $\dfrac{i^3}{1+i} \div \dfrac{-i}{i-1}$?

A) 0

B) $\dfrac{1+i}{i-1}$

C) i

D) $\dfrac{-1}{i+1}$

2

For $i^2 = -1$, $(3 - i)^2 = ?$
A) 2
B) 14
C) $6 - 6i$
D) $8 - 6i$

3

In the complex numbers, where $i^2 = -1$, $i^{37} + i^6 = ?$
A) -1
B) 1
C) $i - 1$
D) $1 + i$

4

$$\dfrac{x - 9i}{yi + 6} = \dfrac{-6}{13} - \dfrac{23i}{26}$$

If in the expression above, x and y are non-zero integers, which of the following could be the value of the quotient of y and x ?
A) 1
B) 2
C) 8
D) 9

5

$$\dfrac{6 - 6i}{i + 3} + (4 + 2i)$$

Which of the following is equivalent to the above expression?

A) $\dfrac{16 + 4i}{i + 3}$

B) $16 + \dfrac{4i}{i + 3}$

C) $6 - 6i + \dfrac{10 + 10i}{i + 3}$

D) $\dfrac{52 - 4i}{10}$

6

For $i = \sqrt{-1}$, what is the sum of $65 - 12i$ and $-3 + 6i$?
A) $62 + 6i$
B) $67 - 30i$
C) $62 - 6i$
D) $30 - 67i$

405

Chapter 4 Practice

COORDINATE GEOMETRY

1

A circle in the coordinate (x,y) plane lies tangential to the x-axis at 9 and the y-axis at 9. What is the equation of the circle?
A) $x^2 + y^2 = 3$
B) $x^2 + y^2 = 9$
C) $(x - 9)^2 + (y - 9)^2 = 81$
D) $(x + 3)^2 + (y + 3)^2 = 9$

2

Square $WXYZ$ lies in the coordinate plane and has vertices $Y(3,2)$ and $Z(8,6)$. What is the slope of side XY?

A) $\dfrac{4}{5}$
B) $-\dfrac{5}{4}$
C) $\dfrac{8}{11}$
D) $-\dfrac{11}{8}$

3

In the coordinate plane, function g has a positive slope and a y intercept of 0, while function f has a negative slope and a y intercept of 8. In which quadrant will the two lines intersect?
A) Quadrant 1
B) Quadrant 2
C) Quadrant 4
D) They won't intersect.

4

What is the area of a circle with the equation $x^2 + y^2 = 64$, on the standard (x,y) coordinate plane?
A) 8π
B) 16π
C) 64π
D) 128π

5

What is the equation of a line passing through the point $(2,5)$ and parallel to the line whose equation is $6x = 2y + 8$?
A) $y = 3x + 1$
B) $y = 3x - 1$
C) $y = 6x - 2$
D) $y = 8x + 2$

6

A circle in the xy-coordinate plane passes through the point $(3,4)$ and is centered at $(8,16)$. Determine the length of its diameter.

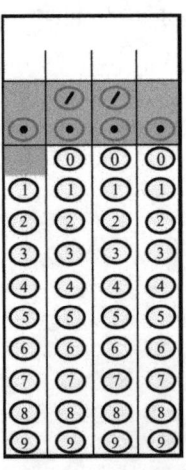

COORDINATE GEOMETRY

Chapter 4 Practice

1

Point *A* is to be graphed in a quadrant, not on an axis of the standard (*x*,*y*) coordinate plane below.

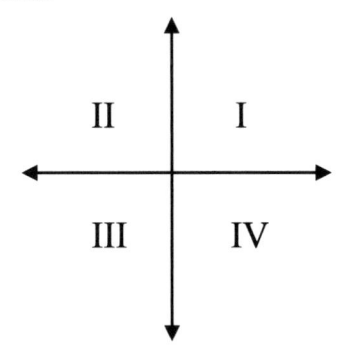

II	I
III	IV

If the *x*-coordinate and the *y*-coordinate of point *A* have the same sign, then point *A* MUST be located in

A) Quadrant I only.
B) Quadrant II only.
C) Quadrant III only.
D) Quadrant I and III only.

2

Which of the following linear equations will NEVER intersect the line $y = .6x + 13$?

A) $y = \frac{3}{5}x - 8$

B) $y = -\frac{10}{6}x + 13$

C) $y = |x|$

D) $y = \frac{x}{3} + 5$

3

In the *xy*-coordinate plane, the graph of the line *P* is $y = 0.75x + 2.5$ and the graph of the line *R* contains the points (-12, -35.4) and (15, 30.75). Lines *P* and *R* intersect at exactly one point, (*a*,*b*). What is the value of *ab*?

A) 10

B) $\frac{130}{11}$

C) $\frac{125}{4}$

D) 100

4

Which of the following graphs contain(s) the point (-2,2) ?

    I. $y = |x|$

    II. $y = \frac{3}{10}|x| + \frac{7}{5}$

    III. $y = 1.5x^2 - 4$

A) II only
B) I and III only
C) I, II, and III
D) None

COORDINATE GEOMETRY

5

The graph of a linear equation contains the points (4,15) and (10,27). Which point also lies on the graph?
A) (-4, -6)
B) (-5, -11)
C) (-12, -10)
D) (-3, 1)

6

What is the y-intercept of the line in the standard (x,y) coordinate plane that goes through the points (8,-6) and (4,-3) ?
A) -6
B) -3
C) 0
D) 4

Chapter 4 Practice

LINES | ANGLES

1

In the figure below, lines *p* and *q* never intersect. Transversals *m* and *n* intersect to form an angle measuring 82 degrees, as shown below. What is the value of the *y* ?

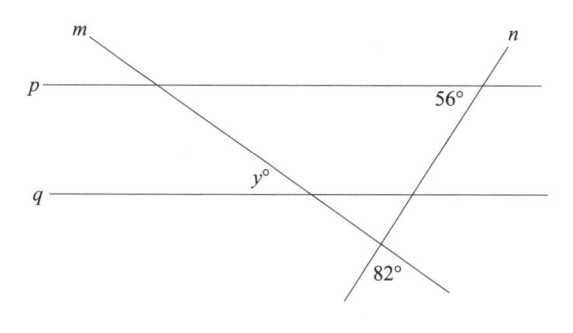

A) 36°
B) 42°
C) 54°
D) 56°

2

In the diagram below, lines *P* and *Q* are parallel. Transversal lines *J* and *K* intersect, forming an angle, marked *x*. Two other angle measures are shown below. What is the measure, in degrees, of angle *x* ?

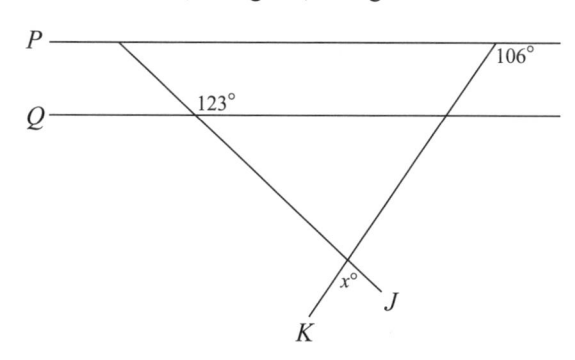

A) 45°
B) 49°
C) 55°
D) 85°

3

In the figure below, what is the value of $A+B+C+D+E+F+G+H+I+J+K+L$?

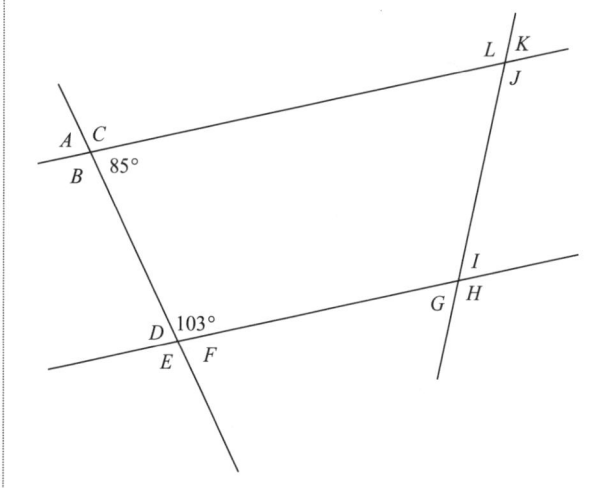

A) 360°
B) 530°
C) 1080°
D) There is not enough information to determine this

4

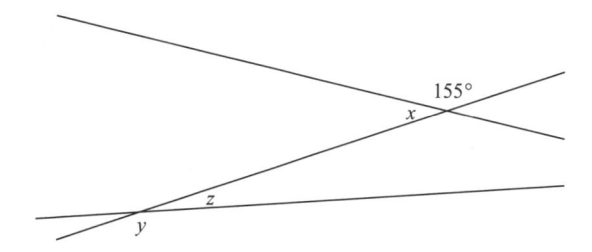

If $y = 4x$ in the figure above, what is the value of *z* ?

A) 25°
B) 80°
C) 155°
D) 180°

Chapter 4 Practice

TRIANGLES   TRIANGLES

1

In the diagram shown below, two similar triangles are shown, with side lengths given in meters. What is the perimeter, in meters, of $\triangle MNO$?

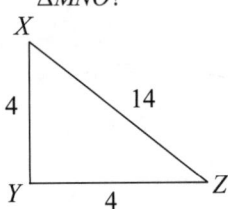

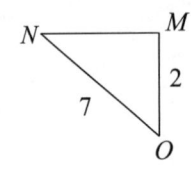

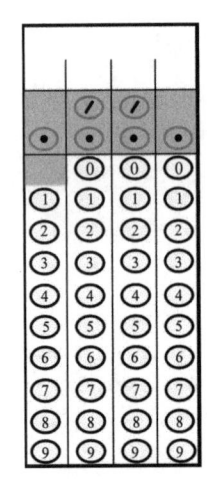

2

3 parallel lines, l_1, l_2 and l_3 are intersected by lines l_4 and l_5 at the points marked on the diagram below. The ratio of segment KL to segment OP is 1:3. The ratio of $\triangle JMN$ to $\triangle JOP$ is 2:3. What is the ratio of JK to KM?

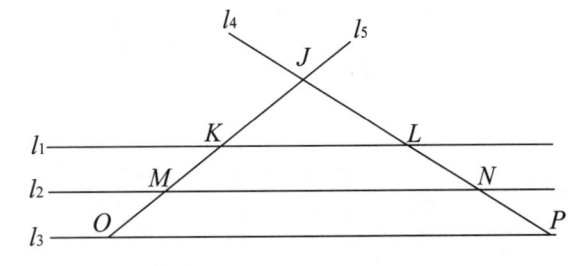

A) 1 : 1
B) 1 : 2
C) 1 : 3
D) 2 : 3

3

In the figure below, A, C, D and F are collinear points. B, D, and E are also collinear. Angles ACB, ABD, BCD and EFD are right angles. Given this information, which of the following statements is NOT justifiable?

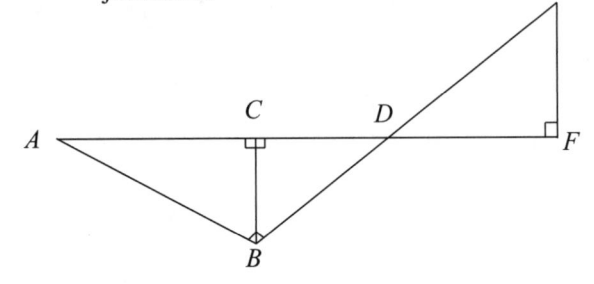

A) Angle CDB is congruent to angle EDF.
B) $\triangle BCD$ is similar to $\triangle EDF$.
C) BD is congruent to AB.
D) AB is perpendicular to BE.

4

In the figure below, two isosceles triangles share a vertex.

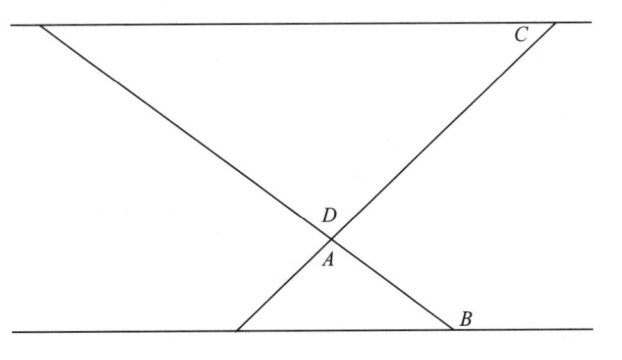

Angle $C = 38°$ and angle $A = 0.25D$. What is the measure of angle B?
A) 38°
B) 77°
C) 103°
D) 104°

CIRCLES

1

Two circles have radii in a ratio of 9:16. What is the ratio of their circumferences?
A) 3 : 4
B) 9 : 16
C) 81 : 256
D) 9 : 16π

2

The diameter of a circle with center S is marked by endpoints Q and R. Point T lies on the circle and angle QST measures 30°. The shortest distance between Q and T is what percent of the distance between Q and R?

A) $8\frac{1}{3}$ %

B) $16\frac{2}{3}$ %

C) $33\frac{1}{3}$ %

D) 50%

3

Kathy used an 8-inch pie pan to bake an apple pie, and then a pumpkin pie. She cut the apple pie into 8 pieces and the pumpkin pie into 6 pieces. If Candace had one slice of each pie, what is the total area of her two pie slices together, rounded to the nearest tenth? (Disregard how thick the pies are.)
A) 3π
B) 4.33π
C) 18.6π
D) 22π

4

The diameter of the earth is 7,917 miles. Passenger airplanes cruise at an average altitude of 39,000 feet. If Miranda decided to fly, non-stop, once around the earth at the same altitude as a passenger airplane, how far would she travel, rounded to the nearest tenth of a mile? (5280feet = 1 mile)
A) 3962.2π miles
B) 7917π miles
C) 7924.4π miles
D) 46,917π miles

5

Triangle ABC is inscribed in circle O where AB is the diameter.

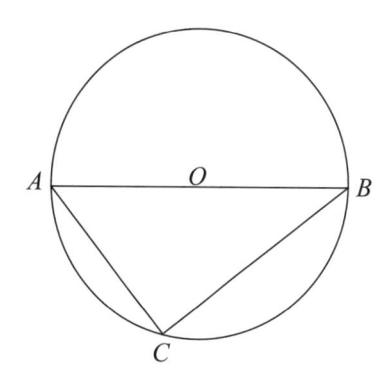

Angle ABC measures 30° and $AC = 4$. What is the measure of the diameter?
A) 4
B) 8
C) $4\sqrt{3}$
D) $22\sqrt{3}$

OTHER POLYGONS — 3D GEOMETRY

1

A small cube has edges that are one fifth the length of those of a large cube. How many times larger is the volume of the large cube than the volume of the small cube?
A) 5
B) 50
C) 75
D) 125

2

The bar of chocolate shown in the diagram is molded in the form of a right triangular prism. All of its sides are going to be coated with a thin layer of cocoa powder. How many square inches of cocoa powder will be needed to coat the entire chocolate bar?

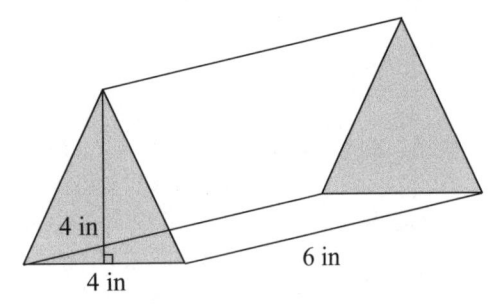

4 in
4 in
6 in

A) $20\sqrt{5}$
B) $20 + 12\sqrt{5}$
C) 22
D) $40 + 24\sqrt{5}$

3

The ratio of the width of rectangle G to a side of square H is 5 : 6. The ratio of a side of square H to the length of rectangle G is 6 : 3. What is the ratio of the area of rectangle G to the area of square H?
A) 4 : 1
B) 5 : 12
C) 9 : 12
D) 12 : 5

4

Samir cut a rectangular piece of fabric. If the length of Samir's fabric is represented by $3x + 4$ and the width is represented by $5x - 12$, then which of the following represents the area of her piece of fabric?
A) $15x^2 - 16x - 48$
B) $8x - 8$
C) $15x^2 + 16x + 48$
D) $16x - 16$

OTHER POLYGONS

5

The equation for the volume of a cylinder is $V = \pi r^2 h$. How can the positive values of r be expressed in terms of h and V?

A) $r = \sqrt{\dfrac{\pi}{Vh}}$

B) $r = \sqrt{\dfrac{Vh}{\pi}}$

C) $r = \sqrt{\dfrac{V}{\pi h}}$

D) $r = \dfrac{V\pi h}{2}$

3D GEOMETRY

6

Tom is building a cylindrical grain silo with a semi circle top, as shown below, to store his corn harvest. If he has enough materials to build a silo 48 feet around the base and have a total height of 70 feet, how many cubic feet of corn can Tom's silo hold? (Round your answer to the nearest foot.)

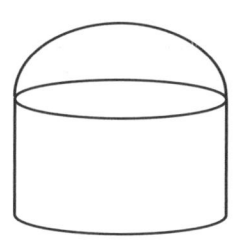

A) 919
B) 8400
C) 10,404
D) 11,323

Chapter 4 Practice

TRIGONOMETRY | TRIGONOMETRY

1

For the right triangle DEF shown below, what is cos F?

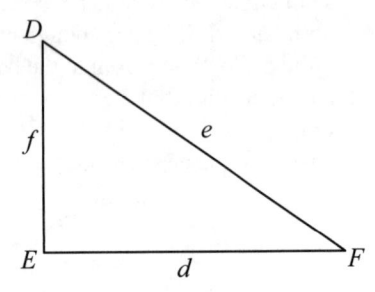

A) $\dfrac{d}{e}$
B) $\dfrac{d}{f}$
C) $\dfrac{e}{d}$
D) $\dfrac{f}{d}$

2

The hypotenuse of the right triangle RST shown below is 20 feet long. The sine of angle T is $\dfrac{5}{8}$. About how many feet long is RS?

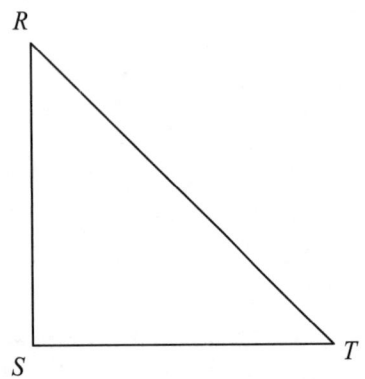

A) 7.5
B) 10.0
C) 12.5
D) 16.0

3

If the two triangles below are similar, but RST is half as large as LMN and sine $X = \dfrac{12}{15}$. What is cosine W?

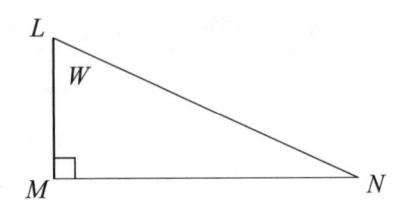

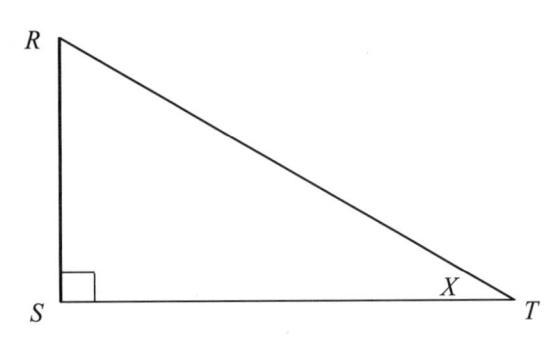

A) 0.8
B) 0.6
C) 1.2
D) 1.25

4

If $\csc x = \dfrac{13}{5}$, then what is the tangent of x?

A) $\dfrac{1}{5}$
B) $\dfrac{5}{13}$
C) $\dfrac{1}{13}$
D) $\dfrac{5}{12}$

414

SAT-R Workbook v. 1.5

Math Test – No Calculator

25 MINUTES, 20 QUESTIONS

DIRECTIONS

For questions 1-15, solve each problem, choose the best answer from the choices provided.
For questions 16-20, solve the problem and enter your answer in the grid. You may use any available space for scratch work.

NOTES

1. The use of a calculator **is not permitted.**

2. All variables and expressions used represent real numbers unless otherwise indicated.

3. Figures provided in this est are drawn to scale unless otherwise indicated.

4. All figures lie in a plane unless otherwise indicated.

5. Unless otherwise indicated, the domain of a given function f is the set of all real numbers x for which $f(x)$ is a real number.

REFERENCE

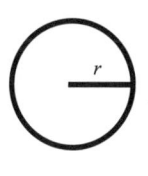

$A = \pi r^2$
$C = 2\pi r$

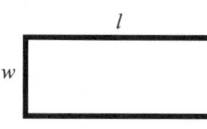

$A = lw$

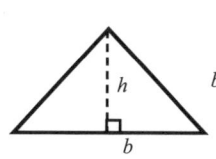

$A = \frac{1}{2}bh$

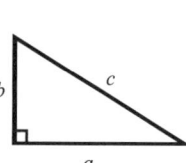

$c^2 = a^2 + b^2$

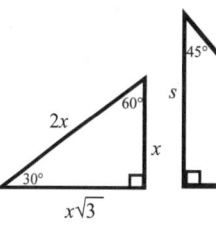

Special Right Triangles

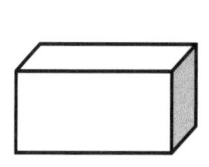

$V = lwh$

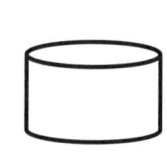

$V = \pi r^2 h$

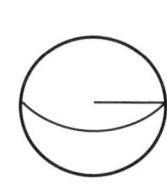

$V = \frac{4}{3}\pi r^3$

$V = \frac{1}{3}\pi r^2 h$

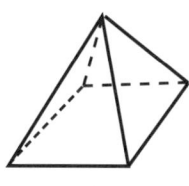

$V = \frac{1}{3}lwh$

The number of degrees of arc in a circle is 360.
The number of radians of arc in a circle is 2π.
The sum of the measures in degrees of the angles of a triangle is 180°.

Chapter 4 Practice

1

If $\dfrac{|2x| + 6}{10} = 2y$ and $y = 10$, which of the following is a possible value of x?

A) -108
B) -97
C) 12
D) 47

2

For $i = \sqrt{-1}$, what is the difference of $-4 + 3i$ and $8 - 6i$?

A) $4 - 3i$
B) $-12 - 3i$
C) $4 + 3i$
D) $-12 + 9i$

3

A taxi company estimates its profits for one day using the expression $2.50p + 0.75md$, where d is the number of drivers working, p is the total number of pick-ups per day and m is the number of miles driven per driver. Which of the following is the best interpretation of the number 2.50 in the expression?

A) The taxi company pays its drivers a base salary of $2.50.
B) Passengers pay a base price of $2.50 for each pick-up.
C) Taxi drivers charge a total of $2.50 per mile driven.
D) Each taxi driver works a shift that is 2.50 hours in total.

4

$$9x^4 + 30x^2y^{\frac{1}{2}} + 25y^{\frac{1}{4}}$$

Which of the following is equivalent to the expression shown above?

A) $(3x^2 + 5y^{\frac{1}{4}})^2$

B) $(3x^2 + 5y^{\frac{1}{2}})^2$

C) $(3x^2 + 5y^{\frac{1}{2}})^4$

D) $(3x^4 + 25y^2)^{\frac{1}{4}}$

5

If $\frac{2x}{7} = \frac{4x+12}{11}$, what is the value of $5x$?

A) -70
B) -7
C) $-\frac{1}{7}$
D) 70

6

$$5x + 2y = 18$$
$$3x + 5y = 7$$

If (x,y) is a solution to the system of equations above, what is the value of $x + y$?

A) 1.8
B) 3.0
C) 6.4
D) 9.2

7

x	$g(x)$
-3	6
-1	0
0	-8
2	-13

The function g is defined by a polynomial. The table above shows some values of x and $g(x)$. Which of the following must be a factor of $g(x)$?

A) $x - 8$
B) $x - 1$
C) $x + 8$
D) $x + 1$

8

$$6x - 2y = 14$$

Which of the following equations represents a line that is perpendicular to the line with the equation above?

A) $7 - y = 3x$
B) $7 + y = -\frac{1}{3}x$
C) $y = 7 + \frac{1}{3}x$
D) $3y = 7x + 1$

9

$$\sqrt{x-3b} = 2x+1$$

If $b = -3$, what is the solution set of the equation above?

A) {-2, 1}
B) {-1, 2}
C) {0, 2}
D) {0, 1, 2}

10

Which of the following equations has a graph in the xy-plane for which y is always less than or equal to -5?

A) $-x^2 - 5$
B) $|x| - 5$
C) $-|x| + 5$
D) $x^2 - 5$

11

$$f(x) = 5x^3 + k^2x$$

For the function f defined above, k is a constant and $f(3) = 183$. What is the value of $f(5)$?

A) 175
B) 645
C) 705
D) 815

12

$$P = \frac{D + S^2}{2I}$$

A scout uses the formula above to calculate a player's rating, P, based on the distance he can throw a ball, D, his speed in a 90 foot sprint, S, and the number of injuries he has had in his career, I. Which of the following expresses the player's speed in a 90 foot sprint in terms of the other variables?

A) $S = \dfrac{2PI - D}{2}$

B) $S = \sqrt{2PI - D}$

C) $S = \sqrt{2PI + D^2}$

D) $S = \dfrac{PI + 2D}{2}$

13

$$0 = -5x^2 + 15x + 20$$

What is the product of all values of x that satisfy the equation above?

A) -20
B) -4
C) 4
D) 20

14

The population of Town X increases at an annual rate of 1.7%. If the initial number of people in the town was 15,680, which of the following functions f models the amount of people in the town after a total of t years?

A) $f(t) = 15,680(1.17)^t$
B) $f(t) = 15,680(.83)^t$
C) $f(t) = 15,680(1.017)^t$
D) $f(t) = 1.17(15,680)^t$

15

$$\frac{a}{4}x^2 + 4q = -12x$$

In the quadratic equation above, a and q are constants. What are the solutions for x?

A) $\dfrac{-24 \pm 4\sqrt{36 - aq}}{a}$

B) $\dfrac{-24 \pm 6\sqrt{-aq}}{a}$

C) $\dfrac{-24 \pm 6\sqrt{aq}}{2a}$

D) $\dfrac{-24 \pm \sqrt{36 + aq}}{2a}$

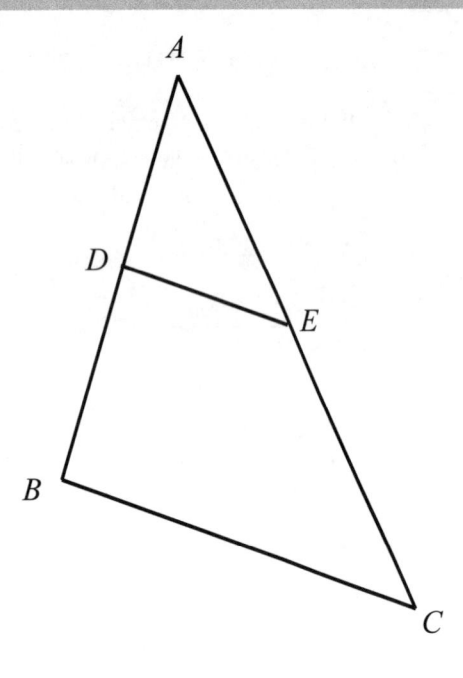

16

In the diagram of *ABC* show above, *BC* ∥ *DE*. Segment *AD* is equal to 7; *DB* is equal to 15 and *AE* is equal to 10.5. What is the measure of segment *EC*?

17

If $\frac{3}{5}x + \frac{11}{15}x = \frac{2}{3} + \frac{4}{6}$, what is the value of x?

18

$$0 = x^3 - 3x^2 + 6x - 18$$

For what real value of x is the equation above true?

19

In a right triangle, angle A measures $y°$, and $\sin A = 0.4$. What is the value of the cosine of the angle complementary to angle A ?

20

$$px + qy = 15$$
$$3x + 6y = 6$$

In the system of equations above, p and q are constants. If the system has infinitely many solutions, what is the value of the product of p and the reciprocal of q ?

4　　　　　　　　　　　　　　4

Math Test – Calculator

55 MINUTES, 38 QUESTIONS

DIRECTIONS

For questions 1-30, solve each problem and choose the best answer from the choices provided.
For questions 31-38, solve the problem and enter your answer in the grid. You may use any available space for scratch work.

NOTES

1. The use of a calculator **is permitted.**

2. All variables and expressions used represent real numbers unless otherwise indicated.

3. Figures provided in this est are drawn to scale unless otherwise indicated.

4. All figures lie in a plane unless otherwise indicated.

5. Unless otherwise indicated, the domain of a given function f is the set of all real numbers x for which f(x) is a real number.

REFERENCE

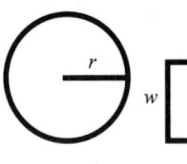

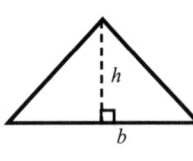

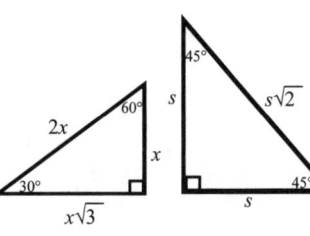

$A = \pi r^2$
$C = 2\pi r$

$A = lw$

$A = \frac{1}{2}bh$

$c^2 = a^2 + b^2$

Special Right Triangles

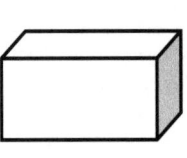

$V = lwh$

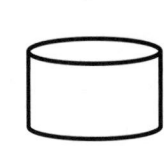

$V = \pi r^2 h$

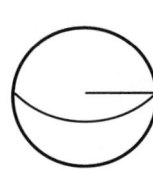

$V = \frac{4}{3}\pi r^3$

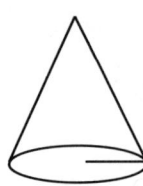

$V = \frac{1}{3}\pi r^2 h$

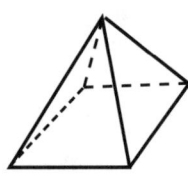

$V = \frac{1}{3}lwh$

The number of degrees of arc in a circle is 360.
The number of radians of arc in a circle is 2π.
The sum of the measures in degrees of the angles of a triangle is 180°.

Chapter 4 Practice

1

Kayla is training for a race and runs at different speeds throughout her training program. Over which interval is the speed at which she runs consistently increasing?

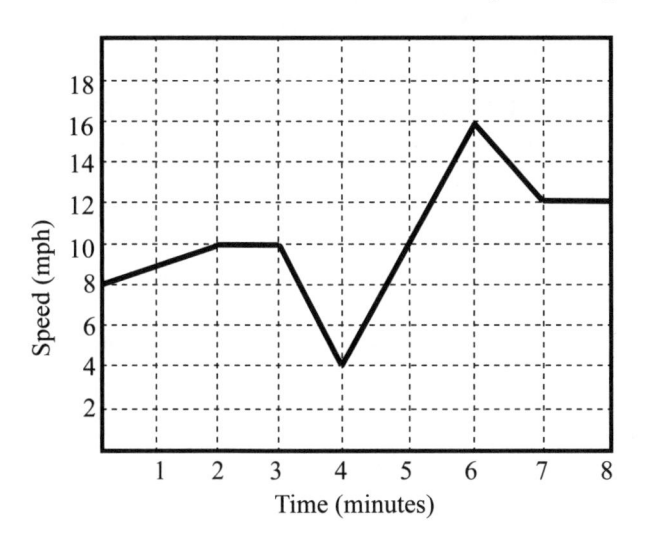

A) Minutes 1 – 3
B) Minutes 3 – 5
C) Minutes 4 – 6
D) Minutes 6 – 8

2

Sheila is in culinary school practicing to become a baker. Her homework assignment is to bake a total of 1,280 muffins. In the first pan of 20 muffins she bakes, she burns a total of 3 of them. At this rate, how many muffins will be burnt out of the 1,280 she must bake?

A) 192
B) 240
C) 252
D) 306

3

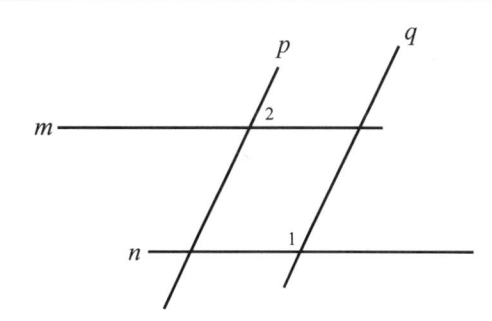

In the figure above, lines m and n are parallel and lines p and q are parallel. If the measure of angle 1 is 102°, what is the measure of angle 2?

A) 54°
B) 62°
C) 78°
D) 258°

4

x	-1	0	1	2
f(x)	-1	-3	-1	5

The table above shows some values of the function f. Which of the following defines f?

A) $f(x) = 3x^2 + 4$
B) $f(x) = 4x^2 - 5$
C) $f(x) = x^2 + 2$
D) $f(x) = 2x^2 - 3$

Questions 5 and 6 refer to the following information.

The amount of a money a tennis player can earn in a tournament is inversely proportional to the number of sets he loses. The tennis players earned a total of $3,025 at a tournament in which he lost a total of 25 sets.

5

How much money will the tennis player earn if he loses a total of 36 sets in his next tournamen? (Round your answer to the nearest cent.)

A) $1,112.48
B) $2,100.69
C) $2,982.25
D) $4,356.00

6

The tennis player must pay his coach 16% of his winnings for each tournament he plays in. On top of that, he must pay 7% of the remaining amount in tournament travel fees. The remaining money he earns is profit. What is his profit at a tournament in which he loses a total of 12 sets? (Round your answer to the nearest cent.)

A) $70.58
B) $3,425.67
C) $3,705.63
D) $4,923.19

7

TV Show Viewership (in thousands) in March 2015

Channel	Type of Show			
	Reality	Talk Show	Comedy	Drama
MTV	17.6	8.3	7.1	3.4
VH1	15.4	12.2	5.8	10
ABC	123.2	56.8	206.3	210.5
FOX	305.7	44.1	195.78	203
NBC	98.4	48.9	180.32	208.4
Total	560.3	170.6	595.3	635.3

The table above represents the viewership numbers, in thousands, for different channels, categorized by show type. What proportion of all show types are comedy shows on ABC and NBC?

A) $\frac{3}{20}$

B) $\frac{1}{5}$

C) $\frac{2}{7}$

D) $\frac{3}{5}$

8

For what value of p is $|-3p^2| - 7$ equal to 5?

A) -4
B) 2
C) 5
D) There is no such value of p.

9

Sabrina owns a clothing company. She can stitch buttons on her shirts at a rate of 36 buttons in 14 minutes. If she continues to work at this same rate, how long will it take her to stitch on 864 buttons?

A) 4 hours, 12 minutes
B) 4 hours, 49 minutes
C) 5 hours, 36 minutes
D) 5 hours, 52 minutes

Questions 10 and 11 refer to the following information.

$$n = \frac{c}{v}$$

The equation above represents the index of refraction, n, which is defined as the amount by which light slows in a given material. The index of refraction is calculated by finding the quotient of the speed of light in a vacuum, c, and the speed of light through a given material, v.

The speed of light in a vacuum is 300,000 km/second.

10

If the speed of light through water is 225,000 km/second, what is the index of refraction of water? (Round your answer to the nearest tenth.)

A) 0.75
B) 1.3
C) 1.8
D) 2.1

11

The index of refraction for glass is 1.5. If the speed of light through lead is 58% as fast as the speed of light through glass, what is the index of refraction of lead? (Round your answer to the nearest tenth.)

A) 1.6
B) 1.9
C) 2.1
D) 2.6

Chapter 4 Practice

12

Number of Fouls Committed by College Basketball Players in March Madness Sweet 16 Round

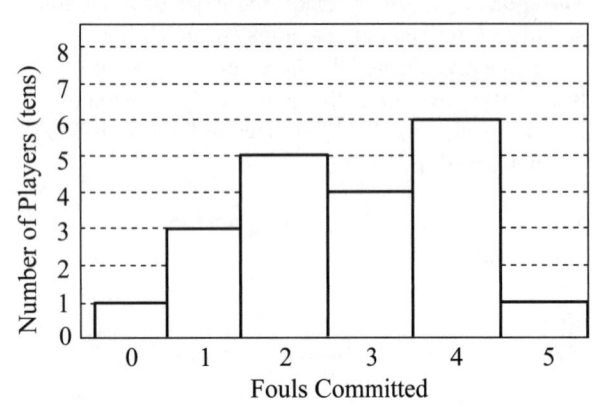

Based on the histogram above, which of the which gives the relationship between the mean and median number of fouls committed by the players?

A) The mean number of fouls is approximately 2.6, while the median number of fouls is 2.5.
B) The mean number of fouls is approximately 2.6, while the median number of fouls is 3.
C) The mean number of fouls is equal to the median number of fouls.
D) The median number of fouls is approximately 2.5, while the mean number of fouls cannot be determined.

13

A researcher conducted a study to determine whether students at a school prefer geometry or trigonometry. The researcher asked 406 students as they walked into the cafeteria. If 286 students responded that they prefer geometry, approximately how many students, out of the total 1,421 students in the school, would the researcher expect to answer that they prefer trigonometry?

A) 420
B) 516
C) 986
D) 1,001

14

Household Median Income in Town X

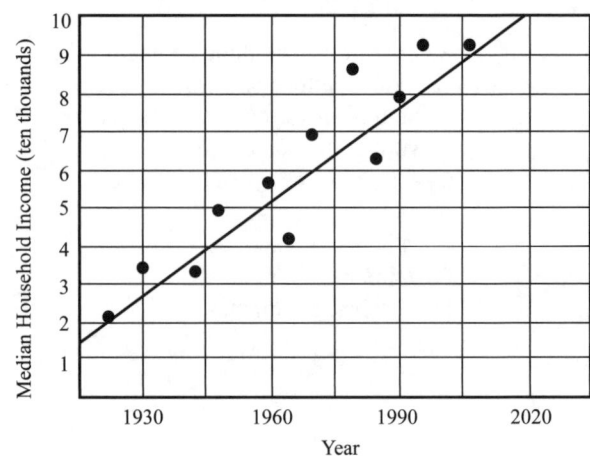

According to the line of best fit in the scatterplot above, which of the following best approximates the median household income in 2005?

A) $67,500
B) $77,000
C) $87,000
D) $91,000

15

The table below shows 70 students' grades in different classes at Basco Middle School.

Class	Grade		
	A	B	C
English	30	27	13
Math	19	40	11
History	26	28	16
Art	51	17	2

If one of those surveyed received an A in English, what is the probability that he or she received an A in History?

A) $\frac{5}{16}$

B) $\frac{3}{7}$

C) $\frac{16}{35}$

D) There is not enough information to determine this.

Questions 16 and 17 refer to the following information.

A clothing company's profits and expenses are functions of the price of fabric, F.

$$P(F) = 1{,}675 - 2F$$
$$E(F) = 3F^2 + 21F - 9$$

The functions above are estimated profit and expense functions for sweaters. The function $P(F)$ gives the company's profit when the price of wool is F dollars, and the function $E(F)$ gives the company's expenses when the price of wool is F dollars.

16

How will the company's profits change if the price of fabric is increased by $20?
A) The profits will increase by $40.
B) The profits will decrease by $40.
C) The profits will decrease by $20.
D) The profits will change by different amounts depending on the original price of fabric.

17

At what price of fabric will the company break even? (Round your answer to the nearest cent.)
A) $12.98
B) $14.55
C) $20.07
D) $32.16

18

Siobhan has a cubic planter box in which she plans to grow a tomato plant. The planter, with a side measuring 6.5 feet, is completely filled with dirt. As a gift, Siobhan's mother gives her a new cylindrical planter that she can have on her desk, with a height of 42 inches and a diameter of 18 inches. If Siobhan transfers dirt from her original planter to completely fill her new planter, how many cubic feet of soil will remain in her original planter? (Round your answer to the nearest tenth.)

A) 179.3
B) 198.6
C) 268.4
D) 428.7

19

A movie theater sells popcorn for $6.95 per bag and tickets for $18.40 per ticket. On Friday night, the theater sold a total of 306 tickets and bags of popcorn, netting them a total revenue of $4,691.50. How many tickets did the theater sell on Friday night?

A) 82
B) 167
C) 224
D) 306

20

The sum of four numbers is 180. The largest number is 5 times the sum of the two smallest numbers. The remaining number is 80% of the largest number. What is the value of the largest number?

A) 18
B) 72
C) 90
D) 112

21

Of the following four situations, which situation represents an example of exponential decay?

A) Each successive month, 2% of the starting population in City Y moves away.
B) Each successive year, 7% of the current value of a savings account is added to the account as interest.
C) Each successive month, 3% of the current population of rats in a laboratory give birth.
D) Each successive year, 6% of the current population in City Z moves away.

22

$$x^2 + y^2 - 18x + 6y = -3$$

The equation of a circle in the *xy*-plane is shown above. What are the values of the center of the circle and the radius of the circle?

A) Center: (9, -3), Radius: 87
B) Center: (-9, 3), Radius: 3
C) Center: (9, 3), Radius: 9
D) Center: (9, -3), Radius: $\sqrt{87}$

23

In Circle *O*, points *P* and *Q* are points on the circumference of the circle. The measure of angle *POQ* is equal to 72° and the measure of minor arc *PQ* is equal to 12π. What is the measure of the diameter of Circle *O* ?

A) 30
B) 46
C) 60
D) 72

24

$$d = -3.2f^2 + 406f$$

The equation above expresses the approximate distance, *d*, a droid will be from the ground after *f* minutes when flying at 406 feet per minute. After appoximately how many minutes will the droid return to the ground?

A) 118
B) 127
C) 143
D) 156

25

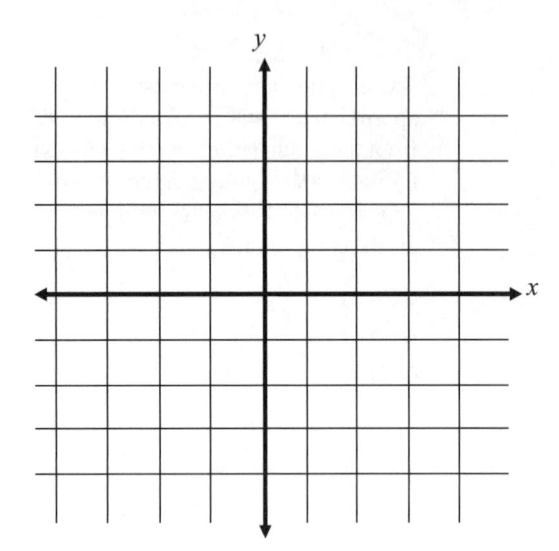

When points A, B, and C are graphed on the xy-plane above, they form a right triangle. Point A has the coordinates (1, 1), and point B has the coordinates (-3, 4). Which of the following could be the coordinates of point C?

A) (1, 4)
B) (-0.5, -1)
C) (1, 3)
D) There is not enough information to determine this.

26

Let x and y be numbers such that $x^2 \leq y^2 \leq y$. Which of the following must be true?

    I. $y + x < 1$
    II. $x < 0$ and $y > 0$
    III. $0 \leq x \leq 1$ and $0 \leq y \leq 1$

A) I and III only
B) I, II and III
C) III only
D) None of the above.

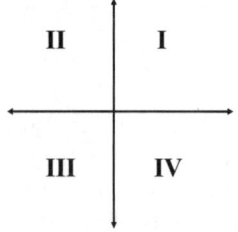

27

If the system of inequalities $y > 3x - 6$ and $y > 2x^2 + 4x + 6$ is graphed on the xy-plane above, which quadrant(s) contain(s) the solution set to the system?

A) Quadrants I and IV
B) Quadrant I and II
C) Quadrants II and III
D) Quadrans III and IV

28

The base of a right triangle is increased by 30%, and the height of the right triangle is decreased by 20%. By what percent did these alterations increase or decrease the area of the triangle?
A) Increased the area by 4%
B) Increased the area by 10%
C) Decreased the area by 8%
D) Increased the area by 104%

29

$$f(x) = (x + 7)(x - 5)$$

Which of the following is an equivalent form of the function f above in which the minimum value of the function appears as a constant or coefficient?
A) $f(x) = (x - 1)^2(x + 36)$
B) $f(x) = (x - 1)(x - 35)$
C) $f(x) = x^2 + 2x - 35$
D) $f(x) = (x + 1)^2 - 36$

30

$$x = -5$$
$$(x - a)^2 + y^2 = b$$

In the system above, a and b are constants. For which of the following values of a and b does the system of equations have more than one real solution?
A) $a = 4, b = 81$
B) $a = -1, b = 25$
C) $a = 1, b = 36$
D) $a = -2, b = 9$

31

A tourism company has been filling its hot air balloon for a total of 3 hours and it currently contains 1,521 cubic feet of air. If the company continues to fill the balloon at this rate, how many additional minutes will it take to completely fill the balloon if it can hold a capacity of 5,779.8 cubic feet of air?

32

GPAs of Students at Hollywood High

Student	GPA	Student	GPA
Dempsey	2.8	Doyle	3.2
Crane	4.0	Moon	3.0
Heck	2.9	Smith	2.8
Brady	3.2	Fawcett	3.7
Matheson	3.7	Welker	2.6
Berenson	3.8	Gore	2.5
Keating	3.5	Manning	3.4

The table above lists the GPAs of 14 students at Hollywood High. According to the table, what is the mean GPA of the students? (Round your answer to the nearest tenth.)

33

Company X Profits

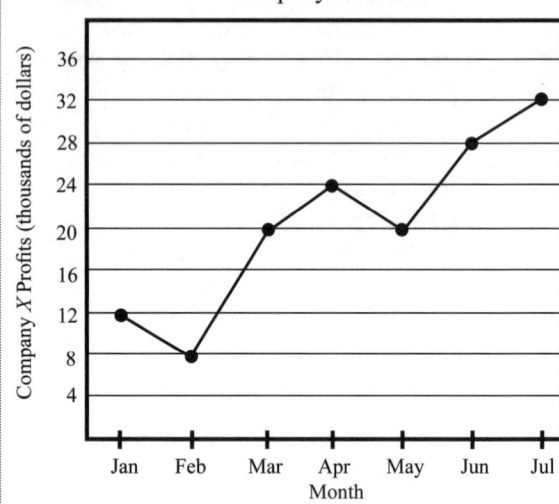

According to the line graph above, what was the percent change in Company X's profits from February to April?

34

In one month, Letica and Simon sold a total of 158 hours of personal training. If Simon sold seven less than 1.5 times the amount of hours that Letica sold, what was the difference between the number of hours Letica sold and the number of hours Simon sold?

35

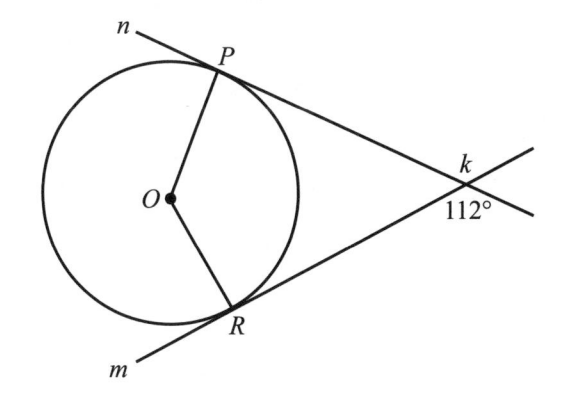

In the figure above, point O is the center of the circle, and line segments m and n are tangent to the circle at points P and R, respectively, and intersect one another at point k. If the area of the circle is equal to 16π, what is the value of the perimeter of sector POR ? (Round your answer to the nearest tenth.)

36

$$\frac{5x + 2}{(x - 4)^2 - 4(x - 1)}$$

What is the sum of all possible values of x for which the function g above is undefined?

Questions 37 and 38 refer to the following information.

Sherry opened a bank account that earns 14% interest compounded annually. Her initial deposit was $65, and she uses the expression $\$65(x)^t$ to model the value of the account after t years.

37

By how much did Sherry's bank account grow between the third and fourth year? (Round your answer to the nearest cent.)

38

Sherry's friend Howard opens a savings account at the same bank on the same day as Sherry, and deposits the same initial amount. However, Howard is locked into receiving a special interest rate of 23% for the first three years he keeps his account at the bank, and then the rate drops to 8% moving forward. What is the difference between the amount of money in Sherry's account and the amount of money in Howard's account after 7 years? (Round your answer to the nearest dollar.)

CHAPTER 5
The Essay

College Knowledge
Admissions Prompts

The Prompts

On this page are the five prompts that the Common Application allows applicants to choose from. Read the following prompts, and look for what common theme ties them together.

1. Some students have a background, identity, interest, or talent that is so meaningful they believe their application would be incomplete without it. If this sounds like you, then please share your story.

2. The lessons we take from failure can be fundamental to later success. Recount an incident or time when you experienced failure. How did it affect you, and what did you learn from the experience?

3. Reflect on a time when you challenged a belief or idea. What prompted you to act? Would you make the same decision again?

4. Describe a problem you've solved or a problem you'd like to solve. It can be an intellectual challenge, a research query, an ethical dilemma-anything that is of personal importance, no matter the scale. Explain its significance to you and what steps you took or could be taken to identify a solution.

5. Discuss an accomplishment or event, formal or informal, that marked your transition from childhood to adulthood within your culture, community, or family.

The Common App's Common Theme

Even though the five prompts seem to cover a range of topics, at their cores they are remarkably similar. What does every one of these essay prompts really want you to focus on?

_____
_____
_____
_____

Chapter 5

The Essay | Overview

The optional SAT essay gives you 50 minutes to critically analyze a text, much like you would in a college class. As with the other parts of the Evidence-Based Reading and Writing Test, reading and analysis are key to achieving a good score. The essay also tests your ability to communicate your ideas effectively. You will have to demonstrate that you can develop and support a position using the fundamentals of standard English grammar and style. Since all the grammar you need to know stems from the Writing and Language Test, you should already be pretty well prepared. The bigger-picture stylistic elements (sentence structure, transitions, organization, etc.) are nothing to fear either, as they use the same skills as argument questions. Let's take a quick look at the structure of the essay and how to approach it.

So, What's It Worth?

The essay does not count towards your overall score. Instead you are given a score by two different graders ranging from 1–4 for each of three different categories: Reading, Analysis, and Writing. To be successful, your essay must fulfill the following criteria:

Reading: Show how well you understand the main point and smaller details of the passage. Use textual evidence smartly.
Total Score: 2–8

Analysis: Evaluate how the author makes his/her argument through use of evidence, logic, and other stylistic techniques. Develop and back up your thoughts with effective textual evidence.
Total Score: 2–8

Writing: Be focused and conscientious with your essay. Use correct grammar and formatting, and ensure that you vary your sentence structure and wording.
Total Score: 2–8

The great part is that as long as you write a legible essay that addresses the topic, you can only gain points on the essay. You cannot lose points on this section!

The Essay | The Rubric

How It's Graded

The essay is graded holistically, based on a rubric that takes multiple factors into account. Below is the rubric for the grades of proficient and advanced, 3 and 4 respectively. Take a look at what the graders are looking for in your essay:

Score	Reading	Analysis	Writing
4	• The response demonstrates thorough comprehension of the source text. • The response shows an understanding of the text's central idea(s) and of most important details and how they interrelate, demonstrating a comprehensive understanding of the text. • The response is free of errors of fact or interpretation with regard to the text. • The response makes skillful use of textual evidence (quotations, paraphrases, or both), demonstrating a complete understanding of the source text.	• The response offers an insightful analysis of the source text and demonstrates a sophisticated understanding of the analytical task. • The response offers a thorough, well-considered evaluation of the author's use of evidence, reasoning, and/or stylistic and persuasive elements, and/or feature(s) of the student's own choosing. • The response contains relevant, sufficient, and strategically chosen support for claim(s) or point(s) made. • The response focuses consistently on those features of the text that are most relevant to addressing the task.	• The response is cohesive and demonstrates a highly effective use and command of language. • The response includes a precise central claim. • The response includes a skillful introduction and conclusion. The response demonstrates a deliberate and highly effective progression of ideas both within paragraphs and throughout the essay. • The response has a wide variety in sentence structures. The response demonstrates a consistent use of precise word choice. The response maintains a formal style and objective tone. • The response shows a strong command of the conventions of standard written English and is free or virtually free of errors.

The Essay | Example

But the Essay Itself?
The essay always consists of a prompt and a passage. The passage will change with each test, and the topics tend to vary broadly, but always argue a specific viewpoint using logical reasoning and evidence. The prompt is split between two boxes before and after the passage and is the same on each test. Pay close attention to the prompt below, so you know exactly what to expect on the day of the test.

As you read the passage below, consider how [the author] uses

- evidence, such as facts or examples, to support claims.
- reasoning to develop ideas and to connect claims and evidence.
- stylistic or persuasive elements, such as word choice or appeals to emotion, to add power to the ideas expressed.

Write an essay in which you explain how [the author] builds an argument to persuade [his/her] audience that [author's claim]. In your essay, analyze how [the author] uses one or more of the features listed above (or features of your own choice) to strengthen the logic and persuasiveness of [his/her] argument. Be sure that your analysis focuses on the most relevant features of the passage. Your essay should not explain whether you agree with [the author's] claims, but rather explain how the author builds an argument to persuade [his/her] audience.

Notice how the essay is explicitly asking for you not to state your opinion. Do not try to present your views on the topic being discussed, but rather concentrate on the author's opinion and how he/she tries to convince us of it. Avoid using "I think" or "in my opinion."

Taking a Look at the Real Thing
On the following pages, we're going to show a a typical SAT passage. As you read it, pay close attention to what the author argues and how he/she builds the case.

The Essay | Example

> As you read the passage below, consider how the author, Sarah Duncan, uses
> - evidence, such as facts or examples, to support claims.
> - reasoning to develop ideas and to connect claims and evidence.
> - stylistic or persuasive elements, such as word choice or appeals to emotion, to add power to the ideas expressed.

Adapted from Sarah Duncan, "Poetry Is Alive." ©2015 by The New York Sun. Originally published February 17, 2015.

1 Poetry is thriving in a myriad of communities throughout the country. Why, then, is journalistic discourse dominated by discussions about its supposed death?

2 This trend began in 1934, when Edmund Wilson asked the world whether or not verse was a dying technique. In 1988, Joseph Epstein inquired as to who it was that killed poetry. In 1991, Dana Gioia wrote an article on poetry's worrisome irrelevance to anyone who was not themselves a poet or creative writing teacher. In 1995, Morris Freedman concluded poetry was nearly dead from an oversaturation of academic and high-brow critical pretension, but not wholly without a fighting chance for the future.

3 These are but a sample. A quick Google search yields over 50 online articles claiming (or combating the claim) that poetry is dead. 2003: Poetry is Dead. Does Anybody Really Care? Newsweek. 2007: The Death of Poetry, Fullspate. 2013: 10 Reasons Poetry's Not Dead, Flavorwire. 2015: Poetry is Going Extinct, The Washington Post. The topic has been exhausted.

4 And yet, little has been said around the vocabulary– namely the words "popular" and "alive" – being used to address this apparent phenomenon. Declarations of poetry's untimely death conflate the popularity of an art form with its life without defining this measurement of appeal or vitality. What does it mean for poetry to be unpopular? And if it is so, can it still be alive?

5 When compared to other arts, poetry does appear to be more marginal than its creative peers. In a 2012 study conducted by the Survey of Public Participation in the Arts, data revealed that only 6.7% of polled Americans had read any poetry in the past year. In contrast, within the past year, 58% of Americans had seen a movie, 44% of Americans had read a novel, and 21% of Americans had attended a theatrical performance.

6 Initially, 6.7% looks like a small number. But the US population is roughly at 320 million; 6.7% of this number works out to be a little less than 22 million people. This number is akin to the populations of a multitude of countries. Australia, for example, has only 23 million people. Chile, The Netherlands, Senegal, Cuba, Israel, Portugal, Jamaica, and more have populations either at or below 22 million. It's seems unlikely that the individuals christening poetry Dead would comfortably say the current inhabitants of Ireland are of a dying nationality solely because their population amasses at a lower number than the USA. Ireland is simply a small country. Poetry, so to speak, is a small country too. Perhaps poets and poetry lovers should found their own.

7 Indigenous cultures across the world have rich histories of oral arts and storytelling. In the 1940s, the Beat Poets took to the stages with their voices and pens to rail against the duplicity of mainstream culture. Spoken word historians Priya Parmar and Bryonn Bain note that during the Harlem Renaissance and the Black Arts Movement of the 1960s and 70s, spoken word poetry and performance art flourished and expanded. In particular, artists like The Last Poets, Gil Scott Heron, Nikki Giovanni, Sonia Sanchez, and others seamlessly linked black liberation with poetic expression.

The Essay | Example

8 Liberation of all marginalized groups is a continued theme on stages in the poetry slam scene, and this is at the very least partly because, as Somers-Willett notes in her book, *The Cultural Politics of Slam Poetry: Race, Identity, and the Performance of Popular Verse in America*, the form invites a democratization of poetry as a whole. As with certain genres of music, individuals who have been denied outlets to process and articulate their experiences find this chance waiting for them in spoken word and the community surrounding it. At a poetry slam, anyone can sign up to directly address their audience through poetic art. As such, everyone can be a poet, regardless of education, race, gender, sexual orientation, income, or ability. The open opportunity for expression creates an atmosphere of poetry as personal as political.

9 I propose, ultimately, a different take on the age old question. Instead of, "Is poetry dead?" we must ask instead: "Is poetry accessible to everyone?" If the answer is yes, or close to yes, then poetry will continue to breathe steadily for whoever finds solace and excitement in it. Whether that is three people, 22 million people, or 300 million, the amount of people who choose to partake is irrelevant outside of industry. What is relevant is that the option of poetry – in all forms – is consistently and readily available.

Write an essay in which you explain how Sarah Duncan builds an argument to persuade her audience that poetry continues to be a vibrant artform. In your essay, analyze how Duncan uses one or more of the features listed in the box above (or features of your own choice) to strengthen the logic and persuasiveness of her argument. Be sure that your analysis focuses on the most relevant features of the passage. Your essay should not explain whether you agree with Duncan's claims, but rather explain how Duncan builds an argument to persuade her audience.

Chapter 5

Drill | Reading

The reading grade on the essay measures your comprehension of the passage. It's not only important to recognize the author's main idea, but also the exchange between those key ideas and supporting details. If this sounds familiar, it is because you have to use similar skills on the SAT Reading Test. Apply the reading comprehension techniques you learned in that chapter to the given passage. The grade also measures how effectively you utilize textual evidence. Make sure your quotations are short and relevant.

Instructions: *Summarize the following passages in 12 words or less. Remember to use language that properly expresses the certainty of the wording and the author's tone. Also avoid inserting your opinion.*

1. Many people categorize Tupac as a gangster rapper from the West Coast. However, these people are unaware of his true origins and musical diversity. Tupac's rap career began as a member of Digital Underground, a group known for its tomfoolery and clownish lead singer Humpty Hump and for the hit, "The Humpty Dance."

   _____

   _____

   _____

   _____

2. During President Obama's time in congress the economy suffered its worst losses in history. Clearly, Obama is ill-equipped to run this country. Once he was elected president not only did the economy continue its downward trend but banks failed at a historical rate, demonstrating Obama's lack of understanding of financial matters. If we are to recover from the economic problems in this country we must return to the policies of George W. Bush.

   _____

   _____

   _____

   _____

3. For decades the selling point of a college education has been the lifetime wage premium that a college degree all but guaranteed. Colleges had a simple marketing pitch: No matter the cost of attendance, getting this credential will provide you benefits for more than one generation. While this dictum may hold true the economic conditions in the country and the rising cost of college has caused many families to demand more tangible evidence of the return on investment.

   _____

   _____

   _____

   _____

4. Many students and families dismiss standardized testing as stressful and time-consuming; some educators agree with this position and point out that it impedes the educational process. While these arguments have merit they overlook that standardized testing provides a uniform measuring stick for diverse groups of individuals and creates guidance and time management tools for teachers.

   _____

   _____

   _____

   _____

Drill I Reading

5. Many students and families dismiss standardized testing as stressful and time-consuming; some educators agree with this position and point out that it impedes the educational process. These arguments, while valid, can be strengthened by highlighting that the reliance on such testing encourages a narrowing of curriculum in order to "teach to the test" and fosters an atmosphere in which dishonesty will likely grow.

_____

_____

_____

6. The conservation movement has been startling both in its suddenness and in its breadth. People who only a decade or two ago were shopping for SUVs are now pressing automotive dealers for information on a vehicle's long term fuel efficiency and bio-diesel compatibility. More adventurous and proactive buyers are flocking to waiting lists for vehicles with "hybrid" engines that run on both gasoline and rechargeable electric batteries. This has become especially true among younger and more educated drivers. There even seems to be an emerging trend among motorists to petition their legislators to set aside funding for the development of distribution stations for ethanol, an "earth-friendly" bio-diesel fuel.

_____

_____

_____

7. The amount paid for the services of professional athletes is unspeakable. Even more absurd is the money athletes receive as signing bonuses. Athletes are paid millions of dollars each year and they often fail to perform to a level that merits such salaries. In the end, clubs end up wasting money in search of the one player who is actually worth his salary, provided it is even possible for someone to deserve ten million dollars for running around a field or a court with a ball. Thus, clubs should negotiate stratified contracts in which players get paid based on performance. This would give players the incentive to perform to their potential and save the clubs billions of dollars in wasted salaries.

_____

_____

_____

8. Even if Dr. Spencer had not accidentally melted a candy bar with a military microwave emitter, the discovery of a household application for microwaves would have only been delayed. This is an unfortunate truth because many Americans suffer as a result of this "modern marvel." The microwave oven helped to accelerate a shift in the traditional family paradigm in the United States. Families do not eat meals as families used to do. Young children no longer wait for their parents to have meals because they are capable of preparing processed meals on their own. The microwave oven is partly responsible for whittling away the family unit. Already weakened by social changes since the 1950s, the American family could have done without the microwave oven.

_____

_____

_____

Drill | Analysis

The analysis grade measures your ability to discern and explain how the author makes his/her case for the stance taken in the passage. In order to do this, you will have to recognize the evidence the author uses and understand the author's reasoning. Like the reading grade, this grade also measures how you use textual evidence. Here your quotations have to display how the author builds and supports his/her claims. <u>Never use a quotation without analyzing it.</u> You do not want to summarize the passage, but instead choose the quotations that are most suitable for your position.

Instructions: *In the following drill, write down from each of the given paragraphs **what** you have been told, **why** the author told it to you, and **how** it was told to you. Remember that this is not an exercise in opinion but in extracting information from what was given to you in the text.*

It has been proven that the SAT essay does not deduct points for factual errors. It has also been widely written that individuals have received perfect SAT essay scores while including information that any fifth grader could tell you was false. Despite the truth of both of these statements test-takers would be wise to take this information with a grain of salt as it does not mean that lying is the preferred approach to writing an SAT essay.

1. List three things the author told the reader:

_____
_____
_____
_____
_____
_____

2. List why the author told the reader these things:

_____
_____
_____
_____
_____
_____

3. How would you describe the way in which the author conveyed his message?

_____
_____
_____
_____

One of the most distinguishable characteristics of a culture is its food. It was one of the few things that identified my family as Ghanaian. We would often eat hkatenkwan (groundnut stew), and my mother served tatale (plantain cakes) with everything. However, even this link to our heritage weakened as time passed. As my family became more assimilated into American culture, we ate less traditional Ghanaian food. My mother started trading recipes with other housewives in the neighborhood during my senior year in high school, and so she began serving Indian and Italian dishes for dinner.

4. List three things the author told the reader:

_____
_____
_____
_____
_____
_____

5. List why the author told the reader these things:

_____
_____
_____
_____
_____
_____

6. How would you describe the way in which the author conveyed his message?

_____
_____
_____
_____

Drill | Analysis

By journey's end, I will not be the person I was last year, yesterday, or even today. My trip to Haiti will have changed me in ways that I cannot anticipate, perhaps in deep spiritual ways, perhaps in superficial physical ways. Perhaps I will change my accent, perhaps I will walk more confidently. Perhaps my accent will become more Haitian and less French, perhaps my worldview will become more Haitian. But for now I am not one of them.

7. List three things the author told the reader:

_____

_____

_____

8. List why the author told the reader these things:

_____

_____

_____

9. How would you describe the way in which the author conveyed his message?

_____

_____

_____

The true value of a college education is beyond a simple conference of a piece of paper certifying a set of acquired knowledge. The true value of college lies in exposure, the exposure for a young girl from a farm in Alabama to the New York fashion industry and the exposure for the urban boy to the concept of the world-wide agricultural industry. The true value of college lies in the opportunity it provides for exposure to networks for many people who may not otherwise have access to these new networks.

10. List three things the author told the reader:

_____

_____

_____

11. List why the author told the reader these things:

_____

_____

_____

12. How would you describe the way in which the author conveyed his message?

_____

_____

_____

The Essay | Writing

The writing grade measures your ability to make your argument in a clear, cogent, and organized fashion. There are some things you should do and others you should simply avoid if you want to write a well-crafted essay. There are not many of them, but each is important. Keep these in mind and you have got a good shot at a high writing score.

Do...	Don't...
...write legibly.	...write sloppily.
...use most or all of the time and space provided.	...stop writing with lots of time and space left.
...pick one side and stick to it.	...try to argue both sides.
...cite appropriate social, historical, or literary examples.	...use inappropriate, immature, or too few examples.
...transition smoothly into, out of, and between ideas.	...jump between thoughts without explanation, introduction, or conclusion.
...follow standard paragraph format.	...write one giant block of unbroken text.
...use appropriate vocabulary, at the highest possible level you are comfortable with.	...use inappropriate vocabulary, or vocabulary of whose definition you are unsure.
...support your ideas and assertions with evidence and explanation.	...list thoughts without backing them up.
...connect your points and examples to the prompt clearly.	...assume the reader will figure you out how you intend what you're writing will relate to the prompt.

The Essay | Writing

Common Corrections

In the chart below, we've compiled some common mistakes and undesirable phrases, along with their revisions. Check them out!

How It's Written...	...How It Should Be Written
the place that & the time that	the place where & the time when
the fact that	that
good & bad	beneficial, valuable, positive & detrimental, negative, worthless
you	one
going on	occur, took place
I myself	I
thing	event, affair, object, matter
pretty much, more or less	fairly, essentially
me as a person	me
the reason for this is (because)	because
really	exceedingly, very
a lot of	many, myriad
for awhile	for a while
irregardless	regardless
the exact same	exactly the same

Chapter 5

The Essay | Critical Analysis

Your essay will depend on your ability to identify the author's main point and the ways in which the author tries to back up this claim. Like the prompt states, you are examining the "evidence...reasoning...and stylistic or persuasive elements" used in the passage.

Finding the Main Point
The main point of the passage should be relatively clear from the passage. It will most likely be in the opening paragraphs or at the very end of the passage. Check your interpretation of the main point against the second part of the prompt, which will explicitly identify it in the "explain how [the author] builds an argument to persuade [his/her] audience that [author's claim]" sentence.

Finding the Appeals
The author will support his/her main point through the use of appeals. Appeals are the different methods the author uses to try to persuade you, the reader. They fall under three categories:

Appeal to Reason
This is the most common type of appeal and potentially the most effective. With appeals to reason, the author attempts to use logic, rhetoric, or facts and figures to make their case. This appeal is known as *logos*.

Types of Support: factual data, statistics, definitions, literary or historical allusions, inductive/deductive reasoning

Appeal to Emotion
This appeal is basically the opposite of the appeal to reason. It depends on connecting with the feelings of the reader. This appeal is known as *pathos*.

Types of Support: personal anecdote, imagery, figurative language, narratives/personal accounts, rhetorical questions, calls to action, irony or humor

Appeal to Credibility
This appeal is designed to establish the author as a reliable source and therefore bolster his/her main point. It does this by citing authorities who are in agreement. This appeal is known as *ethos*.

Types of Support: author's qualifications, references to author's character, quotation of authorities, recognition of alternate views

Drill | Critical Analysis

Instructions: In the exercise below, determine whether each statement is an appeal to reason, emotion, or credibilty. Then, use the space below that statement to write down which type of support that appeal is.

Statement	Type
The chimpanzee, our 98.5% identical genetic relative, has a sophisticated set of social rules and habits.	☐ Reason ☐ Emotion ☐ Credibility
Based on my years as a federal judge, I can say that the action was patently illegal.	☐ Reason ☐ Emotion ☐ Credibility
We must act now to stop this dangerous event from occurring during our lifetime.	☐ Reason ☐ Emotion ☐ Credibility
What would we have done without all your hard work?	☐ Reason ☐ Emotion ☐ Credibility
Experts agree that to proceed with the project, we must follow the guidelines laid out.	☐ Reason ☐ Emotion ☐ Credibility
Consider the tragic story of Tony Conigliario and how one single pitch changed the trajectory of his whole career.	☐ Reason ☐ Emotion ☐ Credibility
Everywhere this economic policy has been utilized in the past has experienced rapid growth, so there is no reason to think the same should not be true here.	☐ Reason ☐ Emotion ☐ Credibility
Looking back, I have nothing but fond memories of the summers I spent there: the cool breeze coming off the mountains at night, and the sun setting hazily over the lake.	☐ Reason ☐ Emotion ☐ Credibility
The opposition does raise several valid issues.	☐ Reason ☐ Emotion ☐ Credibility
In an increasingly isolated world, Donne's "No Man Is An Island" shows the continuing interconnectedness of humanity.	☐ Reason ☐ Emotion ☐ Credibility

The Essay | Action Plan

Now that we've gotten a basic understanding of the essay out of the way, let's define our Action Plan. The following plan is how you will approach every SAT essay. On the next few pages, we will work on making a checklist and an outline.

> 1. **Write Down Your Appeals Checklist.**
>   Recall the three different categories of appeals and the support types for each.
>
> 2. **Read the Passage and Fill Out Your Checklist.**
>   Read actively, looking for the author's main point and the types of support he/she uses.
>
> 3. **Make an Outline.**
>   Write down the author's main point and at least three specific examples of how he/she supports it. Underline brief, effective textual evidence.
>
> 4. **Write Your Essay.**
>   Using your outline, write a four or five paragraph essay analyzing how the author develops his/her argument. Remember to vary your sentence structure and word usage.

The Essay | Action Plan

Let's take a deeper look at the passage we saw earlier in the chapter.

> As you read the passage below, consider how the author, Sarah Duncan, uses
> - evidence, such as facts or examples, to support claims.
> - reasoning to develop ideas and to connect claims and evidence.
> - stylistic or persuasive elements, such as word choice or appeals to emotion, to add power to the ideas expressed.

Adapted from Sarah Duncan, "Poetry Is Alive." ©2015 by The New York Sun. Originally published February 17, 2015.

1 Poetry is thriving in a myriad of communities throughout the country. Why, then, is journalistic discourse dominated by discussions about its supposed death?

2 This trend began in 1934, when Edmund Wilson asked the world whether or not verse was a dying technique. In 1988, Joseph Epstein inquired as to who it was that killed poetry. In 1991, Dana Gioia wrote an article on poetry's worrisome irrelevance to anyone who was not themselves a poet or creative writing teacher. In 1995, Morris Freedman concluded poetry was nearly dead from an oversaturation of academic and high-brow critical pretension, but not wholly without a fighting chance for the future.

3 These are but a sample. A quick Google search yields over 50 online articles claiming (or combating the claim) that poetry is dead. 2003: Poetry is Dead. Does Anybody Really Care? Newsweek. 2007: The Death of Poetry, Fullspate. 2013: 10 Reasons Poetry's Not Dead, Flavorwire. 2015: Poetry is Going Extinct, The Washington Post. The topic has been exhausted.

4 And yet, little has been said around the vocabulary– namely the words "popular" and "alive" – being used to address this apparent phenomenon. Declarations of poetry's untimely death conflate the popularity of an art form with its life without defining this measurement of appeal or vitality. What does it mean for poetry to be unpopular? And if it is so, can it still be alive?

5 When compared to other arts, poetry does appear to be more marginal than its creative peers. In a 2012 study conducted by the Survey of Public Participation in the Arts, data revealed that only 6.7% of polled Americans had read any poetry in the past year. In contrast, within the past year, 58% of Americans had seen a movie, 44% of Americans had read a novel, and 21% of Americans had attended a theatrical performance.

6 Initially, 6.7% looks like a small number. But the US population is roughly at 320 million; 6.7% of this number works out to be a little less than 22 million people. This number is akin to the populations of a multitude of countries. Australia, for example, has only 23 million people. Chile, The Netherlands, Senegal, Cuba, Israel, Portugal, Jamaica, and more have populations either at or below 22 million. It's seems unlikely that the individuals christening poetry Dead would comfortably say the current inhabitants of Ireland are of a dying nationality solely because their population amasses at a lower number than the USA. Ireland is simply a small country. Poetry, so to speak, is a small country too. Perhaps poets and poetry lovers should found their own.

7 Indigenous cultures across the world have rich histories of oral arts and storytelling. In the 1940s, the Beat Poets took to the stages with their voices and pens to rail against the duplicity of mainstream culture. Spoken word historians Priya Parmar and Bryonn Bain note that during the Harlem Renaissance and the Black Arts Movement of the 1960s and 70s, spoken word poetry and performance art flourished and expanded. In particular, artists like The Last Poets, Gil Scott Heron, Nikki Giovanni, Sonia Sanchez, and others seamlessly linked black liberation with poetic expression.

Chapter 5

The Essay | Action Plan

8 Liberation of all marginalized groups is a continued theme on stages in the poetry slam scene, and this is at the very least partly because, as Somers-Willett notes in her book, *The Cultural Politics of Slam Poetry: Race, Identity, and the Performance of Popular Verse in America*, the form invites a democratization of poetry as a whole. As with certain genres of music, individuals who have been denied outlets to process and articulate their experiences find this chance waiting for them in spoken word and the community surrounding it. At a poetry slam, anyone can sign up to directly address their audience through poetic art. As such, everyone can be a poet, regardless of education, race, gender, sexual orientation, income, or ability. The open opportunity for expression creates an atmosphere of poetry as personal as political.

9 I propose, ultimately, a different take on the age old question. Instead of, "Is poetry dead?" we must ask instead: "Is poetry accessible to everyone?" If the answer is yes, or close to yes, then poetry will continue to breathe steadily for whoever finds solace and excitement in it. Whether that is three people, 22 million people, or 300 million, the amount of people who choose to partake is irrelevant outside of industry. What is relevant is that the option of poetry – in all forms – is consistently and readily available.

Write an essay in which you explain how Sarah Duncan builds an argument to persuade her audience that poetry continues to be a vibrant artform. In your essay, analyze how Duncan uses one or more of the features listed in the box above (or features of your own choice) to strengthen the logic and persuasiveness of her argument. Be sure that your analysis focuses on the most relevant features of the passage. Your essay should not explain whether you agree with Duncan's claims, but rather explain how Duncan builds an argument to persuade her audience.

Drill | Appeals Checklist

Instructions: *Based on the passage on the previous pages, fill out your appeals checklist. Name the type of support for each category.*

Appeals to Reason:

_____

_____

_____

_____

Appeals to Emotion:

_____

_____

_____

_____

Appeals to Credibility:

_____

_____

_____

_____

Chapter 5

Drill I Outline

Instructions: *Based on the passage on the previous pages and your Appeals Checklist, create an outline using the method described in the Action Plan. For the appeals, write down the type of support and the line numbers you would quote in your essay.*

Author's Main Point:

_____

_____

_____

Appeal #1:

_____

_____

Appeal #2:

_____

_____

Appeal #3:

_____

_____

454

SAT-R Workbook v. 1.5

The Essay I Introduction

The introduction is your first opportunity to state your case and make an impression on the reader. Therefore, it is very important that your introduction be thoughtful and well-organized. Below we will discuss an effective way to write your introduction. Since you are not given specific instructions on how to write your essay, following a reliable guide is useful for forming your thoughts.

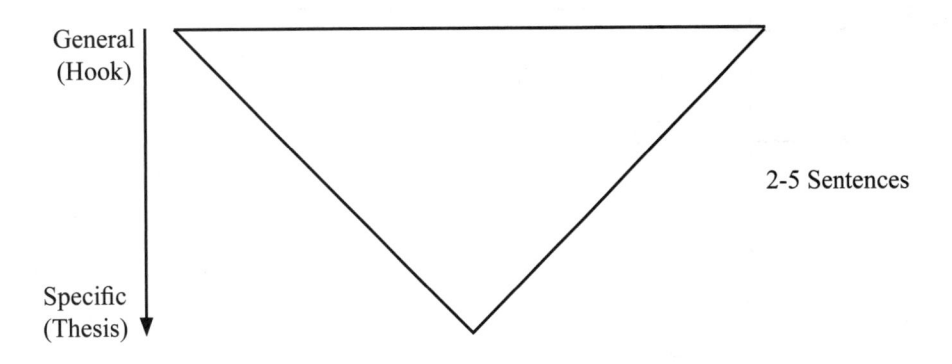

General (Hook) → Specific (Thesis)

2-5 Sentences

The upside down triangle above is a visual representation of how your introduction should progress. The beginning of the paragraph should start out very generally. You should not state your thesis in the very first sentence. Instead, make a general statement about the topic of the passage. This general statement is called the *hook*. Make sure your hook includes the author's name and the title of the work. As your introduction continues, you want to be more and more specific until the last sentence, which should be your thesis. The *thesis* is where you are the most specific, and where you state which appeals and types of support the author uses. Be as explicit as possible in your thesis so the reader knows exactly where you stand.

The Essay | Body

The body paragraphs are really where your essay is made. It is where you define your positions on the passage more exactly and lay out your evidence. It is where the reader will evaluate how you make your case. Therefore, it is centrally important that your body paragraphs are detailed and well developed.

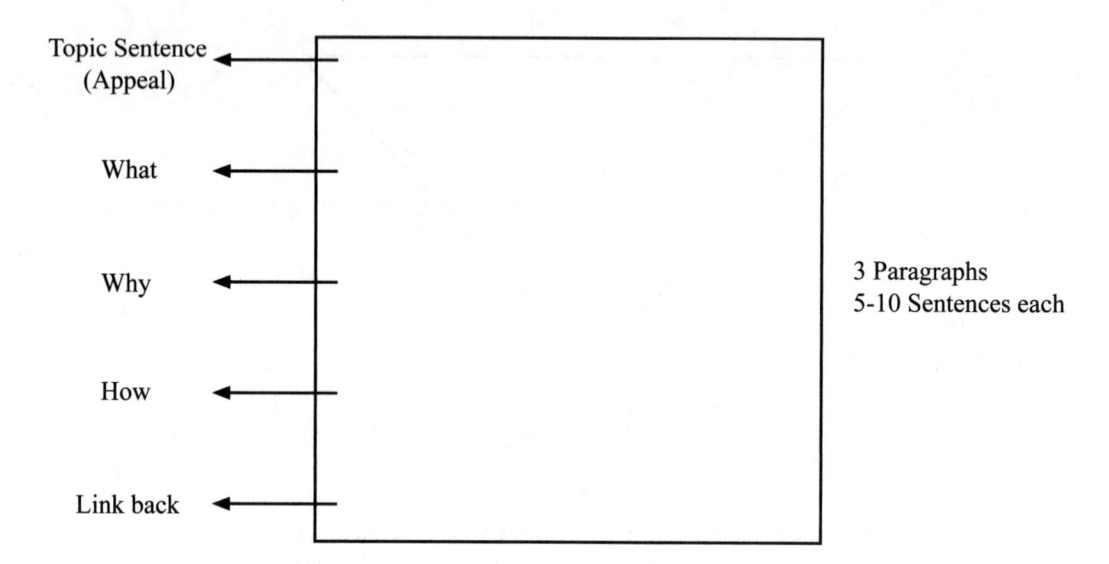

```
Topic Sentence ←──┐
   (Appeal)       │
                  │
    What    ←─────┤
                  │
                  │         3 Paragraphs
     Why    ←─────┤         5-10 Sentences each
                  │
                  │
     How    ←─────┤
                  │
                  │
  Link back ←─────┘
```

Each of your body paragraphs should address one of the appeals you put in your outline. For your three body paragraphs, start with your second strongest appeal, with your weakest appeal sandwiched in the middle, and finish with your strongest. Always begin the paragraph with a *topic sentence*. In this sentence, state the exact type of support the author uses for that appeal that you stated in your thesis. Then, for the remainder of the paragraph, develop your ideas on that appeal through answering the three questions: what, why, and how?

What effect does the appeal want to create? Base the answer to this question on the type of appeal and the response the author is looking for by using it.

Why does the author want to create this effect? This question concerns the author's motivation. It digs a little bit deeper than the what question to ask about the essential intent of the author and the function of the appeal in the argument.

How does the authour use the appeal to strengthen his/her argument? The answer for this question will detail the impact the appeal has on the reader of the passage. This impact is how the author is attempting to support their claim.

Finally, the last sentence of your body paragraph should be a mini-recap of the paragraph, called the *link back*. In the link back, you should restate the type of support and how it attempts to persuade the reader of the author's main point.

The Essay | Conclusion

Though the conclusion is the final paragraph of your essay and usually the shortest, do not disregard its importance to your overall essay. The graders look at your essay holistically, meaning they do not go through line by line looking for mistakes, but rather they judge it based on their impressions of the whole text. The conclusion is the last impression they have of your essay before giving it a grade. Therefore, it is important to leave the graders with a favorable opinion by finishing strongly.

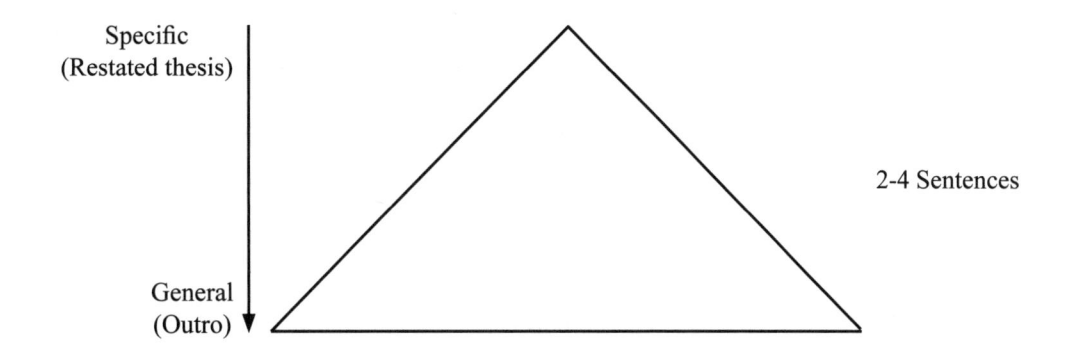

Specific (Restated thesis)

General (Outro)

2-4 Sentences

The conclusion is the opposite of the introduction in the sense that now we are going from specific to general. Start your conclusion with a *restated thesis*. "Restated" does not mean that you say the exact same thing as you did before, but instead write the same concept of your thesis using different words. Complete your conclusion with an outro. An *outro* is a closing statement that ties together the threads of your essay and the passage it's based on. It should be very basic, general, and address the point of view of the author on a broader scale. Be careful not to introduce any new information.

Chapter 5

The Essay | Putting It Together

> As you read the passage below, consider how Dwight Eisenhower, uses
> - evidence, such as facts or examples, to support claims.
> - reasoning to develop ideas and to connect claims and evidence.
> - stylistic or persuasive elements, such as word choice or appeals to emotion, to add power to the ideas expressed.

Adapted from former US President Dwight Eisenhower's Farewell Address. Originally delivered January 17, 1961.

1 We now stand ten years past the midpoint of a century that has witnessed four major wars among great nations. Three of these involved our own country. Despite these holocausts, America is today the strongest, the most influential, and most productive nation in the world. Understandably proud of this pre-eminence, we yet realize that America's leadership and prestige depend, not merely upon our unmatched material progress, riches, and military strength, but on how we use our power in the interests of world peace and human betterment.

2 Crises there will continue to be. In meeting them, whether foreign or domestic, great or small, there is a recurring temptation to feel that some spectacular and costly action could become the miraculous solution to all current difficulties. A huge increase in newer elements of our defenses; development of unrealistic programs to cure every ill in agriculture; a dramatic expansion in basic and applied research -- these and many other possibilities, each possibly promising in itself, may be suggested as the only way to the road we wish to travel.

3 A vital element in keeping the peace is our military establishment. Our arms must be mighty, ready for instant action, so that no potential aggressor may be tempted to risk his own destruction. Our military organization today bears little relation to that known of any of my predecessors in peacetime, or, indeed, by the fighting men of World War II or Korea.

4 Until the latest of our world conflicts, the United States had no armaments industry. American makers of plowshares could, with time and as required, make swords as well. But we can no longer risk emergency improvisation of national defense. We have been compelled to create a permanent armaments industry of vast proportions. Added to this, three and a half million men and women are directly engaged in the defense establishment. We annually spend on military security alone more than the net income of all United States cooperations -- corporations.

5 Now this conjunction of an immense military establishment and a large arms industry is new in the American experience. The total influence -- economic, political, even spiritual -- is felt in every city, every Statehouse, every office of the Federal government. We recognize the imperative need for this development. Yet, we must not fail to comprehend its grave implications. Our toil, resources, and livelihood are all involved. So is the very structure of our society.

6 In the councils of government, we must guard against the acquisition of unwarranted influence, whether sought or unsought, by the military-industrial complex. The potential for the disastrous rise of misplaced power exists and will persist. We must never let the weight of this combination endanger our liberties or democratic processes. We should take nothing for granted. Only an alert and knowledgeable citizenry can compel the proper meshing of the huge industrial and military machinery of defense with our peaceful methods and goals, so that security and liberty may prosper together.

The Essay | Putting It Together

7 During the long lane of the history yet to be written, America knows that this world of ours, ever growing smaller, must avoid becoming a community of dreadful fear and hate, and be, instead, a proud confederation of mutual trust and respect. Such a confederation must be one of equals. The weakest must come to the conference table with the same confidence as do we, protected as we are by our moral, economic, and military strength. That table, though scarred by many fast frustrations -- past frustrations, cannot be abandoned for the certain agony of disarmament -- of the battlefield.

8 Disarmament, with mutual honor and confidence, is a continuing imperative. Together we must learn how to compose differences, not with arms, but with intellect and decent purpose. Because this need is so sharp and apparent, I confess that I lay down my official responsibilities in this field with a definite sense of disappointment. As one who has witnessed the horror and the lingering sadness of war, as one who knows that another war could utterly destroy this civilization which has been so slowly and painfully built over thousands of years, I wish I could say tonight that a lasting peace is in sight.

Write an essay in which you explain how Dwight Eisenhower builds an argument to persuade his audience that the public must guard against the rise of the military-industrial complex. In your essay, analyze how Eisenhower uses one or more of the features listed in the box above (or features of your own choice) to strengthen the logic and persuasiveness of his argument. Be sure that your analysis focuses on the most relevant features of the passage. Your essay should not explain whether you agree with Eisenhower's claims, but rather explain how Eisenhower builds an argument to persuade his audience.

The Essay | Putting It Together

Instructions: *Use the space below for your Appeals Checklist and Outline. Make sure to write your actual essay on the next four pages. You will have a planning page like this on the actual SAT that is **not** read by the graders.*

The Essay | Putting It Together

The Essay | Putting It Together

The Essay | Putting It Together

The Essay | Putting It Together

The Essay | Putting It Together

> As you read the passage below, consider how Carrie Russell, uses
> - evidence, such as facts or examples, to support claims.
> - reasoning to develop ideas and to connect claims and evidence.
> - stylistic or persuasive elements, such as word choice or appeals to emotion, to add power to the ideas expressed.

Adapted from Carrie Russell, "Libraries in Today's Digital Age: The Copyright Controversy." ©2001 by ERIC Digest. Originally published October 1, 2001.

1 Libraries are public institutions committed to equitable access and the free flow of information to meet the needs of the public. For libraries, copyright law, through its incentive model, a rich and robust public domain, fair use, and library and user exemptions-aids in ensuring that information is both created and made accessible. While digital technologies and an ever-expanding communication network infrastructure have enhanced creation and wide distribution of information to the public, these same technologies can be used to control or restrict public access to information.

2 The purpose of the copyright law is to advance the progress of science and the useful arts to benefit the public. It does this by awarding to creators a set of exclusive rights, a limited, statutory monopoly over reproduction, distribution, display, performance, and adaptation of the created work, in order to provide creators an economic incentive to create. The law also sets aside numerous exceptions to creators' right to ensure that users of copyright materials can read and lawfully use the materials in other ways.

3 In recent years, a copyright legislative battle has ensued between copyright holders (primarily represented by the publishing, entertainment, and software business industries) and those who wish to use or have access to copyright materials (primarily represented by library, educational, and public interest communities). Copyright holders argue that they will not make their copyrighted works available to the public in digital formats unless the law is revised to prevent piracy and protect the marketplace for intellectual property by controlling access and use. Libraries argue that users rights to information should be upheld regardless of technological innovation and digital formats. The big question: Can copyright law continue to balance the interests of both copyright holders and users in the digital environment?

4 In an attempt to update the law to encompass new digital environments and to allay copyright holders' fears of widespread piracy, Congress passed the Digital Millennium Copyright Act of 1998 (DMCA), an amendment to the copyright law that has been the source of much controversy. The DMCA has furthered a trend to erode the "balance" of copyright law by awarding more rights to copyright holders while restricting the rights of public who wish to enjoy the same user rights to digital information resources as were enjoyed in the print environment. Thus, copyright law and its adaptability in the digital environment continues to be fraught with uncertainty.

5 For libraries, lending material to library users is a core public service. First sale [the right to distribute the copy after purchase without the permission of the copyright holder] allows libraries to share their lawfully acquired copies with users. Moreover, interlibrary loan is vital to libraries with limited collection development funds. Poorer libraries can borrow copies from bigger libraries to meet user requests. As more materials become available in only digital formats that cannot be loaned, libraries fear that they will be unable to meet the information needs of users. Libraries cannot afford all materials and rely on sharing.

6 Copyright aggregators, those industries that hold the rights to scores of Copyrighted works, like the motion picture and recording industries and the publishing community, parlayed a major victory in the Digital Millennium Copyright Act with the inclusion of a new chapter to copyright law, called Copyright Protection and Management Systems. Many library associations, legal scholars, and public interest groups believe this chapter expands the rights of copyright holders to the detriment of the public.

The Essay | Putting It Together

7 It is now an infringement of copyright (punishable by a fine and jail time) to access a password protected or encrypted work without the prior authorization of the copyright holder. In other words, publishers and other copyright holders can use technological measures to deny access to the public of published works. This allows copyright holders the option of charging a fee for access. Most importantly, copyright holders can use technology to enforce license terms on the public.

8 Libraries remain committed to a balanced copyright law because without it, copyright cannot meet its primary objective, "to advance the progress of Science and the useful arts" for the benefit of the public. Knowledge and discovery are dependent on access to information, and equitable access can only be achieved when independent of the ability to pay. Libraries pay for information to share with their communities. As more information becomes available in only digital formats, it is important that the public can enjoy the same information rights they exercised with print formats.

> Write an essay in which you explain how Carrie Russell builds an argument to persuade her audience that current copyright law restricts the public's access to information. In your essay, analyze how Russell uses one or more of the features listed in the box above (or features of your own choice) to strengthen the logic and persuasiveness of her argument. Be sure that your analysis focuses on the most relevant features of the passage. Your essay should not explain whether you agree with Russell's claims, but rather explain how Russell builds an argument to persuade her audience.

Chapter 5

The Essay | Putting It Together

Instructions: *Use the space below for your Appeals Checklist and Outline. Make sure to write your actual essay on the next four pages. You will have a planning page like this on the actual SAT that is **not** read by the graders.*

© 2016 Bell Curves, LLC

The Essay | Putting It Together

The Essay | Putting It Together

The Essay | Putting It Together

Chapter 5

The Essay | Putting It Together